TYPE SPECIFICATIONS

Normal	Ctrl-Shift-spacebar (F5)
Bold	Ctrl-Shift-B (F6)
Italic	Ctrl-Shift-I (F7)
Underline	Ctrl-Shift-U (F8)
Strike-through	Ctrl-Shift-S
Reverse	Ctrl-Shift-V
Small caps	Ctrl-Shift-H
All caps	Ctrl-Shift-K
Down next size	Ctrl-< (F3)
Up next size	Ctrl-> (F4)
Down one point	Ctrl-Shift-<
Up one point	Ctrl-Shift->

PARAGRAPH ALIGNMENT

Align left	Ctrl-Shift-L
Align center	Ctrl-Shift-C
Align right	Ctrl-Shift-R
Justify	Ctrl-Shift-J
Force justify	Ctrl-Shift-F

EDITING

New line	Shift-Enter
Cut	Shift-Delete (Ctrl-X)
Copy	Ctrl-Insert (Ctrl-C)
Paste	Shift-Insert (Insert; Ctrl-V)
Clear	Del
Select all	Ctrl-A
Undo	Alt-Backspace

Computer users are not all alike.
Neither are SYBEX books.

We know our customers have a variety of needs. They've told us so. And because we've listened, we've developed several distinct types of books to meet the needs of each of our customers. What are you looking for in computer help?

If you're looking for the basics, try the **ABC's** series. You'll find short, unintimidating tutorials and helpful illustrations. For a more visual approach, select **Teach Yourself**, featuring screen-by-screen illustrations of how to use your latest software purchase.

Mastering and **Understanding** titles offer you a step-by-step introduction, plus an in-depth examination of intermediate-level features, to use as you progress.

Our **Up & Running** series is designed for computer-literate consumers who want a no-nonsense overview of new programs. Just 20 basic lessons, and you're on your way.

We also publish two types of reference books. Our **Instant References** provide quick access to each of a program's commands and functions. SYBEX **Encyclopedias** provide a *comprehensive reference* and explanation of all of the commands, features and functions of the subject software.

Sometimes a subject requires a special treatment that our standard series doesn't provide. So you'll find we have titles like **Advanced Techniques, Handbooks, Tips & Tricks**, and others that are specifically tailored to satisfy a unique need.

We carefully select our authors for their in-depth understanding of the software they're writing about, as well as their ability to write clearly and communicate effectively. Each manuscript is thoroughly reviewed by our technical staff to ensure its complete accuracy. Our production department makes sure it's easy to use. All of this adds up to the highest quality books available, consistently appearing on best seller charts worldwide.

You'll find SYBEX publishes a variety of books on every popular software package. Looking for computer help? Help Yourself to SYBEX.

For a complete catalog of our publications:

SYBEX Inc.

2021 Challenger Drive, Alameda, CA 94501

Tel: (415) 523-8233/(800) 227-2346 Telex: 336311

SYBEX Fax: (415) 523-2373

MASTERING
PAGEMAKER 4
ON THE
IBM PC

MASTERING PAGEMAKER® 4 ON THE IBM® PC

REBECCA BRIDGES ALTMAN

WITH RICK ALTMAN

SYBEX®

SAN FRANCISCO ▲ PARIS ▲ DÜSSELDORF ▲ SOEST

Acquisitions Editor: Dianne King
Editor: Marilyn Smith
Project Editor: Janna Hecker
Technical Editor: Maryann Brown
Word Processors: Ann Dunn, Scott Campbell, and Lisa Mitchell
Chapter Art and Layout: Ingrid Owen
Technical Art: Delia Brown
Screen Graphics: Cuong Le and Delia Brown
Typesetters: Bob Myren and Deborah Maizels
Proofreader: Dina F. Quan
Indexer: Nancy Guenther
Cover Designer: Thomas Ingalls + Associates
Cover Photographer: Mark Johann
Screen reproductions produced by XenoFont.

Adobe Type Manager and PostScript are trademarks of Adobe Systems.
Arts & Letters is a trademark of Computer Support Corporation.
Corel Draw is a trademark of Corel Systems.
Microsoft Word, Windows 3.0, Windows Paintbrush, and Windows Write are trademarks of Microsoft Corporation.
PageMaker is a trademark of Aldus Corporation.

XenoFont is a trademark of XenoSoft.

SYBEX is a registered trademark of SYBEX, Inc.

TRADEMARKS: SYBEX has attempted throughout this book to distinguish proprietary trademarks from descriptive terms by following the capitalization style used by the manufacturer.

SYBEX is not affiliated with any manufacturer.

Every effort has been made to supply complete and accurate information. However, SYBEX assumes no responsibility for its use, nor for any infringement of the intellectual property rights of third parties which would result from such use.

Library of Congress Card Number: 90-72077
ISBN: 0-89588-773-8

Manufactured in the United States of America
10 9 8 7 6 5 4

We dedicate this book to each other. If we can write a book together and live to tell about it, we can survive anything.

ACKNOWLEDGMENTS

Books are not written in a vacuum, and *Mastering PageMaker 4 on the IBM PC* is no exception. We would like to thank the following people at SYBEX: Marilyn Smith for her thorough copy and developmental editing, Maryann Brown for her technical expertise, Dianne King for asking us to write the book, and Janna Hecker for coordinating this project. Also, many thanks to Cynthia Uberty, Craig Danuloff, and Freda Cook at Aldus for helping us with logistics and technical issues.

We would also like to thank our good friend Randy Haldeman for allowing us to use his company's brochure for one of the practice exercises in this book.

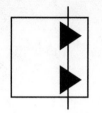

CONTENTS
AT A GLANCE

TABLE OF CONTENTS

APPENDICES

INTRODUCTION

This book features the delightful dichotomy of the grand old desktop publishing program meeting the young, upstart graphical user interface. With PageMaker now running under Windows 3.0, the envelope of free-form page layout and illustration has been pushed to a new horizon on personal computers. While we expect a few oohs and ahs from you over PageMaker's arsenal of features, we won't be a bit surprised if you raise an eyebrow over the background as well. Such elements as the new Clipboard, dynamic data exchange, and the Adobe Type Manager surely place Windows 3.0 near the top of the list of major developments in personal computing and desktop publishing.

HOW TO USE THIS BOOK

Mastering PageMaker 4 on the IBM PC is a tutorial, with easy step-by-step exercises that you can follow at your computer. This book takes a hands-on approach; you will learn by doing. Pictures of the screen are provided at key points so that you can check to make sure you are on the right track.

You can also use this book as a reference guide when you need to review a topic. Use the index or table of contents to locate the subject, and then read through the text to refresh your memory.

NEW FEATURES IN PAGEMAKER 4

This book was written for the latest version of PageMaker, which contains an abundance of new features, as listed below. If you are upgrading from version 3 to version 4, you might want to turn directly to the indicated chapters.

- The *Story Editor* is a built-in word processor that allows you to type, edit, find, replace, and check the spelling of your text. (See Chapter 6.)

- You can *link* imported stories and graphics with their external files so that when you change the original file, the internal file is automatically updated. (See Chapter 9.)

- You can *rotate text* in 90-degree increments. (See Chapter 10.)

- Instead of using the drawing tools to draw lines, you can create horizontal lines with a rules formatting command. Rules can be placed above or below paragraphs. (See Chapter 11.)

- In earlier versions of PageMaker, all graphics were stationary; they were anchored at the location on the page where they were placed. In version 4, graphics can move with the text they are associated with. Graphics that flow with the text are called *inline graphics*. (See Chapters 11 and 12.)

- The *Table Editor* is a stand-alone program that enables you to type columnar information in cells, similar to a spreadsheet. You can perform simple calculations with the numbers and enhance the table with borders and shading. These tables can then be imported into PageMaker. (See Chapter 13.)

- Creating a long document that consists of multiple publication files is now a reality. You can group together related publications into a *book* and automatically number across these publications. You can also create *tables of contents* and *indexes* for your publications. (See Chapter 15.)

These are just the most noteworthy new features in PageMaker 4. There are dozens of other additions that you will discover as you explore the program and read this book.

HOW THIS BOOK IS ORGANIZED

This book is divided into four parts and has four appendices. Because each chapter builds on the material covered in the previous chapter, you will want to read this book in the order it is presented. However, experienced PageMaker users might want to skim through the first introductory chapters. And if you haven't yet installed PageMaker, turn directly to Appendix A.

The chapters in each part are briefly described below.

Part 1: Getting Started

Part 1 introduces the basic procedures for creating publications in PageMaker. This part is the foundation upon which the book is built.

Chapter 1 explains what desktop publishing is and what its goals are, in addition to what PageMaker's capabilities are (and aren't). You will also learn the basic recipe for producing publications.

In Chapter 2, you will learn how to interact with PageMaker. This chapter describes how to start the program, shows you how to use the mouse and give commands, and explains the Microsoft Windows environment in which PageMaker runs.

Chapter 3 provides new PageMaker users with a quick tour of the publishing process. As you follow the steps in this chapter, you will go through the mechanics and maneuvers inherent in building a publication in PageMaker.

Chapter 4 covers two important parts of the desktop publishing process: specifying the layout of your page and printing your publication.

Part 2: Working with Text

Text is the primary ingredient in most publications, and Part 2 will demonstrate the variety of ways you can place and format text.

In Chapter 5, you will type and format a company letterhead. In the process of creating the letter, you will learn how to correct typing errors, move text to another location on the page, and change the size and style of the type.

Chapter 6 describes how to use PageMaker's built-in word processor, the Story Editor. This editor has many of the same capabilities as a word processing program, including finding and replacing text and checking spelling.

Chapter 7 explains the many different ways you can format paragraphs: centering, justification, indentation, hyphenation, spacing, and so on. You will practice paragraph formatting on a three-panel brochure you will create.

Chapter 8 shows you how to automate the formatting process by using the *style* feature. With styles, changing a paragraph's format is only a few mouse clicks away.

Chapter 9 demonstrates another way to place text on the page: by importing it from a file you created in your word processor. You will also learn how to link your publication to an external text file so that when you change the text file, the publication automatically reflects this change.

Chapter 10 describes the different ways you can adjust the spacing between letters and words in PageMaker. You will also learn how to rotate text and create drop caps.

Part 3: Working with Graphics

In Part 3, you will learn how to add numerous graphic elements (lines, boxes, drawings, and so on) to your publications. Graphic elements contribute variety and visual interest to a page. There are two ways to add graphics to a page: by drawing them in PageMaker or by importing them from an external graphics program. Chapter 11 shows you how to create graphics with PageMaker's built-in drawing tools. Chapter 12 explains how to import external images.

Chapter 13 discusses the Table Editor, a stand-alone program included with PageMaker. With the Table Editor, you can create a wide variety of columnar material such as financial reports, forms, calendars, schedules, and price lists.

Part 4: Using Time-Saving Tools

Part 4 presents strategies for managing different types of publishing projects. Chapter 14 describes how to clone a publication that you will be using over and over again, such as a monthly newsletter. Chapter 15 shows you how to manage "monster" (large) projects, such as a book. You will learn how to create a table of contents and an index. Chapter 16 is what we call *The PageMaker Cookbook*. In this chapter, we give you recipes for a variety of projects, from business cards and resumes to menus and invitations.

Appendices

While the appendices are at the back of the book, don't wait until you have finished Chapters 1 through 16 before you read them. Appendix A takes you through the steps of installing PageMaker, so if you haven't yet run the ALDSETUP program, follow the steps in this appendix.

Appendix B is a primer for Microsoft Windows 3.0 neophytes. You will learn how to change the size and position of a window, simultaneously run several applications, and run a DOS application in a window. If you are new to Windows, turn to this appendix to strengthen your windowing skills.

Appendix C discusses many different aspects of using fonts in Page-Maker. It covers beginning as well as advanced issues, including the installation of screen and printer fonts.

Finally, Appendix D explains the process of printing documents on remote PostScript printers and high-resolution typesetting devices. If professional quality is your goal, read this appendix to see how you can achieve it.

PART ONE

▼ ▼ ▼ ▼ ▼ ▼ ▼ ▼ ▼ ▼

GETTING STARTED

Part 1 is dedicated to the novice PageMaker user. The four chapters in this section will introduce you to desktop publishing concepts and the basic procedures for creating publications in PageMaker. Even if you have been using PageMaker for a while, you still might want to read through these chapters because you will undoubtedly pick up a few shortcuts and fill in some gaps in your knowledge about the software.

C H A P T E R

1

INTRODUCING
DESKTOP
PUBLISHING
WITH
PAGEMAKER

This chapter is dedicated to neophytes of desktop publishing and PageMaker. You will learn what desktop publishing is and what its goals are, what PageMaker's capabilities are (and aren't), and tips for becoming a designer.

WHAT IS DTP?

Desktop publishing (also known as *DTP)* is a term that refers to the process of designing and printing documents, using three relatively inexpensive tools:

- Personal computer
- Page-layout program (such as PageMaker)
- Laser printer

With a $5,000 initial investment (perhaps less), you can produce publications that formerly required many thousands of dollars worth of equipment, or the use of an outside design firm and typesetting shop. As you may know from experience, farming out your publications has several disadvantages. First, you are at the mercy of the designer's and typesetter's schedule, and your priorities are not necessarily their priorities. Second, it's expensive, and if you have a lot of publications, perhaps monthly ones, the expense accrues endlessly. Third, each design change requires another round of expense and scheduling conflicts.

It's likely that at least one of the three above reasons is why you are using PageMaker. By publishing it yourself, you have more control over staying within your deadlines and your budget.

THE GOALS OF DESKTOP PUBLISHING

As a desktop publisher, your mission (which you have already chosen to accept) is to design attractive, easy-to-read, professional-looking publications. Your aim is to "sell" your document to your potential readers—to entice them to begin reading your publication and to keep them interested once they have begun.

An integral part of fulfilling your mission is knowing who your audience is. If you are preparing a brochure for a conservative corporation, its design should also be conservative to reflect the company's orientation. On the other hand, if you are creating a flier for a new teenie-bopper boutique, your design can be more avant-garde. If your publication has a design inappropriate for its audience, the reader might not give it more than a cursory glance.

Although creating an attractive design is an important goal of DTP, it should not be your sole purpose. The reason why you are designing a particular publication is not to decorate a page; rather, it is to communicate information in an organized, easy-to-follow manner. Therefore, a second goal of DTP is actually a component of the first goal: to present the text in a way that communicates the relative importance of each piece of information.

The size of each element on the page (such as headlines, subheadings, pictures, captions, and body text) should be determined by its relative importance and the amount of space available. The most important information should stand out in some way: bigger, bolder, boxed, and so on (but not all at once!). You should come up with a hierarchy of headings that allows the reader to easily discern the major headings from the subheadings. As you'll soon see, this is easy to do in PageMaker.

Want an example of this structure? You're holding it. By glancing through this book, you can see that there are three levels of headings, with each level set in a different style. This organized and consistent structure makes it easier for you, the reader, to understand the information.

Contrary to popular belief, maximizing the number of different DTP features used on one page is *not* a goal of desktop publishing. Using many fonts, shades, boxes, and lines is not only unattractive, but it also distracts the readers and inhibits their understanding of the message you are trying to convey. You probably see examples of this everywhere. An order form used to have a bit of bold and a few lines. Now it has rounded rectangles, gray shades all over the place, bold and italic everywhere, fancy borders, and little hands pointing to all the important things. Newsletters used to just have page numbers; now they have little clip-art men holding signs with the page numbers inside. Figure 1.1 is a prime example of how DTP features can be overused.

THE MIRACLE THAT YOU HAVE BEEN WAITING FOR!!!

Yes, YOU, for a *limited time only*, can finally relish the secrets of longevity. For the first time ever in the Western World come the deep dark secrets of the **WALA WALA PLANT**, a special herb that actually slows down the aging process.

And it can be yours for the low, low price of $39.95 per month! But wait--there's more. The price drops to $37.95 once you pass your 80th birthday and then drops by a dollar every five years after that.

Figure 1.1: Overuse of DTP features makes it difficult to read the page

WHAT PAGEMAKER CAN (AND CAN'T) DO FOR YOU

With PageMaker, you can create a wide variety of publications:

- Advertisements
- Business cards
- Resumes
- Letterhead and memo paper
- Brochures
- Fliers
- Newsletters
- Annual reports
- Course outlines and other instructional materials

PageMaker is best known for its handling of short documents such as brochures and fliers. However, with some of the new features added to version 4, you can also produce longer documents, such as books, technical manuals, and catalogs. For example, you can now create tables of contents and indexes that span multiple files.

PageMaker is a page-layout program—a software package whose forte is helping you *position* text and graphics on the page. Although you can do limited word processing and drawing in PageMaker, its strength is not necessarily *creating* the text and graphics.

The program is not a full-blown word processor. Granted, you can type text directly on the page, or use version 4's Story Editor to type and edit in a window. But if you need capabilities beyond simple editing, searching and replacing, and checking your spelling, you should compose your documents in your favorite word processing program. Your word processing documents can be imported directly into PageMaker, as explained in Chapter 9.

Nor is PageMaker a painting or drawing program. Although you can draw lines, boxes, and circular shapes, you cannot rotate graphic objects, draw free-form paintings, or modify a clip-art image. If you need to perform any sophisticated graphic manipulation, you must turn to a separate drawing or painting package, such as Corel Draw or Windows Paintbrush. Then you can import the graphic into PageMaker, as described in Chapter 12.

BECOMING A DESIGNER

PageMaker attracts all types of users: professional graphic artists, secretaries, consultants, your mother, and anyone else who is looking for quality output. PageMaker is popular with professional designers partly because of the program's similarity to their "old-fashioned" paste-up boards. A paste-up board is a work table onto which the page is placed. Typically, designers place all the elements of the document on the edges of the paste-up board and move them onto the page when needed. One by one, photos, captions, headlines, and galleys make their way from the paste-up board onto the page.

You can work the same way in PageMaker. As shown in Figure 1.2, the page appears in the middle of the screen, while the *pasteboard* is the area surrounding the page. As you are designing a publication, you can place objects on the pasteboard temporarily, and then position, or *paste*, them on the page when you are ready.

Although graphic designers make up a good part of PageMaker's user base, you don't have to be in the design profession to use PageMaker. By following a few basic design rules, and with practice and trial and error, anyone can lay out attractive pages in PageMaker.

The first rule for the beginning DTPer is simplicity. Subscribe to the belief that small is beautiful and less is more; don't try to cram as many elements onto a page as is electronically possible. One easy way to be assured of getting an attractive document is by borrowing and recycling good design, as explained in the next two sections.

Borrowing Good Design

Imitation is not only the highest form of flattery, it is often good business. We are not suggesting you republish *Rolling Stone*, articles and all—just that you keep your eye out for advertisements, articles, and newsletters that you think are presented well.

For example, if you like the way a particular brochure is put together, try to recreate it in PageMaker. If you like the clone that you produced, use it for your next similar project. This type of borrowing is completely legal. You can't get sued for look-and-feel infringement of a document's design. Good design belongs to everyone.

There is nothing wrong with adapting an existing design that you find appealing, as long as you don't clone a patented logo or copyrighted slogan. In fact, trying to replicate a successful layout is an excellent way to practice using PageMaker and develop your own sense of design.

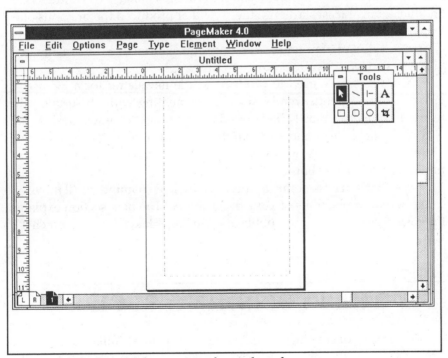

Figure 1.2: The PageMaker page and pasteboard

Recycling Your Successful Designs

Close your eyes and imagine two or three magazines that you think are particularly well-designed: maybe *Newsweek, Life, The Atlantic Monthly,* or *Sports Illustrated.* As you visualize them, certain characteristics might come to mind, such as the way *Life* uses large type, or *Sports Illustrated*'s catchy headlines burned into full-page photos, or *Newsweek*'s section heads that are always white type on red bars.

These magazines aren't well-designed because they do something fabulously different every month; they do the same things over and over again. Each one has found a design that works and has stayed with it for years at a time. That is what makes them distinctive.

Don't think that every document that you create has to be a perfect original—even the famous designers don't try to do that. If you just produced a manual and it happens to look good, bottle it, save it, and use it for your next manual. Maybe you'll decide to change a few things here and there, but at least start with the style that produced the previous one. When something works, get as much mileage out of it as you can. By recycling good design, you will not only produce attractive documents, but you will also reduce your production time.

For example, we used to produce a little newsletter for a PC user's group, and we spent several issues experimenting with all sorts of different design ideas, mostly bad ones. Finally, we settled into a design that was reasonably clean and unencumbered, and used it for every single issue. By recycling this design each month, we pared down a five-hour production job to one hour.

Now that you have some design basics to keep in mind, we'll move on to the actual components of your publications. The next section explains the basic recipe for creating a publication in PageMaker. Put on your chef's hat ....

THE PUBLISHING RECIPE

The process of creating a PageMaker document is similar to following a recipe from your favorite cookbook. To bake a pie, for example, you need a number of ingredients (flour, cherries, sugar, etc.) and various utensils (bowls, spoons, rolling pin, pie dish, and so on). Creating a PageMaker document also requires certain ingredients and special utensils.

The Ingredients

In the beginning, the publishing gods created alphanumeric characters and geometric figures. When you get right down to it, those two heavenly bodies represent the essence of any publishing project. Sure, there is design, inspiration, structure, logic, and no small amount of sweat, but the basic ingredients for the publishing recipe are text and graphics.

Text

There are several ways to include text in a PageMaker document, and we might as well start using the correct terminology; PageMaker calls documents *publications,* and so we will, too. Each publication can comprise one or more stories. A *story* is a continuous block of text that PageMaker recognizes as a single unit. For example, each article in a newsletter is a separate story. A story can be as short as a single headline or as long as a chapter in a book.

You can use one of four methods to include a story in a publication:

- Type it directly onto the page or pasteboard, while in PageMaker.
- Type it into the Story Editor, a simple word processor that appears in its own window.
- Produce a text file in a word processor or text editor and import it into PageMaker.
- Type text in another program, copy the text to Windows' Clipboard, and then paste the text from the Clipboard into PageMaker.

The method you choose depends on the situation, and most of the time your choice will be immediately apparent to you. Let's look at several scenarios.

If all you need to do is create a few headlines or captions, simply type the text onto the page or pasteboard. This technique is explained in Chapter 5.

To type more than a few lines, use either the Story Editor or your word processor. The Story Editor is convenient because it's available inside PageMaker. However, your word processor contains more extensive editing capabilities. You probably will feel more comfortable composing longer stories in your word processor. This is not to say that the Story Editor is worthless. On the contrary, it is quite useful for typing short blocks of text, making revisions, checking spelling, searching for and replacing text, and a few other things you will learn about in Chapter 6.

If the document already exists in a word processing program, you will want to import the file into PageMaker. Importing text files is discussed in Chapter 9.

To bring in part of a word processed document, the Clipboard's cut-and-paste method is your fastest route. See Appendix B for details on using the Clipboard to bring in text.

Regardless of where the text came from, once the story is in a publication, you can edit it directly on the page or in the Story Editor.

Graphics

The second basic ingredient, graphic elements, is usually a part of every publication, even if only in minimal form (such as lines—called *rules* in DTP—above or below headlines). Graphic elements can be incorporated into publications in the following ways:

- Simple geometric figures, such as rectangles, circles, and lines, can be drawn from within PageMaker.

- Shades and rules can be added to text through various Page-Maker formatting commands.

- More complex graphics can be produced in external drawing or paint programs and imported into PageMaker.

- Many types of graphics can be brought across the Clipboard into PageMaker.

You cannot edit an imported graphics file as you can a text file. To make actual changes to a picture, you must return to the program that produced it. However, you can modify the way PageMaker presents a graphic by sizing or cropping it.

To summarize, text and graphics can be created inside PageMaker or produced outside and then imported. Either way, it is in the confines of a PageMaker publication that the stew begins to simmer.

The Appliances

The PageMaker soup kitchen has more utensils than the Galloping Gourmet and Julia Child combined. In fact, some say that there are too many utensils, inviting well-meaning but inexperienced users to overuse them on their way to producing grossly overblown documents. That's where a few well-conceived recipes come in very handy.

Too numerous to list in their entirety, some of PageMaker's more significant tools include the following:

- Automatic flow of text across all the pages of a document
- Weaving and threading of multiple text files across one document
- Newsletter-style flow of text across columns
- Formatting and spacing of any portion of a paragraph, sentence, or word
- Global formatting of text and headlines
- Powerful header and footer controls, including automatic page numbering
- Generation of tables of contents and indexes
- Different ways of wrapping text around a graphic
- Typography tools to control the precise placement of each character on the page
- A Table Editor to help lay out columnar data

These are some of the slicers, the dicers, the skillets, and the casserole dishes of PageMaker. It is with these tools that you shape the two primary ingredients into a document.

The Recipe

Here comes the hard part (or the easy part, depending upon your point of view), the part that comes from your own thoughts and feelings. We won't pretend to teach you the art of publishing because we don't believe any book can, or should even try. We do believe that there is a philosophy associated with using PageMaker. But you cannot practice instinct and you cannot learn feel; they must come to you over time.

Nonetheless, having an understanding of how the ingredients and utensils are used together is absolutely crucial. Developing a sense of the appropriate use of PageMaker's power is equally important, and with these gray areas we will attempt to assist you.

To conclude our culinary analogies, remember back to your high school or college days when you finally got a date with that person of your dreams. You offered to make dinner, despite a long history of burnt toast. Now what did you choose that evening? Did you go for it with Beef Wellington in a wine and mushroom sauce, with stir-fried vegetables sauteed in garlic, butter, and cilantro, or did you play it safe with lemon chicken, salad, and french bread?

If you chose the former, you may be in for a few desktop disasters as a publisher. But if you recognized your limitations back then, maybe you will do so with your publications and stick with the stuff that you *know* you can produce effectively.

Unless you are a professional designer or have a natural sense of illustration and typography, leave the rule-breaking to the experts. At least for now, concentrate on simple recipes that don't get in the way of the intended message of the text. Without exception, the content of your document reigns supreme over its form. It's easy to forget that as you learn a program as rich in fancy features as PageMaker, but try to stay aware of your first reason for wanting to publish something, which is to get across a certain message.

This chapter provided the background you need to start working with a desktop publishing program. By keeping your audience in mind, keeping the design simple enough not to overwhelm the message, and borrowing and recycling good design, you can produce professional-looking publications.

We will present other design tips throughout the book, but now it's time for action. In the following chapter, you will start PageMaker and learn some of the program's basic features.

C H A P T E R

2

INTERACTING WITH PAGEMAKER

Whenever you buy a new electronic toy, whether it's a VCR, a microwave oven, or a PC with PageMaker, the first thing you have to do after plugging it in is to determine what you have to do to make it work. You need to know what all the buttons mean, how to give instructions, and how to read or understand the electronic display. This chapter gives you the information you need to begin working with PageMaker. You will start the program, learn how to use the menus, and learn the significance of what you see in the PageMaker window.

If you are experienced with other Windows applications or Macintosh software, you may find that you are already familiar with much of the information presented here. You may want to skim over the material, looking at the section headings to see if any of the topics are new to you.

WORKING UNDER WINDOWS

We'll begin by discussing the environment in which you will be using PageMaker. PageMaker 4 works under the Microsoft Windows 3.0 program. Windows is a program that has a variety of functions.

To begin, Windows provides a "launching pad" for all your software programs. Instead of loading a program by typing commands at your unfriendly DOS prompt, you click the mouse pointer on a little picture (called an *icon*) on the screen. This launching pad is called *Program Manager.*

Through Windows, you can run more than one software program at a time. Thus, your word processor, a graphics program, and PageMaker can be in memory all at the same time, each in its own window (hence, the name Windows). Just by pressing a couple of keys or clicking the mouse, you can instantly be working in another program. This feature is called *concurrent operation.*

The *Clipboard* is another feature of Windows. This is an area of memory that lets you transfer data between programs by simply cutting and pasting what you see on the screen. The Clipboard is discussed in Chapter 12 and Appendix B.

Windows comes with a file-management utility called *File Manager.* You can use File Manager to copy, move, erase, and rename your files.

Along with Program Manager and File Manager, the Windows package includes a wealth of other programs and accessories. You may find the following useful while you are running PageMaker:

- *Write*, for word processing
- *Calendar*, for keeping track of appointments
- *Notepad*, for jotting down notes
- *Calculator*, for calculating page layout settings
- *Clock*, for checking the time
- *Solitaire*, for when you need a break

To get the most out of PageMaker, it's important that you understand the Windows environment. Because PageMaker has limited features for creating text and graphics, it imports them from other programs. The Windows environment makes this importing process easier. Throughout the exercises in this book, you will get opportunities to practice using some of the Windows features. To learn more about Windows, see Appendix B. If you need further information, refer to a book such as *Mastering Microsoft Windows 3.0.*

STARTING PAGEMAKER

If you haven't yet installed PageMaker on your hard disk, you should turn to Appendix A for instructions and return here when you are finished. You also must have Microsoft Windows 3.0 installed on your computer before you can load PageMaker.

Follow these steps to load Windows and then start PageMaker:

1. At your DOS prompt, type **WIN** and press Enter.

The Program Manager window, with all your program group icons, is displayed on your screen, which should look similar to Figure 2.1. The names of your program groups will be different, although everyone who has installed PageMaker will have an Aldus group. The PageMaker 4

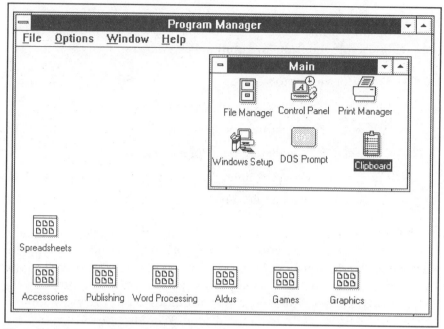

Figure 2.1: The Program Manager Window

program icon should be inside this group. However, your PageMaker icon
may be in a different group if you or someone else moved it elsewhere.
Before you go any further, determine which group PageMaker is in.

2. Check to see if your Aldus group is open. If you see a window
    titled Aldus that contains the PageMaker 4.0 icon, as shown in
    Figure 2.2, proceed to step 5. Otherwise, continue with the
    next step.

3. Move the mouse pointer to the Aldus group icon (or whichever
    group PageMaker is in).

4. Click the left mouse button twice quickly. This is called
    double-clicking.

You will see a window containing the group's program icons. Your
screen should look similar to Figure 2.2. If you got a menu instead of the
window, you didn't click the button correctly. Press Esc and try again.

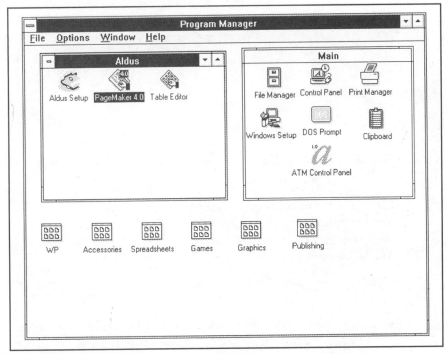

Figure 2.2: The PageMaker 4 icon in the Aldus program group

5. Move the mouse pointer to the PageMaker 4.0 icon.

6. Double-click the left mouse button to load the PageMaker program.

After 30 seconds or so, you will see the menu bar at the top of the screen.

USING THE MENUS

You use the menu bar to give PageMaker instructions on how to lay out your pages. As shown in Figure 2.3, the menu bar contains eight different options:

- File: Use this menu to manipulate your files. You can create, open, close, save, export, and import files. The menu also contains commands for printing.

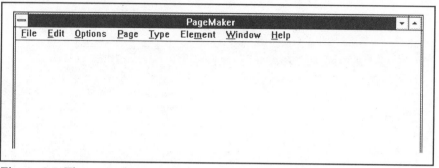

Figure 2.3: The menu bar

- Edit: This menu contains options for cutting and pasting text and graphics. The options are available within PageMaker, as well as in other applications that are running under Windows. The Story Editor commands are also on the Edit menu.

- Options: This menu primarily contains items that can be turned on and off, such as rulers and guides.

- Page: Use this menu to view the page at different levels of magnification. For example, you can see the entire page at once with one option, or you can zoom a section of a page to twice its actual size with another. You can also choose to insert and delete pages.

- Type: The options on this menu allow you to specify the size and alignment of your text. Almost everything related to text is on the Type menu, including fonts, sizes, alignment, type styles, spacing, and indentations. You will probably use this menu more than any other.

- Element: This menu contains options that affect graphic elements.

- Window: Use this menu to control what you see in your window. For example, you can turn on and off the display of a tool box, color palette, and a style palette.

- Help: Use this menu to display an index of different topics on which on-line information is available. You can also press F1 at any time for help.

Of Mice and Menus

How you work with the PageMaker menus depends on whether you want to use the mouse or the keyboard. Some people (namely, those who know how to type) prefer keeping their hands on the keyboard as much as possible. However, if you flunked Typing 1A in high school, you will love the mouse and will only resort to the keyboard when there is no alternative.

The Pull-Down Menus

To use the mouse in the menu bar, move the mouse pointer to the option you want to select, and then click the left mouse button once. You will see a *pull-down menu*, which displays options on a vertical list, directly below the option on the menu bar. For practice, let's look at some of the pull-down menus, without actually choosing any of the options (like going window shopping).

1. Place the mouse pointer on File in the menu bar.
2. Click the left mouse button. The File pull-down menu is displayed.
3. Place the mouse pointer on Type in the menu bar.
4. Click the left mouse button. The File pull-down menu disappears, and the Type pull-down menu is displayed.
5. Pull down the Options menu.
6. Pull down the File menu.

Now take a closer look at the File pull-down menu, which is shown in Figure 2.4. Notice that some of the options are in a different color or shade than the others. The options that are currently unavailable are dimmed (in a faint type). For example, Close and Save are dimmed because you can't close or save a file when you haven't created one yet. However, New and Open are currently available. If you try to choose an unavailable option, your request will be ignored.

Many of the options are followed by ellipses (for example, *Open…*, and *Save as…*). The three dots indicate that a dialog box will appear when you select the option. A *dialog box* is a fill-in-the-blank form that prompts you to supply further information. Later in this chapter, you'll learn how to fill in dialog boxes.

Cascading Menus

Some of the options on the Type and Element menus have a right-pointing triangle next to them. In the Element pull-down menu, the Line and Fill options have this symbol, which indicates that a *cascading menu* will appear when you select the option. A cascading menu displays a list of additional choices. You can experiment with one now:

1. Pull down the Element menu.

2. Place the mouse pointer on the Fill option.

3. Click the left mouse button.

A cascading menu pops out to the right of the option, as shown in Figure 2.5. This particular menu displays the types of patterns that can fill the boxes and circles you draw. The currently selected option has a check

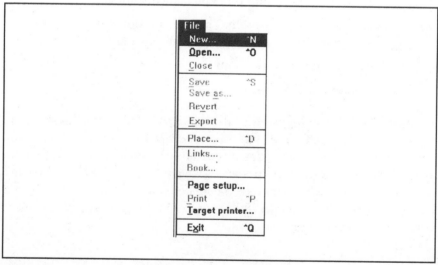

Figure 2.4: Dimmed options are currently unavailable

mark next to it. Thus, None is the *default,* or automatic, setting for the Fill option.

4. To choose a different filling (for example, a 10% shade), click on that option.

5. If you would like additional practice, or just want to explore a bit, continue and select the other options that have cascading menus (but be sure to reset them to their original settings before continuing).

Toggle Options

On the Options menu, some of the options are checked. The check mark indicates that the option is turned on. Some options are *toggles,* which means that the same command turns it both on and off. You will learn later exactly what these options are turning on and off, but for now, let's get accustomed to identifying the current setting (on or off) of an option, and learn how to change it.

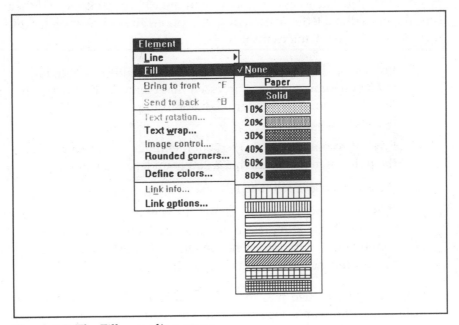

Figure 2.5: The Fill cascading menu

1. Pull down the Options menu. As you can see by the check marks on this menu, Rulers, Guides, and Snap to Guides are all turned on.

2. With the mouse pointer on Snap to Guides, click once. This action turns off the option.

3. Pull down the Options menu again and notice that the Snap to Guides option is no longer checked.

4. While the Options menu is still displayed, turn on the Autoflow option.

5. Return the options to their defaults: turn on Snap to Guides and turn off Autoflow.

Using the Keyboard

For those who would rather not shift their hands from the keyboard to the mouse, PageMaker offers two ways to give commands from the keyboard. First, you can access the menu with the F10 or Alt keys, and then type the underlined letter of each desired option. To see if you prefer this method, try the following example:

1. Press F10. The first option on the menu bar, File, is highlighted to let you know you have accessed that menu. Notice that each option has one letter underlined. For example, the *m* in *Element* is underlined.

2. Press M to pull down the Element menu. Each of the items on the pull-down menu also has a single underlined letter.

3. Press F to choose Fill. The Fill cascading menu pops out.

4. Press the arrow keys to highlight different options, and then highlight None and press Enter. If a cascading menu does not contain items with underlined letters, you must use the arrow keys or the mouse to select an option.

Although the mouse may be more fun to use, expert typists can probably issue commands faster with the keyboard. A fast typist can beat a fast mouser any day.

A second way to give commands with the keyboard is with keyboard shortcuts. These shortcuts usually consist of pressing the Ctrl (Control) key in conjunction with one other key. For example, instead of saving a file by pulling down the File menu and choosing Save, you can hold down Ctrl and press S. For the shortcut to work, the Ctrl key must be depressed the whole time; it is similar to keeping the clutch in while you change gears in a manual transmission car.

Many PageMaker commands can be issued with keyboard shortcuts. How do you know what all these key-combinations are? One way is to look at the complete list on the inside covers of this book. An alternative is to refer to the menus.

Pull down a menu now, such as the File menu, and you will see that some of the options have codes next to them. On the File menu, ^N is next to New and ^S is next to Save. The ^ symbol is an abbreviation for the Ctrl key.

Some of these shortcuts use the Shift key in conjunction with another key or two. On the Edit menu, for example, you can see Sh Del next to the Cut option. Thus, to issue the Cut command, you hold down the Shift key as you press the Del (Delete) key.

The keyboard shortcuts appear on the menu to help you memorize them. As you issue commands from a menu, keep an eye on these codes; maybe the next time you give the command, you can save time by using the keyboard shortcut. Don't expend a lot of effort trying to memorize them—just learn them as you go. We will remind you of the keyboard shortcuts throughout the book.

Conversing with Dialog Boxes

Sometimes when you pull down a menu and make a choice, that's all you have to do. When you instructed PageMaker to turn on the Autoflow option, there was nothing more to the discussion. But to carry out many functions, PageMaker needs further direction, and so it presents you with a dialog box and asks you to fill in a few blanks.

As mentioned earlier, a menu option that has three dots after it displays a dialog box when you select it. A dialog box is the equivalent of a waitress asking you questions after you have given her your order: "Do you want soup or salad?"; "How would you like your steak prepared?"; "Would you prefer rice or baked potato?"

Dialog boxes ask you similar questions—not about food but about the particular command you have selected. For example, if you choose the Open command on the File menu, a dialog box asks you for the name of a file to open.

There are several types of options in a dialog box, which are labeled in Figure 2.6 and described in Table 2.1. Some options (*text boxes*) require you to type in numbers or text, and others have you choose from a list (*list boxes* and *drop-down lists*) or turn a setting on or off (*option buttons* and *check boxes*). Sometimes there are dialog boxes within dialog boxes.

With few exceptions, almost every dialog box has two *command buttons*, labeled OK and Cancel. You click on OK when you are finished filling in the box; click on the Cancel button if you decide to cancel the command you issued. You don't have to memorize the official names of all these types of options, but you should recognize them when you see them.

To practice using a dialog box, let's create a new file.

1. Pull down the File menu.

2. Choose New. The Page Setup dialog box appears (the one shown in Figure 2.6).

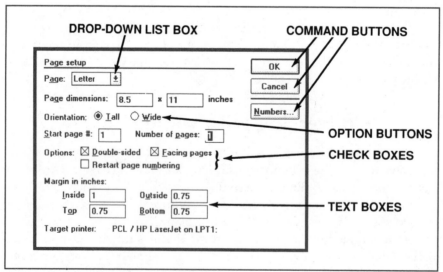

Figure 2.6: The Page Setup dialog box

This dialog box lets you define your page size and layout. These options will be defined in more detail in Chapter 4. For now, we'll concentrate on the techniques to use to fill in a dialog box.

3. The first option in the dialog box, Page, has a down-pointing arrow to the right of the current choice, Letter. Click on this arrow. A drop-down list of page sizes is displayed. This menu is similar to the cascading menu you have already seen.

4. Click on Custom. Now Custom appears next to Page.

5. The next option, Page Dimensions, has two text boxes. The current page width, 8.5, is already highlighted. To enter a new page width, type **5**.

You type in values for many other options in this dialog box: the page length, Start Page #, Number of Pages, and the margins at the bottom

Table 2.1: Dialog Box Options

OPTION TYPE	DESCRIPTION
Drop-down list box	A vertical list of choices that is displayed when you click on the arrow
Text boxes	Rectangles into which you type information
Option buttons	A set of two or three circles that represent mutually exclusive options (only one option can be selected)
Check boxes	A group of squares that represent nonexclusive options (turn on or off as many as you like)
List box	A list of choices from which you can select one item
Command buttons	Boxed words that carry out a command (OK), cancel the command (Cancel), or open another dialog box (Numbers...)

of the box. In order to enter a new value, you must first select, or highlight, the current value. Instead of highlighting the value, you can click to the right of the value and then delete it with the Backspace key.

6. To highlight the page length, double-click just to the right of 11.

7. To replace 11 with a new number, type **7**.

8. Change the value in the Number of Pages field to **2**.

9. The next option, Orientation, has two option buttons: Tall and Wide. Right now the dot is next to Tall. Click on the circle next to Wide (or even the word itself) to specify a horizontal page orientation, (also known as *sideways* or *landscape*). The dot jumps to Wide.

10. The Double-Sided and Facing Pages options have check boxes next to them. Click on the box next to Facing Pages. The X disappears as the option is turned off.

Think of the check boxes as on/off switches. Click on the description or check box, and the option turns on or off, depending on its current state. If an X appears in the box, the option is turned on.

11. Click on the OK command button to accept all the choices you have entered. A page appears with the dimensions you specified.

Using the Keyboard with Dialog Boxes

You can also use the keyboard to choose dialog box options, as follows:

- Use the Tab key to move between the options in a dialog box.

- To go directly to an option, press Alt and type the underlined letter. For example, to choose the Wide option in the Page Setup dialog box, hold down Alt and press W.

- Press Enter instead of clicking on the OK button.

- Press Esc instead of clicking on the Cancel button.

Note that even if you are an avid mouser, it often makes more sense to press Enter than to click on OK. As instructors, we frequently observe students typing in a value, taking a hand off the keyboard, reaching for the mouse, moving the pointer to OK, and clicking the mouse button. The basic rule of thumb to follow is if you have your hands on the keyboard, press Enter; if you are selecting options with the mouse, click on OK.

UNDERSTANDING
THE PAGEMAKER WINDOW

Before you go any further, you should understand the PageMaker window. As you read this section, refer to Figure 2.7, which points out the important areas.

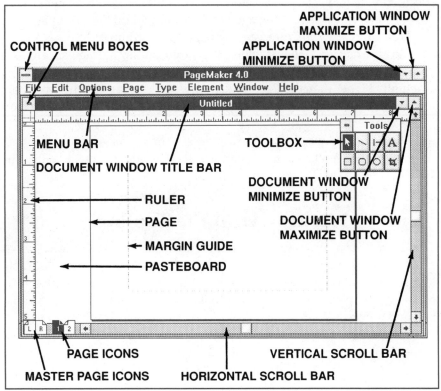

Figure 2.7: The PageMaker window

Some of the areas of the screen are identical in all Windows applications; others are unique to PageMaker. As in other Windows applications, you can click on the document window maximize button (marked in Figure 2.7) to enlarge the area you have available for your page. You will see that we did this for most of the figures in this book. For more information about Windows icons (maximize button, minimize button, and control menu), see Appendix B.

The current page or page spread appears in the middle of the window. (A *page spread* consists of two pages side by side in a double-sided publication.) The dashed lines inside the page are your *margin guides*, which separate the body of the page from the margins. Although PageMaker will let you type in the margin area, usually your text and graphics will go inside the rectangle formed by the margin guides.

The margins, along with the page size and orientation (tall or wide) are specified when you create the publication. However, you can later change the page layout by using the Page Setup command on the File menu.

The empty area surrounding the page is called the *pasteboard*. As you learned in Chapter 1, the pasteboard is a temporary storage spot where you can place objects before you paste them onto the page. The pasteboard is actually bigger than the PageMaker window. You can use the scroll bars to view nonvisible parts of the pasteboard. You will practice scrolling later in this chapter.

The name of your publication appears in the *document window title bar*. Because you haven't assigned a name to the file you just created, the title bar displays *Untitled*.

Working with the Toolbox

The *toolbox* appears in the upper-right corner of the window. Just as graphic designers have a box of tools, containing rulers, T-squares, exacto knives, blue pens, and so on, PageMaker users have a tool box that rests on top of the pasteboard. The PageMaker tools let you create or modify text and graphics on the page. Table 2.2 describes each of these tools.

To practice using the toolbox, let's draw a box with the rounded-corner tool.

Table 2.2: The Tools in the Toolbox

ICON	NAME	FUNCTION	KEYBOARD SHORTCUT
▸	Pointer tool	Selects objects on the page or pasteboard	F9
╲	Diagonal-line tool	Draws lines in any direction	Shift-F2
⊢	Perpendicular line tool	Draws lines restricted to 45-degree angles	Shift-F3
A	Text tool	Enters, edits, and selects text	Shift-F4
□	Square-corner tool	Draws rectangles with square corners	Shift-F5
▢	Rounded-corner tool	Draws rectangles with rounded corners	Shift-F6
○	Circle/oval tool	Draws circles or ellipses	Shift-F7
⌗	Cropping tool	Crops (trims) a graphic	Shift-F8

1. Click on the rounded-corner tool. The pointer turns into a crossbar when you move it onto the pasteboard or page.

2. Place the crossbar somewhere in the upper-right corner of the page. The exact position is not important in this example.

3. Click and hold down the left mouse button. Do not release the button until you have finished drawing the box. If you let go of the button too soon, you will need to start over.

4. Drag the mouse in the direction you want to draw the box: down and to the right. As you move the mouse, a box forms in that direction.

5. Release the mouse button.

6. Since you don't want to draw any more boxes, click on the pointer tool. Your screen should look similar to Figure 2.8.

The technique you used to draw the box is called *click-and-drag*. You will use this technique frequently in PageMaker.

If you prefer to use the keyboard, you can press key combinations to access the tools in the toolbox. Table 2.2 also lists the keyboard shortcuts for selecting tools. Because you will frequently switch back and forth between the pointer and other tools, PageMaker offers a function key toggle, F9, which switches between the pointer tool and the last tool you were using.

Moving and Removing the Toolbox

If the toolbox ever gets in your way, you can easily move it elsewhere on the screen. You move the toolbox the same way you move any window.

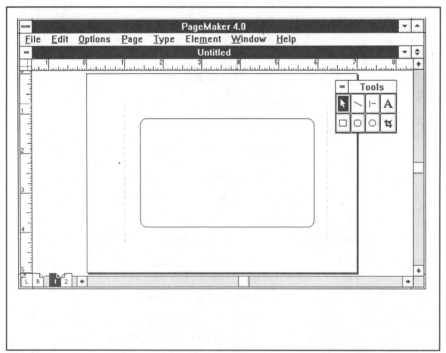

Figure 2.8: A box drawn with the rounded-corner tool

To see how this works, we'll move the toolbox to the lower-right corner of the screen.

1. Place the mouse pointer on the window's title, anywhere in the word *Tools*.

2. Click and hold down the left mouse button, and then drag the mouse down. As you move the mouse, an outline of the toolbox moves in the same direction.

3. Release the mouse button. The toolbox moves into the location you specified.

4. Repeat the procedure to move the toolbox back to its original position.

An alternative to moving the toolbox is getting rid of it altogether. Sometimes you will find that no matter where you move the toolbox, it keeps getting in the way. As long as you don't need to change tools, why not clean up your screen and just turn it off? To remove it, choose the Toolbox option on the Window menu or press Ctrl-6. Later, when you need to change tools, turn the Toolbox option back on using the same command you used to turn it off.

Moving to Other Parts of the Screen with the Scroll Bars

The horizontal and vertical *scroll bars* allow you to use the mouse to see different parts of the page and pasteboard. Right now, you can see the entire page on the screen, but if you were zoomed in on part of the page, you would need a way to scroll the screen. The scroll bar offers one way of repositioning what you see on the screen. Table 2.3 describes how to use the scroll bar, and Figure 2.9 points out the different parts of the horizontal and vertical scroll bars.

You should practice using the scroll bars until you feel comfortable with the mechanics of scrolling. This process can be a bit confusing at first because the screen scrolls in the opposite direction of the scroll arrows. For example, when you click on the down arrow, the screen shifts up. But keep in mind that the scroll arrows let you view something that exists in the

Table 2.3: Using the Scroll Bar

DIRECTION OF SCROLLING	ACTION
Down	Click on down arrow in vertical scroll bar
Down one screen	Click on vertical scroll bar underneath the scroll box
Up	Click on up arrow in vertical scroll bar
Up one screen	Click on vertical scroll bar above the scroll box
Right	Click on right arrow in horizontal scroll bar
Right one screen	Click on horizontal scroll bar to the right of the scroll box
Left	Click on left arrow in horizontal scroll bar
Left one screen	Click on horizontal scroll bar to the left of the scroll box
Top of pasteboard	Click and drag scroll box to top of vertical scroll bar
Left edge of pasteboard	Click and drag scroll box to beginning of horizontal scroll bar

direction of the arrow. In other words, clicking down shows you what's down there. This becomes easy with practice.

If your page disappears, it has probably scrolled off the screen, leaving you with just the pasteboard. To get your page back on the screen, you can scroll the screen in the opposite direction. However, an easier way is to use the command to fit the page in the window: choose Fit in Window from the Page menu or press Ctrl-W.

Viewing the Page

While we are on the subject of page views, let's review some of the other options on the Page menu (you might want to pull down this menu as we discuss these options).

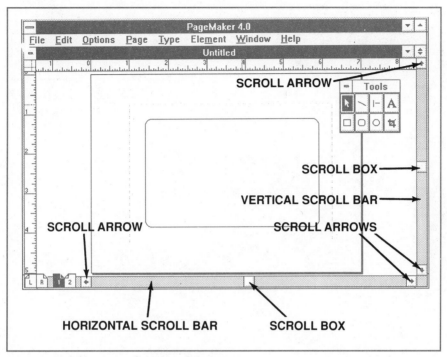

Figure 2.9: Elements of the scroll bars

The Fit in Window option lets you see the entire page or page spread inside your document window, as shown in the example in Figure 2.10. Notice that you can't read most of the text in this view.

The Fit in Window view is the default. It gives you an overall feel of the page layout. However, you can't see much detail unless you have one of those fancy oversized display monitors. To read small type or to precisely position an object on the page, you need to choose one of the other view magnifications.

The Actual Size option displays the elements on your page at their actual printed size. Use this or the 75% Size option to read small type. Figure 2.11 shows the same document that appears in Figure 2.10, but in the Actual Size view. The right mouse button toggles between Actual Size and Fit in Window view.

To see your page larger than life, use the 200% Size or 400% Size option. With these superzoomed views, it is easy to make sure two objects are

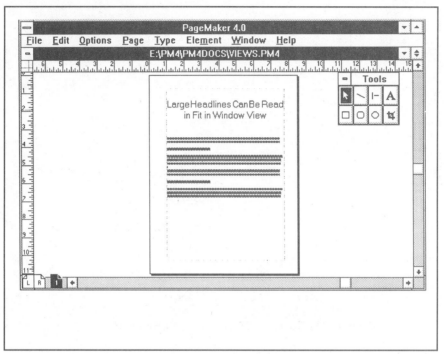

Figure 2.10: The Fit in Window view

aligned with each other. We recommend that you use the Actual Size, 200%, or 400% view for precise positioning.

If you are interested in seeing more of the pasteboard, use the 25% Size option. The 25% view, shown in Figure 2.12, is helpful if you tucked something away on the pasteboard, and you don't see it on your screen. While you can't see the entire pasteboard at once, you can view most of it, and you can use your scroll bars to display the outer edges.

To see the entire pasteboard, use the Fit in World view. You're probably saying "Hey, dream on—there's no Fit in World option on the Page menu." You're right. Aldus buried it in the documentation for reasons only the programmers know for sure. To see the Fit in World view, hold down the Shift key as you select the Fit in Window option from the Page menu.

As you can see on the Page menu, each of the page views has a Ctrl-key shortcut. These key combinations are listed in Table 2.4. Since most of

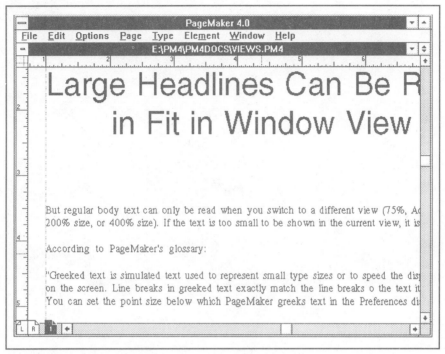

Figure 2.11: The Actual Size view

these codes are mnemonic, they are fairly easy to memorize. Starting with the 25% view, practice each of the keyboard commands in Table 2.4. See how you gradually zoom in with each view.

After you give a page view command, you will most likely need to move the page around so that you can zero in on a particular area. That's where the scroll bars come in handy. Let's practice using the scroll bars to see each of the four corners of the page in 200% view.

1. To switch to 200% view, press Ctrl-2. The section of the page you see right now depends on where you scrolled the last time you used the scroll bars.

2. View the upper-left corner of the page. You may need to click on the up arrow in the vertical scroll bar and the left arrow in the horizontal scroll bar.

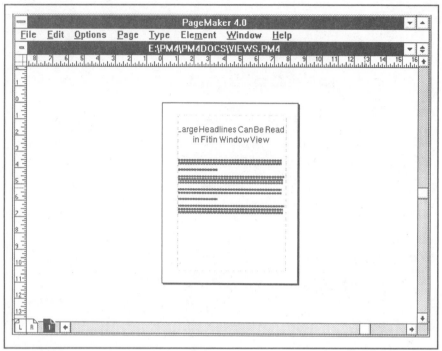

Figure 2.12: The 25% view

Table 2.4: Keyboard Commands for Page Views

VIEW	KEY COMBINATION
Fit in Window	Ctrl-W
25% Size	Ctrl-0 (zero)
50% Size	Ctrl-5
75% Size	Ctrl-7
Actual Size	Ctrl-1
200% Size	Ctrl-2
400% Size	Ctrl-4

3. Click on the down arrow in the vertical scroll bar until you can see the lower-left corner of the page.

4. Click in the horizontal scroll bar (to the right of the scroll box) to see the lower-right corner of the page.

5. View the upper-right corner of the page.

6. Press Ctrl-W to fit the page in the window.

Moving the Page with the Grabber Hand

The *grabber hand* is another way to move the page around the screen. With it, you can grab and move the screen in any direction. While the scroll bars are restricted to horizontal and vertical movement, the grabber hand lets you move diagonally as well. The grabber hand requires teamwork between keyboard and mouse, as follows:

- Hold down the Alt key and keep it down through the entire procedure.

- Click and hold down the left mouse button. A pudgy little hand appears. This is the grabber hand.

- Drag the mouse in the direction you want to move the page. As you move the mouse, the hand and the page move in that direction.

- When you have finished moving the page, release the Alt key and the mouse button.

Before clicking the mouse, you need to position the pointer on the screen. Place the pointer on the opposite side of the direction you want to move. For example, if you want to move the page to the right (so that you can see what's on the left), you should click on the left side of the screen and drag to the right. In the larger view magnifications (200% and 400%), you may need to repeat the process several times until you see what you want to view.

Now, let's use the grabber hand to move the page in Actual Size view.

1. To switch to Actual Size view, press Ctrl-1.
2. Place the mouse pointer in the lower-right corner of the screen.
3. Hold down the Alt key.
4. Click and hold down the left mouse button. The grabber hand appears.
5. Drag the mouse up and to the left.
6. Release the Alt key and the mouse button. You should now see the lower-right corner of the page.

Displaying Other Pages

To the left of the horizontal scroll bar are the page icons. A page number appears for each page in a publication. Since you specified that your document has two pages (by setting the Number of Pages field in the Page Setup dialog box to 2), the numbers 1 and 2 appear inside the page icons. You can move between pages by clicking on the appropriate number.

Next to the numbered page icons are the master page icons. The master pages contain elements that appear on each page of the document, for example, chapter titles or vertical rules between columns. The L refers to the left-hand pages and the R refers to the right-hand pages in double-sided publications. Chapter 14 discusses master pages in detail.

In this chapter, you learned how to interact (or *interface* as they say in the computer world) with PageMaker. You used both the mouse and the keyboard to make selections from the menus and to fill in dialog boxes. You also explored the PageMaker window, familiarizing yourself with the important parts of the screen (the toolbox, scroll bars, page icons, and so on), and experimented with several techniques for scrolling the screen.

In the next chapter, you will take a quick tour of the PageMaker publishing process.

C H A P T E R

3

A
QUICK
TOUR

This chapter provides a quick, abridged tour for the new user. As you follow the steps in this chapter, you will go through the mechanics and the maneuvers inherent in building a publication in PageMaker.

During this tour, we won't stop to explain everything fully; all these topics will be covered in later chapters. Our goal here is to give you an overview, eschewing for the moment all the details that could get in the way. Maybe you'll get everything you need out of this chapter and save the rest of the book for a rainy day. On the other hand, if you already know how to produce a publication and would rather read about the specific features of the program, you might want to pass over this chapter, or just give it a quick skim.

In this tour, you will create a new file, type and format some text, and add geometric shapes. You will then save, print, and close the file. The publication you will create is not complicated or fancy; it is the simple name tag you see in Figure 3.1.

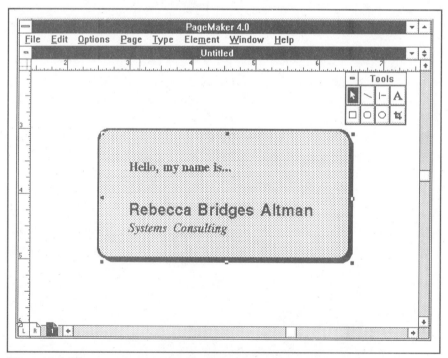

Figure 3.1: The name tag you will create in this chapter

FOLLOWING
THE PUBLISHING RECIPE

Remember the publishing recipe you learned in Chapter 1? Well, you are going to follow that recipe to create your name tag. Before you start, you need to make sure you have all the necessary ingredients at your fingertips.

The main ingredients for any publication are text and graphics. In some publications, you will need to get these ingredients from other programs. For example, the text may come from a word processing file and a piece of clip art may come from a graphics drawing package. However, in our sample publication, all the ingredients will come from Page-Maker itself. You will type the text and create the graphics using PageMaker's tools.

Creating a New File

In the process of learning how to fill in dialog boxes in Chapter 2, you also learned how to create a new file. Let's create a file for your new publication.

1. Pull down the File menu and choose New. The Page Setup dialog box appears.

Normally, you would give your page layout a lot of thought and set its dimensions carefully. But in this practice publication, the default settings will work just fine.

2. Click on the OK button. A letter-size page appears in tall orientation.

Entering Text

Your name tag consists of three short lines of text. To type text in Page-Maker, use the text tool, the one with the letter A in the toolbox.

1. Click on the text tool. When you move the pointer onto the page or pasteboard, it changes into an I-beam to let you know you have selected the text tool.

2. Click anywhere on the page. A small cursor appears next to the margin guide.

3. Begin typing the word **Hello**. You can't read what you are typing in Fit in Window view, so you should switch to Actual Size view.

4. Pull down the Page menu and select Actual Size, or press Ctrl-1. Isn't it nice being able to read what you type?

5. Finish typing **Hello, my name is**…, and then press Enter.

6. Press Enter two more times to insert a couple of blank lines.

7. Type your name and press Enter.

8. Type your company name and press Enter. Your screen should resemble Figure 3.2.

Formatting Characters

The text in each of these lines needs to be formatted differently. Your name is to be set in large, bold type, and your company name should be italicized. You will make these formatting selections through the Type menu. Before you can format text, you must select (or highlight) it first, using the click-and-drag technique you learned in Chapter 2. Let's first format your name.

1. Click the I-beam just to the left of the first letter in your name.

2. Hold down the mouse button and drag to the right until your entire name is selected.

3. Release the mouse button. Your selected name should look similar to Figure 3.3. If you released the mouse button too early, you will need to repeat the steps to select it.

4. Pull down the Type menu and select Font. A cascading menu of fonts appears.

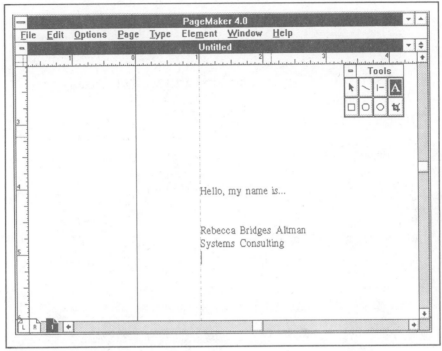

Figure 3.2: The text in your name tag

In PageMaker, a *font* is a specific typeface, such as Helvetica, Times Roman, or Courier. Depending on your printer, you may have these or other fonts.

5. If it's available, select Helv (Helvetica). If not, choose a different font.

6. Pull down the Type menu and select Size. A cascading menu of available type sizes appears. The current size has a check mark next to it.

The variety of sizes in your list depends on your printer and how many sizes you have installed. See Appendix C for information about installing fonts.

7. Choose a larger size, such as 18. If your menu doesn't list 18, choose the closest available size.

Your name is now the largest element on this page (just as it should be!). The text is still selected, so we will take advantage of this fact and format it some more.

8. Pull down the Type menu and select Type Style. A cascading menu appears.

9. Choose Bold.

It's difficult to see this effect while the text is still selected. To unselect text, you simply click the mouse elsewhere on the page.

The other two lines also need to be formatted. We'll set them in a smaller size.

10. Select the first line of text.

11. Set the size to 14 (or the closest available size).

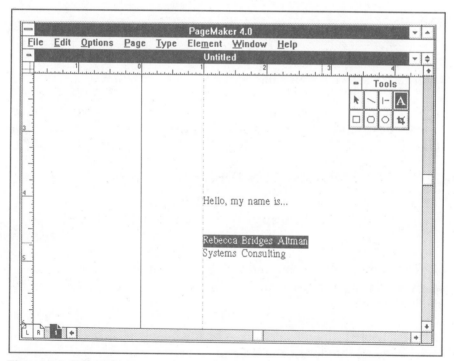

Figure 3.3: Selected text

12. Set the type style to Bold.

13. Select the last line of text.

14. Set the size to 14.

15. Set the type style to Bold.

16. Set the type style to Italic. Your screen should look similar to Figure 3.4.

In this exercise, you had to go through the Type menu several times to specify the format of the selected text. In Chapter 8, you will learn how to assign multiple styles and set the size with one trip to the menu.

Indenting Text

Because you are going to eventually draw a box around this text, you need to provide some extra room to the left of each line. The easiest way

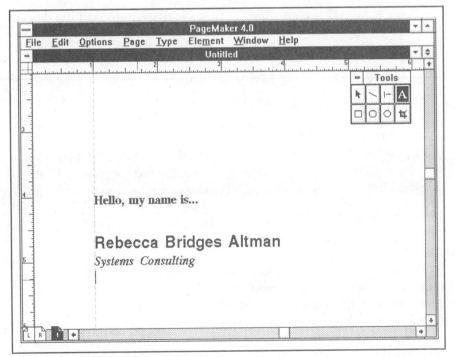

Figure 3.4: Formatted text

to insert this extra space is to indent the text from the margin.

1. Use the click-and-drag technique to select all the text.

2. Pull down the Type menu and select Paragraph. The Paragraph Specifications dialog box appears. Chapter 7 explains these options in detail; in this example, we are concerned only with the first option, which sets the left indent.

3. Next to the Left field, type **2**, and then press Enter. This indents the selected lines 2 inches from the left margin.

4. To see how the text looks on the page, switch to Fit in Window view. (Press Ctrl-W or use the Page menu.)

5. Click elsewhere on the page to unselect the text. Your screen should look similar to Figure 3.5.

Moving a Text Block

You used the Paragraph Specifications dialog box to position the text horizontally on the page. Now you will position the text vertically by picking it up and moving it with the pointer tool.

1. Click on the pointer tool in the toolbox.

2. Click anywhere in your text.

Boundaries, called *window shades,* appear above and below the text block. The window shades indicate the block is selected. As you can see, the pointer tool selects objects differently than the text tool. You will use the now-familiar click-and-drag method to move this text block.

3. With the pointer inside the window shades, click and hold down the mouse button.

Now the text block is completely enclosed with dashed lines, and a four-headed arrow appears inside the block. Look carefully at the vertical ruler, and you will see lines that correspond to the top and bottom of the text block. Use these lines for reference when you want to position a block a certain number of inches down the page. In this exercise, we want to place the top of the block 3½ inches from the top of the page.

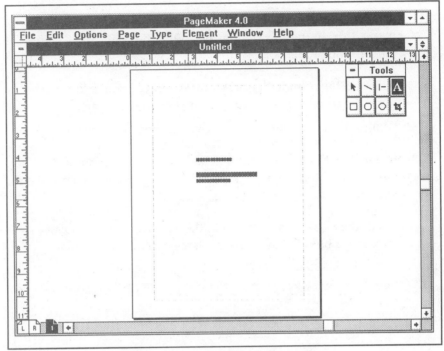

Figure 3.5: Text indented 2 inches from the left margin

4. Drag the mouse until the block begins 3½ inches down the page. Remember, watch the lines in the ruler.

5. Before releasing the mouse button, make sure you haven't shifted the block horizontally. The block should be within the margin guides.

6. Release the mouse button.

Adding Graphics

Although it may not be immediately obvious, your name tag will contain two graphic figures: the shaded box and the shadow that appears around the shaded box. You can easily create these graphics with Page-Maker tools and commands.

Drawing a Box

First, we'll draw the box, using the rounded-corner tool. Figure 3.6 shows the location of this box.

1. Click on the rounded-corner tool. When you move the pointer onto the page or pasteboard, it turns into a *crossbar*.

2. Without clicking the button, move the crossbar around the page.

Notice that lines in the horizontal and vertical rulers indicate where the crossbar is on the page. Use these lines as a guide to positioning the box as you draw.

3. Place the crossbar above and to the left of your text block. To draw a box the same size as the one in Figure 3.6, place

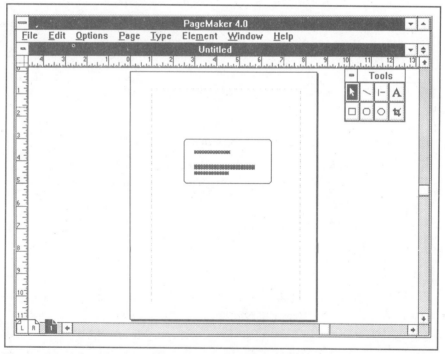

Figure 3.6: A box drawn with the rounded-corner tool

the crossbar at the 3-inch mark on the vertical ruler and the 2½-inch mark on the horizontal ruler.

4. Click and drag the mouse to the right and below your text block. As you drag, a box is drawn on your screen. Again, if you want your box to match the one in the figure, place the crossbar at the 5-inch vertical mark and the 6½-inch horizontal mark.

5. Release the mouse button. Small rectangular boxes surround the edges of your graphic.

The rectangular boxes, called *handles,* indicate the graphic is selected. You will learn more about what you can do with a selected graphic in Chapter 11.

Formatting a Graphic

There are several ways to enhance a box. For our name tag, we'll change the line width used for the box and fill it with a pattern.

1. Change to 75% view so that you can see your formatting changes more clearly.

2. If necessary, use the scroll bars or grabber hand to position your name tag in the center of the screen.

3. Pull down the Element menu and select Line. A cascading menu of line widths and styles appears. The current selection, 1pt, has a check mark next to it.

4. Select 2pt, which produces a slightly wider line.

5. Pull down the Element menu and select Fill. A cascading menu of shades and patterns appears. The current filling is None.

6. Select the lightest shade available, 10%. What happened to your text?

Don't worry, your text is still there. It's hiding out behind the shaded box. Because you added the box *after* you typed the text, the box is on top of, or in front of, the text. This positioning didn't matter when the box wasn't filled with a pattern, but the 10% shade you added now covers the text. In order to make the text visible again, you must put it on top of the box.

7. Pull down the Element menu and select Send to Back. Your text reappears, as shown in Figure 3.7.

Drawing a Shadow Box

To create a drop-shadow effect, you draw a solid box that slightly off-sets the main box and then send it to the back. Figure 3.8 shows the position of the second box for your name tag.

1. Check to make sure the rounded-corner tool is still selected in your toolbox.

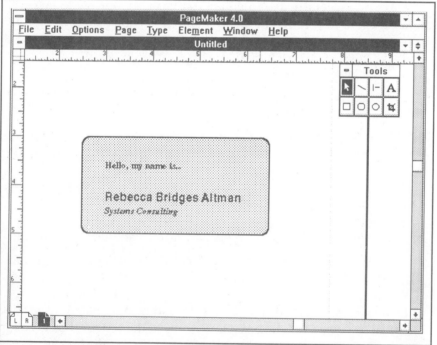

Figure 3.7: A shaded box that is sent to the back so that the text can be seen

2. Place the crossbar slightly below and to the right of the upper-left corner of the first box.

3. Click and drag to the right and down. Place the crossbar slightly below and to the right of the lower-right corner of the first box.

4. Release the mouse button. Now you can fill this box with a solid shade.

5. Pull down the Element menu and select Fill.

6. Choose Solid. Now the solid box lays over the shaded box, obscuring the text. You need to send this box to the back.

7. Pull down the Element menu and select Send to Back.

Your name tag is now complete and should look like Figure 3.1. In the following sections, you will save and then print it.

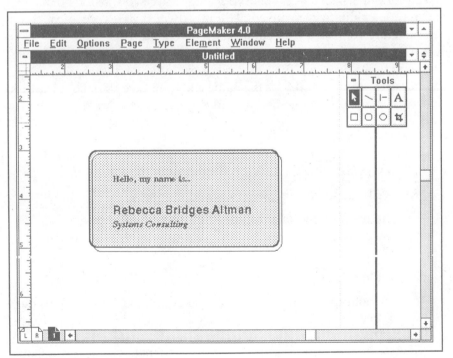

Figure 3.8: The second box

MANAGING YOUR FILES

This section explains basic file operations, including saving, printing, closing, and opening publications. The options for file handling are on the File pull-down menu.

Some programs allow you to work with more than one file at a time, but PageMaker is *not* one of them. You can only have one publication open at once. If you have a document on the screen when you tell PageMaker to open or create another file, the current publication is automatically closed.

Saving Your Work

Save your file to disk about every 15 minutes, or when you complete an important task. It doesn't take very long to save your work, but it could take a long time to recreate something. Always save your most recent work before you leave your computer unattended.

The File pull-down menu offers both the Save and Save As options. The first time you save a file, you can choose either of these options. Page-Maker first prompts you for a file name and then saves the file to the disk.

All the usual DOS file-naming rules apply to PageMaker file names, as follows:

- A file name can be up to eight characters long. Try to make the name descriptive of what is contained in the file.

- A file name can contain letters and numbers.

- Many of the special symbols (such as the * and ?) are not allowed. If you type an invalid character, PageMaker displays an error message.

- A file name cannot include spaces or periods.

- Do not type an extension. PageMaker automatically assigns the extension .PM4.

If you continue working on the document and make changes, you should resave the document. The Save option saves the file with the same name you gave it previously. The Save As option lets you assign a new name to the file. Thus, if you want to replace the previously saved version with the new version, choose Save (or press Ctrl-S). If you want to keep the original file and create a different file from the new version, choose Save As.

Follow these steps to save the publication you just created:

1. Pull down the File menu.

2. Choose Save As. The Save Publication As dialog box appears, as shown in Figure 3.9.

3. Type the name **NAMETAG**. If necessary, you can change where the file will be saved, as described below.

4. Click on OK or press Enter. The path and file name now appear as the window title.

If you take a look at the Save Publication As dialog box, you can see exactly where this file will be saved. The Path (right above the Name field) indicates the drive and subdirectory in which the file will be saved. For example, in Figure 3.9, the current path is e:\pm4. Thus, the file will be saved on the E: drive in the PageMaker 4 subdirectory. But what if you don't want to save your file here? No problem—use the Directories list to change the path to another subdirectory or drive.

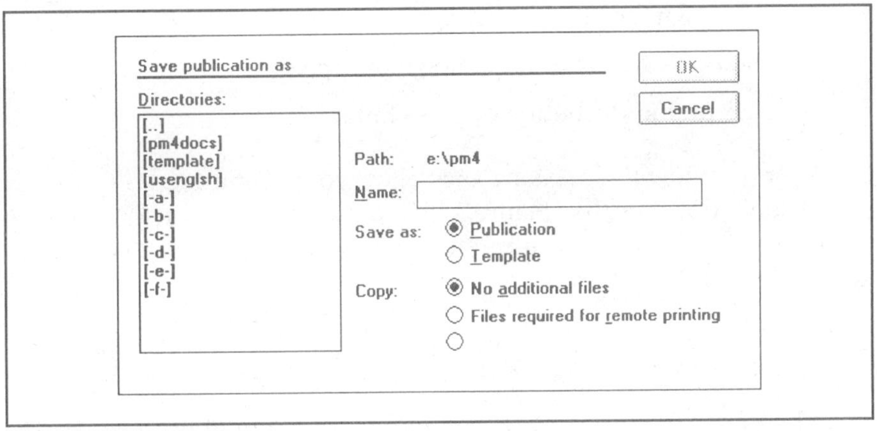

Figure 3.9: The Save Publication As dialog box

If you have never navigated a Directories list, you are probably wondering what each of the bracketed items in the list box stands for. Here is an explanation:

- The first item, [..], refers to the parent directory. Choose this item to go back to the previous subdirectory.

- The words, such as [template] and [usenglsh], are subdirectory names.

- The single letters, such as [-a-] through [-f-], refer to disk drives.

To change to another drive or subdirectory, double-click on the bracketed item. The Directories list will then reflect the subdirectories in the new drive/subdirectory. Keep your eye on the Path to see exactly where you are.

Printing a File

Chapter 4 covers PageMaker's printing options in detail. In the following steps, you will print your name tag without specifying any special options. We are assuming that your printer has been set up in Windows.

1. Make sure your printer is turned on, switched on-line, and has paper.
2. Pull down the File menu.
3. Choose Print. The Print dialog box appears.
4. Click on the OK button or press Enter.

After a moment of flashing messages, your name tag will print. It should look something like Figure 3.10. What are you going to do with this masterpiece? Let's see … you can frame it, wear it, stick it on your door, or toss it out. Take your pick.

Closing a File

When you are finished working with a file, you will want to close it. The process of closing a file removes it from the screen and the computer's temporary memory. Fortunately, if you haven't saved your file, Page-Maker will warn you and ask if you want to save it.

PageMaker offers several ways to close a file:

- Pull down the File menu and choose Close.

- Click on the document window's Control-menu box and choose Close.

- Double-click on the document window's Control-menu box.

- Create a new file.

- Open an existing publication.

When you are closing a file with the Control-menu box, be careful that you don't click on the wrong box. The top box controls your PageMaker application; the second box controls your document window. If you close the application window, you will exit your publication *and* the PageMaker program.

Now you should close your NAMETAG publication:

1. Pull down the File menu.

2. Choose Close.

Hello, my name is...

Rebecca Bridges Altman
Systems Consulting

Figure 3.10: The printed name tag

Opening a File

To work with a publication you have previously created and saved, use the Open option on the File pull-down menu (or press Ctrl-O). The Open Publication dialog box, shown in Figure 3.11, is similar to the Save Publication As dialog box.

You type the name of the publication you want to work with next to the Name field, or select the name from the Files/Directories list. The names of your publications are listed alphabetically, but only ten file names can be displayed at a time. If the file you want to open is not shown, use the scroll bar in the Files/Directories list to view additional names. Either click on the down-pointing scroll arrow or click inside the scroll bar. Once you have found the name, double-click on it to open the file.

If you still can't locate a file on the list, it might be stored in another drive or subdirectory. As in the Save Publication As dialog box, the current path is indicated above the Name field. To change the path, you can navigate the Files/Directories list, just as when you are saving your work. Because the subdirectory names and drive letters are listed at the end, you may need to use the scroll bar to change the path.

Follow these steps to open your NAMETAG publication:

1. Pull down the File menu.

2. Choose Open.

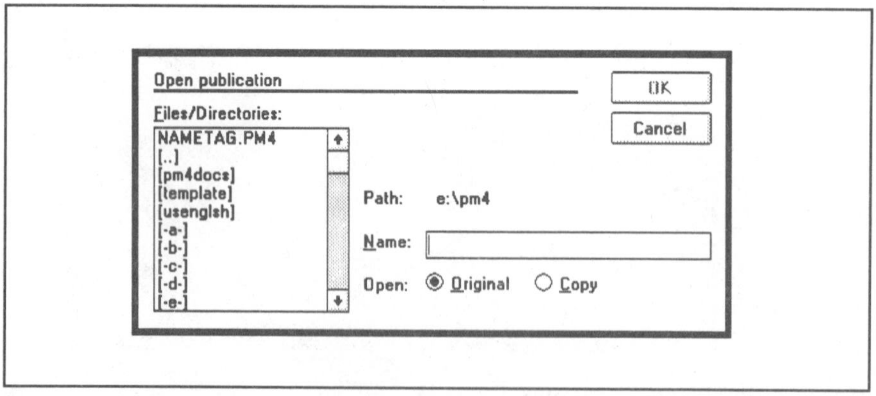

Figure 3.11: The Open Publication dialog box

3. In the Files/Directories list, double-click on NAMETAG.PM4.

After a moment, your name tag will reappear.

GETTING HELP

PageMaker has a comprehensive on-line Help facility that provides you with instant information about any command, as well as explanations of many different topics.

Using the Help Index

One way to use the Help feature is to select a command or topic from an index. Let's use the Help Index to print a list of keyboard shortcuts.

1. Press F1 or pull down the Help menu and select Index. You will see the Help window shown in Figure 3.12.

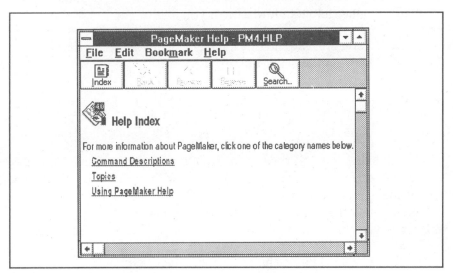

Figure 3.12: The Help Index

The Help window has its own menu, and it can be moved, sized, or scrolled like any other window.

2. Move the pointer to an option on the Index list. As you position the pointer, it changes to a hand with a pointing finger.

3. Click on Topics. An extensive list of topics is displayed.

4. Use the scroll bar to peruse this list.

5. Click on Keyboard Shortcuts (at the beginning of the list).

6. Read over the list of keyboard shortcuts and see how many you have learned already. Use the scroll bar to see additional text.

7. Pull down Help's File menu and choose Print Topic. After a moment, this Help topic, the list of keyboard shortcuts, is printed.

Underneath the menu are a series of buttons. Use the Index option to go back to the initial Help index. Back displays the Help window you just looked at. The >> Browse option displays the next related topic, and the << Browse option displays the previous related topic. Use the Search option to specify which command or topic you want to find out about. Feel free to explore the Help window more if you like.

8. When you are ready to exit the Help facility, choose Exit from the Help window's File menu.

Getting Information about Dialog Box Options

Occasionally, you will need an explanation of one or more of the options in a dialog box. To see a Help window with information about the current dialog box, hold down Shift and click on the background of the dialog box (not on an option) with the *right* mouse button. For example, here's how you can get help on an option in the Page Setup dialog box:

1. Pull down the File menu and choose Page Setup.

2. Hold down Shift and click the right mouse button in an empty area of the dialog box.

3. Read this screen. From here, you can proceed to see Help information about any other related topics that interest you.

4. Choose Exit from the Help window's File menu to leave the Help system.

5. At this point, you would normally finish filling in the Page Setup dialog box. But since you were just practicing, choose Cancel.

After this quick tour, you should have a better sense of the process of producing a publication in PageMaker. Here is the recipe:

- Create a file.
- Add your basic ingredients: text and graphics.
- Spice it with up some formatting.
- Save and print the publication.

In the next chapter, you will learn more about setting up your page layout and printing your documents.

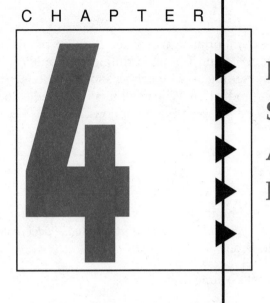

C H A P T E R

PAGE
SETUP
AND
PRINTING

This chapter covers two important parts of the desktop publishing process: specifying the layout of your page and printing your publication. Defining the page layout and setting up your printer should be done in the initial stages of publication production. When you finally print the document, you can select from the available printing options.

SETTING UP THE PAGE LAYOUT

You should give careful thought to your page setup when you are creating a publication. *Before you add any text or graphics to the page,* make the following important decisions:

- Paper size of the final document
- Margin settings
- Whether you want the page orientation to be tall (vertical, its normal position) or wide (sideways)
- Whether the final printed document will be double- or single-sided
- How many columns your publication will have (this topic will be covered in Part 2)

Most of the page layout options are set from the Page Setup dialog box that appears when you select New on the File menu. This dialog box is shown in Figure 4.1. If you want to change any of these settings after you have created the publication, choose Page Setup from the File menu to see a dialog box that is almost identical to the one you see when you choose New.

If PageMaker offers a way to change settings after the fact, then why are we lecturing you on the importance of determining your page setup before you create the document? (No, it's not because we like to nag.) Although you can change the settings after you have added text and graphics to the page, if you do so, you may need to manually resize and reposition those items that already existed on the page. In a short one- or two-page document, this repositioning takes only a few minutes. But if you have a long publication, you're in for a long, tedious task.

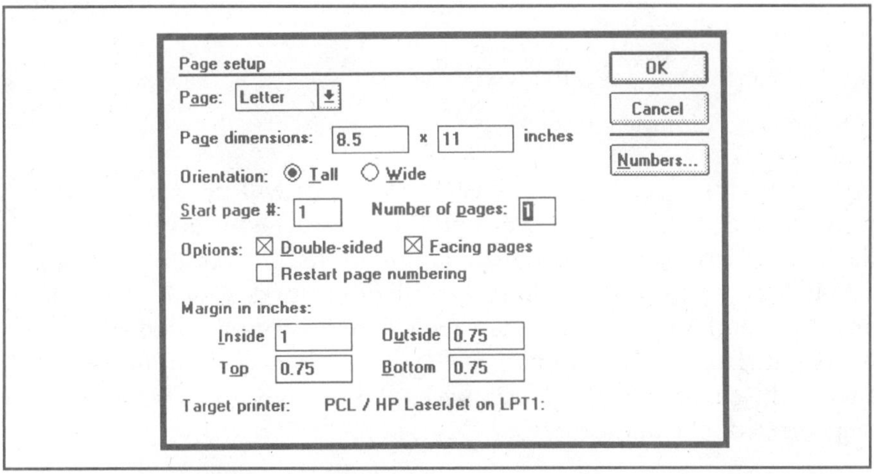

Figure 4.1: The Page Setup dialog box

Most of the options in the Page Setup dialog box are fairly straightforward, but for some, there are special considerations.

Choosing a Page Size

Three predefined page sizes are offered: Letter (8½ by 11 inches), Legal (8½ by 14 inches), and Tabloid (11 by 17 inches). If your page doesn't fall into one of these categories, you can enter your own page dimensions. Follow these steps to change the page size.

1. Pull down the File menu and choose New.

2. Display the drop-down list by clicking on the down arrow next to Letter.

3. Click on Tabloid. Notice that the page dimensions, 11 by 17 inches, are automatically entered.

4. Change the page size to Custom.

Your previous page width and length are still listed next to Page Dimensions. When you select a custom page size, you need to change these values yourself. The width is already selected for you.

5. Type **3.5** for the width.

6. Press Tab to go to the next field.

7. Type **5** for the length.

When your document is a custom size, you will probably print the page on letter-size paper anyway and then instruct your print shop to cut the finished print job to your custom dimensions. To indicate your page's actual dimensions, you should print with crop marks. *Crop marks* are thin lines that mark the corners of the page when the page size is smaller than the paper size. It is an option in the Print dialog box, which is described later in the chapter. Figure 4.2 shows crop marks around a 3½-by-5-inch page printed on letter-size paper.

Setting the Orientation

You should be aware of how the Orientation setting impacts other PageMaker options. First of all, when you select the Wide orientation, the two page dimension values switch. For example, if the current page dimensions are 8.5 by 11, they become 11 by 8.5 when you choose Wide. Thus, when the page is switched from a vertical to a horizontal orientation, the width becomes the length and the length becomes the width. PageMaker switches these values for you.

An option that is not changed automatically is the print orientation. When you choose a wide orientation for your page setup, you must also choose the wide orientation (called *landscape*) for your printer setup. The print orientation is specified through the File menu's Target Printer or Print option, as discussed later in this chapter.

Another consideration when you choose a wide orientation is your printer fonts. To print text in wide orientation, you must have landscape fonts available. See Appendix C for information about using fonts.

Numbering Pages

Unlike most of the other options in the Page Setup dialog box, the two page numbering fields, Start Page # and Number of Pages, and the Numbers

The secret is out

For centuries, humans have searched for magical potions that will increase their life spans--the mythical fountains of youth. Silver-haired Americans have spent over three billion dollars on various "if-you-act-now" schemes that claim never-ending youth for clients.

But now the secret is out.

If you want to live longer, you don't need to pay anyone or eat exotic herbs or chant unrecognizable hymns. If you want to live longer, do this:

Stop smoking
Eat good foods
Don't overeat
Exercise regularly

That's the secret.

Figure 4.2: Crop marks indicate the page size

button are not crucial to your page setup; they can easily be changed at any time.

The Start Page # field indicates the first page number in the publication. This option is useful when you have split a long document into several smaller publications. To have continuous page numbering across the publications, you can change the starting page number. Let's say you're producing a book with 10 chapters, each one produced as its own publication. If the first chapter has 17 pages, you would enter 18 for the second chapter's Start Page # option. If you use the book feature, as described in Chapter 15, the starting page number is changed automatically.

The value you enter for the Start Page # field controls both the numbers that appear inside the page icons at the bottom of the window and the numbers that print on each page when you specify page numbering on your master page. The latter topic is discussed in Chapter 14.

The Numbers command button displays the Page Numbering dialog box, where you can change the style of your page numbers. This dialog box is shown in Figure 4.3. By default, your pages are numbered with arabic numerals (1, 2, 3, etc.). But if the publication is a preface, forward, appendix, or index, you may want roman numerals (such as i, ii, and iii) or alphabetic characters (A, B, C, and so on). The numbering style you choose here does not affect what you see in the page icons; the icons always display arabic numbers.

The Number of Pages option is straightforward. Just enter the total number of pages that your publication will have. Sometimes you will know exactly how many pages you need, such as when you are creating a two-page brochure. However, other times, you won't be sure how many

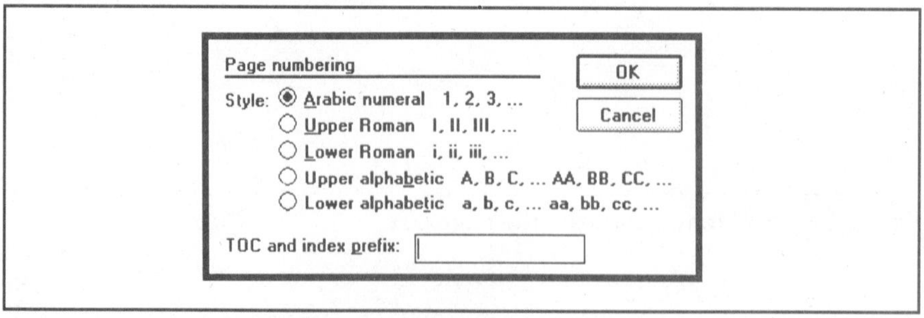

Page numbering   OK

Style: ● Arabic numeral 1, 2, 3, ...   Cancel
       ○ Upper Roman I, II, III, ...
       ○ Lower Roman i, ii, iii, ...
       ○ Upper alphabetic A, B, C, ... AA, BB, CC, ...
       ○ Lower alphabetic a, b, c, ... aa, bb, cc, ...

TOC and index prefix: [   ]

Figure 4.3: The Page Numbering dialog box

pages your publication will have until it is finished. This is often the case with longer documents such as manuals and books.

If you aren't sure how many pages your publication will have, don't worry; you can use the Insert Pages or Remove Pages option on the Page pull-down menu to add or delete pages as necessary. In addition, PageMaker can automatically insert pages when you import text, as you will see in Chapter 9. This capability, called *autoflow,* is invaluable when you are inserting a word processed document and don't know how many PageMaker pages it will need. Just leave Number of Pages set at 1, and PageMaker will create new pages when the text is imported.

Creating Double-Sided Publications

If your final publication will be printed on both sides of the page, leave the Double-Sided check box alone, because its default setting is on. You will need to create double-sided publications when the pages are going to be bound together in some way: in a three-ring binder, spiral-bound, *perfect-bound* (glued at the spine), or folded and *saddle-stitched* (stapled once or twice in the fold).

However, when you have the Double-Sided option turned on, your printer will not necessarily automatically print on both sides of the page. In fact, very few printers have this capability; the Hewlett-Packard (HP) LaserJet IID is one that does print on both sides of the page. Use the Duplex option in the Print dialog box to specify double-sided printing if your printer has this feature.

Even if your printer does not have this capability, you can still print double-sided pages by following these general steps:

1. Tell PageMaker to print only the odd-numbered pages (in the Print dialog box).

2. Flip these printed pages over and reinsert them into the printer. (Be prepared for a bit of trial and error to determine in which direction you should place the sheets into the paper tray.)

3. Tell PageMaker to print all the even-numbered pages.

If you will be giving your publication to a print or copy shop for final production, you do not need to give them double-sided originals. Leave the Double-Sided option on, but print the document single-sided. Then simply instruct the shop to print it double-sided (or *back-to-back*, as it is sometimes called).

So why leave the Double-Sided option on if you are going to print it single-sided? For one very good reason: in a double-sided publication, the pages on the right and left side might not be layed out the same way. For example, you might need different margins to accommodate the binding, and the printed page numbers could appear near the left margin on a left-hand page and near the right margin on a right-hand page. With the Double-Sided option on, you can set up your right and left pages differently.

In conjunction with the Double-Sided option, you may want to use the Facing Pages option, which is also turned on by default. This option shows you the left and right pages that appear side by side in a double-sided publication. The two facing pages create what is called a page spread. Figure 4.4 shows pages 2 and 3 in a page spread. In a bound, double-sided publication, it's important to consider how facing pages look together. As you are designing the publication, you should see how the two pages in a spread interact, and perhaps even think of the spread's design as a single entity. Make sure a page's design and layout complement, rather than conflict with, its facing page.

Here are a few things to be aware of when you are creating double-sided publications that have facing pages:

- Even-numbered pages are displayed on the left, and the odd-numbered pages are on the right.

- Page 1 cannot be part of a page spread. Since it is an odd-numbered page and appears on the right, it cannot have a facing page on the left.

- You can only turn on the Facing Pages option if you have turned on the Double-Sided option.

- You should make your inside margins large enough to accommodate your binding method. Setting margins is discussed in the next section.

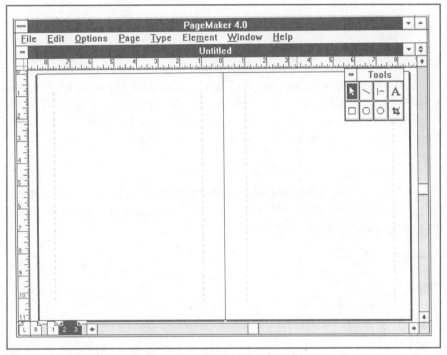

Figure 4.4: A page spread

Setting Margins

The margins you set in the Page Setup dialog box define the white space around the edges of the page. As mentioned in Chapter 2, these margins are marked with dotted lines, called margin guides. Although you can place text and graphics inside the margins, most of your elements will be confined to the body of the page. That's why you set margins—to define the work area of the page.

In the dialog box area titled Margin in Inches, the following margins and default values are listed (assuming the Double-Sided option is on):

Inside   1 inch

Outside   0.75 inch

Top   0.75 inch

Bottom   0.75 inch

The most common elements that influence top and bottom margins are headers and footers, because you need to allot more space if you intend to have them. Professional designers use a complex grid, closely linked to the size of the text, to determine top and bottom margins. For a more complete discussion of setting vertical spacing, see Chapter 7.

Inside and Outside Margins

The Inside and Outside settings apply to double-sided publications only. Pages are bound together at the inside margins in a double-sided publication, as illustrated in Figure 4.5.

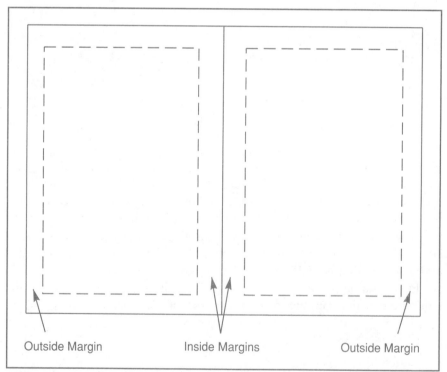

Outside Margin   Inside Margins   Outside Margin

Figure 4.5: Inside and outside margins in a double-sided publication

The inside margin is on the right side of a left-hand page and on the left side of a right-hand page. The outside margin is the space on the outer edges of the page spread. It's the left margin on the left-hand page, and the right margin on a right-hand page.

Depending on your binding method, you may want the inside margin to be slightly larger than the outside margin in order to accommodate the binding. If you forget to specify a larger inside margin, the text close to the binding may actually get cut off (the worst case), or the outer margins will look noticeably larger than the inner margins (undesirable, but not the end of the world).

A single-sided publication does not have inside and outside margins. It simply has the normal garden-variety left and right margins that you are accustomed to setting in your word processor. If you turn off the Double-Sided option (try this now), you see the Left and Right options listed instead of Inside and Outside.

Units of Measurement

PageMaker's default measurement system is inches. You can choose one of the other available measurement systems by selecting the Preferences option on the Edit menu. For example, if you're from outside the United States, you might prefer entering your measurements in millimeters. Those who are familiar with the typesetting world may prefer the pica/point system. (There are about 6 picas to an inch and 72 points to a pica.) Once you change the default, you can enter the value in your preferred measuring system when a dialog box prompts you for a measurement (for margins, indentations, spacing, and so on).

If it's easier for you to enter inches for some measurements and picas for others, you can override the default system and specify a different system on the spot. For example, if your default system is in inches, but you want to specify a 3-pica indent, type 3p. The abbreviations to use to specify the measurement systems are as follows:

System	Abbreviation
Inches	**i** after the value
Millimeters	**m** after the value
Picas	**p** after the value

System	Abbreviation
Points	**p** before the value
Picas and points	**p** between the values

After you enter the value, PageMaker will convert it to the default measuring system. For example, if you enter 3p for the top margin, and then return to the Page Setup dialog box, you will see that the value is converted to 0.5 (½ inch).

Changing the Default Page Setup

If you find that you are frequently changing the page setup to the same values and options, you may want to modify your default page setup. Follow these general steps to change the default settings:

1. If a publication is open, close it. (This first step is crucial to creating a new default setting in PageMaker.)

2. Pull down the File menu and choose Page Setup.

3. Adjust the dialog box settings to reflect the options you use most frequently.

4. Click on the OK button.

From this point on, any new publication you create will automatically have this page setup. As with the original default settings, you can change your new defaults whenever necessary.

The procedure described above works for many PageMaker options. When you change a setting on the Options menu *while a file is not open,* you are changing the program's defaults. Thus, the key to resetting a PageMaker default is to not have a file open when you make the change.

SETTING UP YOUR PRINTER

Another important consideration before you begin adding text to the page is your *target printer*, which is the printer that will print the final publication. The fonts you can use in your publication are determined by your target printer. In many cases, the printer currently connected to your computer is your target printer.

Follow these steps to see what is set as your current target printer:

1. Pull down the File menu.

2. Choose Target Printer.

3. Look at the bottom of the dialog box, next to Current Printer. This is your current target printer.

If you installed more than one printer in Windows, you will have several choices in the printer list. Figure 4.6 shows three printers listed. To select a different printer, click on its name.

Each of the printers shown in Figure 4.6 has a different status:

- LPT1 (or LPT2, COM1, or COM2) indicates that the printer is connected to your computer, and Windows (and therefore Page-Maker) considers it your active printer.

- None indicates that the printer has an inactive status. To use this printer in PageMaker, you must activate it in the Windows Control Panel. (See your Microsoft Windows *User's Guide* for additional information.)

- FILE indicates that you will be printing to disk. These disk files can then be printed on a high-resolution typesetter or laser printer not directly connected to your computer.

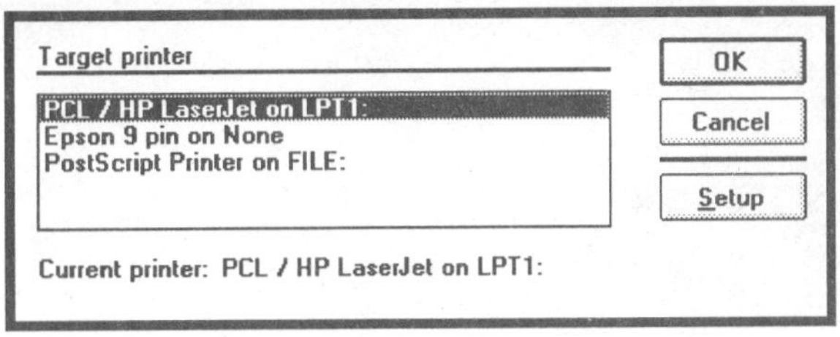

Figure 4.6: A list of printers installed in Windows

A typical example of using the FILE status is to create an *Encapsulated PostScript file,* which is then given to a service bureau for printing at very high resolution (for example, 1200 or 2400 dots per inch, as opposed to 300 dots per inch on most laser printers.) See Appendix D for further information.

Specifying Target Printer Options

As part of the setup for your target printer, you can specify a variety of options. Click on the Setup command button to see a box of printer options.

The specific printer options you are offered depend on your target printer. Figures 4.7, 4.8, and 4.9 show dialog boxes for the HP LaserJet II, Epson 9-pin printer, and a PostScript printer, respectively. These dialog boxes display different options because each type of printer has unique capabilities. The following sections discuss various target printer options; skip over those that are not applicable to your printer.

Paper Source or Paper Feed

Your printer may have several different ways you can feed paper. For example, a laser printer has one or more trays, and can also be fed manually.

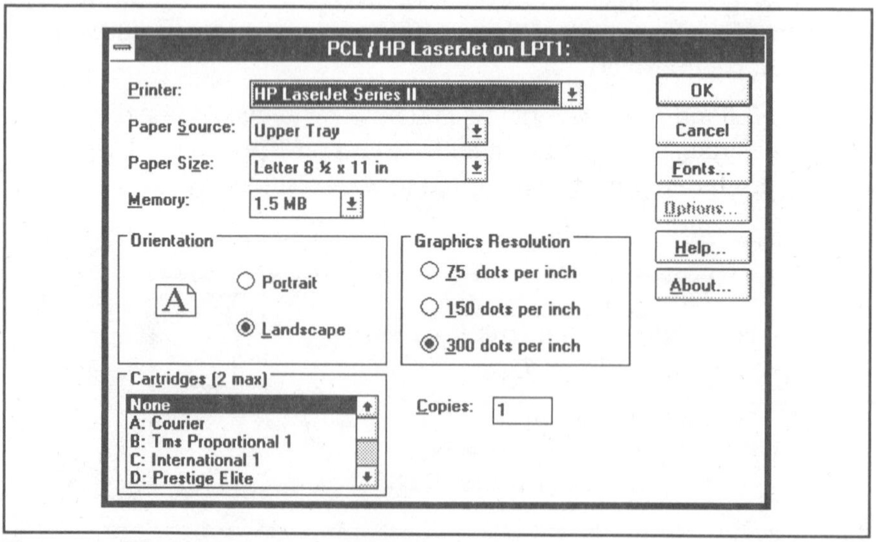

Figure 4.7: The HP LaserJet II dialog box

The Paper Source or Paper Feed option lets PageMaker know which feeding mechanism you are using.

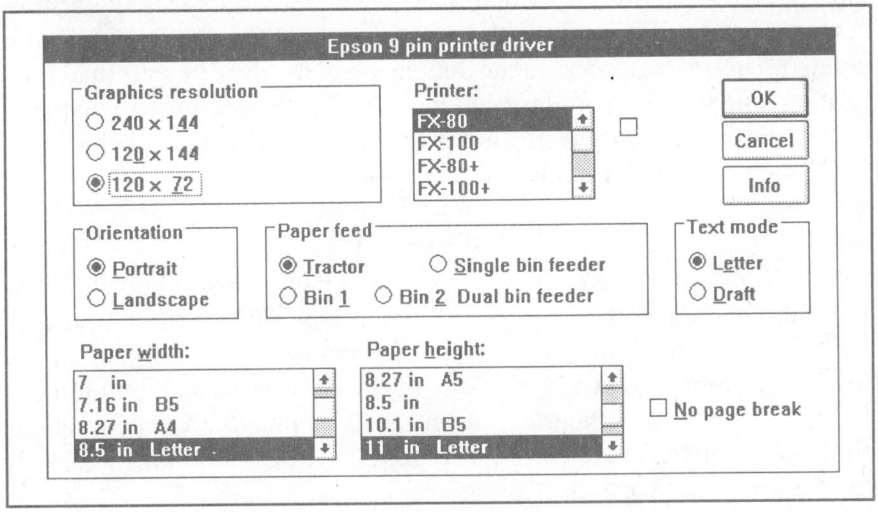

Figure 4.8: The Epson 9-pin printer dialog box

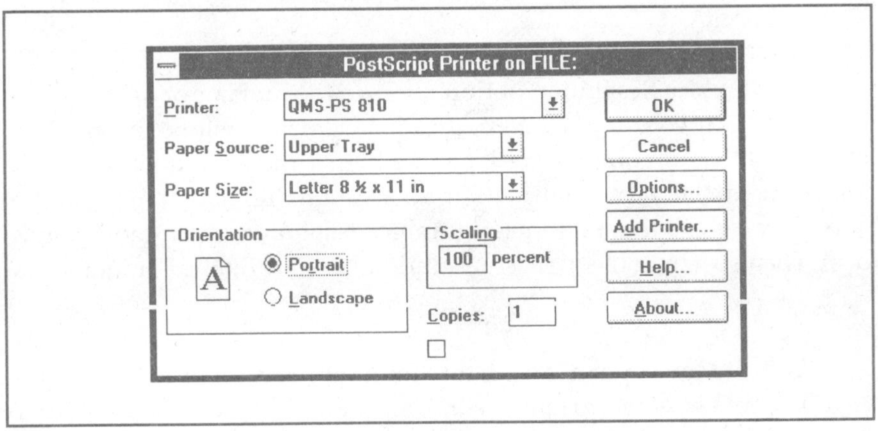

Figure 4.9: The PostScript printer dialog box

Paper Size, Paper Width, and Paper Height

The Paper Size setting in the Target Printer Setup dialog box does not have to be the same as the Page dimensions in the Page Setup dialog box. As mentioned earlier, a page can be smaller than the paper on which it is printed. The *page size* refers to the dimension of the page in your final publication. The *paper size*, on the other hand, is the physical size of the paper in the printer. Therefore, if you are printing a 5-by-7-inch page on an 8½-by-11-inch piece of paper, choose Letter for the Paper Size option.

Orientation

As you were warned when we discussed page setup, if you chose the Wide orientation in the Page Setup dialog box, make sure you specify Landscape for orientation in the Target Printer Setup dialog box. Make this change before you add any text to the publication so that your font list (displayed when you choose Font on the Type menu) accurately reflects the landscape fonts you have available. Fonts are discussed more thoroughly in Chapter 5 and Appendix C.

Choose Portrait for Orientation when Tall is selected in the Page Setup dialog box.

Graphics Resolution

The Graphics Resolution option refers to the number of dots per inch (dpi) at which your publication's graphic elements will be printed. The more dots that are printed per inch, the higher the print quality, but the longer the time it takes to print. For your rough drafts, you may want to save time by printing at a lower graphics resolution (for example, at 75 dpi). Then switch to the highest resolution for your final printout.

Text Mode

The Text Mode option is similar to the Graphics Resolution option, except it applies to the printed text. Some printers (namely dot-matrix printers) offer two print modes: letter-quality and draft. The letter-quality mode either prints more dots or prints over each line several times to produce darker, higher quality type. The draft mode has poorer resolution but prints faster.

Cartridges

With some printers, you can purchase *cartridges* that plug into the printer and offer additional typefaces. For example, with the HP LaserJet II, the B cartridge (the second one on the list in Figure 4.7) lets you use the Times Roman and Helvetica typefaces in your publications. You can choose up to two different cartridges from the list.

Scaling

The Scaling option applies only to printers with scalable fonts (fonts that can be set to any size). PostScript printers, LaserMaster printers, and the HP LaserJet III have built-in scalable fonts. Other printers can use scalable soft fonts, such as those included with Adobe Type Manager and FaceLift.

To use this option, enter the percentage at which you want to reduce or enlarge the entire page. At 100 percent, the page prints at its actual size. If you change the percentage to 50, for example, everything on the page will be reduced to half the actual size. If you enter a number larger than 100, the page will be enlarged.

Saving the Target Printer Setup Options

After you have made all the necessary changes to set up your target printer, do the following:

1. Click on OK in the Setup dialog box.
2. Click on OK in the Target Printer dialog box.

If you currently have a publication open, sometimes you will be asked if you want to recompose it for your new target printer, even if you didn't select a new printer name (the target printer is actually comprised of the printer's name and all of its setup options). The recomposing process applies the new target printer option to your current publication. For example, let's say you change from a PostScript printer to an HP LaserJet. When you indicate that you want to recompose the publication for the new target printer, PageMaker changes your PostScript fonts to similar fonts on the LaserJet.

3. Click on OK.

The options you changed in the target printer's setup are permanent and will apply to any document you print. Therefore, it's a good idea to check these settings (especially the Orientation) before you print to make sure they apply to the current publication.

PRINTING A PUBLICATION

If you can't get your document onto paper, having the most beautiful design in the world is worthless. As long as PageMaker is installed for your printer, printing is a breeze. Follow these general steps:

1. Make sure your printer is turned on, ready to print (on-line), and has paper.

2. Open the file you want to print.

3. Pull down the File menu and choose Print (or press Ctrl-P) to display the Print dialog box, shown in Figure 4.10.

4. Change any options in the Print dialog box, which are described in the following sections.

5. Click on OK.

Various messages then pop up on the screen, letting you know that the document is in the process of being printed. After these messages disappear, your publication prints in the background, so you can continue working on the current file, open another file, or create a new publication. Depending on the complexity of the publication and the speed of your printer, each page takes from 1 to 15 minutes to print.

Selecting Printing Options

The Print dialog box contains many different options. Don't let this option-packed dialog box intimidate you. Most of the time, you won't need to change a single option. Also notice that a number of the options in the Print dialog box are dimmed. This means that your printer is not capable of using the option. For example, only PostScript printers can take advantage of the Thumbnails option.

Here, we'll discuss the options for printing multiple copies, specifying the pages you want to print, and choosing the printer. The other options will be covered in later chapters.

Multiple Copies

Enter the total number of copies you want to print for the Copies option. If you print multiple copies of a multiple-page document, you might want to turn on the Collate option. When this option is checked, Page-Maker will print all the pages in the publication before printing another copy. However, collated printing is extremely slow, so you might prefer collating by hand.

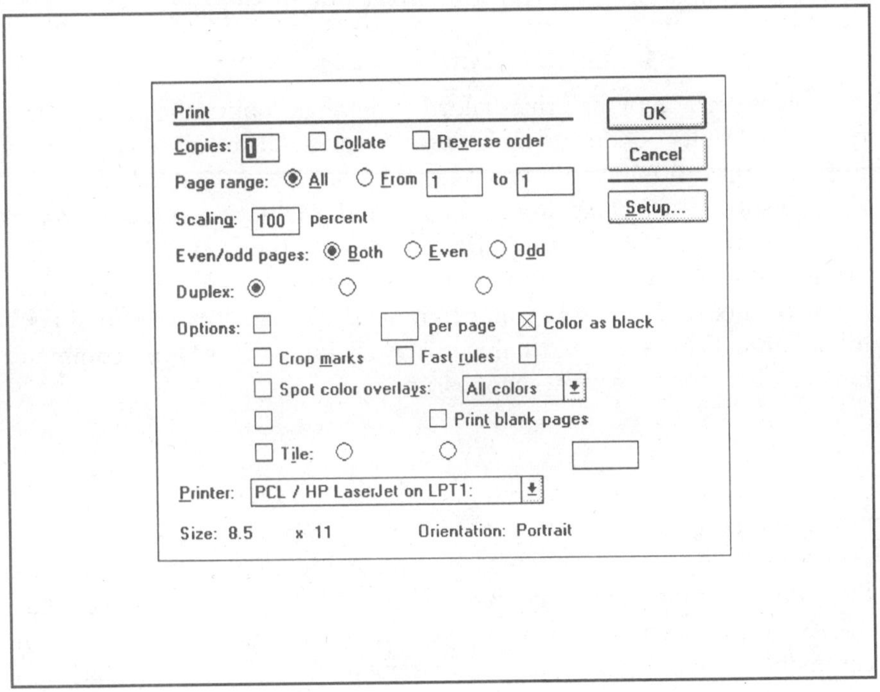

Figure 4.10: The Print dialog box

Specifying Which Pages to Print

In the Page Range field, you can specify which pages to print. By default, PageMaker prints the entire publication. Because the printing process is relatively slow, regardless of how fast your printer is, you will never want to print a page if you don't have to.

To print a range of pages, enter the numbers of the first and last pages you want to print in the From and To text boxes. Note that this page range is saved with the publication, and the next time you print, this same specific range will be in effect. Be sure to double-check your print range before you click on the OK button.

As discussed earlier in the chapter, you can use the Even/Odd pages option to help you print double-sided publications. Click on the Odd option button to print the odd-numbered pages or the Even button to print the even-numbered pages. Choose Both to print single-sided.

By default, blank pages in your publication will not print. Turn on the Print Blank Pages option if you want to include these pages.

Checking Your Printer Setup

Before you accept the Print dialog box settings, look at the printer name next to the Printer option and make sure it is correct. If not, click on the arrow to display the drop-down list and select the printer you want to use.

You should also check the paper size and orientation at the bottom of the dialog box. If these settings are not correct, you need to change your printer setup. However, you do not have to cancel your Print command and then choose the Target Printer command. Instead, you can go directly to the Target Printer's Setup dialog box by clicking on the Setup command button. Make the necessary changes, and then click on OK.

Using Print Manager

After you click on OK in the Print dialog box, PageMaker sends the document to Microsoft Windows for printing. More specifically, Windows' Print Manager program handles the printing of your PageMaker documents.

As you've seen, several messages appear when you give the Print command. While these messages are displayed, the publication is in the process of being sent to Print Manager. If you change your mind about printing this document while the dialog box is displayed, you can click on Cancel. But what if you want to discontinue printing after the dialog box has disappeared and before the document is finished printing? Because PageMaker's role in the printing process is completed, you need to take this issue up with Print Manager.

Print Manager works with print jobs, which it places in a print queue. A *print job* is a single print request you make in PageMaker or any other Windows application. For example, if you tell PageMaker to print your name tag, that request becomes a print job in Print Manager. The program can handle multiple print requests from any number of Windows applications.

Each print job is lined up in a *print queue* and printed in the order it was requested. Let's say, for example, that you want to print pages 1 and 5 in a PageMaker publication. Because these pages are not consecutive, you must issue two Print commands, specifying the appropriate page range each time. Page 1 would become the first print job in the queue (assuming you requested this page first), and page 5 would become the second job in the queue.

Canceling a Print Job

Just for practice, you will print your name tag, and then cancel this print job in Print Manager. To stop a document from printing, you must delete the print job from the queue.

1. If necessary, open your NAMETAG file.

2. Pull down the File menu and choose Print.

3. Click on the OK button.

4. Read the screen messages that appear. They might make more sense now that you know that the file is being sent to Print Manager.

5. After the messages disappear (in other words, once the file has been sent to Print Manager), press Ctrl-Esc to bring up your Task List. (If you can see the Print Manager icon at the bottom of your screen, you can double-click on it instead of going through the Task List.)

6. Double-click on Print Manager. The Print Manager window should look similar to Figure 4.11. The queue contains only one print job: PageMaker4.0-NAMETAG.PM4.

7. Click on the print job to highlight the line.

8. Click on the Delete button.

9. Click on the OK button to confirm that you want to remove the job from the queue.

10. To exit from Print Manager, pull down the Options menu and choose Exit.

Other Print Manager Functions

Besides deleting a print job, you can use Print Manager for other print-related tasks, such as the following:

- See how much of a print job has been sent to the printer. The percentage appears next to the document name in the queue.

- Change the order in which print jobs are printed. (Use the Options pull-down menu.)

- Resume printing after pausing. For example, Print Manager pauses the printer when you run out of paper. Click on the Resume button to continue printing.

For additional information about Print Manager, use its Help feature or refer to the chapter about printing in your Microsoft Windows *User's Guide*.

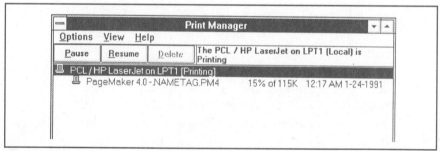

Figure 4.11: The Print Manager window

Setting up your page and your printer are two important initial steps to producing a publication. If you take the time and effort to do these steps properly—before you begin placing text and graphics on the page— you will avoid tedious extra work as you build your publication. Because producing a professional-looking, attractive document is one of your goals as a desktop publisher, knowing the ins and outs of printing is imperative.

This chapter concludes Part 1 of the book. In Part 2, you are going to learn more about one of the publishing recipe's key ingredients: text.

PART TWO

WORKING
WITH
TEXT

Part 2 will demonstrate the variety of ways you can place and format text in your publications. Because text is such an integral part of publishing, this is the longest section in the book. There are three chapters devoted to getting text onto the page: typing it with the text tool, placing it from PageMaker's Story Editor, or by importing it from an external file. The other chapters concentrate on enhancing the appearance of your text.

C H A P T E R

5

**USING
THE
TEXT
TOOL**

This chapter describes how to use PageMaker's text tool to work with text. Regardless of which method you used to place the text—through the text tool, the Story Editor, the Windows Clipboard, or importing a word processor document—you can use the text tool to correct and format it.

Using this tool, you can insert new text, delete unwanted characters, and cut and paste. You can also change fonts, adjust type sizes, and add type styles such as bold and italic. There are quite a few other formatting options that you can specify while you are using the text tool, and these are covered in Chapters 7 through 10.

WORKING WITH THE TEXT TOOL

To activate the text tool when you are working on a publication, click on the A in the toolbox. When the text tool is active, you will notice two changes on your screen:

- The A in the toolbox is reversed (white on black).
- The mouse pointer turns into an I-beam when you move it onto the page or pasteboard.

Before you can type with the text tool, you need to place the I-beam where you want to type.

Moving the Cursor

To position the I-beam, move it to where you want to begin entering text and click the left mouse button. You will see a blinking vertical bar, called the *insertion point*—PageMaker's fancy name for a cursor. The location of the insertion point indicates where text will appear as you type. Once you have an insertion point, you can slide the mouse to move the I-beam out of the way. From here on, we will refer to the insertion point as your cursor.

When you click inside the margin guides, the cursor appears just to the right of the left margin guide, regardless of where you clicked.

You can also move the cursor using the keyboard. The arrow keys move the cursor (not the I-beam) one character or line at a time. Table 5.1

lists other keyboard controls for moving the cursor. These keystrokes may be the same ones used in your word processor.

Selecting Text

After you've entered text with the text tool, many of the changes you might make to it, such as formatting and rearranging, require that you select the text to be affected first.

PageMaker offers several ways to select text while you are using the text tool:

- Click and drag across the text.
- Click at the beginning of the text, place the I-beam at the end of the text, and press Shift as you click.
- Place the I-beam on a word and double-click to select the word.
- Place the I-beam on a paragraph and triple-click to select the entire paragraph.

Table 5.1: Keystrokes for Moving the Cursor

MOVEMENT OF CURSOR	KEYSTROKE
Right one word	Ctrl-→
Left one word	Ctrl-←
Beginning of line	Home
End of line	End
Next sentence	Ctrl-End
Previous sentence	Ctrl-Home
Next paragraph	Ctrl-↓
Previous paragraph	Ctrl-↑
Next screen	PgDn
Previous screen	PgUp
Beginning of story	Ctrl-PgUp
End of story	Ctrl-PgDn

FORMATTING CHARACTERS

The three primary qualities you can assign to characters are font, size, and type style. The following sections define these formatting options. We'll also explain how to determine which particular fonts and sizes are available on your printer.

Using Fonts

PageMaker defines the word *font* differently than the rest of the world. In PageMaker, a font refers to a specific typeface, such as Helvetica, Times Roman, Courier, and Line Printer. It does *not* refer to a character's size or style (bold, italic, and so on).

There are two basic types of fonts: serif and sans serif. *Serif* fonts have tiny decorative tails at the ends of the strokes of each character. *Sans serif* fonts do not have these decorative touches.

Figure 5.1 compares a serif font (Times Roman) with a sans serif font (Helvetica). Times Roman is commonly used for body text, Helvetica for headlines or subheads. However, this is not written in stone. In fact, many books use serif fonts for all type: body text, headlines, and subheads. Whatever you do, do not mix two different serif (or sans serif) fonts on a page. Instead of providing variety, it will look like you substituted a similar font because you didn't have the right size available in a font.

The spacing of a particular font is either proportional or fixed. In a *fixed-space font,* each character is assigned the same amount of space, regardless of how thin or fat the character is. In a *proportional font,* the space each character consumes depends on the size of the character. For example,

> This is a serif font (Times Roman).
>
> This is a sans serif font (Helvetica).

Figure 5.1: Serif and sans serif fonts

a lowercase *i* or *t* takes up much less space than an uppercase *M* or *W*. Figure 5.2 compares a fixed-space font (Courier) with a proportional font (Times Roman). Proportional fonts are used most often in professional publications.

In order to follow the exercises in this book, you need two fonts. To see which fonts you have, pull down the Type menu and choose Font. The cascading menu lists the fonts available on your target printer. The one that has a check mark is the currently selected font.

The fonts used in the exercises are Helvetica and Times Roman. If you don't have Helvetica (or Helv) and Times (or Tms Rmn) listed, you must choose two other fonts. See Appendix C for information about installing fonts.

Selecting Sizes

Character sizes are measured in *points*. Points refer to a character's height and width in a given font. The larger the point size in a particular font, the larger the character. There are 72 points to an inch. Body text is usually in the 10- or 12-point range; subheads are usually around 14 points; and headlines are 20 points and up.

The Other option on the Size cascading menu lets you enter type sizes that are not on the list. You can enter type sizes in increments as small as a tenth of a point. However, this option only works if your printer has the capability of producing *scalable fonts*. PostScript printers, LaserMaster printers, and the HP LaserJet III have their own internal font outlines that can be scaled to any point size. To produce scalable fonts on a LaserJet II or other PCL printer, you can use soft fonts such as those included with Adobe Type Manager or Bitstream's FaceLift.

```
            Courier is a fixed-space font.


            Times Roman is a proportional font.
```

Figure 5.2: Fixed-space and proportional fonts

Applying Styles

To emphasize key words and phrases in your documents, you can use a variety of type styles. These styles are listed on the Type Style cascading menu. Figure 5.3 shows examples of each style in Times Roman.

You are probably familiar with the styles and have a good idea when to use them. However, applying the reverse type style requires some special considerations.

Using Reversed Type

The reverse type style switches the character color from black to white. If these characters are on a white background (such as the paper), the result is white text on white paper—invisible type. Therefore, when you specify a reverse type style, you must also change the background to black

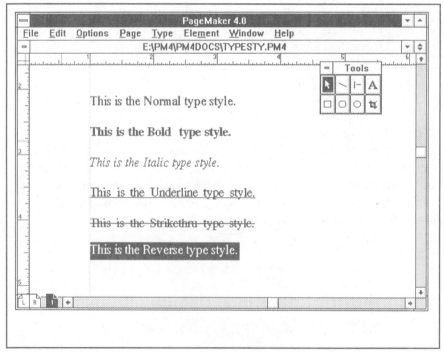

Figure 5.3: The type styles

or some other color or shade. To shade the background of reversed type, draw a shape around the text with one of the drawing tools, and then fill this shape. Chapter 11 explains this process in detail.

Large, bold, sans serif fonts are the easiest to read in the reverse type style. When reversed, small and serif typefaces tend to be difficult to read.

The reverse type style does not work on all printers. If your reversed text appears as a solid black box when you print it, your printer does not have reversing capability. PostScript printers, LaserMaster printers, and the HP LaserJet III can print reversed text. Certain soft fonts, such as those included with Adobe Type Manager, also can produce reversed text. If you have your heart set on reversed type but don't have the equipment, you can create the reversed text in a graphics package and save it as a .PCX, .MSP, or .TIF file. You can then import the file into a PageMaker document, and it will print correctly. See Chapter 12 for details on importing graphics.

Assigning Type Characteristics

PageMaker offers several ways to assign fonts, sizes, and styles. You have already worked with the cascading menus that appear when you choose Font, Size, or Type Style from the Type pull-down menu. Use this method if you need to make a single change to the type. For example, if the current font and style are correct and all you want to do is change the size, use the Size option.

Using the Type Specifications Dialog Box

If you need to make more than one change to the type (for example, change its font and size or specify bold and italic), choose Type Specs from the Type menu, or press Ctrl-T. This displays the Type Specifications dialog box, shown in Figure 5.4, which offers drop-down lists for specifying the font and size, as well as check boxes for selecting type styles.

The Type Specifications dialog box provides additional ways to format characters. The Case option's default setting is Normal, which means that the characters will appear in the case in which they were entered. The other options are All Caps and Small Caps.

Using the Case option called Small Caps, you can capitalize all characters, with lowercase letters 70 percent of the size of the uppercase letters.

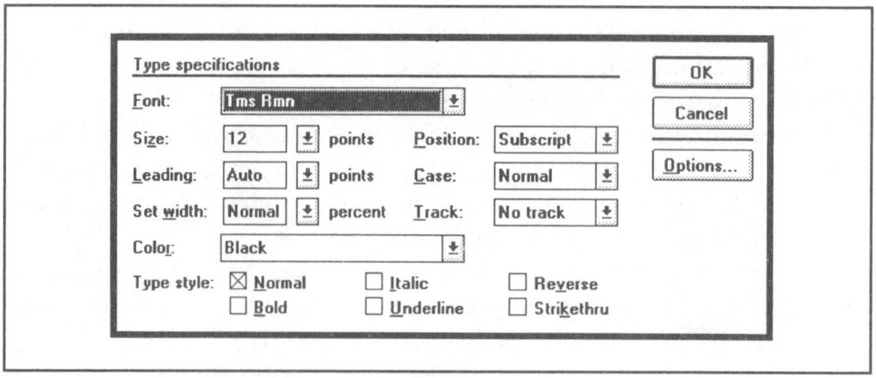

Figure 5.4: The Type Specifications dialog box

For example, if you formatted uppercase and lowercase 20-point characters as Small Caps, the lowercase letters would be 70 percent of the point
size, or 14 points. To change this percentage, click on the Options button
in the Type Specifications dialog box. You can then fill in a different
percentage next to Small Caps Size. A higher percentage value brings the
size of the small caps closer to the size of the type.

The Small Caps option works best with scalable fonts since it involves
percentage scaling. Without scalable fonts, you might not have the appropriate type size available, and a different size would be substituted.

The other options in the Type Specifications dialog box will be covered
in later chapters.

Using Keyboard
Shortcuts for Styles and Sizes

Another way to specify styles and sizes is with keyboard shortcuts.
The shortcuts for changing type styles are listed in Table 5.2. Notice that
most of the styles have two keyboard shortcuts. The shortcuts that use Ctrl
and Shift are mnemonic (for the most part), but the function keys are faster
and easier (if you can remember them).

The normal style clears all other styles. For example, if the selected text
is bold and italics, you can press F5 to choose normal and cancel both
styles at once. To cancel only one of the styles, press the appropriate function key or key combination. For instance, to clear only the bold from
selected text, use the Bold command (press F6 or Ctrl-Shift-B).

Table 5.2: Keyboard Shortcuts for Applying Type Styles

STYLE	KEY COMBINATION	FUNCTION KEY
Normal	Ctrl-Shift-spacebar	F5
Bold	Ctrl-Shift-B	F6
Italic	Ctrl-Shift-I	F7
Underline	Ctrl-Shift-U	F8
Strikethru	Ctrl-Shift-S	
Reverse	Ctrl-Shift-V	

Two of the shortcuts for changing type sizes are Ctrl-Shift-> and Ctrl-Shift-<. Each time you press Ctrl-Shift->, the type size increases by one point. Ctrl-Shift-< decreases the type size one point at a time. For example, if the current type size is 12 points, the first time you press Ctrl-Shift->, the size increases to 13 points. The second time, it increases to 14 points. These shortcuts allow you to play "what-if" games with your type sizes when you aren't sure which size you want. Each time you use the shortcut key, you will immediately see how the selected text looks in the new type size.

You shouldn't use Ctrl-Shift-> and Ctrl-Shift-< with bit-mapped (non-scalable) fonts because they might increase or decrease the type size to one that is unavailable on your printer. For example, if you increase the type to 13 points and you don't have a 13-point font, the text will be printed with the closest size that is available (probably 12 points) but with additional spacing between the lines. Thus, as you are pressing Ctrl-Shift-< or Ctrl-Shift->, the size of the characters might not change, but the space between the lines of type will. Instead, you should use the other shortcuts for size, Ctrl-> and Ctrl-<.

The Ctrl-> and Ctrl-< keyboard shortcuts work like the combinations with Shift, except that they only increase or decrease to type sizes on your font list. For example, suppose you are using bit-mapped soft fonts, such as those included with Bitstream's Fontware, and you have generated fonts in 12-, 14-, and 20-point sizes. If the selected text is currently 12 points and you press Ctrl->, the text will increase to 14 points. Press Ctrl-> again, and the text becomes 20 points. In other words, it skips over the point sizes that are unavailable.

You should be aware that each time you press the key combination, you must wait for the screen to be redrawn. If you have only a few lines selected, or if you are increasing or decreasing the size by one or two points, you won't mind the wait. If you are making wider changes, you may want to take a trip to the Size cascading menu.

PRODUCING A BUSINESS LETTER

Now you will use the techniques we've described so far to type, edit, and format a business letter, a rejection letter from a personnel director. After completing the exercises in this chapter, your final letter will look similar to Figure 5.5. You will also save the letterhead in its own file so that you can use it again with other letters.

Creating a Letterhead

In the following exercise, you will create the letterhead for a company called Blue Chip Realty.

1. Pull down the File menu and choose New.

2. Turn off the Double-Sided option.

3. Specify **1.25** inches for the Left and Right margins.

4. Specify **.5** inch for the Top and Bottom margins.

5. Click on OK.

6. Activate the text tool (the A in the toolbox).

7. Click the I-beam in the upper-left corner of the page (just under the top margin guide and to the right of the left margin guide). The cursor appears at the beginning of the line.

8. Type **Blue Chip Realty** and press Enter.

9. Press Ctrl-1 to switch from Fit in Window view (where the text is greeked) to Actual Size view (where you can read your text).

BLUE CHIP REALTY

January 15, 1991

Ms. Betty Johnson
1234 State Street
San Francisco, CA 95123

Dear Ms. Johnson:

Thank you for sending us your resume. Your experience is impressive, and you seem to be very qualified. However, the position has already been filled.

We will keep your resume on file in case another position for which you are qualified becomes available.

Sincerely Yours,

Jody Peterson
Personnel Director

P.O. Box 1234
Menlo Park, CA 55555
(415) 555-CHIP

Figure 5.5: At least disappointing news can be presented well

10.　Type the remaining lines of the letterhead, pressing Enter after each line (press Backspace to erase mistakes as you are typing):

P.O. Box 1234
Menlo Park, CA 55555
(415) 555-CHIP

The completed text for the letterhead is shown in Figure 5.6. Now it's time to format this text. First, you'll format the company name.

11.　Place the I-beam anywhere in the line *Blue Chip Realty* and triple-click to select the paragraph. Because you pressed Enter at the end of this line, PageMaker considers the single line to be a paragraph.

12.　Press Ctrl-T to display the Type Specifications dialog box (Figure 5.4).

13.　Display the Font drop-down list and choose Helvetica (or Helv).

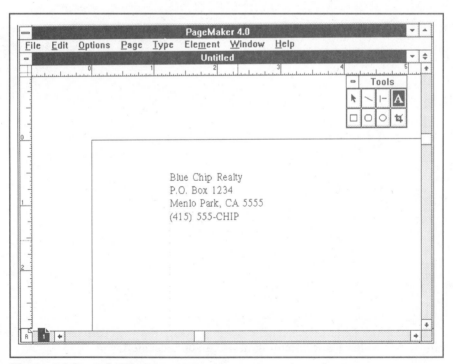

Figure 5.6: Letterhead text

14. Display the Size drop-down list and choose 14.

15. Turn on the Bold check box.

16. Display the Case drop-down list and choose All Caps.

17. Click on OK.

As another enhancement, we'll enlarge the first letter of each word in the company name.

18. Click-and-drag across the letter *B* in *Blue.*

19. Pull down the Type menu and choose Size.

20. Choose 20. If 20 is not listed, choose Other, type **20**, and press Enter.

21. Repeat steps 18, 19, and 20 to enlarge the letters *C* and *R.*

Figure 5.7 shows the formatted name. Note that you could achieve a similar effect by selecting the entire line and choosing 20-point type with the Small Caps option.

Now let's format the remainder of the letterhead as 12-point Helvetica with the italic type style.

22. Click right before *P.O. Box.*

23. Hold down Shift and click right after *555-CHIP.* The address and phone number should be selected.

24. Press Ctrl-T, display the Font drop-down list, and choose Helvetica (or Helv).

25. If necessary, display the Size drop-down list and choose 12.

26. Turn on the Italic check box.

27. Click on OK.

Your letterhead is now complete and should look like Figure 5.8.

28. Use the Save option on the File menu to save the file with the name **LETHEAD1**.

Typing the Letter

Now that the letterhead is complete, you can type the letter. As with a word processor, the text you create in PageMaker automatically *word wraps* as you type, so you do not need to press Enter at the end of each line in a paragraph. You only need to press the Enter key at the end of short lines (such as *Dear Ms. Johnson:*), to create blank lines, and at the end of paragraphs.

When typing this letter, press the spacebar only once between sentences. We know that your high school typing instructor taught you to insert two spaces after the period, but this rule does not apply to typeset documents. Extra spaces can cause large ugly gaps between sentences (especially when text is justified).

For your letterhead, you formatted existing text. Since the entire letter is going to be one font and one size, it will be easier to make the specifications before you start typing.

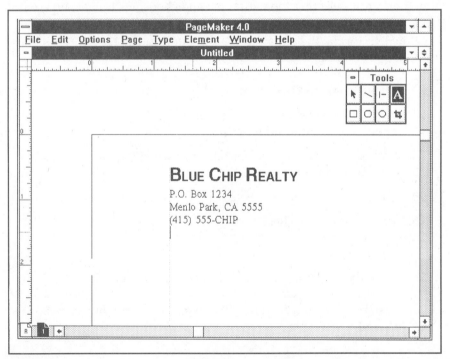

Figure 5.7: The first letter in each word is in a larger type size

1. Click an inch or so below the letterhead. Precise positioning is unimportant because you can adjust the text placement later.

2. Specify 12-point Times Roman (this font and size might already be set).

3. Type the following text (remember, press the spacebar once, not twice, between sentences):

    January 15, 1991

    Ms. Betty Johnson
    1234 State Street
    San Francisco, CA 95123

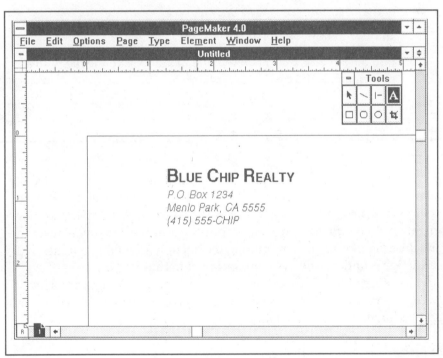

Figure 5.8: The formatted letterhead

Dear Ms. Johnson:

Thank you for sending your resume. Your experience is quite impressive, and you seem to be very, very qualified. However, the job has already been filled. (It seems that the president's daughter was also quite qualified.) We will keep your resume in case another position for which you are qualified becomes available.

Very Sincerely Yours,

Jody Peterson
Personnel Director

4. Italicize *Personnel Director* at the bottom of the letter. Figure 5.9 shows the completed letter.

5. Use the Save As option on the File menu to save the file with a new name: **JOHNSON**.

TYPING SPECIAL CHARACTERS

The only time you should press the spacebar is between words. Do not insert two spaces between sentences or use the spacebar to align text. Many novices make the mistake of trying to align text with the spacebar. They might spend hours inserting spaces, printing out the document, inserting and deleting more spaces, reprinting the document, pulling out their hair, screaming—until finally everything almost lines up.

However, there are occasions when you may want extra spaces between letters or words; for example, between the state and zip code in an address or after a numbered step.

To insert additional space, use one of these special characters instead of pressing the spacebar:

- An *em space* (Ctrl-Shift-M) is equivalent to the amount of space a capital M consumes in the current point size.

- An *en space* (Ctrl-Shift-N) equals half an em space.

- A *thin space* (Ctrl-Shift-T) is a quarter of an em space.

Although it's easier to use the spacebar than to remember all these keystrokes, inserting special spacing characters is the only way to know exactly how much space will be added when you are using a proportional font. The space created with the spacebar is variable because its actual size depends on the font and type size you are using.

In addition to spacing characters, PageMaker offers other special characters that you can insert into your text. For example, typographical quotation marks that look more professional than the ones on your keyboard. Also, you can use an em-dash (—) instead of two hyphens, and an en-dash instead of a single hyphen to specify a range of values (for example, 1–5). The keystrokes for special characters are listed in Table 5.3. (At the time of the writing the Ctrl-Shift-= keystroke produced two

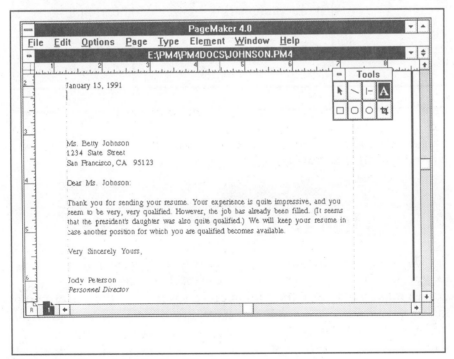

Figure 5.9: Completed body of the letter

Table 5.3: Keystrokes for Inserting Special Characters

CHARACTER	DESCRIPTION	KEYSTROKES
"	Opening quotation mark	Ctrl-Shift-[
"	Closing quotation mark	Ctrl-Shift-]
'	Opening single quotation mark	Ctrl-[
'	Closing single quotation mark	Ctrl-]
—	Em dash	Ctrl-Shift-= or Alt-0151 (numeric keypad)
–	En dash	Ctrl-=
©	Copyright mark	Ctrl-Shift-O
®	Registration mark	Ctrl-Shift-G
§	Section mark	Ctrl-Shift-6
¶	Paragraph mark	Ctrl-Shift-7
•	Bullet	Ctrl-Shift-8
	Em space	Ctrl-Shift-M
	En space	Ctrl-Shift-N
	Thin space	Ctrl-Shift-T

hyphens instead of an em-dash; if you encounter this problem, hold down Alt and type 0151 on the numeric keypad.)

CORRECTING MISTAKES

The three most common typing mistakes are to leave out characters, to type the wrong characters, or to type extra characters.

An important part of the editing process is moving the cursor to the mistakes you want to correct. You have already learned how to scroll the screen using the scroll bar or grabber hand. Once the screen displays what you want to correct, you can click the I-beam or use the keyboard controls to place the cursor in the text.

Inserting Text

PageMaker is always in insert mode. Whatever you type, wherever you type it, the text is added to what is already there. To insert text, click the I-beam to the left of where you want to add characters and start typing. Text to the right of the cursor is pushed forward as you type.

Now we'll insert some words and spaces in the business letter. The words you will insert are underlined in Figure 5.10 to help you locate them (the text on your screen should *not* be underlined).

1. Place the I-beam just to the left of the word *your,* click, type **us,** and press the spacebar.

2. Move the cursor just to the right of the word *qualified* in the sentence in parentheses, press the spacebar, and type **for this position**.

3. Insert the words **on file** after *resume* on the last line.

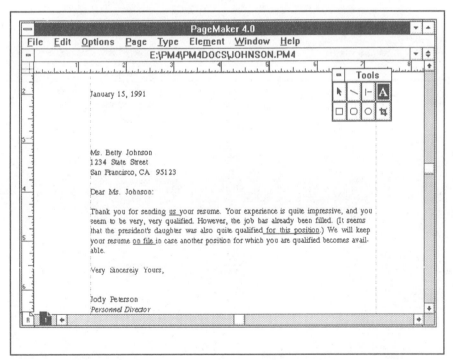

Figure 5.10: The letter, with words to insert (underlined)

4. To insert an extra blank line after *Very Sincerely Yours,* click the I-beam at the end of this line (or on one of the blank lines below it) and press Enter.

5. To divide the letter into two paragraphs, click the I-beam on what will be the beginning of the second paragraph, *We will keep*, and press Enter twice.

Figure 5.11 shows the letter with the words and line spaces inserted.

Deleting Text

PageMaker offers two ways to delete text while you are using the text tool. To delete a single character, click the I-beam to the right of the incorrect character and press the Backspace key. To delete larger amounts of text, select the text and then press Del (or Delete). Unlike most software

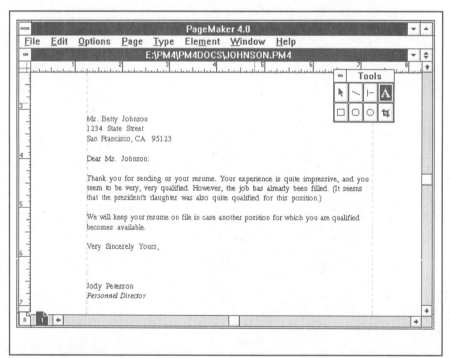

Figure 5.11: A single paragraph divided into two paragraphs

packages, you cannot delete a single character with the Del key, unless you select it first.

Let's continue working on the business letter, and delete the words that are crossed out in Figure 5.12.

1. Delete the word *quite* in the first line of the letter by double-clicking on it and pressing Del.

2. Delete *very,* on the second line. Be sure to delete the comma and space.

3. Select the whole sentence in parentheses (including the parentheses) and press Del to remove it.

4. Double-click on the *Very* in the closing and press Del.

When you are finished, your letter should have the same text as Figure 5.5 (except for the word *position* instead of *job*, which you'll do next).

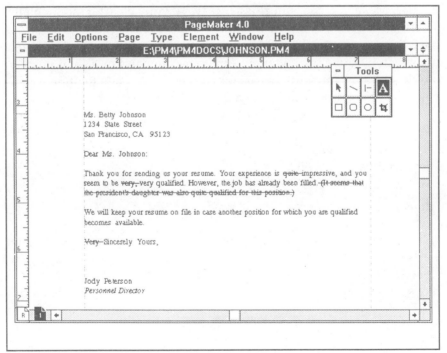

Figure 5.12: The document, with words to delete

Replacing Text

Sometimes you might want to replace one word or phrase with another. Rather than selecting the text, deleting it, and inserting the new text, you can simply select the text you want to replace and then type the new text. The selected text immediately disappears as soon as you begin typing.

Follow these steps to replace a word in the JOHNSON letter:

1. Place the I-beam on the word *job* and double-click to select the word.

2. Type **position** and press the spacebar.

To replace multiple occurrences of a word throughout a story, you can use the Story Editor's Change command, as explained in Chapter 6.

Undoing Mistakes

PageMaker's Undo feature is a lifesaver if you delete text accidentally. To bring back text you deleted with Del or Backspace, choose Undo from the Edit menu or press Alt-Backspace. You must issue the Undo command immediately, however. If you give another command or even reposition the cursor, you cannot restore the text. When it's too late to undo a command, the Undo option is dimmed on the Edit menu.

The Undo feature is not limited to restoring deleted text. You can also undo other types of editing you've done with the text tool, such as inserting, replacing, and cutting and pasting. However, you cannot undo type specifications.

Cutting and Pasting Text

To move text such as a sentence or a paragraph, you can use an electronic cut-and-paste method. Select the text to be moved, choose Cut from the Edit menu (or press Shift-Del), click the I-beam where you want to move the text, and then choose Paste from the Edit menu (or press Shift-Ins).

In the following steps, you'll use the Cut and Paste commands to move part of the letterhead to the bottom of the page.

1. Position the screen so that you can see the letterhead at the top of the page. (You should be in 75% or Actual Size view.)

2. Select the address and phone number (but not *Blue Chip Realty*).

3. Pull down the Edit menu and choose Cut (or press Shift-Del). The text is removed from the page.

4. Scroll down until you can see the bottom-left corner of the page.

5. Click the I-beam about an inch above the bottom margin guide. Don't worry about the exact position; you will place it more precisely later.

6. Pull down the Edit menu and choose Paste (or press Shift-Ins).

The address and phone number are now positioned near the bottom of the page.

When you cut the text out of the document, it is sent to Windows' Clipboard. The *Clipboard* is a temporary storage area that holds data that you want to transfer elsewhere—to another location in the same publication, to a different publication file, or even to a different software application. Here are a few examples of ways you can use the Clipboard:

- In the previous exercise, you cut several lines from your letter and then pasted them in another location on the same page. You could also have pasted them on another page in the document (if there were multiple pages).

- You can cut or copy a block of text or a graphic from one PageMaker publication and paste it into another PageMaker publication. Copy the element from one document, close that publication, open another, position the cursor, and then paste.

- You can cut or copy an image from a graphics program and paste it into a PageMaker publication. For example, copy the drawing in Corel Draw, switch to PageMaker, and paste it into a publication. Because Windows allows you to have several applications running at once, you can perform this transfer quickly.

- You can cut or copy text from any program (word processor, spreadsheet, database, and so on) and paste it into a PageMaker publication.

The Clipboard only holds the last thing you cut or copied to it. Once you cut or copy something else, the previous Clipboard contents are thrown out. Therefore, make sure you don't cut or copy a second item before pasting the first item, or you will lose the first thing you sent to the Clipboard. To see the contents of your Clipboard, go back to Windows' Program Manager and double-click on the Clipboard icon in the Main program group. For more information about the Clipboard, see Appendix B.

WORKING WITH TEXT BLOCKS

In the previous section, you used the text tool's cut-and-paste method to move text to another spot on the page. Another way to move text is to use the pointer tool to reposition an entire text block.

A *text block* is a rectangular body of text. Originally, your JOHNSON letter had two text blocks: the letterhead and the body of the letter. When you moved the address and phone number to the bottom of the page, you created a third text block.

To see the boundaries of a text block, click the pointer anywhere in the text. Let's try it.

1. Click on the arrow in the toolbox to switch to the pointer tool.

2. Press Ctrl-W to see the entire page at once.

3. Click anywhere in the body of the letter. This text block is now selected and can be moved, sized, or deleted.

Solid lines appear above and below the text block, and window shade handles are attached to these upper and lower boundaries. These handles can be clicked and dragged to lengthen or shorten the text block. The corners of the block contain *text block handles*. You can click and drag these handles to widen, narrow, lengthen, or shorten the text block. Figure 5.13 points out these two types of handles.

Moving a Text Block

The easiest way to get the address and phone number aligned at the bottom margin guide is to move the text block. You might remember that you moved a text block (your name on the name tag) in Chapter 3. Follow these steps to move this block:

1. Switch to 75% view.

2. Position the screen so that you can see the bottom of the page.

3. Click inside the address block and hold down the mouse button. If you do this correctly, dashed lines surround the text block and a four-headed arrow appears.

4. Drag the box down so that its bottom border touches the margin guide at the bottom of the page. Make sure the box's left border touches the left margin guide.

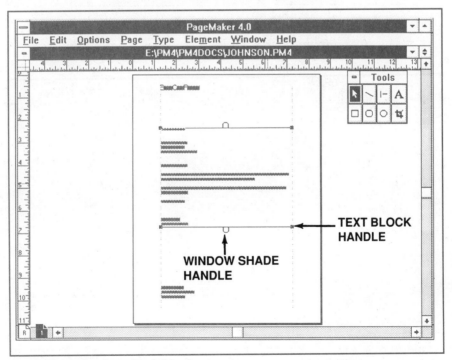

Figure 5.13: A selected text block

5. Release the mouse button. This text block should be positioned as shown in Figure 5.14.

6. You may also want to reposition the middle text block, the one containing the body of the letter. In Fit in Window view, move the text block so that it is centered on the page.

Using a Ruler Guide to Align Text Blocks

You can use PageMaker's *ruler guides* to align elements in the same way you would use a T-square or a ruler. These guides can be horizontal or vertical, and you are allowed up to 40 ruler guides per publication. Like your margin guides, the ruler guides do not print.

To insert a vertical ruler guide, click in the vertical ruler and drag the guide to the right. To insert a horizontal ruler guide, click in the horizontal ruler and drag the guide down onto the page. (If your rulers are not

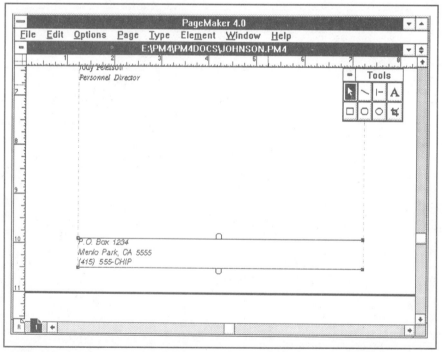

Figure 5.14: The address text block positioned at the bottom of the page

displayed on the screen, choose the Rulers option on the Options menu.)

As you can see in Figure 5.15, the two letterhead text blocks have been moved into the left margin. To align the two blocks with each other, you need a vertical ruler guide at the 1/2-inch mark. Follow these steps to insert this ruler and then move the text:

1. Press Ctrl-7 to switch to 75% view, and scroll the screen until you can see the upper-left corner of the page.

2. Click in the vertical ruler and drag to the right. As soon as you move the pointer (a double-headed arrow) onto the pasteboard, you will see the vertical ruler guide.

3. Continue dragging until the guide is at the 1/2-inch mark in the horizontal ruler. Your ruler guide should be positioned as shown in Figure 5.16.

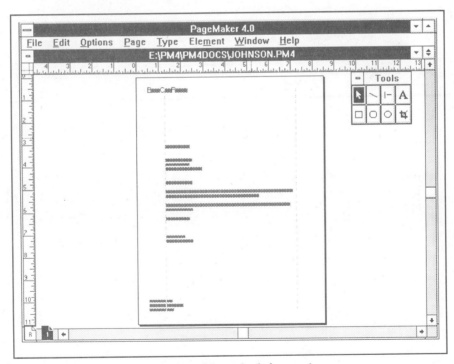

Figure 5.15: The letterhead moved into the left margin

4. Release the mouse button.

If you release the button too soon, you can use the click-and-drag technique to move the ruler to the correct position.

5. Now that you have the ruler guide in place, move the two letterhead blocks (one at a time) so that the left edge touches the ruler guide.

Positioning these blocks is even easier if the Snap to Guides option is turned on. This option creates a magnetic effect between the object you are moving and the various guides on the page (ruler, margin, and column).

6. To see if the Snap to Guides option is turned on, pull down the Options menu. If a check mark appears next to Snap to Guides, it is turned on.

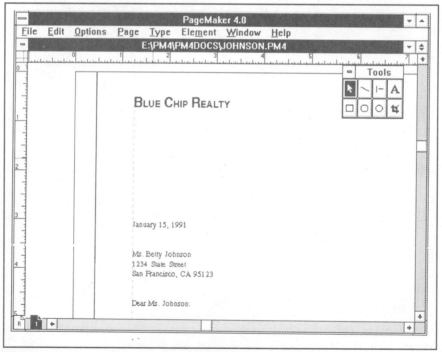

Figure 5.16: A vertical ruler guide at the ½-inch mark

When you are finished with a ruler guide, you can either leave it on the page or drag it back into the ruler.

Resizing a Text Block

If you change your margins *after* you have placed text on the page, you must resize the text blocks so that they fit within the new margin guides. To see how this works, let's change the left and right margins in the letter from 1¼ to 1 inch.

1. Pull down the File menu and choose Page Setup.

2. Enter **1** for the Left and Right margins.

3. Click on OK.

4. Press Ctrl-W to see the entire page.

As Figure 5.17 shows, the margin guides have shifted to the new settings you specified, but the text blocks are still in their original locations. In this example, you need to resize the middle text block so that the boundaries touch the left and right margin guides. To resize a block, you click and drag the text block handles until the block boundary touches the margin guide.

5. Click on the middle text block (the body of the letter) to select it.

6. On the left side of the text block, click on either the top or bottom text block handle (the small black dots) and hold down the mouse button. If you do this correctly, the pointer turns into a double-headed, diagonal arrow.

7. Drag until the left border touches the left margin guide.

8. Release the mouse button.

9. Repeat the procedure to move the right side of the text block. The text rewraps to fit in the new text block size.

10. Press Ctrl-S to save the file.

11. Press Ctrl-P to print the final letter.

Deleting a Text Block

In the beginning of this chapter, you saved your letterhead under the name LETHEAD1. You have since revised the letterhead, placing the company name at the top and the address at the bottom. Now you will save this version of the letterhead in a file with a different name, LETHEAD2. Before you do this, however, you will delete the body of the letter, so the file will become a template to be used with other letters.

You can delete a text block using either the text tool or pointer tool. With the text tool, click and drag across the entire text block (in the letter, from the date through the signature block), and then press Del. The pointer tool offers a faster way: simply click on the text block and press Del.

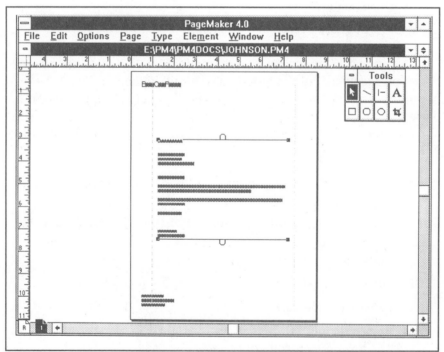

Figure 5.17: The text blocks do not automatically conform to the new
margin guides

Follow these steps to save your second version of the letterhead:

1. Click on the body of the letter.

2. Press Del. The text block is removed.

3. Use the Save As option on the File menu to save the file with the name **LETHEAD2**.

You now have two styles of letterhead that you could use on different business documents. Be sure to keep LETHEAD1 and LETHEAD2, because you will be using them in later chapters.

In this chapter you learned how to type and format characters with the text tool. Although you can correct typing mistakes with this tool, the Story Editor is the editing specialist. The next chapter introduces you to this powerful feature included in PageMaker 4.0.

C H A P T E R

6

USING
THE
STORY
EDITOR

The Story Editor is yet another way to type and edit text in PageMaker. Just click on the text you want to edit, press Ctrl-E, and your story appears in its own word processing window. All the text tool's editing commands (insert, delete, cut, and paste) are available in the Story Editor.

The Story Editor is also equipped with two powerful features that aren't offered when you use the text tool: a spelling checker and a search-and-replace feature. You are probably familiar with these features from your word processing program, and you will see that they work much the same way in PageMaker.

WHAT THE STORY EDITOR CAN (AND CAN'T) DO

You will probably not format text very often in the Story Editor (even though you are allowed to) because it does not display most formatting effects on the screen. When you are in the Story Editor, you are concerned about content, not form. You view only the text, not the page layout, formatting, or graphics.

When you are in the Story Editor, you are in what is referred to as *story view*, as opposed to the view you have been using so far, *layout view*. Figure 6.1 shows the story view of the business letter you created in Chapter 5.

While the story looks different in the two views, it contains exactly the same text. Any editing changes you make in story view are automatically made in layout view, and vice versa. Each view simply shows the same text in a different form. Story view focuses on the publication text; layout view shows you the big picture.

There are a couple of ways you may want to use the Story Editor. First, you can use it to edit text that is already placed in your publication. You can correct typing mistakes, check the spelling in the story, or use the search-and-replace feature.

Although you won't want to do your initial formatting in story view, you may want to use the Story Editor to *change* your formatting. For example, if you underlined ten different titles throughout your document,

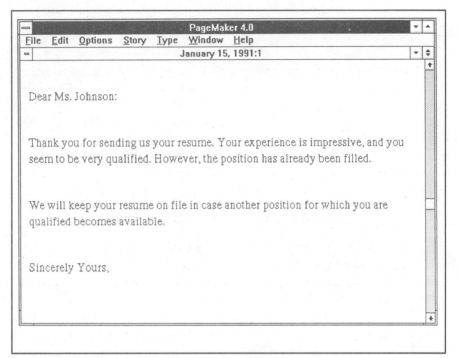

Figure 6.1: The JOHNSON letter in story view

and you decide you want those titles in italics instead, the Story Editor can substitute the italic style for the underlining. Or if your subheads are in 14-point Times Roman, the Story Editor can automatically change them to 16-point Helvetica.

Another way to use the Story Editor is to create and type an entire story from scratch. So, instead of typing the text directly on the page (as you did in the last chapter) or in your word processor, you can create a publication and then type its text in the Story Editor.

The Story Editor offers several advantages. You can type and edit much faster in story view than in layout view because the Story Editor does not display fonts and graphics on the screen, nor does it concern itself with line or page breaks. Furthermore, you do not need to load a separate piece of software to create a story—you can type it right in PageMaker.

LOADING THE STORY EDITOR

To create a new story in the Story Editor, press Ctrl-E without any text or text blocks selected. Ctrl-E is the keyboard shortcut for the Edit Story option on the Edit menu.

To load the Story Editor and edit an existing story, click in the text with the text tool, or select the text block with the pointer tool, and press Ctrl-E. You can also load an existing story in the Story Editor by triple-clicking on the text block with the pointer tool.

The Story Window

When you load the Story Editor, you are actually opening a window. Your story window lays on top of your publication window, and it has its own buttons and scroll bars. Most of the time, you will want to click on the maximize button so that your story window fills the screen.

When you are creating a new story, the title bar says *Untitled*. When you edit an existing story, the first few words of the story are entered into the title bar as the story name. In Figure 6.1, the name is shown as *January 15, 1991*, the beginning text in the JOHNSON letter. The *:1* after the story title indicates that this is the first open story with that name. If you were to open a second story that began with the same exact words, the title bar would show *:2* after the name.

The Story Editor's menu bar is slightly different than the one you see in the publication window because you have different capabilities in each view. A new option, Story, is available. The Element menu is not offered because you do not see graphics in story view. The Page menu is gone because it is also irrelevant in story view; you work with a continuous stream of text rather than with pages.

The story window is partitioned into two vertical areas separated by a solid line. The right area is where you type your story; the left area displays style names. (Chapter 8 describes the style feature.)

Typing in the Story Editor

As when you are using the text tool, you have an insertion point (the cursor) and an I-beam (the mouse pointer) in story view. You should keep the following in mind when you are typing in the Story Editor:

- Press the spacebar once—and only once—between sentences.

- Let the text word wrap as you type. Press Enter only at the end of paragraphs.

- Do not double-space between paragraphs. To add interparagraph spacing, use a paragraph formatting command (see Chapter 7). You may notice that the Story Editor automatically puts a little extra space between paragraphs so that you can more easily identify your paragraphs. This extra space appears only in story view; it disappears in layout view (and on your printout).

- Do not press Tab at the beginning of paragraphs. If you want the first line of each paragraph indented, use a paragraph formatting command (see Chapter 7).

Type styles are one of the few formatting options that display in story view. As in layout view, you specify the style (bold, italic, and so on) in story view by turning it on and off as you type the text, or by selecting the text after it is typed and then turning on the style.

CREATING A BROCHURE

If you want to use the Story Editor to type a story from scratch, you must first open or create a publication. In this chapter, you will begin creating a three-panel brochure that, when folded, fits into a standard business envelope. The final brochure, shown in Figure 6.2, is for the same company for which you designed the letterhead, Blue Chip Realty. You will type most of the text in the Story Editor.

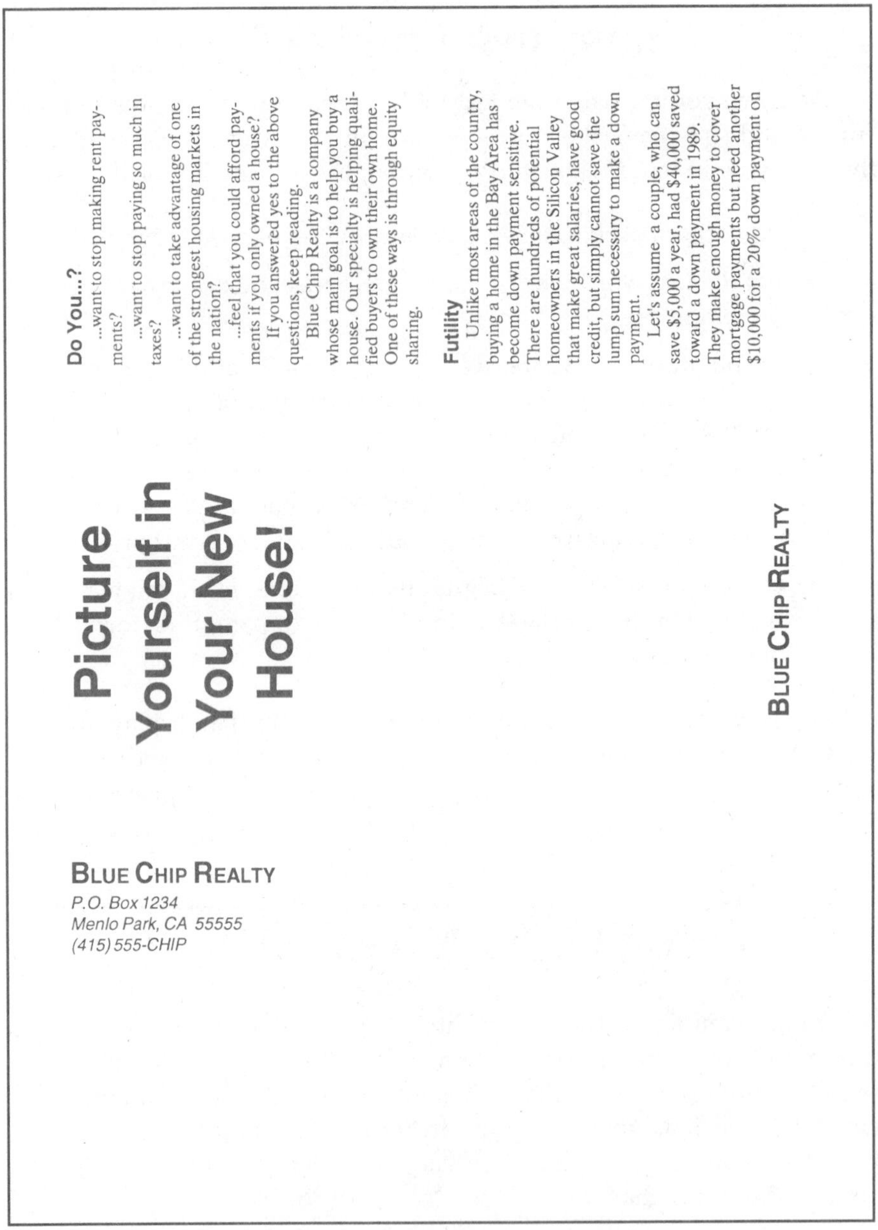

Picture Yourself in Your New House!

Do You...?

...want to stop making rent payments?

...want to stop paying so much in taxes?

...want to take advantage of one of the strongest housing markets in the nation?

...feel that you could afford payments if you only owned a house?

If you answered yes to the above questions, keep reading.

Blue Chip Realty is a company whose main goal is to help you buy a house. Our specialty is helping qualified buyers to own their own home. One of these ways is through equity sharing.

Futility

Unlike most areas of the country, buying a home in the Bay Area has become down payment sensitive. There are hundreds of potential homeowners in the Silicon Valley that make great salaries, have good credit, but simply cannot save the lump sum necessary to make a down payment.

Let's assume a couple, who can save $5,000 a year, had $40,000 saved toward a down payment in 1989. They make enough money to cover mortgage payments but need another $10,000 for a 20% down payment on

BLUE CHIP REALTY
P.O. Box 1234
Menlo Park, CA 55555
(415) 555-CHIP

BLUE CHIP REALTY

Figure 6.2: The brochure for Blue Chip Realty

a $250,000 house. So they decide to wait and save.

In the two years it took them to save $10,000, the house appreciated $100,000. Now it's 1991 and they need $70,000 for a down payment on the same house, and they only have $50,000. What can they do? Save another four years? By then the house might be worth $450,000. Chances are they'll never catch up. They need money today. Equity sharing can provide it.

Concepts

Equity sharing is an arrangement where an investor puts up money toward a portion of the down payment. In return, he/she will receive a share of the equity from the home buyer.

For example, suppose a buyer, with the help of an investor, purchases a house in 1991 for $300,000. Here's a hypothetical breakdown of the up-front costs:

	Investor	Buyer
Down Payment	$40,000	$20,000
Closing Costs	5,000	5,000
House Payments	None	All
% of Appreciation	40	60

Numerous benefits accrue to you, the buyer, in return for the portion of the appreciation you relinquish in an equity sharing deal. First, you get to fulfill your own American dream: home ownership.

Other benefits include large tax deductions, saying goodbye to rent payments, and getting a leveraged investment in one of the strongest real estate markets in the world. If these benefits sound good to you, then Blue Chip Realty can help.

Our Focus

Blue Chip Realty specializes in serving home buyers. We do not list property. Instead, we simply act as agents to help people like you find a house here on the Peninsula. So how do we get paid? By receiving a percentage of the commission that the home seller pays to the listing agent. That's all.

We are members of several Multiple Listing Services (MLS) throughout the region. Our geographic area spans Santa Clara and San Mateo counties. Here's an outline of our services:

- **We help determine your price range.** By analyzing your income and savings, Blue Chip Realty uses a computerized worksheet to determine the range of home prices you can reasonably afford.
- **We arrange equity sharing.** If you need cash for a down payment, Blue Chip Realty will match you with an investor.
- **We help you shop for your house.** Blue Chip Realty will work with you to find a house that's just right for you.
- **We handle the transaction.** Blue Chip Realty will write up the offer, negotiate to your advantage, and arrange inspections.
- **We hand you the house keys.**

Matchmaking

Because investors supply the majority of cash, they define most of the terms of the transaction. Blue Chip Realty simply acts as a matchmaker. An investor looks for buyers who have solid cash flow, are credit worthy and debt-free, and are eager to buy a house. Buyers look to match with an investor who fits the buyers' financial needs and desires.

Results

If you are interested in owning your own home and would like Blue Chip Realty to help you achieve this goal, call for an appointment now.

Figure 6.2: The brochure for Blue Chip Realty (continued)

Changing Your Measurement System

Starting with this chapter, the remaining exercises in the book will use the pica/point measuring system. Because your fonts are measured in this system, you will find it much easier to measure everything in picas and points. If you are not from the typesetting world, the pica/point measuring system may seem like a foreign language. You will probably find it helpful to invest in a pica/point ruler. Remember, there are 6 picas to an inch, 12 points to a pica, and therefore 72 points to an inch.

Follow the steps below to change your default measuring system and vertical ruler:

1. If necessary, close the current publication.

2. Pull down the Edit menu and choose Preferences. The Preferences dialog box appears.

3. Change the Measurement System to Picas.

4. Change the Vertical Ruler to Picas.

Note that the bottom of this dialog box has two options pertaining to the Story Editor: Font and Size. These options control the font and type size of the text on the screen in story view, not how the text will print.

5. Select OK in the dialog box.

Until you change them, these settings will apply to all future publications you open or create. If you ever want to go back to working in inches or centimeters, select those measurements in the Preferences dialog box.

Setting Up the Page

To get the brochure to fold in the white space between columns (called the *gutter*), you need to give careful consideration to your page setup. The rule is that your gutters should be twice the size of your left and right (or inside and outside) margins, and your left and right (inside and outside) margins must be identical.

Now that your measurement system is in picas, you are ready to create a new publication with the appropriate margin and column settings.

Strangely enough, the column settings are not in the Page Setup dialog box; they are in their own dialog box (accessed from the Options menu), so you'll have to go through two dialog boxes to set up the page.

Follow these steps to set the page specifications for the brochure:

1. Pull down the File menu and choose New. The Page Setup dialog box appears.

Notice the current page size is now in picas. If you are wondering where the 51 × 66 measurement came from, follow this math lesson: multiply 8.5 inches by 6 picas/inch to get 51; 11 inches multiplied by 6 picas/inch equals 66.

2. Specify a Wide orientation.

3. Enter **2** for the number of pages.

4. Enter **3** for both the Inside and Outside margins (3 picas = 0.5 inch).

5. If necessary, enter **4p6** for the Top and Bottom margins (4 picas, 6 points = 0.75 inch). Your Page Setup dialog box should match the one in Figure 6.3.

6. Choose OK. The first page of your brochure appears in landscape orientation. Also, your rulers are in pica increments.

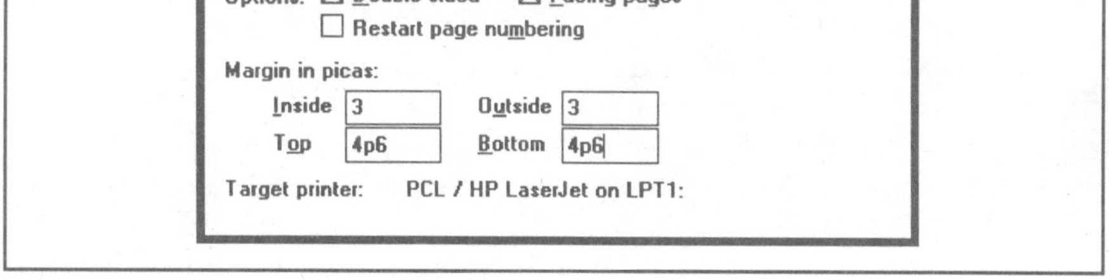

Figure 6.3: The brochure's page setup

7. Pull down the Options menu and choose Column Guides.

8. Type **3** for the Number of Columns.

9. Type **6** (picas) for the Space Between Columns.

Notice that this setting follows our basic rule: the gutter is twice the size of the inside and outside margins. This setting will ensure that you can fold the brochure in the gutters.

10. Choose OK. Page 1 now displays three columns, each surrounded by column guides, as shown in Figure 6.4.

11. Click on the page 2 icon to move to page 2.

12. Repeat steps 7 through 10 to place the column guides on the second page.

13. Click on the page 1 icon to return to the first page.

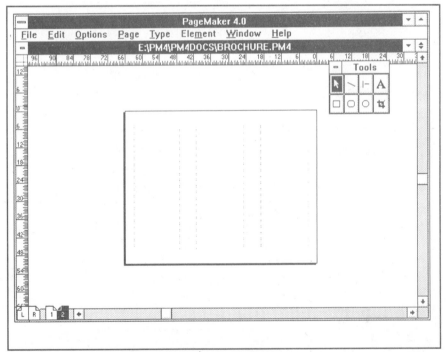

Figure 6.4: The page layout for the brochure

In Chapter 14, you will learn how to use master pages so that you don't have to place column guides individually on each page.

Since you changed the orientation to Wide when you created the publication, you should change the target printer to Landscape before you go any further. As explained in Chapter 4, this step is necessary because you may have different font choices in landscape orientation than you do in portrait.

14. Pull down the File menu and choose Target Printer. Make sure the correct target printer is current (look at the bottom of the dialog box).

15. Click on the Setup command button.

16. In your Target Printer dialog box, click on the Landscape option button, and then click on OK.

17. Choose OK to close the Target Printer dialog box.

18. Save your publication with the name **BROCHURE**.

Entering the New Story

The story you create in the Story Editor uses your publication's default font and size (probably 12 points). The text should be 11-point Times Roman, and you can format it as such while in the Story Editor, even though you won't see the formatting in story view.

Follow these steps to format and enter the text:

1. To load the Story Editor, press Ctrl-E or pull down the Edit menu and select Edit Story.

2. Click on the maximize button so that your story window fills the screen. Your window should look similar to the one shown in Figure 6.5.

Since our story will not have any styles, you can eliminate the style name area so the story can take up the whole window.

3. Pull down the Options menu and select the Display Style Names option to turn it off.

4. Press Ctrl-T and specify the Font as Times Roman and the Size as 11 points.

5. Choose OK.

Now you are ready to type the text of the brochure, which is shown in Figure 6.6. As you are typing, remember not to press Enter at the end of lines, just at the end of paragraphs. Don't try to match the line endings shown in the figure.

6. Type the text shown in Figure 6.6. Be sure to make the sub-headings bold (you can use the keyboard shortcuts, F6 or Ctrl-Shift-B). You'll see the bold format in story view.

After you type the text, you can go back and make corrections. The techniques for moving the cursor and editing text in the Story Editor are

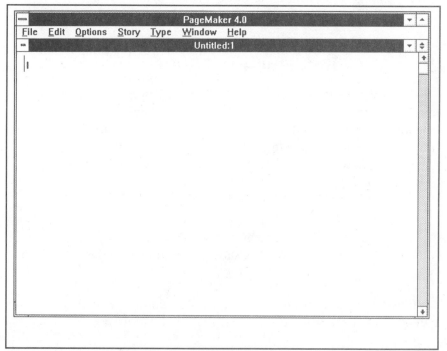

Figure 6.5: The maximized story window

identical to those that you use with the text tool. Refer to Chapter 5 if you need to refresh your memory. Unlike in layout view, the Del key deletes the character to the *right* of the cursor.

Do You...?

...want to stop making rent payments?

...want to stop paying so much in taxes?

...want to take advantage of one of the strongest housing markets in the nation?

...feel that you could afford payments if you only owned a house?

If you answered yes to the above questions, keep reading.

BCR is a company whose main goal is to help you buy a house. Our specialty is helping qualified buyers to own their own home. One of these ways is through equity sharing.

Futility

Unlike most areas of the country, buying a home in the Bay Area has become down payment sensitive. There are hundreds of potential homeowners in the Silicon Valley that make great salaries, have good credit, but simply cannot save the lump sum necessary to make a down payment.

Let's assume a couple, who can save $5,000 a year, had $40,000 saved toward a down payment in 1989. They make enough money to cover mortgage payments but need another $10,000 for a 20% down payment on a $250,000 house. So they decide to wait and save.

In the two years it took them to save $10,000, the house appreciated $100,000. Now it's 1991 and they need $70,000 for a down payment on the same house, and they only have $50,000. What can they do? Save another four years? By then the house might be worth $450,000. Chances are they'll never catch up. They need money today. Equity sharing can provide it.

Concepts

Equity sharing is an arrangement where an investor puts up money toward a portion of the down payment. In return, he/she will receive a share of the equity from the home buyer.

Figure 6.6: Brochure text

7. Press Ctrl-PgUp to go to the beginning of the story.

8. Proofread your document and correct some of your typing mistakes, but be sure to leave in a few typos so the spelling checker

---

For example, suppose a buyer, with the help of an investor, purchases a house in 1991 for $300,000. Here's a hypothetical breakdown of the up-front costs:

(insert table here)

Numerous benefits accrue to you, the buyer, in return for the portion of the appreciation you relinquish in an equity sharing deal. First, you get to fulfill your own American dream: home ownership.

Other benefits include large tax deductions, saying goodbye to rent payments, and getting a leveraged investment in one of the strongest real estate markets in the world. If these benefits sound good to you, then BCR can help.

Our Focus

BCR specializes in serving home buyers. We do not list property. Instead, we simply act as agents to help people like you find a house here on the Peninsula. So how do we get paid? By receiving a percentage of the commission that the home seller pays to the listing agent. That's all.

We are members of several Multiple Listing Services (MLS) throughout the region. Our geographic area spans Santa Clara and San Mateo counties. Here's an outline of our services:

(insert list here)

Matchmaking

Because investors supply the majority of cash, they define most of the terms of the transaction. BCR simply acts as a matchmaker. An investor looks for buyers who have solid cash flow, are credit worthy and debt-free, and most of all, are eager to buy a house. Buyers look to match with an investor that fits the buyers' financial needs and desires.

Results

If you are interested in owning your own home and would like BCR to help you achieve this goal, call for an appointment now.

Figure 6.6: Brochure text (continued)

can find mistakes when you use this option later. (If you are a perfect typist, make a few mistakes to give the spelling checker something to do!)

9. Press Ctrl-S to save the file.

SEARCHING FOR TEXT

Using the Story Editor's Find command is probably the fastest way to move your cursor in a long story. You can use this feature to go directly to a word or phrase you need to correct or to move the cursor quickly to the heading of a section you want to work on. Use the Find command instead of scrolling through your story, scanning for the passage you need to correct. Your eyes will thank you.

Using the Find Command

The Find command searches for the specified characters from the cursor location forward through the story. To begin a search from the top of the story, press Ctrl-PgUp before you initiate the Find command. If you begin the search from somewhere in the middle of the story, the Story Editor will ask you

Continue from beginning of story?

when it reaches the end, so you can search through the entire story if necessary.

In the following steps, you will use the Find command to move the cursor to the Matchmaking subhead in the brochure text you just entered. Once there, you can correct some mistakes in this section.

1. Move the cursor to the beginning of the story.

2. Pull down the Edit menu and choose Find (or press Ctrl-8). You will see the Find dialog box, as shown in Figure 6.7.

3. If necessary, drag the title bar so that you can see the entire dialog box.

4. To the right of Find What, type **matchmaking** (in either upper-case or lowercase letters).

5. Make sure that the Current Story button is selected. (We'll explain the other options in the next section.)

6. Click on the Find command button.

Matchmaking has been found, and it is selected on your screen. When the Story Editor cannot locate a word, perhaps because you mistyped the text in the Find dialog box or in the story, it will display the message

Search complete

When this happens, check your typing and try again.

7. To exit the Find feature, double-click on the control-menu box in the Find dialog box.

Now you can edit the text in this portion of the story.

8. Delete the text *most of all,* in the first paragraph of the Match-making section. This text is selected in Figure 6.8.

9. In the last sentence of the Matchmaking section, replace the word *that* (underlined in Figure 6.8) with *who.*

In this example, there was only one occurrence of *matchmaking,* so the cursor moved right where you wanted to go. If a story contains multiple occurrences of the word you want to find, continue the search by clicking on the Find Next button in the Find dialog box. If the dialog box is no

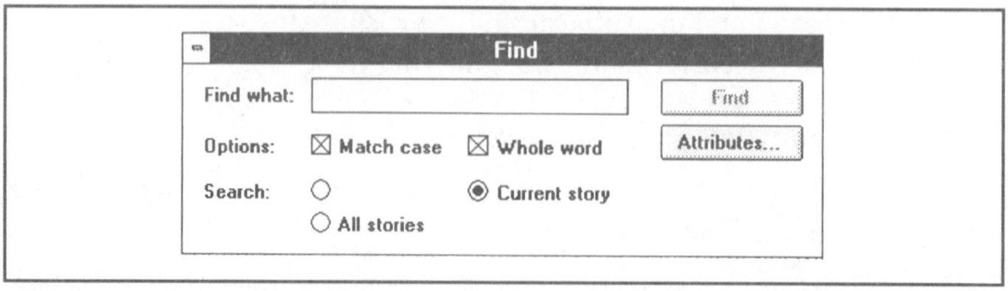

Figure 6.7: The Find dialog box

longer displayed, you can use the Find Next command on the Edit menu or press Shift-Ctrl-9.

Narrowing the Search

To save yourself the effort of choosing the Find Next command many times, make the text you enter in the Find What box—the *search string*—as unique as possible.

One way of narrowing the search is to enter a phrase rather than a word. For example, if you want to find where the list is to be inserted in your brochure, don't search for the word *insert* because it appears more than once. Instead, search for *insert list*.

Another way to reduce the number of occurrences that the Story Editor finds during a search is to use the Whole Word and Match Case

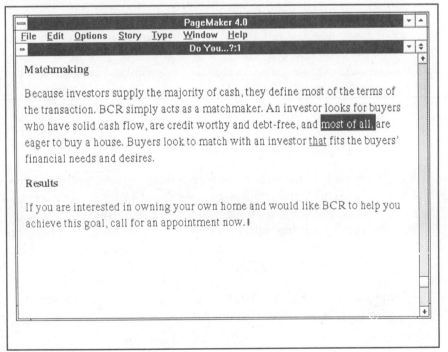

Figure 6.8: Delete the selected text

options in the Find dialog box. The Whole Word option finds your search string only if it appears as a complete word. Without this option, Page-Maker locates the word even if it's in the middle of another word. For example, if you search for *other* using this option, you will just find that complete word, not *another, smother,* or *others.*

The Match Case option only finds text in the story that matches the exact case you enter. So, if you search for *Matchmaking,* the Story Editor will not locate *MATCHMAKING* or *matchmaking.*

You can choose both of these options at the same time to narrow your search even further. The options remain selected for subsequent searches unless you turn them off or exit PageMaker.

CHECKING YOUR SPELLING

The Story Editor's spelling checker scans your story and stops at words that are potentially misspelled, allowing you to correct them. Even if you won all your school spelling bees, you still may want to use the spelling checker because it also locates typing mistakes (unless you were also the school typing champ). If you have ever used your word processor's spelling checker, you realize the value of this feature.

Correcting Unknown Words

Pull down the Edit menu and choose Spelling, or press Ctrl-L, to have the Story Editor check the spelling of each word in your story against PageMaker's 100,000-word dictionary. If a word is not in the dictionary, the Story Editor stops at the word and presents a dialog box to let you correct it. Figure 6.9 shows the spelling checker dialog box displayed for the unknown word *strongst.* This dialog box contains the following options:

- Ignore: Leaves the word as it is, and bypasses all future occurrences of the word throughout the story.

- Replace: Replaces the word with the corrected spelling that appears in the Change To box.

- Add: Inserts the word in the dictionary so that the Story Editor will recognize it as correctly spelled the next time you check any story in any publication.

Like your word processor's spelling checker, PageMaker's checker sometimes stops at words that are correctly spelled. Proper names, abbreviations, acronyms, and technical terms may not be in the dictionary. Thus, the spelling checker would think the words *Rumpelstiltskin, DMV,* and *sulfathiazole* are misspelled. When the spelling checker finds these types of words, you can choose either the Ignore or Add option. If you are not likely to use a particular word in other stories, choose Ignore. If you will use the word frequently, add it to the dictionary by choosing Add.

When the word is indeed misspelled, you can choose the correct spelling from the list by double-clicking on it. The list displays scroll bars if additional suggestions are available. If the correct spelling is not in the list, you will need to edit the word in the Change To text box. Click the I-beam in the text box to place the cursor there, and then use the regular editing keys to correct the mistake. After you've chosen the correct spelling from the list or edited the word in the Change To box, press Enter or click on the Replace button.

Using the Spelling Checker

The spelling checker starts correcting at the cursor location and checks all words after that point in the story. If your cursor is not at the beginning when you start the spelling check, the Story Editor checks

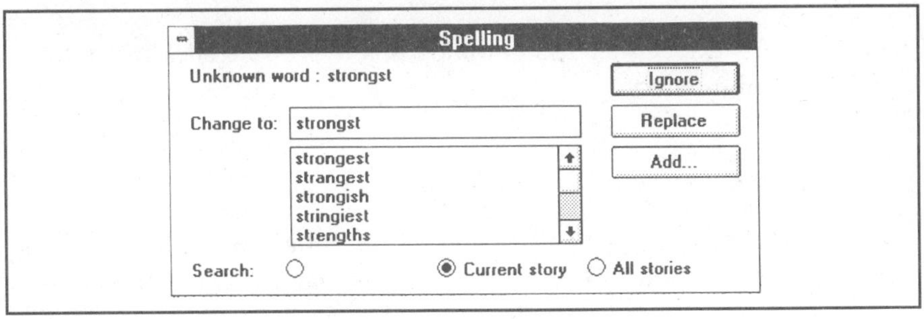

Figure 6.9: The Spelling Checker dialog box

the words from the cursor to the end of the story and then asks you if you want to continue the check at the beginning of the story.

Now you can use the spelling checker to check your brochure text. Follow these steps:

1. Move the cursor to the beginning of the story.

2. Pull down the Edit menu and choose Spelling, or press Ctrl-L.

3. If necessary, drag the title bar so that you can see the entire dialog box.

4. When the spelling checker dialog box appears, make sure the Current Story option button is turned on.

5. Click on the Start command button.

The Story Editor highlights (selects) the first word that is not in the dictionary. Figure 6.10 shows the word *BCR* selected. This word is actually an abbreviation for Blue Chip Realty; it is not misspelled, so it should be ignored.

6. Click on the Ignore button.

7. As the spelling checker proceeds to find words, choose to correct or skip them, as explained in the previous section.

When the spelling checker can't find any more misspelled words, it displays the message

Spelling check complete.

8. Close the spelling checker dialog box by double-clicking on its control-menu box.

Checking a Single Word's Spelling

On occasion, you might want to check a single word to see if you spelled it correctly. Follow these general steps to check a word:

1. Select the word (for example, double-click on it).

2. Press Ctrl-L.

3. Select the Start button.

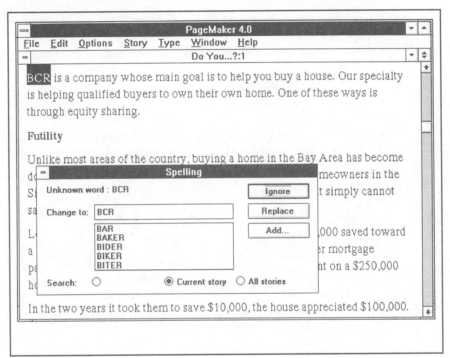

Figure 6.10: An unknown word

PLACING A NEW STORY

The story you have been editing exists only in the Story Editor right now. For it to be part of your publication, you must switch to layout view and place it on the page. PageMaker offers five ways to do this:

- Pull down the File menu and choose Place (or press Ctrl-D).

- Pull down the Edit menu and choose Edit Layout (or press Ctrl-E).

- Pull down the Window menu and choose the name of your publication (near the bottom of the menu).

- Pull down the Story menu and choose Close Story.

- Double-click on the control-menu box in the story window.

If you use one of the last two methods, you see an alert box warning

Story has not been placed

Choose the Place command button to confirm that you want to insert the text on the page. If you choose Discard, all the text in the story window will be lost. To return to layout view without placing the text, you must minimize the story window.

Putting Your Text on the Page

Your brochure text will begin in the third column of page 1 and continue onto page 2. The first column is actually the back page of the brochure, and the second column is the cover page.

Follow these steps to place your brochure text onto the page:

1. Save your file with the same name.

2. Pull down the File menu and choose Place.

The story window disappears, and the cursor turns into a *loaded text icon.* This icon is like a gun, and your mouse button is like a trigger. You aim by placing the icon at the top of a column. You pull the trigger by clicking the mouse. Once you have done this, you have shot the text into a column.

First, let's turn the text gun into an automatic weapon by turning on the Autoflow feature. When you turn on the Autoflow option, you do not need to pull the trigger for each column. You just pull the trigger once, and the text automatically flows into other columns, even on different pages. (Autoflow is discussed in more detail in Chapter 9.)

3. Pull down the Options menu.

4. Check to see if Autoflow is checked. If it is, press Esc twice to cancel the command. If it's not, choose Autoflow to turn it on.

The text icon changes to indicate the Autoflow feature is on. Now you can shoot the text into the third column on page 1. Because the first two columns are the front and back covers of the brochure, you do not want the story to flow into those columns.

5. Place the loaded text icon at the top-left corner of column 3 and click.

The text flows into the third column of page 1 and then continues flowing into the first two columns of page 2. Figure 6.11 shows the text placed on page 2. Notice the window shade handles in each selected text block. (Remember, a text block is the text between window shade handles.)

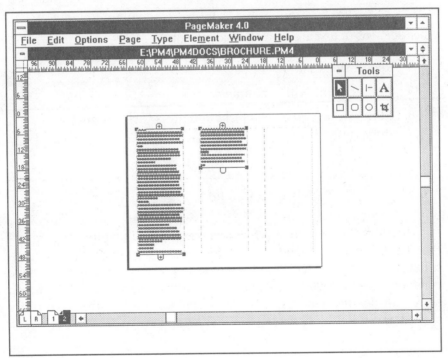

Figure 6.11: The text flowed onto page 2

A plus sign (+) in a top handle indicates the story is continued from another text block. A plus sign in the bottom handle indicates the story continues to another text block. An empty bottom handle appears at the end of a story, and an empty top handle appears at the beginning. These handle symbols let you know which part of the story you are viewing.

Formatting the Story in Layout View

Now that the text is in layout view, you can see formatting effects as you format. Format the brochure's six subheads as follows:

1. Select the text tool.

2. Switch to 75% view.

3. Select each subhead and increase the size to 14 points.

In Chapter 8, you will learn how to speed up the formatting process when sections of text are formatted identically.

4. Repeat steps 2 and 3 for page 1.

5. Save your file with the same name.

6. Click on one of the text blocks and press Ctrl-E to switch to story view.

CHANGING TEXT

The Story Editor's Change feature takes the Find feature one step further. The Change command searches for a word, phrase, or formatting attribute and replaces it with another. For example, if you find that you have consistently misspelled someone's name throughout a story, you can search for the incorrectly spelled name and replace it with the correctly spelled one.

Replacing Text Automatically

Another way you can use the Change command is to have it replace shorthand codes typed throughout the story. If a cumbersome word or phrase, such as a company name or a technical term, appears frequently in a story, type an abbreviation in its place.

In the brochure text, you typed *BCR* as a shorthand code for *Blue Chip Realty*. Now you will replace the code with the complete name in one easy procedure.

1. Move the cursor to the beginning of the story.

2. Pull down the Edit menu and select Change, or press Ctrl-9.

3. If necessary, drag the title bar so that the entire dialog box is visible.

4. Next to Find What, type **BCR**.

5. Next to Change To, type **Blue Chip Realty**.

6. Turn on the Match Case and Whole Word options. (These options work the same way as they do with the Find command.) Your dialog box should match the one shown in Figure 6.12.

7. Choose the Change All command button to replace all occurrences of *BCR* with *Blue Chip Realty*.

8. Double-click on the control-menu box in the Change dialog box.

You can scroll through the story and notice that *Blue Chip Realty* now appears throughout.

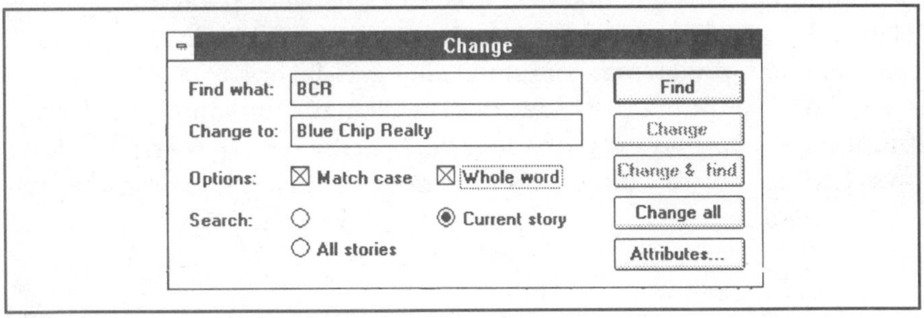

Figure 6.12: The Change dialog box

Be very careful when you use the Change All command button. If you are not 100 percent certain that you want every occurrence automatically replaced, do *not* use Change All; instead, choose the Find and Change & Find command buttons, as described in the next section.

Replacing Words One by One: Playing It Safe

If you do not want every occurrence of a word replaced, or you aren't sure if you do, play it safe and use the Find and Change & Find command buttons. For example, suppose that you want to replace all occurrences of *her* with *him* in a story. If you forget to turn on the Whole Word option and you choose Change All, the Story Editor replaces the letters *her* in *here*, forming the word *hime*. The word *other* becomes *othim* and *there* becomes *thime*.

You would then have to use the Change command again to search for *him* and replace it with *her*—but this time do not choose *Change All*.

After filling in the Change dialog box, choose the Find button. Page-Maker then stops at the first occurrence of the word. If you want to replace the word, choose the Change & Find button to change the word and find the next occurrence. If you don't want to replace the word, choose Find Next to search for the next occurrence.

Replacing Special Characters

The Change command can also find and replace special characters, such as carriage returns and tabs. This capability is invaluable when you have imported a text file that has two returns between paragraphs, or has a tab at the beginning of each paragraph. As you will learn in Chapter 7, this is not how you format paragraphs in PageMaker.

To rid a text file of extra codes, use the Change command. The carriage return code is ^p, and the tab code is ^t. Actually type the caret (^); don't press Ctrl. To replace a double carriage return with a single return, search for ^p^p and replace it with ^p. To remove tabs, search for ^t and don't type anything in the Change To text box, because you want to replace the tab space with nothing.

Replacing Formatting Attributes

An extremely powerful use of the Change command is to search for and replace formatting attributes. You can replace fonts, sizes, type styles, and paragraph styles (this last feature is covered in Chapter 8). This capability makes it easy to revise a story's formatting.

To replace one or more attributes, use the Attributes command button in the Change dialog box. The Change Attributes dialog box is shown in Figure 6.13. In the left half of the box, you indicate the attributes you want to locate. In the right half, you specify the new attributes.

In our brochure, the subheads will be in Helvetica instead of Times Roman. Rather than switching to layout view and formatting each subhead individually, you can replace the 14-point Times Roman with 14-point Helvetica. Follow these steps to change the attributes:

1. Save the file. It's always a good idea to save your work before you use the Change command, just in case you make a mistake along the way.

2. Move the cursor to the beginning of the story.

3. Pull down the Edit menu and choose Change.

4. Delete the text next to Find What and Change To.

5. Click on the Attributes command button.

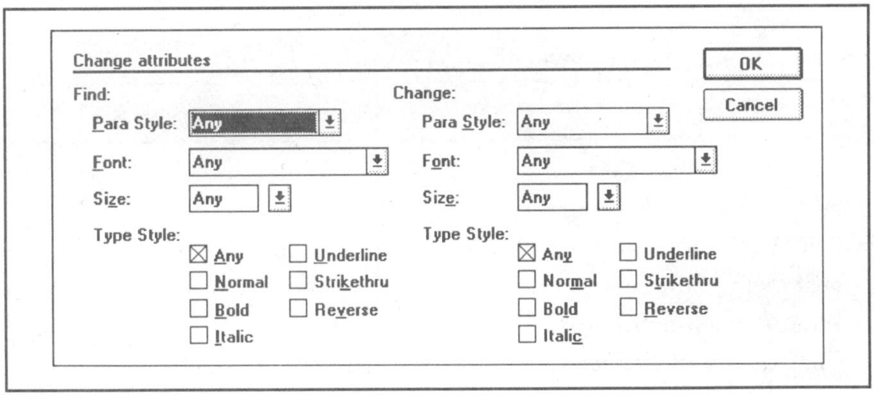

Figure 6.13: The Change Attributes dialog box

6. In the Find section of the dialog box (the left side), specify Times Roman for the Font and 14 for the Size.

7. In the Change section (the right side), specify Helvetica for the Font and 14 for the Size.

8. Choose OK to close the Change Attributes dialog box.

9. Choose the Change All command button to replace the attributes automatically.

10. Close the Change dialog box.

Since story view doesn't display formatting attributes, it's best to switch to layout view to make sure the Change command worked properly.

SWITCHING TO LAYOUT VIEW

Earlier in the chapter, you learned a number of ways to switch to layout view so that you could place your story on the page. These same methods will switch you back to layout view after you have placed the text. However, some of the commands close the story window, and others leave it open, as summarized in Table 6.1.

All these different methods of switching between story and layout view may seem overwhelming. When you are first learning to work with

Table 6.1: Commands for Switching to Layout View

COMMAND	WINDOW STATUS
File menu, Place/Replace (or Ctrl-D)	Closed
Story menu, Close Story	Closed
Double-click on control-menu box	Closed
Edit menu, Edit Layout (or Ctrl-E)	Open
Window menu, publication name	Open
Click on minimize button	Open

the Story Editor, you might want to stick to one method; for example, use Ctrl-E because it switches you both in and out of the Story Editor. If you are not sure whether a story window is still open, pull down the Window menu and check to see if any story names are listed.

Follow these steps to switch to layout view and check the format of your subheads:

1. Press Ctrl-E to switch to layout view.

2. Switch to Actual Size view. The subheads should be displayed in Helvetica (sans serif) instead of Times Roman (serif).

3. To double-check the format, select the heading and press Ctrl-T to display the Type Specifications dialog box. Helvetica or Helv should appear in the Font box.

4. Press Esc.

Keeping the Story Window Open

If you leave the story window open, it lies under your publication window, and you may see part of it hiding underneath. If you can see the story window, you can simply click on it to return there. If you can't see the story window, you must use the Window pull-down menu to go back to it.

After you have left story view, you don't see the story window or the story icons unless the publication window is smaller than the PageMaker application window. In other words, your publication window cannot be maximized. Figure 6.14 shows an example of the story window behind the publication window. Figure 6.15 shows a minimized story icon in the application workspace underneath the publication window.

There are a few minor advantages to keeping the story window open rather than closing it. First, you do not need to select the story before you edit it. Just click on the story window, double-click on its minimized icon, or choose the story name from the Window pull-down menu. Also, if your publication has multiple stories, you can keep each story in its own window. Then, to edit a particular story, you don't have to go to that page and select it. You just select the story name from the Window menu.

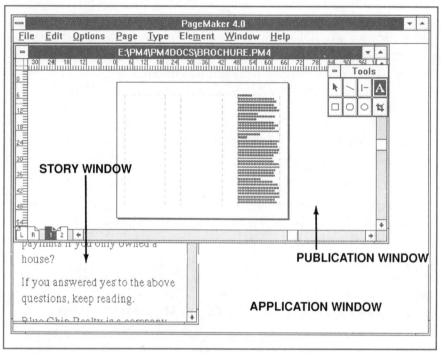

Figure 6.14: The story window behind the publication window

Each of PageMaker's views, story and layout, has its unique capabilities and advantages. In the story view, you can type and edit text quickly, without having to wait for the page layout to adjust as you make changes. You also have access to the powerful Find and Change features, as well as the spelling checker. Although you can't see formatting in the Story Editor, you can use the Change command to make fast, global formatting changes.

The layout view lets you see the actual page layout with its formatting and graphics. The next chapter describes additional ways to format your page.

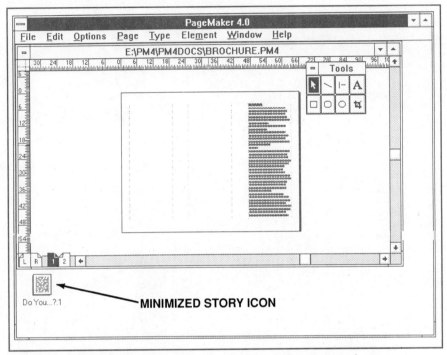

Figure 6.15: The minimized story icon in the application workspace

FORMATTING PARAGRAPHS

In Chapter 5, you used the text tool to format individual characters. You changed fonts, sizes, and type styles. In this chapter, you will learn how to use formatting options that affect paragraphs. Most of these options are in the Paragraph Specifications dialog box, accessed by choosing Paragraph from the Type menu or by pressing Ctrl-M.

The formatting options that apply to entire paragraphs or groups of paragraphs include centering, justification, and indenting. You can also control vertical spacing, hyphenation, and paragraph breaks at the end of a column or at the end of a page. In this chapter, you will get an opportunity to practice setting these formatting options for the brochure you created in the last chapter.

SELECTING PARAGRAPHS TO FORMAT

A *paragraph* is defined as a block of text that ends in a carriage return. A paragraph can be made up of multiple lines that are word-wrapped, a single line, or even a blank line that you created with the Enter key.

In the Story Editor, you can see your paragraph marks by turning on the Display ¶ option on the Options menu. Figure 7.1 shows a story window with paragraph marks displayed. You cannot display paragraph marks in layout view.

All the paragraph formatting options require you to select the paragraphs with the text tool. If you are using the pointer tool when you give a paragraph formatting command, you change the publication's default format, and any new paragraphs you type will have this format.

Depending on how many paragraphs you want to format, choose the appropriate selection technique below:

- To format a single paragraph, you don't even need to select it; just place the cursor anywhere in the paragraph before you initiate the paragraph command. (You can triple-click to select the entire paragraph, but it's not necessary.)

- To format all the paragraphs in a story, place the text cursor anywhere in the story and choose the Select All command on

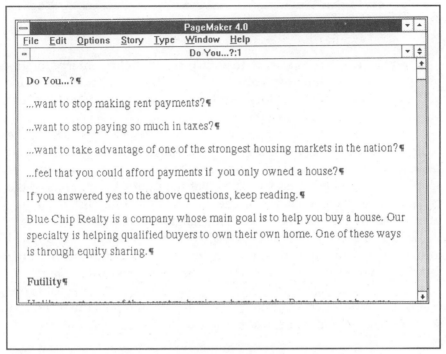

Figure 7.1: Paragraph marks displayed in the Story Editor

the Edit menu (or press Ctrl-A). The entire story, even text blocks that are continued on other pages, is selected.

- To format consecutive paragraphs, select all the paragraphs in the range by using the click-and-drag technique or by clicking at the beginning and Shift-clicking at the end. You do not need to select every character in the range; just make sure at least part of each paragraph is selected. You cannot simultaneously select paragraphs that are not consecutive.

You can also format paragraphs before you type them. Make sure the cursor is not in any existing text and that no text is selected, and then choose your formatting options and begin typing. As you type, your paragraph will be formatted properly.

ALIGNING PARAGRAPHS

PageMaker offers four ways to align text: left, right, centered, or justified. The default paragraph alignment is left; that is, text is lined up at the left edge of the text block. And, unless you have moved the text block, its left edge is at the left column guide.

Left-aligned text is sometimes referred to as *ragged-right* because the right side of the paragraph is uneven. To eliminate this ragged look, you can choose justified alignment. With this alignment, small amounts of space are inserted between words so that the right and left ends of the paragraph are even and smooth. The last line of a paragraph is not justified unless you choose the Force Justify alignment option.

The other types of alignment, centered and right, are usually applied to single-line paragraphs or special text designed to stand out from the rest. Centered alignment is popular for headlines and titles. Designers typically use right alignment to create a special effect. The Force Justify option is also most often used on a single-line paragraph so that the text spans the entire width of the text block (usually the column width).

Changing Alignment

You can change the alignment of a paragraph several different ways: by using the Alignment cascading menu, filling in a dialog box, or pressing key combinations.

If the only paragraph formatting option you need to change is alignment, use the Alignment option on the Type menu. Or, if you have a good memory, memorize the keyboard shortcuts for paragraph alignment shown in Table 7.1.

If you know that you want to change other paragraph formatting options in addition to alignment, display the Paragraph Specifications dialog box by pressing Ctrl-M or by choosing Paragraph from the Type menu. Click on the down arrow next to the Alignment option to display the dropdown list of alignment choices.

Table 7.1: Keyboard Shortcuts for Paragraph Alignment

SHORTCUT	DESCRIPTION
Ctrl-Shift-L	Align left
Ctrl-Shift-C	Align center
Ctrl-Shift-R	Align right
Ctrl-Shift-J	Justify
Ctrl-Shift-F	Force justify

Centering Text

In the following steps, you will type and center the paragraphs on the cover page of the brochure.

1. Open the BROCHURE publication you created in Chapter 6 and display page 1.

2. Activate the text tool and click at the top of the second column.

3. Specify the font as Helvetica, the size as 36 points, and the type style as Bold.

4. Pull down the Type menu and choose Alignment.

5. From the cascading menu, choose Align Center. The cursor centers itself between the column guides.

6. Type **Picture Yourself in Your New House!** Let the text wrap, and PageMaker will automatically center it as you type. Compare your title to the one shown in Figure 7.2.

Now you will center the company name at the bottom of the cover page. This time, you'll enter the text and then format it.

7. Click right above the bottom column guide in the second column, and switch to 75% view.

8. Type **BLUE CHIP REALTY** (in all caps).

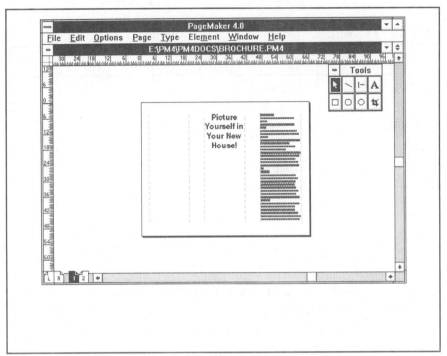

Figure 7.2: The centered title on the brochure's cover page

To establish consistency between the brochure and the letterhead you created in Chapter 6, the company name should be formatted the same way in both publications.

9. Specify the font as Helvetica, the size as 14 points, and the type style as Bold. Also make the first character in each word 20 points.

10. Press Ctrl-Shift-C to center the company name.

11. Switch to the pointer tool and move the text block so that the baseline of the text is aligned with the bottom margin guide, as shown in Figure 7.3.

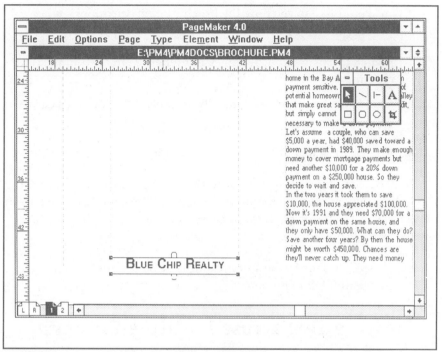

Figure 7.3: The company name aligned at the bottom margin guide

Justifying Text

Just because it's easy to do, don't feel that you need to justify your body text. The main advantage to justified text is that you can fit more text on the page because more words are hyphenated. If space is a precious commodity in your publication, you might want to justify the text.

Left-aligned text is the easiest to read because fewer words are hyphenated and because the eye doesn't have to skip over extra spaces between words. Furthermore, uneven line endings create white space, which lightens the page.

If you insist on the more formal look of justified text, make sure the Hyphenation option on the Type menu is turned on (the default setting) so that you don't get large gaps between words. These gaps can create unattractive rivers of white space that run through your paragraphs.

If you would like to see how the brochure body text looks when it is justified, follow these steps:

1. Switch to the text tool and click anywhere in the text in the third column.

2. Pull down the Edit menu and choose Select All (or press Ctrl-A).

3. To see that all the text in the story is selected, go to page 2.

4. Press Ctrl-Shift-J to justify the selected text.

Notice that the story is a little shorter when it is justified. However, the brochure has enough space for its contents, and Blue Chip Realty wants to project a warmer and friendlier image, so you should switch back to left-aligned paragraphs.

5. Press Ctrl-Shift-L (the story should still be selected) to return to the default left alignment.

Flowing Text across Multiple Columns

By default, PageMaker flows your text between the column guides. To flow text across two columns, or across the entire page when you have multiple columns, you stretch the text block.

Just for practice, you'll stretch the brochure's 36-point cover page title across columns 1 and 2. You would want to do this for the head of a two-column newsletter article, for example.

1. Go to page 1 and position the title on the screen.

2. Select the title with the pointer tool.

3. Click on one of the left handles and drag it to the left until it touches the left column guide of column 1. Release the mouse button.

The text is now centered between columns 1 and 2, as shown in Figure 7.4. But this format won't work for the brochure. To put the title back into column 2, you simply reverse the process.

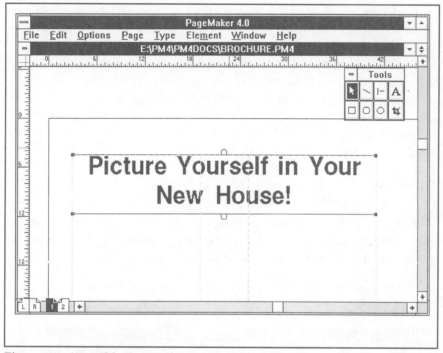

Figure 7.4: A text block stretched across two columns

4. Click on one of the left handles and drag it to the right until it touches the left column guide of column 2. Release the mouse button.

5. If you don't see all the text in your title, pull down the bottom window shade to lengthen the text block.

You can use this same technique to stretch any type of text across columns. The text does not have to be centered.

INDENTING PARAGRAPHS

An *indent* is extra space on the left or right side of the paragraph. For example, if you have a quotation or a list, you will want to indent it on the left (and perhaps the right) so that it stands out from the rest of the text. Figure 7.5 shows examples of the different types of indents available in PageMaker.

PageMaker offers two ways to set indents: numerically, with the Paragraph Specifications dialog box; or visually, with the on-screen ruler. Use the dialog box when you know the numeric value of your indent (for example, 0.25 inch or 1 pica). Use the on-screen ruler (Ctrl-I) to set the indents with respect to the text. You will try both techniques in the following sections.

Setting a First-Line Indent

Frequently, the first line of each paragraph of body text is indented. On a typewriter, you press the Tab key to indent a paragraph; in PageMaker, you specify a *first-line indent*.

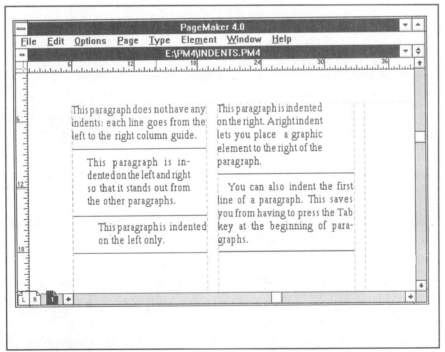

Figure 7.5: Paragraph indents

After you set up a first-line indent, you don't need to press Tab at the beginning of each paragraph. And, if you later decide you want more or less space, you don't need to insert tabs or adjust tab stops; you simply change the amount of the indent.

In the following steps, you'll set a 1-pica first-line indent for the brochure body text. For wider columns (when you have a two-column grid, for example), you would probably want to set a larger first-line indent.

Since we know the numeric value of the indent, the quickest way to set the indent is to type it in the Paragraph Specifications dialog box. Follow these steps to set the indent:

1. Switch to the text tool and click anywhere in the main story.

2. Pull down the Edit menu and choose Select All (or press Ctrl-A).

3. Pull down the Type menu and choose Paragraph (or press Ctrl-M).

4. In the Indents section in the dialog box (upper-left corner), next to First, type **1**.

5. Choose OK.

6. If necessary, switch to 75% view to see the indents.

Figure 7.6 shows some of the indented paragraphs on page 2. Notice that every paragraph is indented, even the subheads that aren't supposed to be. You could remove the subhead's indent now by selecting each heading and changing the first-line indent to zero. However, we will be adding other formatting to the subheads later, so let's wait and do all the subhead formatting at once.

Setting Indents in the Ruler

If you want to "eyeball" your indent settings, the ruler is the way to go. With the Indents/Tabs option, you can set indents and tab stops by clicking and dragging symbols in a ruler.

Figure 7.7 points out the various symbols in the ruler. The default tab stops are set every 3 picas, or 1/2 inch. You will learn about tab stops shortly.

To change an indent, you click and drag the appropriate symbol. The text box in the middle of the dialog box indicates the amount of

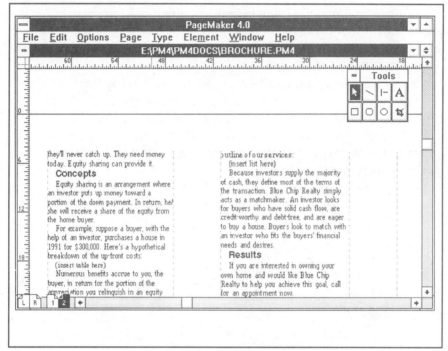

Figure 7.6: Paragraphs with a 1-pica first-line indent

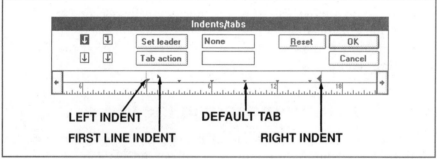

Figure 7.7: The indent/tab ruler

indent (for example, 2p0 for 2 picas) as you drag the symbol. The best way to understand how the ruler works is to experiment with it. Follow these steps:

1. On page 1, switch to Fit in Window view.

2. Click anywhere in column 3 and press Ctrl-A.

3. Pull down the Type menu and choose Indents/Tabs (or press Ctrl-I).

A ruler and dialog box appear on the screen. Notice that the beginning of the ruler (the zero point) is at the beginning of the column. This positioning lets you set the indents with respect to the text. All indents are set relative to the edges of the text blocks.

4. Drag the first-line indent symbol to 2p0.

5. To indent the text 1 pica from the right margin, drag the right indent symbol to 1p0.

6. Drag the left indent symbol to 1p0.

You'll note that the left indent and first-line indent symbols are linked. When you move the left indent symbol, the first-line indent also moves, so that it keeps the same relative distance from the left indent (2 picas, in this case).

7. Move the left and right indents back to 0p0. (Watch the number inside the box as you drag the symbols.)

8. Move the first-line indent back to 1p0.

9. Click on OK.

Creating Hanging Indents

Another type of indent is called a *hanging indent* because text (such as a bullet or a number) "hangs" to the left of the indented paragraph. Figure 7.8 shows the bulleted list with hanging indents that you will add to your brochure. To create this type of indent, you need to set a left indent, a first-line indent, and a custom tab stop. The first-line indent is where the bullet will go. It is always a negative value because it is set as the distance from the left indent, not from the left column guide. The left indent and the tab stop are set at the same place: where you want the text to wrap.

- **We help determine your price range.** By analyzing your income and savings, Blue Chip Realty uses a computerized worksheet to determine the range of home prices you can reasonably afford.
- **We arrange equity sharing.** If you need cash for a down payment, Blue Chip Realty will match you with an investor.
- **We help you shop for your house.** Blue Chip Realty will work with you to find a house that's just right for you.
- **We handle the transaction.** Blue Chip Realty will write up the offer, negotiate to your advantage, and arrange inspections.
- **We hand you the house keys.**

Figure 7.8: A bulleted list with hanging indents

Follow these steps to type the bulleted list in the brochure:

1. Select the text *(insert list here),* which is in the second column of page 2, and delete it. You should still have a blank line, and the cursor should be on this line.

2. Press Ctrl-I to display the Indents/Tabs dialog box and ruler.

3. Drag the left indent to 2p0 (the first-line indent travels with it since these two indents are linked).

4. Drag the first-line indent to the left until the text box reads −1p0.

5. To set a tab at the same spot as the left indent, place the mouse pointer on the left indent symbol and click once. The text box

should read 2p0. Then click on the Tab Action button and choose Add Tab.

A tab symbol appears. Note that custom tabs have different symbols than the default tabs. Your ruler should match the one shown in Figure 7.9.

6. Click on OK.

The cursor is already at the first-line indent. You are now ready to type the bulleted list.

7. Press Ctrl-Shift-8. This key combination is PageMaker's code for inserting a bullet. The bullet is quite small, but you'll enlarge it soon.

8. Press Tab.

9. Press F6 to turn on the bold type style and type **We help determine your price range.** Press F6 to turn off the bold style.

10. Type the rest of the paragraph: **By analyzing your income and savings, Blue Chip Realty uses a computerized worksheet to determine the range of home prices you can reasonably afford.**

11. Press Enter to complete the paragraph. The tab and indent settings from the preceding paragraph automatically carry forward to the next paragraph when you press Enter.

12. Repeat steps 7 through 11 to enter the remaining bulleted items shown in Figure 7.8. Do not press Enter after the last item; if you did, delete the blank line.

13. Save the file.

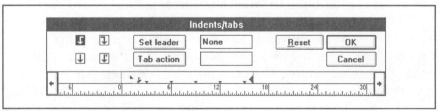

Figure 7.9: A ruler set for hanging indents

14.   Switch to 75% view.

The bullet in the Times Roman font is tiny. The Symbol font, built into PostScript printers and available in soft fonts, creates many different special characters, such as Greek letters (α, β), the British pound sign (£), and mathematical symbols ($\div$, $\approx$). It also offers larger bullets.

15.   One by one, select each bullet, and choose Symbol from the Font cascading menu.

16.   The bullets are the same point size as your body text (11 points). If you feel they are too large, reduce the size of each bullet by pressing Ctrl-Shift-< until you like the way it looks.

Another way to format the bullets is with the Story Editor's Change command. For the Find What and Change To text strings, enter ^8, the code for a bullet. Then, on the Change side of the Change Attributes dialog box, specify Symbol for the font and 8 for the size.

CREATING COLUMNAR TABLES

If you have a columnar table or list that you want to include in a publication, you can either type it directly in the publication, use the Table Editor, or import it from a file. This section describes how to type the table with the text tool. Chapter 13 discusses the Table Editor and Chapter 9 explains how to import text files.

There are two things to remember when typing a table with the text tool. First, set and use tab stops for each column. Do not use the spacebar to align text because it won't work with proportional fonts. You will also want to specify the appropriate tab alignment.

The second rule for typing tables is to use the *line break* command (Shift-Enter) instead of pressing Enter at the end of each line in the table. The line break command moves the cursor down to the next line without creating a new paragraph. That way, the table is a single paragraph, and you can format it without having to select every line in the table. Because tables often require special formatting and fine tuning, you will find it more efficient to select it by clicking anywhere in the table, rather than clicking and dragging across all its lines.

Setting, Adjusting, and Deleting Tabs

PageMaker provides four kinds of tab alignments:

- A left-aligned tab aligns the column on the left.
- A right-aligned tab lines up the column on the right.
- A centered tab centers the text around the tab stop.
- A decimal tab lines up numbers at the decimal point.

By selecting the appropriate tab alignment, your columns will be properly aligned without any fudging with the spacebar.

The default tab alignment is left. To specify the other tab types, you need to click on the appropriate icon in the Indents/Tabs dialog box. The icons are labeled in Figure 7.10.

Setting Up and Typing a Table

Now you will set up and enter a three-column table, which requires two right-aligned tabs. Follow these steps to add the table to your brochure:

1. On page 2, switch to the text tool and 75% view.

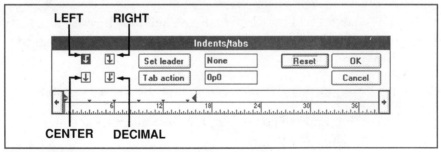

Figure 7.10: The tab alignment icons in the ruler

2. Select the text *(insert table here)*, which is in the first column of page 2, and delete it. You should still have a blank line, and the cursor should be on this line.

3. Press Ctrl-I to display the Indents/Tabs dialog box and ruler.

4. Drag the first-line indent to 0p0 to remove the indent.

5. Click on the right-align tab icon.

6. Move the pointer to the 10-pica mark on the ruler and click. A right-aligned tab symbol appears. If you didn't click in the right spot, you can drag the symbol to 10p0.

Notice that when you set a custom tab stop, the default tab stops to the left of your new tab disappear.

7. Set a right-aligned tab stop at 14p0.

8. Click on OK.

Before you begin typing the table, you should consider your type specifications. In order to fit a multiple-column table in a single column, you will frequently need to specify a smaller type size. For this table, a 10-point font will work fine.

9. Specify the font as Times Roman, the size as 10 points, and the type style as Bold.

10. Press Tab to go to the first tab stop, and then type **Investor**. As you type, the text moves to the left. Because the tab is right-aligned, the text is lined up on the right.

11. Press Tab to go to the second tab stop and type **Buyer**. Press F6 to turn off the Bold style. These bold entries are the headings for the table's columns.

Do not press Enter! If you already did, press Backspace to remove it.

12. Press Shift-Enter to go to a new line without creating a new paragraph.

13. Press Shift-Enter again to create a blank line.

14. Beginning at the left column guide, enter the following table. The most important thing to remember is to press Shift-Enter at the end of each line instead of Enter. Do not press Shift-Enter or Enter at the end of the last line.

Down Payment	$40,00	$20,000
Closing Costs	5,000	5,000
House Payments	None	All
% of Appreciation	40	60

While the column spacing is sufficient, the extra space at the end of each line indicates there's enough room to spread the columns out a little more. You can do this by manipulating the existing tab stops.

Adjusting Tab Settings

To adjust a tab setting in a table, first make sure the table is selected. Because you set up the table as a single paragraph (by pressing Shift-Enter at the end of each line), you can easily select the whole table by clicking anywhere in it with the text tool. If you press Enter at the end of each line instead, you will have to select all the lines in the table to change the tab stops. After the table is selected, you adjust a tab stop by simply clicking and dragging the tab symbol in the ruler.

If your ruler contains extra tab stops that you no longer need (or that you set accidentally), you can remove all the custom tabs or delete them one by one. The Reset button in the Indents/Tabs dialog box clears all the custom tabs and displays the default tab stops. To delete a single tab, click on the tab symbol in the ruler, click on the Tab Action button, and then choose Delete Tab.

1. Click anywhere in the table and press Ctrl-I to display the Indents/Tabs dialog box and ruler.

2. Drag the second tab symbol to 15p0.

3. Click on OK. Now the columns are spaced evenly, as shown in Figure 7.11.

4. Save your file.

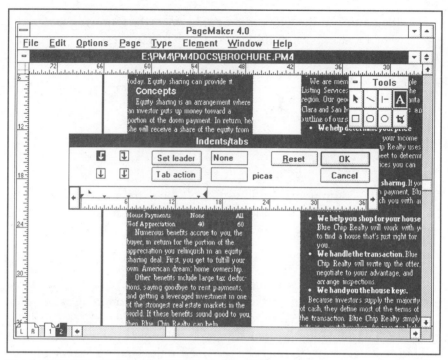

Figure 7.11: The table, with adjusted tab settings

If only part of your table contains the new tab settings, you have hard returns in your table instead of line breaks. To replace a return with a line break, place the cursor at the beginning of the line following the hard return, press Backspace, and then press Shift-Enter.

Flowing the Extra Text

Now you can check how the page looks with the new table.

1. Switch to Fit in Window view.

You will see that the text in column 2 now goes past the bottom margin. The text overflowed when you inserted the table. Now you need to resize the text block and flow the extra text into the third column.

2. Select column 2 with the pointer tool and drag the bottom window shade handle up until it is aligned with the bottom column guide.

3. Click on the bottom handle to load the text gun.

4. Place the text gun icon at the top of column 3 and click to shoot the text into the column.

Scrolling the Ruler

When you set the indents and tabs in the preceding exercise, the zero point in the ruler was automatically aligned with the left column guide. However, sometimes the ruler does not begin at the edge of a column. This happens, for example, when you have selected text in multiple columns, as illustrated in Figure 7.12.

Because it's difficult to set your indents and tab stops when the ruler is not lined up over the column, you should scroll the ruler horizontally. The scroll arrows appear at either end of the ruler. Click on the left scroll

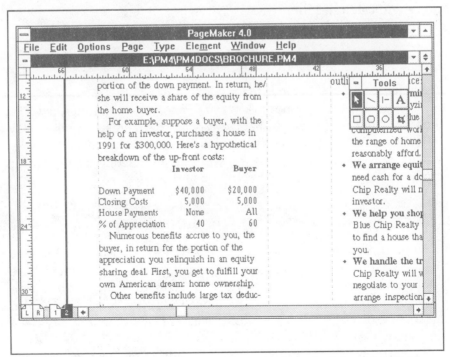

Figure 7.12: A ruler whose zero point doesn't begin at the left column guide

arrow until the zero point is aligned with the left column guide. If you go too far, click on the right scroll arrow to go back.

ADJUSTING VERTICAL SPACING

So far, we have been ignoring the vertical spacing in the brochure. None of the elements on the page (body text, subheads, or the columnar table) have any extra space around them. However, a well-designed page uses white space liberally. Extra space around the subheads and the table will help differentiate them from the body text. Furthermore, white space helps break up the "sea of gray syndrome."

PageMaker offers three ways to control the vertical spacing on your page:

- Adjust the leading

- Add extra space before or after the paragraph

- Use the Align to Grid feature

You will use all three methods to format your brochure.

One golden rule: Do not insert extra space with the Enter key. The problem with hard returns is that they are always there, even when they land at the top of a column. When you use any of the three methods described above, you do not have to worry about deleting space at your column tops.

Changing the Leading

Leading controls the amount of space between successive lines of type. In PageMaker, leading is measured from the tops of capital letters. Those who are from the typesetting world will recognize that this definition differs from the traditional one. Traditionally, leading is measured from the baseline of one line of type to the baseline of the next. The *baseline* is the imaginary line on which your characters sit.

Regardless of how you measure the leading, the amount of space between lines of type is increased when you increase the leading value.

Figure 7.13 displays several examples of text with the same font and size but with different leading. As you increase the leading, some of the extra space goes above the character and some goes below. To be precise, two-thirds of the leading is above the baseline and one-third is below.

Unless you specify otherwise, PageMaker automatically sets your leading as 120 percent of the type size. Thus, 10-point type has 12-point leading; 12-point type has 14.4-point leading. If your line of type contains multiple type sizes, the leading is based on the largest type size. The automatic leading ensures that two lines of type will never be too close together, although it may not always look right or be appropriate for your layout.

You can change the leading by choosing the size from the Leading cascading menu, or by entering it in the Type Specifications dialog box. If the only type specification you want to change is the leading, choose the Leading

This paragraph is typed in
12-point Times Roman
with 12-point leading.

This paragraph is typed in
12-point Times Roman
with auto leading (14.4).

This paragraph is typed in
12-point Times Roman
with 16-point leading.

This paragraph is typed in

12-point Times Roman

with 24-point leading.

Figure 7.13: Examples of different amounts of leading

option from the Type menu. Frequently, however, you enter the leading as you are specifying the font and type size, so you will want to go through the Type Specifications dialog box and do everything at once.

Using a Leading Grid

On a professionally produced page, all textual and graphic elements have depths that are numerically related. They are multiples of a predetermined magic number. If the magic number is 12, all headlines, callouts, graphic boxes, and other page elements have depths of 12, 24, 36, 48, and so on.

This magic number is the size of the leading for your body copy. Don't think of your page's dimensions in terms of inches or points. Instead, think of your page as being divided in increments that match your magic number. Designers refer to this as a *leading grid.*

When all your elements are multiples of your magic number, something magical happens: the baselines in one column exactly line up with the baselines in the adjacent column. Figure 7.14 has a ruler pulled down so that you can see that the baselines match. If your baselines are not aligned, as in Figure 7.15, you might be advertising to discerning eyes that your publishing efforts are less than professional.

In our brochure, we are going to use 14 as our magic number. Fourteen-point leading is just slightly larger than the automatic leading for 11-point type (13.2), and it is infinitely easier to work with a whole magic number. We will therefore specify 14-point leading for the body text and subheads. The extra space around the subhead will also be 14.

But what do you do when an element cannot conform to your magic number? For example, the table is in 10-point type, and 14-point leading would generate too much interline spacing. A leading of 12 points would look better, but it is not a multiple of 14. PageMaker's Align to Grid option comes to the rescue here. This option adds extra space to make sure the body text that follows the element aligns to the leading grid. You'll see how this works later on in the chapter.

Your top and bottom margins are key players in your leading grid, although they do not have to be multiples of your leading. Your goal is to get the active area of your page (your page size minus the margins) to be a multiple of your leading. The exact margin size is the amount left over after subtracting the active page area from the page size.

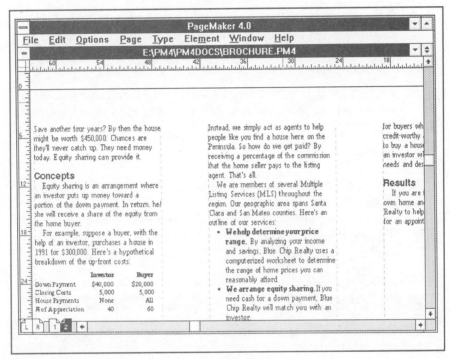

Figure 7.14: Perfectly aligned baselines of text

With a handheld or pop-up calculator close by, follow this mathematical progression to determine your active page area and margins:

1. Decide approximately what margins you want. For instance, let's say we want about 4-pica (48-point) top and bottom margins for the brochure.

2. Subtract both of these margins (96 points) from the page size (612) to get 516 points for the active page. A landscape letter-size page has a total of 612 points—8½ inches multiplied by 72 points per inch. (A portrait letter-size page has 792 points.)

3. Divide the 516 points by your leading (14) to get 36.86 lines. If the number of lines results in an even number, you lucked out and can stop here—your initial margins will work perfectly on the leading grid. If not, continue on.

4. Take the integer of the number of lines calculated in step 3 (36) and multiply it by your leading (14) to get an active page size that is a multiple of your magic number. Your active page size in this example is 504 points.

5. Subtract the active page size (504) from the total page size (612) to get the total area available for top and bottom margins (108).

6. Divide the total margins (108) by two to get the value for each of the margins (54 points).

These are the top and bottom margins you set in Chapter 6. Figure 7.16 shows a page set to this leading grid.

Although calculating your leading grid requires quite a bit of math, you will find that the time it saves you as you lay out your page makes it well worth the initial effort.

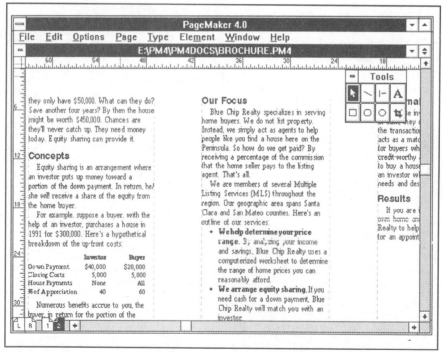

Figure 7.15: Misaligned baselines of text

Specifying Fixed Leading

As mentioned previously, we want 14-point leading for the main story in the brochure and 12-point leading for the table. Follow these steps to change the leading:

1. Switch to Fit in Window view on page 2. This is only so that you can see how the length of the text automatically adjusts with the leading change.

2. Click anywhere in the story with the text tool.

3. Press Ctrl-A to select all the text.

4. Pull down the Type menu and choose Leading.

5. From the cascading menu, choose 14. The text adjusts to 14-point leading, and the story is now a bit longer.

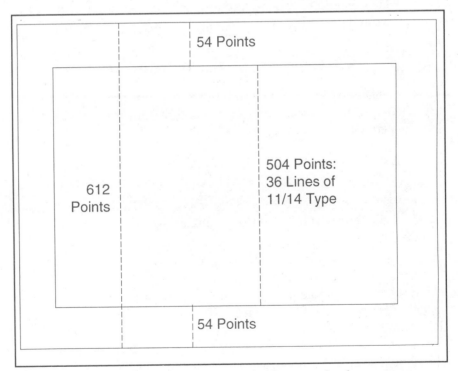

Figure 7.16: The leading grid for 14-point leading on a landscape page

6. Switch to 75% view and select the table (you can triple-click on it since it is one paragraph). Notice that there is currently too much space between lines in the table when 10-point type has 14-point leading.

7. Specify 12-point leading.

There is still too much space between the column headings and the rest of the table. You should now adjust the leading of this single line.

8. Double-click on the blank line to select it.

9. From the Leading cascading menu, choose Other.

10. Type **2**.

11. Press Enter.

Your table should now be spaced as shown in Figure 7.17. You'll add space above and below the table in the next section.

Adding Paragraph Spacing

As mentioned earlier, you shouldn't press Enter to insert an extra space between paragraphs. There are several reasons for avoiding blank lines created with a carriage return:

• If the blank line lands at the top of a column, this extra space will cause the column to start lower than the other columns.

• The blank lines could possibly throw off the leading grid, so that the baselines of the type do not align.

• You cannot precisely control the amount of space—one carriage return might not add enough space and two might add too much.

None of these problems arise when you use PageMaker's paragraph spacing options. In the Paragraph Specifications dialog box, you can set the amount of space before and after your paragraphs.

In determining how much space to add before and after a subhead, you should keep in mind that a subhead introduces a new topic and should therefore be separated from the text above it and tied to the text

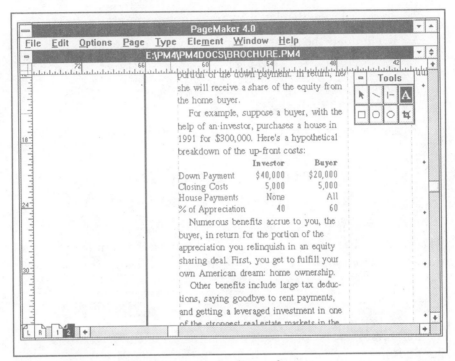

Figure 7.17: The table with the new leading values

below it. You can show this relationship by placing more space above the subhead than below it.

Exactly how much space? The leading of your subhead plus the space above and below it should be a multiple of your magic number (the leading of the body text). Once you determine the appropriate paragraph spacing for your subheads, use this spacing for all subheads in the publication. This consistency and uniformity not only looks more professional, but it helps your readers visually identify each level of subheading. PageMaker's style feature offers an easy way to apply consistent formatting to your subheadings (see Chapter 8).

In your brochure, the leading of the body text is 14. The leading of the subhead is also 14. To keep on the leading grid, you will add 14 points above the paragraph. Follow these steps to format your subheads:

1. Click on one of the subheads.

2. Press Ctrl-M to display the Paragraph Specifications dialog box.

3. To eliminate the paragraph indent, type **0** next to First.

4. Next to Before, type **0p14** (14 points) or **1p2** (1 pica, 2 points).

5. Press Enter. Your subhead should be spaced as shown in Figure 7.18.

6. Repeat steps 1 through 5 for the remaining five subheads.

Formatting a Table
with the Align to Grid Option

Because the table uses a different leading (12 points) than the body text (14 points), the baselines of type will not line up on the leading grid. If you examine the text below the table in 75% view, you will see this misalignment.

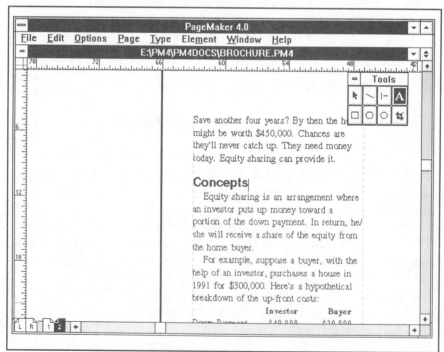

Figure 7.18: The properly spaced subhead

You could get out your calculator and determine how much space is required above and below the table to keep the body text on the leading grid, but that would be a grueling job. It would also be frustrating, because you would have to constantly adjust the spacing each time you altered the number of lines in the table. Instead, you can use the Align to Grid option. This option, when applied to a paragraph (such as the table), will position the following paragraph on the leading grid.

You access the Align to Grid option through the Paragraph Specifications dialog box, but it is hidden several dialog boxes deep in the Paragraph Rule Options box (although it has absolutely nothing to do with paragraph rules).

The table also needs extra space around it. Since you typed it as a single paragraph, you can specify the paragraph spacing as you would for any other paragraph.

Follow these steps to add spacing and then align the paragraph after the table to the grid:

1. With the text tool, click anywhere in the table and press Ctrl-M.

2. Specify **0p6** before and **0p6** after, and then choose OK.

Now that the paragraph spacing is set, you can return to the Paragraph Spacing dialog box and find the Align to Grid option.

3. Click in the table and press Ctrl-M.

4. Click on the Rules button.

5. Click on the Options button.

6. Click on the Align to Grid option.

7. Next to Grid Size, type **14**.

8. Hold down Alt and click on OK to close all three dialog boxes.

Now all the baselines should be perfectly aligned. You can see this in your document by pulling down a ruler guide.

9. Click on the horizontal ruler.

10. Drag the ruler guide down to a line of type underneath the table. All the baselines across the page should sit on this guide.

11. Switch to the pointer tool and drag the ruler guide back into the ruler.

Use the Align to Grid option with discretion. Don't use it for repeating elements, such as subheads, because you may get different amounts of spacing around them. You cannot be assured of consistent spacing from one element to the next when you use Align to Grid. Save this feature for special cases or exceptions.

GIVE YOURSELF A BREAK

PageMaker offers a number of ways to control how your lines, paragraphs, columns, and pages break. For example, you can tell PageMaker not to split a paragraph between two columns, or to always place certain paragraphs at the top of a column or page. Most of these options are in the Paragraph Specifications dialog box, although Hyphenation has its own dialog box.

Hyphenation

By default, the hyphenation feature is turned on for all paragraphs. You may have noticed that a few hyphens appear throughout the main story.

You can turn off hyphenation for single paragraphs or for an entire story. If you turn off hyphenation before you type the story, none of the text will be hyphenated. If you type a story and then decide you don't want hyphenation, you must select all the paragraphs (Ctrl-A) before you turn off hyphenation. For a single paragraph, simply click in the paragraph and then turn off hyphenation.

Types of Hyphenation

When you select Hyphenation from the Type menu or press Ctrl-H, you will see the dialog box shown in Figure 7.19. This dialog box offers three different types of hyphenation: Manual Only, Manual Plus Dictionary, and Manual Plus Algorithm. Each option progressively puts more hyphens in your text.

When you initially select the Manual Only option, it is as if you turned off hyphenation; no hyphens are used. However, you can add your own hyphens when and where you want by inserting *discretionary hyphens* (Ctrl-hyphen). Use this option if you want very light hyphenation or if you want total control over the hyphenation.

If you see a big gap at the end of a line, you can hyphenate the word at the beginning of the next line. Just place the cursor where you want the hyphen to go and press Ctrl-hyphen to insert a discretionary hyphen. The first part of the word will be hyphenated and move up to the previous line, assuming there's enough room for it. If you change the text and a hyphen is no longer needed (the word does not appear at the end of a line any more), the discretionary hyphen disappears. However, the hyphen is simply hidden, and if it is ever needed again, it will reappear.

Wait until the final stage of your publication production before you insert discretionary hyphens. If you insert them too early in the process, the line endings will inevitably change, and you will find that different hyphenation is required.

The Manual Plus Dictionary option (the default) also lets you enter discretionary hyphens, but it automatically hyphenates other words when necessary, using its 100,000-word hyphenation dictionary. This is actually the same dictionary that the Story Editor's spelling checker uses. If a word is not in the dictionary, it will not be hyphenated.

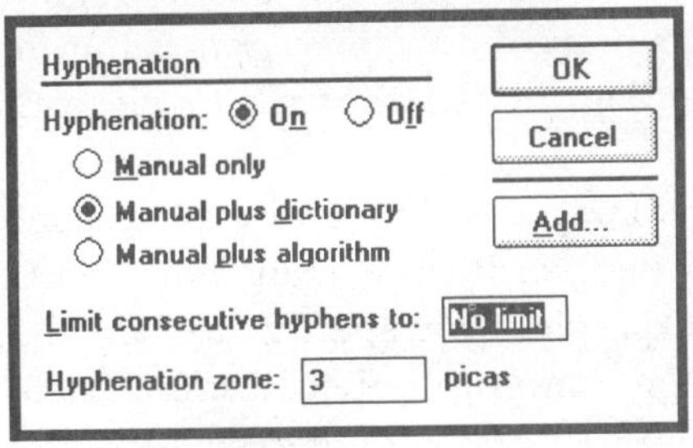

Figure 7.19: The Hyphenation dialog box

Of the three types of hyphenation, the Manual Plus Algorithm option inserts the most hyphens. Along with your discretionary hyphens and the dictionary hyphens, it also inserts hyphens in words not found in the dictionary by following a set of guidelines (an algorithm) for their placement.

Other Hyphenation Controls

Another way to control the amount of hyphenation in a paragraph is with the two options at the bottom of the Hyphenation dialog box.

We highly recommend you limit the number of consecutive hyphens. By default, the setting for the Limit Consecutive Hyphens To option is No Limit, which means you can have an *unlimited* number of hyphens in a row. Because a stack of hyphenated words is unattractive and hard to read, you should limit the number of consecutive hyphens to 2.

The Hyphenation Zone option tells PageMaker the maximum amount of white space you will accept at the end of a line. It therefore does not apply to justified text. The default zone is 3 picas ($\frac{1}{2}$ inch). If you want a less ragged right margin, enter a smaller value for Hyphenation Zone; it will hyphenate more words. To hyphenate fewer words, enter a larger value for Hyphenation Zone.

Figure 7.20 shows three paragraphs, each with a different hyphenation zone. The first paragraph has a 2-pica hyphenation zone, the second has the default zone of 3 picas, and the third has a 4-pica zone.

Avoiding Widows and Orphans

In PageMaker, widows and orphans are straggling words that appear at the top or bottom of a column. A *widow* is the beginning of a paragraph that sits at the bottom of a column. An *orphan* is the end of a paragraph at the top of a column. Figure 7.21 shows a lonely orphan at the top of a column.

By default, PageMaker's widow and orphan controls are turned off. However, you can define exactly how many lines constitute a widow or orphan (1, 2, or 3). For example, if you specify 2 for both the widow and orphan control options in the Paragraph Specifications dialog box, PageMaker will not permit two lines of a paragraph to end up at the top or bottom of a column. Thus, if the first two lines of a paragraph begin at the bottom of a column, the lines will be placed at the top of the next column. Or, if

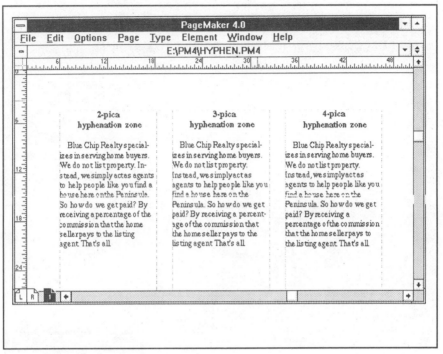

Figure 7.20: Comparing hyphenation zones

the last two lines of a paragraph land at the top of a column, a line from the previous column will be brought up, so that three lines are at the top.

When widow or orphan control is activated, your columns may end up with ragged bottoms, but most designers prefer ragged bottoms to widows and orphans. In fact, the white space created from ragged bottoms might contribute to a friendlier, more open feeling to your page.

You can look through your brochure for single-line widows and orphans in 75% view. Regardless of whether you find any, let's turn on the widow/orphan control. That way, if you change the page layout in the future, you won't have to worry about straggling lines.

1. Select the entire story with the text tool and press Ctrl-M.

2. Turn on Widow Control and Orphan Control.

3. Click on OK.

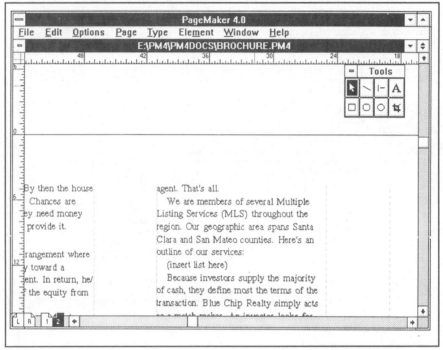

Figure 7.21: An orphan

Note that single-line paragraphs, such as subheads, are *not* considered widows. So, even if you have widow/orphan control turned on, your subheads might fall at the bottom of the column. However, PageMaker offers a different way to avoid this kind of problem, as described in the next section.

Paragraph Breaks

The Paragraph Specifications dialog box offers a variety of options for controlling your paragraph breaks.

The Keep with Next ___ Lines option in the Paragraph Specifications dialog box will prevent your subheads from being stranded at the bottom of a column. It essentially glues two paragraphs together so they won't be separated. When you check this option, the number 1 automatically appears as the number of lines. This setting works fine as long as the paragraph of body text is indeed on the next line. If an extra carriage return somehow found its way between the subhead and body text, the Keep with Next value would have to be 2 lines.

The Keep Lines Together option prevents a paragraph from being split between columns. This option is ideal for tables whose lines shouldn't be separated. If you don't want any paragraphs to be split between columns, you could select the entire story and specify this formatting option. (Keep in mind that your columns will be very uneven and your text will be longer.)

To start a particular section of your story on a new page or column, use the Page Break Before or the Column Break Before option. Click in the single paragraph that should appear at the top of the page or column before turning on the option. These types of breaks are sometimes referred to as *hard*, or *forced, breaks*. Your other column and page breaks are *soft*, and their positions will vary according to the amount and format of text in the column.

The position of a hard break is always the same. It appears before the paragraph formatted with Page Break Before or Column Break Before.

Now you will use the paragraph break options to control the breaks in the brochure.

1. Select a subhead and press Ctrl-M.

2. Turn on the Keep with Next 1 Lines option and click on OK. This will keep the subhead with the body text.

3. Repeat steps 1 and 2 for each subhead.

4. Select the table, press Ctrl-M, turn on the Keep Lines Together option, and click on OK. Now the list will never be divided between columns.

5. Turn on the Keep Lines Together option for the paragraphs in the bulleted list.

As shown in Figure 7.22, the subhead *Our Focus* starts near the bottom of the column. You should put a column break there.

6. Click on the Our Focus subhead, press Ctrl-M, choose Column Break Before, and click on OK. This forces that subhead to move to the beginning of the next column.

7. Press Ctrl-S to save the file.

8. Press Ctrl-P to print the brochure.

The printed page 2 of the brochure should look similar to Figure 7.23.

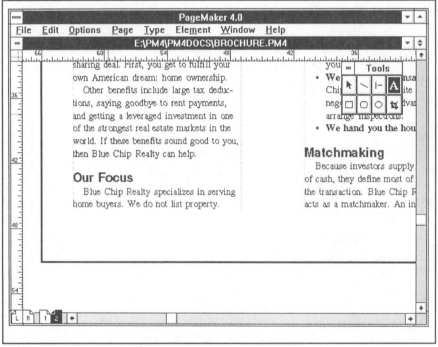

Figure 7.22: Insert a column break so a subhead doesn't appear at the end of the column

Save another four years? By then the house might be worth $450,000. Chances are they'll never catch up. They need money today. Equity sharing can provide it.

Concepts

Equity sharing is an arrangement where an investor puts up money toward a portion of the down payment. In return, he/she will receive a share of the equity from the home buyer.

For example, suppose a buyer, with the help of an investor, purchases a house in 1991 for $300,000. Here's a hypothetical breakdown of the up-front costs:

	Investor	Buyer
Down Payment	$40,000	$20,000
Closing Costs	5,000	5,000
House Payments	None	All
% of Appreciation	40	60

Numerous benefits accrue to you, the buyer, in return for the portion of the appreciation you relinquish in an equity sharing deal. First, you get to fulfill your own American dream: home ownership.

Other benefits include large tax deductions, saying goodbye to rent payments, and getting a leveraged investment in one of the strongest real estate markets in the world. If these benefits sound good to you, then Blue Chip Realty can help.

Our Focus

Blue Chip Realty specializes in serving home buyers. We do not list property. Instead, we simply act as agents to help people like you find a house here on the Peninsula. So how do we get paid? By receiving a percentage of the commission that the home seller pays to the listing agent. That's all.

We are members of several Multiple Listing Services (MLS) throughout the region. Our geographic area spans Santa Clara and San Mateo counties. Here's an outline of our services:

- **We help determine your price range.** By analyzing your income and savings, Blue Chip Realty uses a computerized worksheet to determine the range of home prices you can reasonably afford.

- **We arrange equity sharing.** If you need cash for a down payment, Blue Chip Realty will match you with an investor.

- **We help you shop for your house.** Blue Chip Realty will work with you to find a house that's just right for you.

- **We handle the transaction.** Blue Chip Realty will write up the offer, negotiate to your advantage, and arrange inspections.

- **We hand you the house keys.**

Matchmaking

Because investors supply the majority of cash, they define most of the terms of the transaction. Blue Chip Realty simply acts as a matchmaker. An investor looks for buyers who have solid cash flow, are credit worthy and debt-free, and are eager to buy a house. Buyers look to match with an investor who fits the buyers' financial needs and desires.

Results

If you are interested in owning your own home and would like Blue Chip Realty to help you achieve this goal, call for an appointment now.

Figure 7.23: Page 2, printed on an HP LaserJet II

When we refer to paragraph formatting, we are talking about commands that affect entire paragraphs, not single lines or characters. Alignment, indents, tabs, hyphenation, and extra space above and below are some of the ways you can format your paragraphs.

This chapter discussed one topic that is not actually a paragraph format: leading. Because leading is closely associated with the type size, this specification is officially a character format, and it is an option in the Type Specifications dialog box. However, except in rare cases, a paragraph has the same leading throughout.

In the next chapter, you will learn how to apply both character and paragraph formats quickly and uniformly throughout a publication.

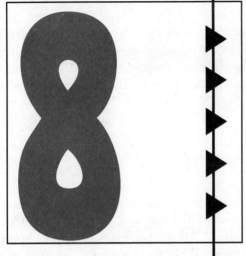

C H A P T E R

8

GOING
IN
STYLE

In the previous chapters, you've learned how PageMaker formats blocks of text and individual paragraphs. Now you will take a giant leap forward and learn how to use a very powerful method of formatting: paragraph styles. By creating and applying styles, you not only make formatting more efficient, but you also give yourself the flexibility to reformat your publication quickly and easily.

THE BENEFITS OF USING STYLES

Paragraph styles allow you to automate the formatting, and the inevitable reformatting, of your publication. Remember how you had to individually format each subhead in your BROCHURE publication with its specifications: 14-point Helvetica bold with 14 points of leading, 14 points of space above, and kept with the next paragraph. With styles, you only have to format one paragraph. You can then apply this exact formatting to any other paragraph with just two mouse clicks.

Imagine that you decided that the body text would look better in a 12-point type size instead of an 11-point type. Making this formatting change without styles would be a tedious process, requiring you to increase the point size of each group of consecutive paragraphs of body text (making sure you don't change the type size of the subheads or table). However, if you had assigned a style to all the paragraphs of body text, you could simply edit the style to automatically change the type size of every paragraph of body text.

Another benefit to using styles is that they ensure consistent formatting. When you are formatting paragraphs one at a time, you risk forgetting to turn on a particular option. Although you might not notice this inconsistent formatting right away, you probably will see it clearly in the final printout. With styles, on the other hand, every paragraph associated with a certain name will be formatted identically.

The set of styles in a publication is called a *style sheet*. This might sound like the styles are stored in a separate file, but they are not; styles are stored within the publication.

USING THE STYLE PALETTE

While you are formatting your publication and creating styles, you will want to turn on the *style palette*. This is a box that lists the styles contained in your publication. The name of the style of the currently selected paragraph is highlighted. You can use the style palette to create, assign, and edit styles. Figure 8.1 shows an example of a style palette.

Turning on the Style Palette

To begin, follow these steps to turn on the style palette for the brochure you created and edited in the previous chapters:

1. Open the BROCHURE.PM4 publication.

2. Pull down the Window menu and choose Style Palette, or press Ctrl-Y.

Like the toolbox, the style palette can be dragged anywhere on the screen to keep it out of the way of your document. It also can be lengthened if your publication has many style names.

Applying the Default Styles

Even though you haven't created any styles yet, several style names are already listed in the palette: Body text, Caption, Headline, Subhead 1, and Subhead 2. These are the default styles included with all publications.

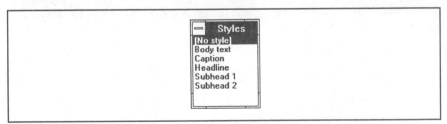

Figure 8.1: A style palette

The first item in the palette, [No style], applies to paragraphs to which no style is assigned. This currently applies to all the paragraphs. Just for practice, let's assign styles to different paragraphs in your brochure.

1. Save your document.

2. Switch to 75% view.

3. With the text tool, click in any paragraph of body text. (You must use the text tool to create and apply styles.)

4. Click on Body text in the style palette. PageMaker reformats the paragraph to the default Body text style: 12-point Times Roman, with a 2-pica first-line indent.

5. Assign the Caption style to this same paragraph. The default settings for this style are 10-point Times Roman italic, with no indent.

6. Click on one of the subheads.

7. See how your subhead looks in the following default styles: Headline, Subhead 1, and Subhead 2.

We are not going to keep these style assignments; in fact, we'll remove all the default names in the next section. Let's start over with the original file.

8. Pull down the File menu and choose Revert.

9. Choose OK.

The Revert option on the File menu recalls the last saved version of your publication. Using this option is faster than reopening the file.

REMOVING STYLES

Because we will not be using the default styles in the brochure, you should delete them so they won't be confused with the ones you will create.

In the following steps, you will remove the style names.

1. Pull down the Type menu and choose Define Styles (or press Ctrl-3). You will see the Define Styles dialog box, as shown in Figure 8.2.

2. Click on the first style name, Body text.

3. Click on the Remove command button.

4. Repeat steps 2 and 3 to remove the remaining style names.

5. Click on OK. The style palette is now empty except for the [No style] item.

If you remove a style name accidentally, and you discover the error before you choose OK in the Define Styles dialog box, click on the Cancel button. Any styles you removed will be restored.

To eliminate the default styles from all new publications you create, remove the style names when no publication is open. Your new publications will then have empty style palettes.

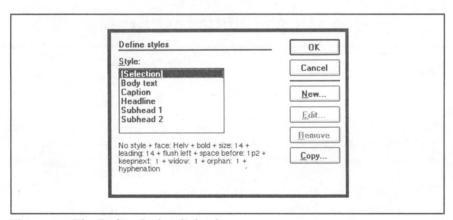

Figure 8.2: The Define Styles dialog box

CREATING A STYLE SHEET

Creating a style is easy. You simply use the Define Styles dialog box to assign a style name to a formatted paragraph, and the formatting contained in that paragraph is then associated with the name. The style contains instructions on character formatting (such as font, size, leading, and type style), as well as paragraph formatting (such as indents, space above and below, hyphenation, widow/orphan control, and column breaks). Note that only one font can be associated with a style.

You can create styles at any point in the design and layout process, but the earlier the better. If the publication already has text, you can create the style as you come across the various elements. For example, the first time you encounter a subhead, format it as fully as you can, and then create a style for it. You can always refine the style later.

In the following exercises, you will create four styles for the brochure. These will contain formats for the body text, subheads, bulleted list, and table.

Creating a Body Text Style

First, you'll create a style for your body text, appropriately named Body Text.

1. Switch to the text tool and, in 75% view, click anywhere in a paragraph of body text.

2. Pull down the Type menu and choose Define Styles (or press Ctrl-3).

When the dialog box appears, [Selection] is highlighted. This indicates the style is based on the formatting in the selected paragraph. The paragraph's formats are listed at the bottom of the dialog box. We'll explain how to decipher and change these formats later in the chapter.

3. Click on the New button. The Edit Style dialog box, shown in Figure 8.3, appears.

4. Next to Name, type **Body Text**.

5. To finish creating the Body Text style, hold down Alt and click on OK to close both dialog boxes.

Body Text is now listed in your style palette. However, this style is not yet applied to any paragraph, not even the current one, because creating a style does not apply that style.

Specifying the Next Style

The Next Style option in the Edit Style dialog box specifies the style of the paragraph that follows the current style. When you created the Body Text style, you accepted the default setting for the Next Style option, Same Style, because body text usually follows body text. This is not the case with subheadings, however, because subheadings are normally followed by body text.

In your brochure, a paragraph of body text always follows a subhead, so you can specify Next Style as Body Text. Follow these steps to create the Subhead style:

1. Click on any of the subheads, except *Our Focus*, which contains the column-break formatting.

2. Press Ctrl-3 to display the Define Styles dialog box.

3. Click on the New button.

4. Type the name **Subhead**.

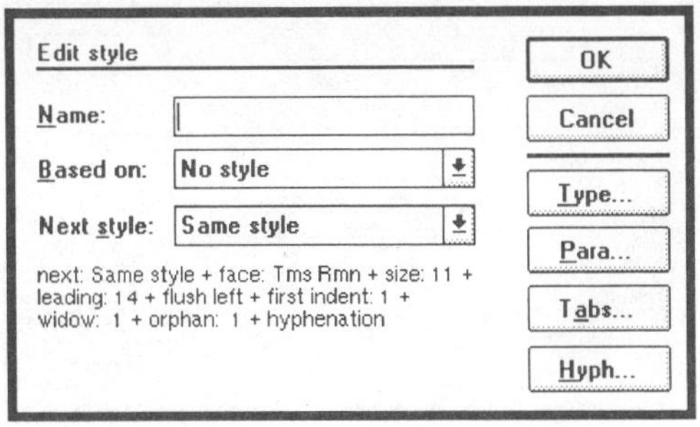

Figure 8.3: The Edit Style dialog box for Body Text

5. Pull down the drop-down list to the right of Next Style.

6. Select Body Text. Your dialog box should match the one shown in Figure 8.4.

7. To finish creating the Subhead style, close the dialog boxes.

Subhead is now listed along with Body Text in your style palette.

Note that the Next Style has no effect when you apply styles to existing text. The only time it takes affect is when you are creating new paragraphs. For example, if you formatted text with the Subhead style and pressed Enter to go to the next paragraph, that next paragraph would be formatted with the Body Text style. But if the paragraphs were already typed, assigning the subhead style would *not* format the next paragraph with the Body Text style.

Basing a Style on Another Style

The Based On option in the Edit Style dialog box creates a link between the current style and an existing style. When you change the format of the Based On style, you automatically change the format of all styles that are linked to it.

The bulleted paragraphs are perfect candidates for the Based On option because they are supposed to have the same font, size, and leading as the Body Text style. By linking the Bullet List style to the Body Text style, you will save time when you make formatting changes. If you change the

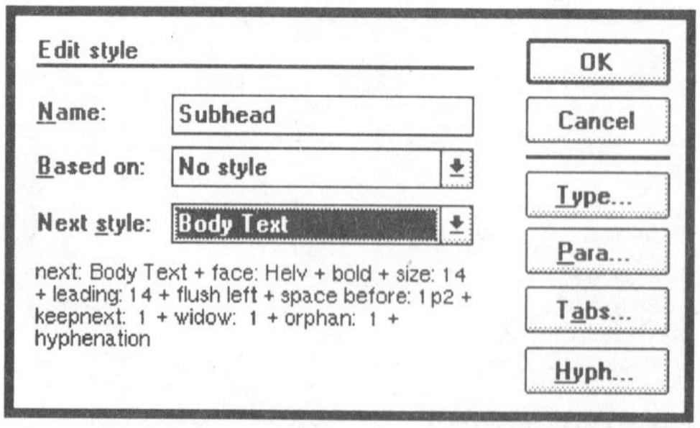

Figure 8.4: The Edit Style dialog box for the Subhead style

type size associated with the Body Text style, this change will be automatically reflected in the Bullet List style.

Follow these steps to create the Bullet List style:

1. Click anywhere in one of the bulleted paragraphs, *except* in the first sentence (or the style will have the bold type style associated with it).

2. Press Ctrl-3 and click on the New button in the Define Styles dialog box.

3. Type the name **Bullet List**.

4. Pull down the drop-down list to the right of Based On.

5. Select Body Text. Your Edit Style dialog box should match Figure 8.5.

The format list at the bottom of the dialog box changes to reflect this new setting. All formatting characteristics that match those in the Body Text style are replaced with the style name. The formatting specifications that are not a part of Body Text, such as the hanging indent settings and the tab stop, are still listed.

6. Close dialog boxes.

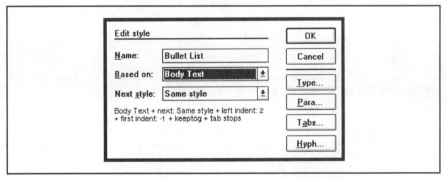

Figure 8.5: The Edit Style dialog box for the Bullet List style

Using a Shortcut to Create Styles

We will create the style for the table by using a shortcut. This method bypasses the menu and is even faster than the Ctrl-3 keyboard shortcut.

Follow these steps to create the Table style:

1. Click anywhere in the table, except in the line with the bold type style.

2. Hold down Ctrl and click on [No style] in the style palette. This takes you directly to the Edit Style dialog box.

3. Type **Table** for the style name.

4. Select Body Text as the Next Style. The dialog box should match the one shown in Figure 8.6.

5. Click on OK.

6. Save your file.

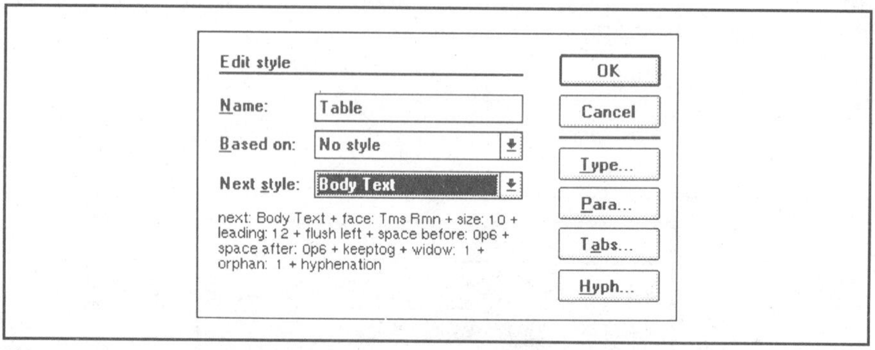

Figure 8.6: The Edit Style dialog box for the Table style

ASSIGNING STYLES

Now that you have created a style for every element in your main story, you can begin assigning styles. This is sometimes called *paragraph tagging* (*tag* is another word for style). You already learned how to use the style palette to tag paragraphs. You can also use the Style option on the Type pull-down menu, but the style palette is quicker and more convenient.

Tagging the Body Text

Since most of the text is body text, you will assign this style first.

1. Click anywhere in the story with the text tool.
2. Press Ctrl-A to select the entire story.
3. Click on Body Text in the style palette.

All your text is now formatted with the Body Text style, including the subheads, table, and bulleted list. This is not the disaster that it appears to be. You have created styles for these other elements and will soon apply them to restore the formatting. Do *not* apply a style for body text to all the text until you have created styles for the other items!

Applying Other Styles

To format the rest of the brochure, follow these steps:

1. In 75% view, click on one of the subheads.
2. Click on Subhead in the style palette. The paragraph is instantly reformatted.
3. Repeat steps 1 and 2 to reformat the remaining subheads.

If you have trouble formatting a subhead, select it, press F5, and then apply the Subhead style again. This clears any local formatting, which we'll discuss later in the chapter.

4. The bulleted paragraphs are consecutive, so select all of them together, and then click on Bullet List in the style palette. All the selected paragraphs are formatted at once.

The Symbol font formatting for the bullets is now lost because a style can have only one font associated with it.

5. Select each bullet and format it with the Symbol font (or use the Story Editor's Change command, as described earlier).

6. Click anywhere in the table, which is a single paragraph, and choose Table from the style palette.

7. Press Ctrl-S to save the file.

Your publication is now completely tagged and formatted. It should look exactly like it did before you began creating styles. You might be wondering what you have gained from all this work—the end result is exactly the same. The real value of a style sheet becomes apparent when you make formatting changes.

EDITING A STYLE

When you change one of the formatting characteristics associated with a style, the change affects all the paragraphs that have been assigned that style. This global and automatic reformatting lets you quickly and easily play what-if games with your page layout. How would the page look if the subheads were in Avant Garde instead of Helvetica? Edit the Subhead style, and you will instantly see this change. How would the page look if a 12-point font was used for text instead of an 11-point font? Just edit the Body Text style.

To make a formatting change to a style, you do not edit the actual text; you revise the style. If you format the text, you only change the local format of that text. A global change must be made through the Edit Style dialog box.

Before you edit a style, you should be able to read the list of the formats it contains. The bottom of the Edit Style dialog box lists the formats as follows:

- The various formats are separated by plus signs.

- Most formats have a short, sometimes abbreviated, description followed by a colon and a value. For example, *face: Tms Rmn* and *size: 11* indicate the paragraph is typed in 11-point Times Roman.

- Formats that don't require a value are simply listed with a brief description. For example, *flush left* indicates the text is left-aligned.

To revise the formatting associated with a style, click on the appropriate button—Type, Para, Tabs, or Hyph—and make your changes.

One way to get to the Edit Style dialog box is by choosing Define Styles on the Type menu. You then select the style name from a list and click on the Edit button. A faster way is to hold down the Ctrl key as you click on the style name in the style palette.

Changing the Type Size

Let's see how the brochure looks with 12-point body text.

1. Hold down Ctrl and click on Body Text in the style palette. You will go directly to the Edit Style dialog box for the Body Text style.

2. Click on the Type button.

3. Change the type size to 12.

4. Close the dialog boxes.

All the body text is now reformatted in 12-point type. The paragraphs in the bulleted list are also in 12-point type because you based the Bullet List style on the Body Text style. If you had not applied styles, you would have had to select each portion of body text and make the formatting change.

You might suspect that the story consumes more space in 12-point type. If you switch to Fit in Window view on page 2, you will see that the story is indeed longer, but it still fits on the page with a little room to spare. (Later in the book, we will use this extra space for a graphic.)

Changing the Spacing

Next, let's change the first-line indent of Body Text to 1.5 picas.

1. Hold down Ctrl and click on Body Text in the style palette.

2. Click on the Para button.

3. Change the first-line indent from 1 to 1.5 picas.

4. Close the dialog boxes.

5. Save the file.

Figure 8.7 shows a paragraph with the new specifications for the Body Text style. The additional indent adds a bit more definition to the body text paragraphs.

You can continue to explore the possibilities. Try changing the font of the Subhead style to Times Roman. Which do you prefer: Helvetica or Times? Print the page and see what you think.

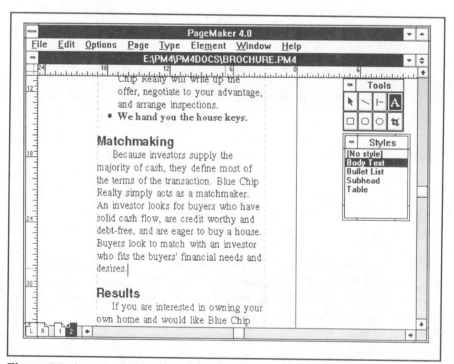

Figure 8.7: A paragraph formatted with the new Body Text style

WATCHING
FOR LOCAL FORMATTING

Local formatting refers to formatting specifications within a paragraph that are not part of the style. You apply a local format by selecting and editing the text. Your changes have no effect on other paragraphs with the same style.

The bulleted list in your brochure contains two instances of local formatting: the first sentence is in the bold style, and the bullet is formatted with the Symbol font. These formats are not associated with the Bullet List style. If they were, the entire paragraph would either be boldfaced or in the Symbol font (quite a sight!).

As you are creating your styles, pay close attention to where the cursor is positioned in the paragraph. If the cursor is on a character that is locally formatted (in bold or italic, for example), this formatting will be part of the style. Then, when you apply the style, the entire paragraph will have this unintentional formatting.

When you see a plus sign next to the style name in the style palette, the current paragraph contains some kind of local formatting. You will only see the plus sign when the cursor is positioned on the locally formatted text. To see how this works, click inside one of the paragraphs in the Bullet List style. You will see the plus sign when you click within the bold sentence or on the bullet itself, as shown in Figure 8.8.

If you find that your style is not formatting the way it should, the text's local formatting may be overriding the style's formatting. To correct this problem, select the entire paragraph and press F5 to clear all type specifications. Then reapply the style.

Figure 8.8: Bullet List+ indicates that the paragraph contains local formatting

USING STYLES IN THE STORY EDITOR

When you use the style palette in the Story Editor, you can see the style names next to each paragraph—a feature unavailable in the standard layout view. Another advantage of using styles in the Story Editor is that you can find and change style names.

Turning On the Style Bar

In story view, style names appear in a sidebar, the *style bar,* to the left of the text. The style bar only appears when the Display Style Names option on the Options menu is turned on.

To see how the style bar looks, load your story into the Story Editor.

1. Click anywhere in the story.

2. Press Ctrl-E.

3. Maximize the story window.

4. If you don't see the style bar, as shown in Figure 8.9, pull down the Options menu and choose Display Style Names.

5. Scroll through the document and look at the different names in the style bar. When a paragraph has no style associated with it, a small dot appears in the style bar. As you scroll through your story, make sure every paragraph has a style name.

As in layout view, you can assign styles by clicking on the style name in the style palette. Keep in mind that you won't actually see the formatting until you return to layout view. Use the style bar to keep track of the styles.

Finding and Changing Style Names

The Story Editor's Find and Change commands can search for and replace paragraph styles. Here are a few examples of how you can use these commands:

- Use the Find command to quickly discover whether a certain style is used in the story.

- Search for the Subhead style to jump from one section to the next.

- If many paragraphs were tagged incorrectly, just replace one style name with another using the Change command.

To locate a style name, click on the Attributes button in the Find or Change dialog box. Then choose the style from the Para Style drop-down list. Figure 8.10 shows the style list in the Find Attributes dialog box.

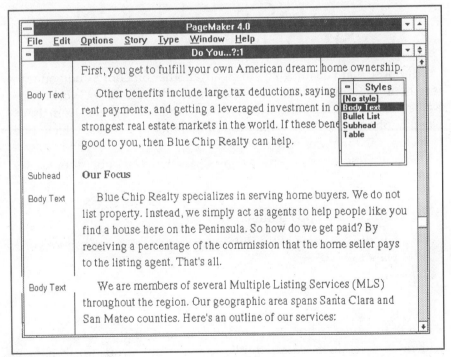

Figure 8.9: The style bar

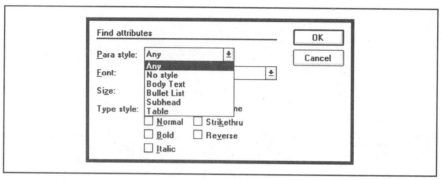

Figure 8.10: The Find Attributes dialog box

COPYING STYLES FROM ANOTHER PUBLICATION

Suppose that you are going to create another brochure, and you want it to be in the same format as the brochure you have been working on. Rather than recreating these styles, you can simply copy them from the existing publication to the new one. You cannot pick and choose which styles to include; all the styles will be copied.

Follow these general steps to copy styles between publications:

1. Pull down the Type menu and choose Define Styles.

2. Click on the Copy button.

3. Choose the name of the publication that contains the styles you want to copy.

4. Click on OK.

These styles are added to the current publication's style sheet. You can then edit the styles in the new publication or immediately format the text with these styles. In the case of duplicate style names, you are asked if you want to copy over the existing styles. If you choose OK, the imported styles will replace the existing styles with the same name. If you choose Cancel, none of the styles will be imported.

In this chapter, you learned that the most efficient way to format a publication is with paragraph styles. Global formatting changes are a couple clicks away when you have assigned styles to your paragraphs; formatting revisions can be an absolute nightmare without styles.

Not only are styles a big time saver, but they also promote formatting consistency. When you use styles, each subhead is formatted exactly like every other subhead. Styles also make it easier to work with imported text files, as you will see in the next chapter.

C H A P T E R

9

IMPORTING
AND
FLOWING
TEXT

So far, you have learned two ways to place text on the page: with the text tool and with the Story Editor. Another, perhaps more common, way is to import text from your word processor. PageMaker can import files from a wide variety of word processors, such as Microsoft Word, Word-Perfect, and MultiMate. You can even import stories from other Page-Maker documents. A publication can contain any number of imported text files; each file becomes a separate story within the publication.

After we explore techniques for importing text, we'll cover some ways to handle text blocks. By manipulating the text blocks, you can control the flow of text in the publication.

HOW TO IMPORT FILES

The Place option on the File menu is PageMaker's command for importing both text and graphic files. This option is called *Place* and not *Import* to stress that a key part of bringing in an external file is indicating where it is to be *placed* in the publication. Actually, this concept should already be familiar to you. In Chapter 6, you used the Place command to place the text you typed in the Story Editor.

And speaking of the Story Editor, you can import text into story view as well as layout view. The Import option on the Story menu brings the file into the Story Editor instead of placing it on the page. If you know that the file needs editing (for example, you need to find and remove extra carriage returns), it makes sense to import the file into the Story Editor before placing the story on the page. After your editing is finished and you exit from the Story Editor, you are automatically prompted to place the text.

IMPORTING
STORIES FROM OTHER
PAGEMAKER PUBLICATIONS

You could copy a story from one PageMaker publication to another by opening one document, copying the text to the Clipboard, opening the second document, and pasting the story. However, an easier way is to use the Place command on the File menu to import the story. Note that you can import stories from other PageMaker publications only if you chose the PageMaker Pub Import filter when you installed the software (see Appendix A).

In the brochure you've been working on in previous chapters, the company name and address will appear on the back page. This will be the same text that is in the letterhead you created in Chapter 5. Because this text requires special formatting, importing the LETHEAD1 publication will be quicker than retyping the address.

Follow these steps to import the PageMaker story:

1. Open the BROCHURE publication and display page 1 in Fit in Window view (press Ctrl-W).

2. Choose Place from the File menu (or press Ctrl-D) to display the Place File dialog box.

In the Place File dialog box, you'll see a list of your files in the current path (shown next to Path). We'll explain how to work with the Files/Directories list and the options at the bottom of the dialog box later in the chapter.

3. Choose LETHEAD1.PM4. You will see the Place PageMaker Stories dialog box, shown in Figure 9.1.

This dialog box lists the first few words of each story in the publication. This particular publication has only one story (the letterhead). To see

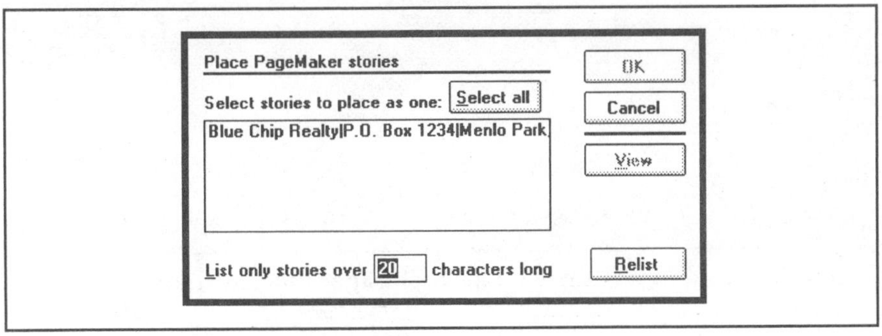

Figure 9.1: The Place PageMaker Stories dialog box

the contents of a story, click on the story name (the first few words of the story) and choose the View button.

You can control which stories are listed by specifying the minimum length of the stories. To do so, change the default of 20 characters at the bottom of the dialog box, and then choose the Relist button.

4. Click on the story name (Blue Chip Realty. . .) and choose OK.

Your text is now loaded into a text gun. You saw this same text gun when you placed the text from the Story Editor in Chapter 6.

5. Place the loaded text gun at the top of column 1 and shoot the text.

6. Switch to 75% view. Your screen should resemble Figure 9.2.

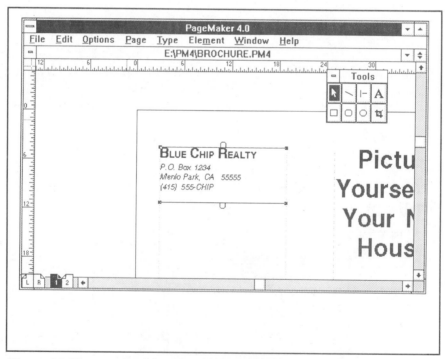

Figure 9.2: The return address on the back page of the brochure

7. Save the file.

In the next chapter, you will position the address more precisely.

IMPORTING
WORD PROCESSOR FILES

Before you bring in a word processor file, you should make sure that you have set up PageMaker to import that type of file. You should also be sure that the file has been properly prepared to minimize the work you'll have to do after the text is in PageMaker. When you import the file, you can control its placement and format it as necessary.

Checking Which Files Can Be Imported

When you used the Aldus Setup program to install PageMaker on your hard disk, you were asked to specify which file filters you want to use, so that PageMaker can import files from other programs. (See Appendix A for information about installing filters.) For example, if WordPerfect is your word processor of choice, you should choose this filter in the Aldus Setup program. You can run the Setup utility, located on Disk 1, any time you need to install more filters.

Table 9.1 lists the word processors for which PageMaker offers filters and the three-character file extension PageMaker expects for each program. If your file has a different extension from the one listed in the table, it will not automatically appear in the Files/Directories list in the Place File dialog box, and you will have to specify that file yourself. (You will learn how to do this later.)

If you don't want to use the file extension PageMaker assigns to your word processor, and you get tired of having to specify the extension and file type yourself, you can change the default file extension. The filters and their file extensions are stored in a file called ALDUS.INI in your PageMaker directory. You can change the default extension by editing this file.

In the following steps, you will open the ALDUS.INI file so that you can see which filters you have installed in PageMaker. While the file is

Table 9.1: Word Processing Import Filters

WORD PROCESSOR	FILE EXTENSION
Ami Professional	SAM
Microsoft Word	DOC
Microsoft Word for Windows	DOC
MultiMate	DOC
Ollivetti	OTX
PC Write	PCW
Wang	DOC or IWP
Windows Write	WRI
WordPerfect 5.0–5.1	WP5
WordPerfect 4.2	WP
WordStar	WST or WS

open, you can change the default file extensions if you like. Follow these steps:

1. From the Windows Program Manager, open the Accessories group window (or whatever group the Notepad has been moved into) and double-click on the Notepad icon.

2. Pull down the File menu and choose Open.

3. Check the current directory (it is probably C:\Windows).

4. In the Directories list, navigate to the drive and directory where your PageMaker program is stored (for example, C:\PM4), and then change to the [usenglsh] directory.

5. Next to Filename, type *.INI, and then press Enter.

6. Select ALDUS.INI.

7. Pull down the File menu and choose Print. Keep this printout; you will refer to it again later.

8. If desired, change the file extension for your word processor and be sure to save the file. Since the change does not take effect until

the next time you load the program, you must reload Page-Maker to see the new default extension listed.

9. Close the Notepad application and return to PageMaker.

Figure 9.3 shows a sample ALDUS.INI file on the screen. Your file will have different contents but will be structured similarly. The first set of lines, under [AldusImports], lists your import filters. The next group of lines, titled [AldusExports], shows your export filters.

The import filter lines contain coded information. For example, here is the WordPerfect line in Figure 9.3:

WordPerfect 5.0–5.1 Import=WP5IMP.flt,wp5

The line begins with a brief description of the import filter (WordPerfect 5.0–5.1 Import). After the equal sign is the name of the filter file (WP5IMP.flt). The

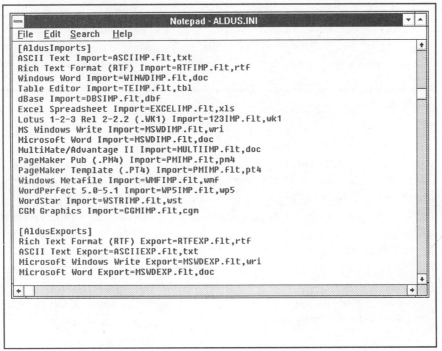

```
[AldusImports]
ASCII Text Import=ASCIIMP.flt,txt
Rich Text Format (RTF) Import=RTFIMP.flt,rtf
Windows Word Import=WINWDIMP.flt,doc
Table Editor Import=TEIMP.flt,tbl
dBase Import=DBSIMP.flt,dbf
Excel Spreadsheet Import=EXCELIMP.flt,xls
Lotus 1-2-3 Rel 2-2.2 (.WK1) Import=123IMP.flt,wk1
MS Windows Write Import=MSWDIMP.flt,wri
Microsoft Word Import=MSWDIMP.flt,doc
MultiMate/Advantage II Import=MULTIIMP.flt,doc
PageMaker Pub (.PM4) Import=PMIMP.flt,pm4
PageMaker Template (.PT4) Import=PMIMP.flt,pt4
Windows Metafile Import=WMFIMP.flt,wmf
WordPerfect 5.0-5.1 Import=WP5IMP.flt,wp5
WordStar Import=WSTRIMP.flt,wst
CGM Graphics Import=CGMIMP.flt,cgm

[AldusExports]
Rich Text Format (RTF) Export=RTFEXP.flt,rtf
ASCII Text Export=ASCIIEXP.flt,txt
Microsoft Windows Write Export=MSWDEXP.flt,wri
Microsoft Word Export=MSWDEXP.flt,doc
```

Figure 9.3: A sample ALDUS.INI file

next entry, after the comma, is the file extension (wp5).

Look through the list of import filters and locate your word processor. If you can't find it, you may need to run the Aldus Setup program. See Appendix A for details.

Preparing the Text in Your Word Processor

As you are creating a PageMaker-bound document in your word processor, concentrate on the content of the document. Don't worry about how the text is formatted—you will be doing most of your formatting in PageMaker. In general, the less formatting you do in your word processor, the less clean-up work you will have to do in PageMaker.

Here are a few things to *avoid* when typing a document that will be imported into PageMaker:

- Two spaces between sentences
- Regular spaces (inserted with the spacebar) to line up columns
- Tabs at the beginning of paragraphs
- Hyphenation
- Justification
- Double-spacing

If you type the text single-spaced without tabs (as the above list implies), you will need some way to see where one paragraph ends and the next begins. The easiest way to differentiate your paragraphs is to insert a blank line between each; in other words, press Enter twice at the end of each paragraph. Later, you can remove the extra carriage returns with your word processor's search and replace feature before the text is imported, or with the Story Editor's Change command after the text is in PageMaker. Chapter 6 explains how to find and remove carriage returns in story view.

Don't waste time specifying document layout settings, such as margins, page size, headers, and footers, because these settings will be ignored when the file is imported.

Including Formatting to be Retained

While you are creating text in your word processor, you may choose to do some light formatting, such as boldfacing or italicizing words. This formatting can be imported if you turn on the Retain Format option in the Place File dialog box. The option is turned on by default. You cannot select which formatting to import; it's all or nothing. The type of formatting that is imported depends on your word processor. We tested five of the most popular word processors to see how much formatting is imported. Table 9.2 shows the results.

But there is a major drawback to importing formatting: you give up the capability to preformat the text in PageMaker. Before importing the text, you can set default type and paragraph specifications for the story. For example, you can specify 11-point Times Roman with a 1-pica first-line paragraph indent before you choose the Place command. Then, when you import the text, it will automatically be formatted the way you specified. This preformatting is ignored if the Retain Format option is turned on.

Table 9.2: Retained Formatting

FORMAT ATTRIBUTE	WORD-PERFECT 5.0	WORD-STAR 5.0	WORD FOR WINDOWS 1.0	WORD 5.0	MULTI-MATE ADVAN-TAGE II
Centering	Yes	No	Yes	Yes	Yes
Justification	Yes	Yes	Yes	Yes	Yes
Left indents	Yes	No	Yes	Yes	Yes
Hanging indents	No	No	Yes	Yes	Yes
Bold, underline	Yes	Yes	Yes	Yes	Yes
Italics	Yes	Yes	Yes	Yes	No
Fonts and sizes	Yes	Yes	Yes	Yes	No
Leading/line spacing	Yes	No	Yes	Yes	Yes

Figure 9.4 shows a WordPerfect file that was imported twice. The text in the column on the left was imported without formatting. That is, the Retain Format option and the Convert Quotes option were turned off. Convert Quotes transforms inch marks (") and apostrophes (') into the more professional-looking typographical opening and closing quotation marks (" "). For the text in the right column, both of these default options were left on. Compare the text in the two columns. In particular, notice the difference in apostrophes.

Placing Imported Text

When you are ready to insert your word processor file into a Page-Maker publication, choose the Place option from the File menu and navigate the Files/Directories list to change to your word processing directory.

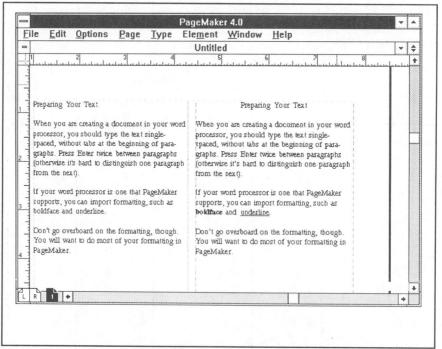

Figure 9.4: The text in the second column was imported with formatting, and quotes were converted

If the file you want to import does not have the default extension used by PageMaker (see Table 9.1), it will not be listed in the Files/Directories list. In this case, either type the complete file name next to the Name field (if you know the name), or use DOS wildcards to display files with a different file extension. In Figure 9.5, we displayed a list of all files with the .WS extension by typing *.WS next to the Name field and pressing Enter.

When you use nonstandard file extensions or file extensions intended for another type of word processor, PageMaker doesn't automatically recognize what type of file it is. You will see a dialog box with a message indicating that PageMaker doesn't know how to place the file. This message does not mean that PageMaker is unable to place the file. It just indicates that PageMaker needs to know the file type of this nonstandard name. As shown in Figure 9.6, a list of filters is displayed so that you can select the appropriate file type.

Flowing Imported Text

PageMaker offers three ways to flow text into columns: automatically, manually, or semiautomatically.

In the following sections, you'll use each of these methods. For the exercises, you need a short (one- or two-page) single-spaced text file. Either choose an existing file or make up a new one. Since you will use this file to practice different text flow techniques, we will refer to it as FLOW.

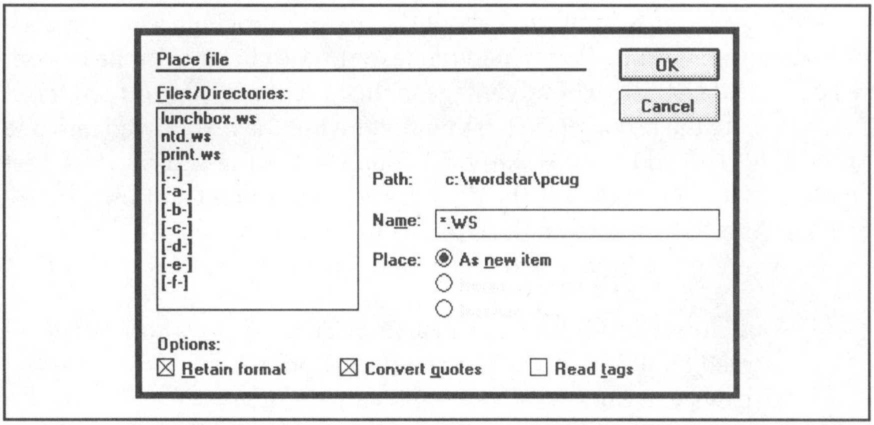

Figure 9.5: Listing files that have an extension of .WS

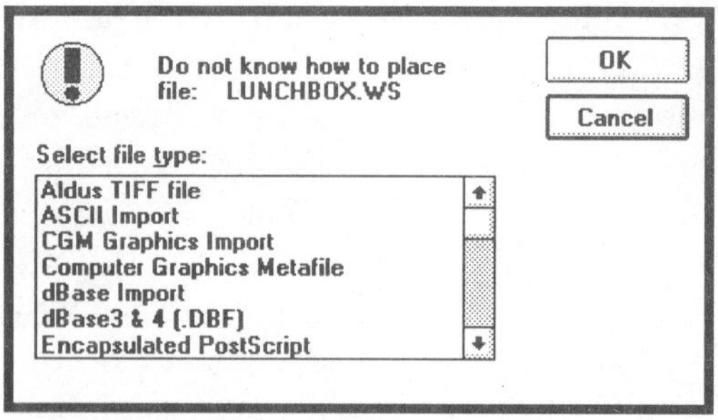

Figure 9.6: A list of import filters

(Be sure to assign the appropriate file extention to your file.)

Set up your PageMaker publication as follows:

1. Create a new publication with the following specifications: tall orientation, two pages, and 3-pica margins all the way around.

2. Create four column guides on each page.

3. Change the type size to 10 points. By making this change before you import the text file, the text will automatically be formatted in this type size.

4. Save the publication as **FLOWTEST**.

Manual Text Flow

With manual text flow, you shoot the text into each column, on each page. Before each shot, you reload the text gun by clicking on the bottom window shade handle. The advantage to this method is that you can select exactly where the text is placed. If you don't want the text flowed into one of the columns, you simply skip over it and shoot the text into the next column. Manual text flow is the default. When manual text flow is in effect, the Autoflow option on the Options menu is not checked.

Now let's place the imported text using manual text flow.

1. Pull down the Options menu and check to see if Autoflow is turned on. If it's checked, turn off the option. Otherwise, press Esc twice to cancel the command.

2. Pull down the File menu and choose Place (or press Ctrl-D).

3. If necessary, navigate the Files/Directories list to change the path to your word processing directory.

4. Click on the FLOW file. (Don't double-click or you won't have a chance to select the Place File options).

5. Turn off the Retain Format option. If you don't do this, the text will not be formatted to your earlier specification of 10 points.

6. Click on OK.

If PageMaker did not recognize your file type, you are presented with a list of import filters. Choose the appropriate filter before continuing.

After a few seconds, you will see the manual text flow icon, which looks like a box of greeked text.

7. Go to page 1 and shoot the text at the top of column 1.

The text flows into this one column and is enclosed in window shades, as shown in Figure 9.7. The triangle inside the bottom handle indicates there is more text to flow. Notice that you no longer have a text gun.

8. To reload the text gun, click on the bottom window shade handle. The text gun reappears.

9. Shoot the text at the top of the next column.

10. Repeat steps 8 and 9 until all the text is placed. When the bottom window shade handle is empty, there is no more text to flow.

Semiautomatic Text Flow

Semiautomatic text flow gives you the best of both worlds. You can select which columns to flow the text into, but you don't have to reload the text gun for each column. Unfortunately, there is no menu option for turning on semiautomatic text flow. You must hold down the Shift key as you shoot the text into each column. You can use semiautomatic text flow regardless of whether Autoflow is turned on or off.

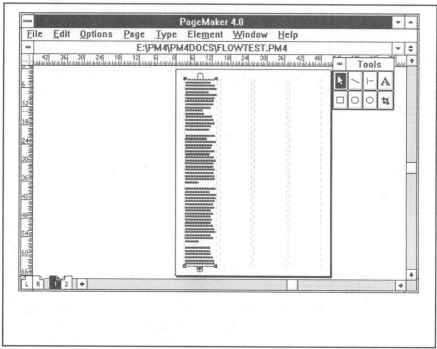

Figure 9.7: Text flowed into column 1

Since manual text flow is a bit tedious, let's flow in the same file using the semiautomatic technique. First, get rid of the text you imported.

1. Choose the Revert option from the File menu. (You could also select all the text with the text or pointer tool and press Del.)

2. Go to page 1. There should be no text on the page.

3. Press Ctrl-D to display the Place File dialog box.

4. Click on the FLOW file.

5. Turn off the Retain Format option.

6. Click on OK.

7. Hold down Shift, and the text gun appears as a semiautomatic text icon—a squiggly, dotted-line arrow. Keep the Shift key

down as you click the text icon at the top of column 1. The text flows into this one column, and the text gun is still loaded.

8.   Hold down Shift as you shoot the text at the top of each column.

When all the text is flowed, the text gun disappears, and the bottom window shade of the text block is empty.

Automatic Text Flow

With automatic text flow, you shoot the text only once, in the first column into which you want the text to flow. Text automatically ripples into subsequent columns on subsequent pages. If the text is longer than the number of pages in the publication, PageMaker creates the necessary number of pages. This type of text flow is ideal for long documents. You turn on automatic text flow by choosing Autoflow on the Options menu.

Revert back to your last saved version and try the third way of flowing text:

1.   Select Revert from the File menu and go to page 1.

2.   Pull down the Options menu and choose Autoflow.

3.   Press Ctrl-D to display the Place File dialog box.

4.   Click on the FLOW file.

5.   Turn off the Retain Format option.

6.   Click on OK. The autoflow text gun appears.

7.   Click the autoflow text gun at the top of the first column. The text automatically flows onto subsequent columns.

Drag-Placing Text

When you click the text gun at the top of a column, the text flows into the entire column. But what if you want the text to flow across two columns, or into part of one column? The point-and-shoot technique of flowing text will not work in these circumstances. Instead, use the *drag-place* method.

With the drag-place technique, you define the shape of the block by clicking and dragging. The shape can be any rectangular size and can span multiple or partial columns. Figure 9.8 shows a text block that is placed across two columns. Here is the general procedure for drag-placing text.

1. Place the loaded text gun in the upper-left corner of where you want the text placed.

2. Hold down the Shift key (if you want to keep the text gun loaded).

3. Use the click-and-drag method to draw a box the size of the desired text block.

4. Release the mouse button.

This technique works regardless of the type of text flow in effect.

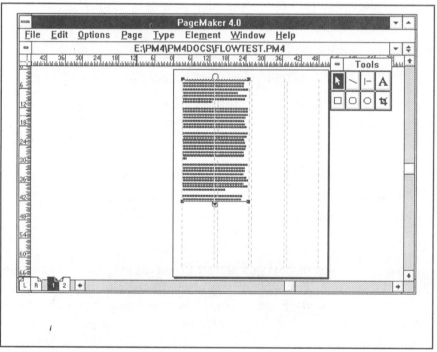

Figure 9.8: A text block placed across two columns

IMPORTING STYLES

Because PageMaker can import styles, the assignment of paragraph styles can begin right in your word processor. When you embed style names in your word processing document, the text is imported with style names already assigned to each paragraph. If you get in the habit of tagging paragraphs in the word processing stage, all you have to do in Page-Maker is define the formatting associated with each style.

Bear in mind that assigning style names in your word processor is not the same thing as formatting the text; you will usually wait to do most of the formatting in PageMaker. In your word processor, just assign names to the major elements in the story, such as body text and headings.

PageMaker offers two ways to import styles from a word processing document into a PageMaker publication, depending on whether your word processor has a style feature.

Using Your Word Processor's Style Feature

Microsoft Word for Windows, Word 5.0, and WordPerfect are several word processors that allow you to define and assign styles. Figure 9.9 shows an example of a style list in Word for Windows. If you aren't familiar with how to create styles in your word processor, refer to your documentation or a book about the software.

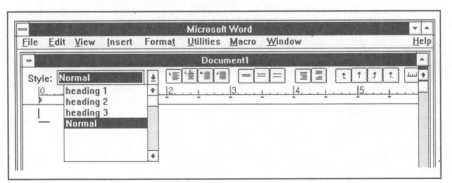

Figure 9.9: A Word for Windows style list

After you place the file, the style palette will then list the imported styles. An asterisk appears next to each style that wasn't previously defined in the current publication. The asterisk will disappear when you define the style's formatting in the Edit Style dialog box.

Note that if the Retained Format option in the Place File dialog box is turned off, style names will still be imported and applied, but the formatting will be lost.

Embedding Style Tags

If your word processor doesn't have its own style feature, you can type style names directly into your word processing document. Figure 9.10 shows a WordStar document that contains PageMaker style names.

Follow these rules for embedding style names in your word processing documents:

- Enclose the name in angle brackets.

- Type the tag at the beginning of the paragraph.

- Do not tag a paragraph if it uses the same style as the preceding paragraph. In other words, you only need to enter tags when the style changes.

Notice that the third paragraph in Figure 9.10 does not have a tag. This paragraph will automatically be assigned the same tag as the previous paragraph (Body text).

To import a tagged file, turn on the Read Tags option in the Place File dialog box. When a tag name matches an existing style name, the style is automatically assigned to the paragraph, and it is formatted accordingly.

When the tag name doesn't already appear in the publication's style sheet, the style name will still be imported, and the paragraph will be tagged. However, since PageMaker doesn't know how to format this new style, its name appears in the style palette with an asterisk next to it. After you edit the style to format the text, the asterisk disappears.

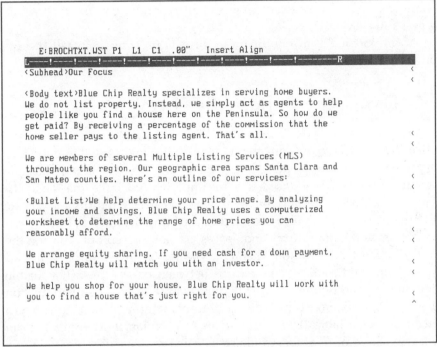

Figure 9.10: A WordStar document with embedded style names

IMPORTING ASCII FILES

If PageMaker does not provide a filter for your word processor (it's not listed in Table 9.1), don't despair. PageMaker can import files that are in standard text format. The most common of these formats is ASCII (American Standard Code for Information Interchange). An ASCII file contains only text. Any special formatting, such as fonts, bold, centering, and indents, are stripped out when you save the file in ASCII format. Almost every program has a way of creating an ASCII file; check your software's documentation for details.

Two other types of standard file formats are DCA (Document Content Architecture) and RTF (Rich Text Format). Unlike ASCII, these file formats retain some of the file's formatting. Not all programs can create these file types, however.

To import a file in one of these formats, you must install the appropriate filters in Aldus Setup (see Appendix A).

Using the Smart ASCII Import Filter

After you specify the name of the ASCII file you want to place (in the Place File dialog box), you are presented with the Smart ASCII Import Filter dialog box, shown in Figure 9.11. This dialog box allows you to reduce the amount of clean-up work needed on the imported ASCII file (that's why it's smart). ASCII files typically contain unwanted carriage returns and spaces. This dialog box lets you filter them out as you bring the text into PageMaker.

By default, extra returns and spaces are not filtered out. Turn on the At End of Every Line option when your file has carriage returns at the end of each line and two carriage returns between paragraphs. (If your file does not contain double-spacing between paragraphs when you turn on this option, the file comes in as one gigantic paragraph!) Also be sure to turn on the But Keep Tables, Lists, and Indents As Is option, if necessary. You can imagine what a mess a table would be if its line endings were removed.

When the ASCII file has two carriage returns between paragraphs (but does not have returns at the end of each line), turn on the Between Paragraphs option.

Two of the dialog box options deal with extra spaces. Let's say you create an ASCII file in your database program. Instead of a tab between each column, the ASCII file might have a series of spaces. If you set this text in

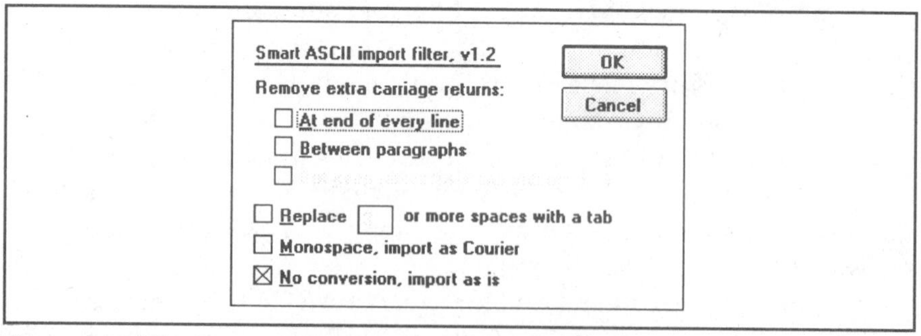

```
┌─────────────────────────────────────────────────────────────┐
│        ┌───────────────────────────────────────────┐         │
│        │ Smart ASCII import filter, v1.2   ┌──────┐ │         │
│        │                                   │  OK  │ │         │
│        │ Remove extra carriage returns:    └──────┘ │         │
│        │   ☐ At end of every line          ┌──────┐ │         │
│        │   ☐ Between paragraphs             │Cancel│ │         │
│        │   ☐                                └──────┘ │         │
│        │                                             │         │
│        │   ☐ Replace [   ] or more spaces with a tab │         │
│        │   ☐ Monospace, import as Courier            │         │
│        │   ☒ No conversion, import as is             │         │
│        └───────────────────────────────────────────┘         │
└─────────────────────────────────────────────────────────────┘
```

Figure 9.11: The Smart ASCII Import Filter dialog box

a proportional font, the columns will not line up. In this case, you could either import the file in a fixed-space font (the Monospace option), or have PageMaker replace the spaces with tabs.

In order to determine which options you should use, you must know what is in your ASCII file. If you aren't sure of the structure of the ASCII file, import the file directly into the Story Editor, but don't use any conversion options. Turn on the Display ¶ option so that you can see where the carriage returns and tabs are.

You can see that the story in Figure 9.12 has carriage returns at the end of every line and two carriage returns between paragraphs. In this example, you would want to choose the At End of Every Line option. You can then discard the story and import it again with the appropriate options.

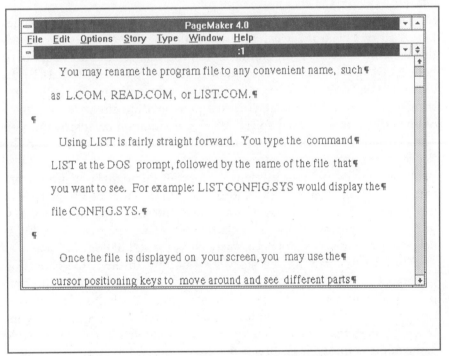

Figure 9.12: Display paragraph codes in the Story Editor so you know which ASCII import options to use

RELATING STORIES TO TEXT FILES

Normally, an imported text file is a one-way street. Once you import the file, there is no further connection between the text file and the publication; if you edit the text in the publication, the text file is not altered. Likewise, if you edit the text file after it's imported, the publication does not change. PageMaker offers several ways to change this and make text-editing a two-way street.

Creating a Text File from a Story

The Export option on the File menu creates a text file out of a Page-Maker story. This text file can be exported using any of the export filters that were installed with the Aldus Setup program (refer to the printout of your ALDUS.INI file to see which export filters you have installed). If you export the file to Word format, you can then edit the file in Microsoft Word. If you export to ASCII format, you can open the file in any word processor or text editor (refer to your software's documentation for instructions on retrieving an ASCII file). After you export a file, you can return it to the PageMaker publication by placing it again.

When you export a file, some of the formatting might be stripped from the file; it depends on the type of formatting in the story and what type of exporting procedure you use. If you export the story, add more text to it in your word processor, and then place it in the same PageMaker publication, the new story will not necessarily be formatted like the original.

The key to retaining the story's formatting through the exporting process is to use paragraph styles instead of local formatting wherever possible. Then, when you export the file, turn on the Export Tags option to create a file with embedded tag names. Figure 9.13 shows part of your brochure story that has been exported to a Windows Write file. Each style name appears inside angle brackets.

When you place the new version of the story, make sure you turn on the Read Tags option in the Place File dialog box. Notice how the Export Tags option tags *every* paragraph, including consecutive body text paragraphs that don't actually need to be tagged.

The import–export–import routine could become tedious were it not for one important time-saver: When you place the same story in the same location in a publication, you don't have to delete the text before importing the new story. Just click anywhere in the story, display the Place File dialog box, and then turn on the Replacing Entire Story option.

One common reason to use the Export command is because you changed the page layout. If you change the margins or columns after you have placed the text, the text blocks will not automatically adjust to fit the new column guides. Rather than adjusting the size of each text block (which could take an hour or so in a lengthy publication), you can export the file with its tags, delete the story, and then place the file again. (Because the text block is a different size, you can't use the Replacing Entire Story option here.) Although this sounds like a lot of work, it is much faster than moving and sizing many text blocks. Let's try this on your brochure.

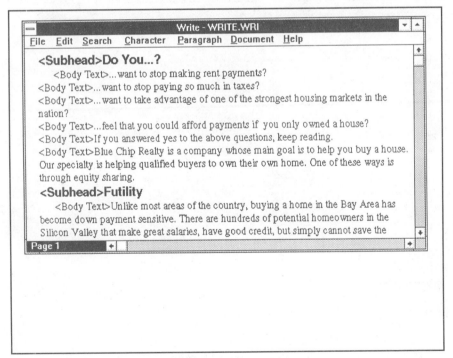

Figure 9.13: An exported text file with tag names

(*Do not* save any of the changes you make to BROCHURE.PM4 in the remainder of this chapter.)

1. Open BROCHURE.PM4.

2. Change the top and bottom margins to 0p40. As Figure 9.14 shows, the text blocks do not span the new top and bottom margins.

3. Switch to the text tool and click anywhere in the story.

The text cursor must be in the story you want to export. If you are using the pointer tool, the Export option is unavailable.

4. Pull down the File menu and choose Export.

5. Type **BROCHTXT** for the file name.

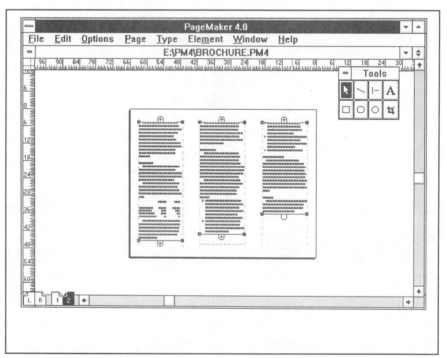

Figure 9.14: After changing margins, text blocks are too small

6. Turn on the Export Tags option.

7. Select a file format.

8. Choose OK.

When the export operation is complete, you have a file that can be viewed and edited in a word processor. The file is assigned an extension appropriate to the file type to which you exported (for example, .TXT for ASCII or DOC for Word). If you want to check, you can switch into your word processor now and look at this file. If you created an ASCII file, you can open it in Notepad. (Remember, local formatting is stripped from an ASCII file.)

Once the text is exported with its tag names, you can delete the story and import it again.

9. Press Ctrl-A to select all the text.

10. Press Del to delete the selected text.

11. Pull down the File menu and choose Place.

12. Select the BROCHTXT file from the list.

13. Turn on the Read Tags option.

14. Choose OK.

15. Using the Autoflow feature, place the text beginning in column 3 of page 1.

When you are finished, the text blocks conform to the new margins.

Establishing Links to Your Text Files

Another way to connect your PageMaker story with its external text file is with PageMaker's Links option. When a link is established, changes in the text file are reflected in the story inside the publication. This feature is especially useful when other people are supplying you with stories for your publication. If someone makes a change to a text file after you have placed it, file linking can save you from having to import the file again. It also ensures that the publication story matches the contents of the external file.

To display the Links dialog box, choose Links from the File menu or press Shift-Ctrl-D. Your dialog box should be similar to the one shown in Figure 9.15. As you can see, PageMaker automatically lists BROCHTXT and LETHEAD1 as linked files.

The process of file linking is automatic, but the process of updating the story to match the linked file is not—you must explicitly issue that command. Right now your text file matches your story, so the Status message reads

This item is up to date.

When you make a change to the external file, the Status message reads

The linked file has been modified since the last time it was placed.

The Update All button reimports all linked files.

You can also tell PageMaker to automatically replace the internal version of the story with the changed external file. Click on the Link Options command button in the Links dialog box to display the Links Options dialog box, and then turn on the Update Automatically option. Whenever you open the publication, the story will automatically reflect any changes made in the text file. You may also want to turn on the Alert Before Updating option, so that as you open a file, PageMaker notifies you

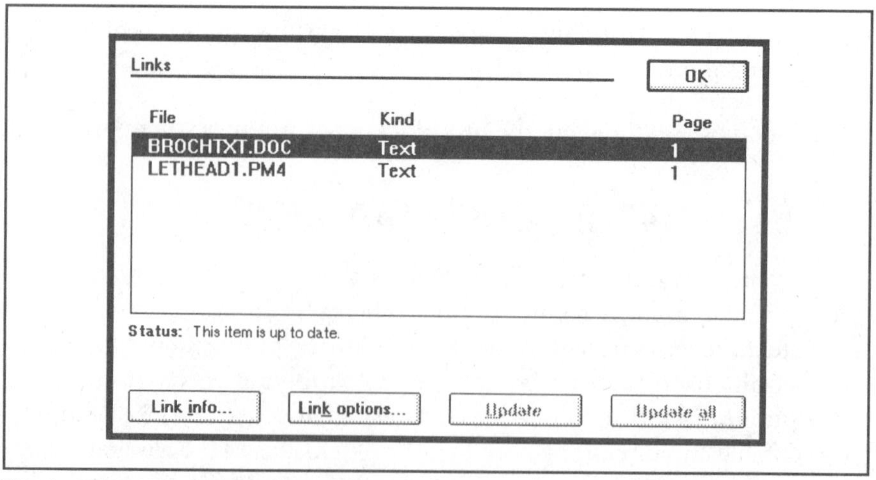

Figure 9.15: The Links dialog box

when a story needs updating. You can then cancel the updating if you want to leave the story as it is.

You might *not* want the story updated with the new external file if you have made any changes to it in PageMaker. If both the internal story and the external text file have been changed, you have a problem: which version do you go with? If you replace the story with the linked file, you lose any edits you made to the internal story. With the Update Automatically option turned on, PageMaker always warns you when the internal and external versions of the text have both been modified. Figure 9.16 shows this dialog box.

To get information about the text file, click on the Link Info command button in the Links dialog box. The Link Info dialog box, shown in Figure 9.17, lets you know when the file was originally placed, when it was last modified, and when (if applicable) the contents of the internal copy were last modified. You can also use this dialog box to link and import a different text file in the place of the current one; just select a different file in the Files/Directories list.

Another way to get to the Link Info and Link Options dialog boxes is through the Element menu. You must select part of the story (with either the pointer or text tool) before choosing these commands. If you don't, the Link Info option will not be available, and the changes you make to the Link Options dialog box will change the defaults for any new stories you place, but they won't affect existing stories.

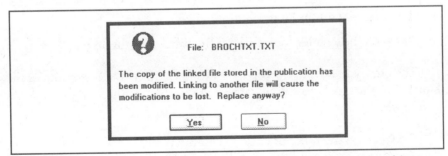

Figure 9.16: A warning box that appears when both the internal and external versions of the text have been changed

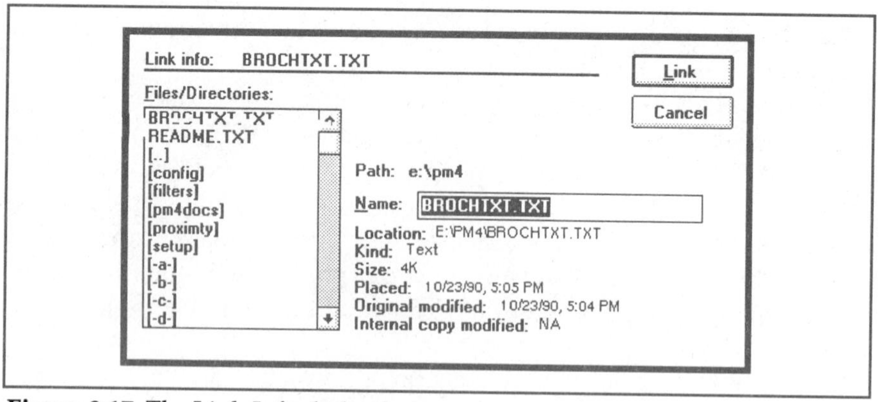

Figure 9.17: The Link Info dialog box

PLAYING WITH TEXT BLOCKS

As you flow text into different columns, the story is divided into multiple text blocks, one text block per column. These text blocks are connected to one another, as indicated by the plus sign (+) in the window shade handles. When you see a + in the handle, the text block is *threaded* (connected) to another text block in the same story. Threaded text blocks are part of the same story.

Let's take a look at the text blocks in your BROCHURE publication.

1. Go to page 1, in Fit in Window view.

2. With the pointer tool, click on the third column on page 1.

The empty handle at the top indicates that this is the beginning of the story. The + at the bottom indicates that the story is threaded to another text block.

3. Click on the brochure title in column 2.

The empty window shade handles indicate that this text block is not connected to any other block. This text block is a complete story (albeit, a short one).

4. Go to page 2, and switch to Fit in Window view.

5. Click on each column and look at the window shade handles at the top and bottom of the text block.

You'll see that all the text blocks are threaded together. The advantage to threaded text blocks is that the copy flows freely from one block to another. When you format the text or change the size of a text block, the text automatically reflows between text blocks. If, for example, you shorten a text block, the overflow is automatically sent to the next block, which then pushes text into the third block. This rippling effect continues to the end of the story. If the last text block is not large enough to accommodate the additional text, a triangle appears in the bottom window shade handle, notifying you that additional text needs to be placed.

Shortening Text Blocks

Now let's shorten a text block in your brochure so that you can see the automatic reflow of threaded text. Follow these steps:

1. Switch to 75% view.

2. Select the first column on page 2.

3. Drag the bottom window shade up until the text block is about half its original length.

When you release the mouse button, you can see that the text reflowed into the other columns.

Separating a Text Block

There are several situations in which you will need to divide a text block into two smaller, separate blocks. Adding a graphic or pull-quote to a column is probably the most common reason to separate a text block. Figure 9.18 shows two separate text blocks in the first column, with space in between.

Try this technique with your brochure so that the second page resembles Figure 9.18:

1. If you haven't done so already, follow the steps in the previous section to shorten the text block in the first column of page 2.

2. Click on the bottom window shade handle to load the text gun.

3. Shoot the gun where you want the second block to go. You can also drag-place the text if you don't want the text to fill the rest of the column.

Combining Text Blocks

Sometimes, after you have separated a text block into multiple blocks, you will want to recombine them into a single text block. Your first instinct

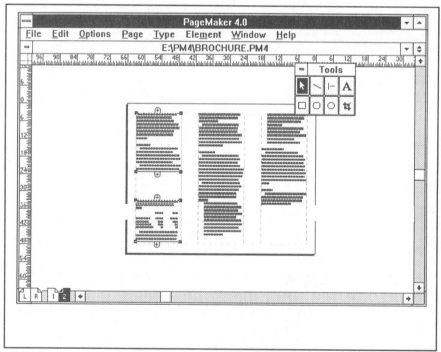

Figure 9.18: A text block that has been divided into two

might be to move the text blocks so that they are close together, but this technique still leaves two separate text blocks. Your second instinct might be to delete the lower text block and resize the upper one, but this deletes the text in the lower block. The process of combining text blocks is not at all intuitive, so you will just have to memorize the steps or refer back to this section when you need to do it.

Follow these steps to recombine the two text blocks in the first column:

1. With the pointer tool, select the second text block.

2. Drag the bottom window shade up until it meets the top window shade.

If you do this correctly, the text in the block disappears (although it is still there). Make sure your text block looks like Figure 9.19 before you

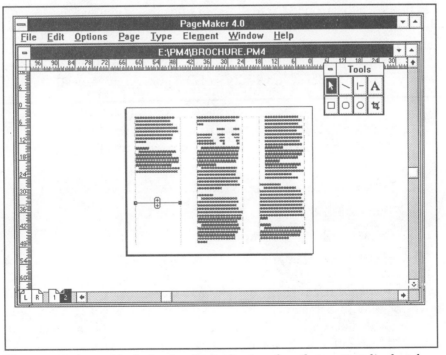

Figure 9.19: A text block that has been shortened so that no text displays between window shade handles

proceed. If you still see a line or two of text, shorten the block until it is entirely collapsed upon itself.

3. Select the first text block.

4. Drag the bottom window shade handle to the bottom of the column.

When you release the mouse button, the text is now contained in a single block in column 1. To summarize, in order to combine two text blocks, you must collapse the lower block into nothingness and then run over it with the upper block.

Threading a Text Block

Occasionally, you will inadvertently create a separate text block that was supposed to be connected to the main story. If, say, you click the I-beam outside a text block to which you intended to add the text, that text becomes its own story in its own block, not threaded to the main story.

The best way to understand this mistake is to make it. In the following steps, you will add Blue Chip Realty's phone number underneath the last paragraph in the story.

1. With the text tool in Actual Size view, click underneath the last paragraph in the third column, allowing about a line of white space above the cursor.

2. Press F6 to turn on the bold style.

3. Type **(415) 555-CHIP**.

4. Press Ctrl-Shift-C to center the line.

5. Switch to the pointer tool and click on the phone number.

The empty window shade handles indicate that this text block is its own story. Because it is not threaded to the preceding paragraph, it will not flow with the main story. This could create future problems when you change the size of other text blocks or reformat the text. As Figure 9.20

shows, text from the main story could actually flow over this unthreaded text block.

To make the unthreaded text block part of the main story, you need to cut the block with the pointer tool and then paste it with the text tool. The phone number should already be selected with the pointer tool.

6. Pull down the Edit menu and choose Cut. The text block is sent to the Clipboard.

7. Switch to the text tool.

8. Click at the end of the last paragraph in the main story and press Enter twice.

This is actually what you should have done before typing the phone number in the first place. If you had, you would not have created the separate text block.

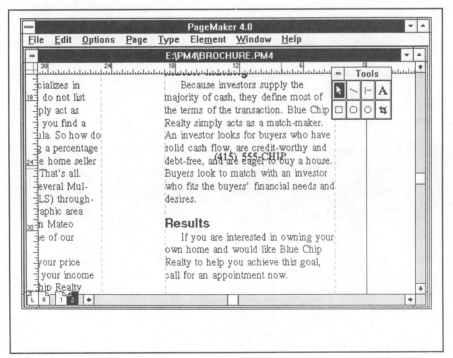

Figure 9.20: One story flowing over another

9. Pull down the Edit menu and choose Paste. The phone number is pasted from the Clipboard.

10. Switch to the pointer tool and click on the phone number.

As you can see from the text block handles, the phone number is now part of the main story. If the text you want to rethread is in more than one text block, select all text blocks (by pressing Shift as you click on each block) before cutting it to the Clipboard.

11. Since we are finished working on the brochure for now, close BROCHURE.PM4 without saving the changes you made in this chapter.

Unthreading a Text Block

In the previous exercise, you "accidentally" created an unthreaded text block. There may be times, however, when you want to purposely disconnect text from a story. For example, you may have imported a text file that is made up of two articles. When you place this file, it is a single, threaded story. Because you want to place each article separately, you need to unthread one of the articles so that it is in its own story.

To unthread text, follow these general steps:

1. With the pointer tool, select the text blocks you want to unthread.

2. Cut the text blocks to the Clipboard.

3. Display the first page on which you want the unthreaded text to appear.

4. With no text selected, paste from the Clipboard.

After you perform the above steps, the group of pasted text blocks becomes its own story, completely unrelated to the original story.

Drawing a Text Box

At the beginning of this book, we mentioned that you could use the pasteboard as a temporary storage area for text and graphics until you are ready to place them on the page. For example, you might want to type a headline or caption on the pasteboard and then move it into position later.

When you type text to the right of the page, the width of the text block is equivalent to the active page area (the area between the margin guides). The first text block in Figure 9.21 shows you how wide this block is—much wider than it needs to be. Because this extra-wide block would be cumbersome to work with, you would want to drag one of the right text block handles to narrow the block, either before or after you moved the block onto the page.

An alternative is to draw a *text box* the approximate width of the text before you begin typing. The second text block in Figure 9.21 was created with this method. To draw a text box, follow these general steps:

1. Switch to the text tool.

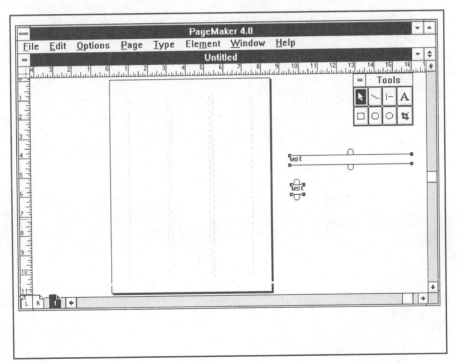

Figure 9.21: The first text block is the default width; the second block's width was defined before the text was typed

2. Click on the page or pasteboard where you wish to type the text, and then draw a box by dragging down and to the right.

3. When the box is the size of the text block you will be typing, release the mouse button.

Although the text box disappears as soon as you release the mouse button, PageMaker remembers its size when you type. If the text is longer than the invisible text box, it will word wrap, just as if you were typing the text between column guides.

In the previous chapters in this book, you have used PageMaker in somewhat of a vacuum. All text and graphics came from inside PageMaker. In this chapter, you started bringing the outside world into PageMaker. In most publications, especially the longer ones, the main text will be imported from an external text file, so the techniques and concepts discussed in this chapter are important ones.

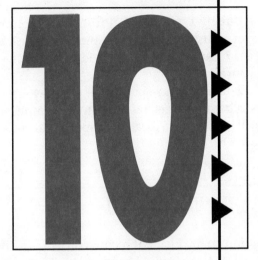

ADVANCED
TEXT
FORMATTING
TECHNIQUES

You have already learned many typographical formatting controls, such as the ones in Chapter 5 for adjusting fonts, sizes, and type styles, and the leading controls in Chapter 7. But PageMaker provides more ways to fine tune the appearance of your type.

This chapter describes how to adjust the spacing between letters and words in PageMaker. However, before we get into these more complicated aspects of typography, you will learn how to create two special effects with your type: rotated text and drop caps.

ROTATING TEXT

With the Text Rotation option on the Element menu, you can flip a text block in 90-degree increments. Use this option when you want part of the page oriented differently. Figure 10.1 shows an example of using rotated text for a headline.

Note that this option is not for rotating all the text in a publication; if this is what you have in mind, change the page orientation in the Target Printer Setup dialog box. Also, if you want slanted rather than rotated text, create it in your graphics program and import it as a graphic.

In Chapter 9, you placed the company name and address in column 1 of the brochure. If you rotate this text, it becomes a return address, and you can use the brochure as a self-mailer. Follow these steps to rotate the text on the brochure's back panel:

1. Open the BROCHURE.PM4 publication.

2. With the pointer tool, select the address block.

3. Pull down the Element menu and choose Text Rotation.

The Text Rotation dialog box, shown in Figure 10.2, illustrates the only ways PageMaker can flip the text block. The first option is the current rotation (none). The second option rotates the block 90 degrees counterclockwise. The third option flips the text upside down. The fourth option rotates the block 90 degrees clockwise.

4. The return address needs to be rotated 90 degrees clockwise, so choose the fourth option.

5. Choose OK.

6. Switch to 75% view so that you can see the rotated text.

Notice that the text block no longer has window shades; instead, it has small selection boxes around it. These are the same handles that appear on

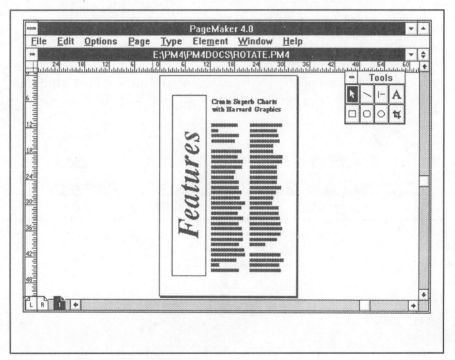

Figure 10.1: A rotated headline

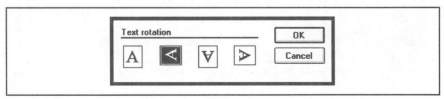

Figure 10.2: The Text Rotation dialog box

a selected graphic. Rotated text is similar to an imported graphic in that you cannot edit or format it with the text tool. However, unlike imported graphics, you can edit the rotated text in the Story Editor.

7. Move the rotated text block so that it lines up with the column guides in the upper-right corner, as shown in Figure 10.3.

8. Save the file.

9. Print page 1 to see how the rotated text looks.

Note that you cannot rotate part of a text block, text selected with the text tool, or a threaded text block (the text block must be a complete story). Also, on some printers, rotated text has a lower print quality. The characters look somewhat spindly on the HP LaserJet II and other PCL printers, unless you are using a type manager such as Adobe Type Manager or Facelift.

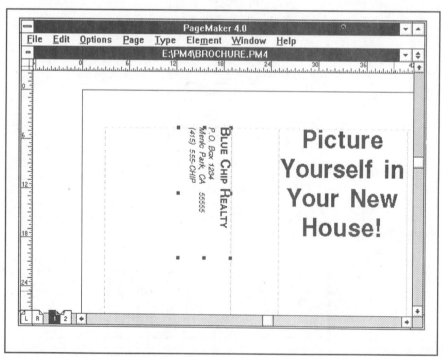

Figure 10.3: The rotated address block

CREATING DROP CAPS

A dropped capital letter, called a *drop cap,* is the first character of a paragraph that has been enlarged and hangs down into the body of a paragraph. They are frequently used at the beginning of a story or to introduce new sections of a story, as shown in Figure 10.4. When set correctly, drop caps add a professional touch to your publication.

There are several ways you can produce drop caps in PageMaker, but none of them are easy or elegant. The PageMaker *Reference Guide* suggests that you make the drop cap a separate text block, but this causes problems if the text reflows, because the drop cap will not flow with its paragraph. A different method, which uses typographical position controls, creates a drop cap that flows with the paragraph.

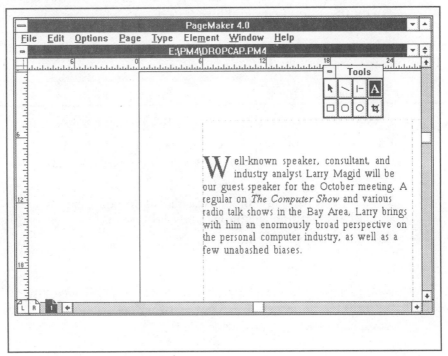

Figure 10.4: A drop cap

In the following steps, you will create two different types of enlarged caps: a drop cap and a standing cap. But first you need to do some preparation.

1. In a new publication, create two column guides.

2. In the first column, type the following paragraph, formatting the text as 12-point Times Roman with 14-point leading.

   Well-known speaker, consultant, and industry analyst Larry Magid will be our guest speaker for the October meeting. A regular on *The Computer Show* and various radio talk shows in the Bay Area, Larry brings with him an enormously broad perspective on the personal computer industry, as well as a few unabashed biases.

3. Copy the paragraph and paste it somewhere else, such as in column 2. (At the end of this section, you will create a standing cap for this second paragraph.)

Now that your housekeeping is out of the way, you are ready to create the drop cap shown in Figure 10.4.

4. Select the first letter of the first paragraph (the *W*).

5. Press Ctrl-T to display the Type Specifications dialog box.

6. Enlarge this character to three times the size of the body text: 36 points. (Drop caps are typically two to four times the size of the body text.)

7. Make sure the leading is the same as that of the body text: 14 points. (Auto leading will throw off the spacing of the paragraph.)

8. In the Position drop-down list, choose Subscript.

9. Choose the Options command button.

10. Next to Super/Subscript Size, type **100**. This setting makes the subscripted character 100 percent of the point size; in other words, the actual point size specified.

11. Next to Subscript Position, type **42**. (After the exercise, we will discuss how we arrived at this value.)

12. Hold down Alt and choose OK.

At this stage, the drop cap is embedded in the paragraph, and the text overlaps the enlarged letter. To wrap the text around the drop cap, you will use tabs.

13. Place the cursor before the *e* in *Well* and press Tab.

14. Press Ctrl-I and set a tab at 3p0. This position will vary according to the size of the character. The *W* is one of the widest characters, so it requires a bigger tab setting than most.

15. Close the Indents/Tabs dialog box.

16. Press End to go to the end of the line, and press Shift-Enter to create a line break.

17. Press Tab to indent the next line.

If part of the *W* disappears, redraw the screen by issuing a page view command. You don't have to switch to a different view. For example, if you are in Actual Size view, press Ctrl-1 to redraw the screen. The drop cap will then appear in entirety.

For larger drop caps, you may have to indent additional lines of text. Repeat steps 16 and 17 as necessary.

Now that your drop cap is finished, you can experiment with a much simpler effect: a standing or raised cap. As shown in Figure 10.5, a standing cap simply has a larger point size than the body text. Just select the *W* and enlarge it—that's all there is to it. You don't have to worry about subscript settings or tabs. Again, the capital letter should have the same leading as the body text.

18. To create the standing cap shown in Figure 10.5, select the *W* in the second copy of the paragraph. Press Ctrl-T and set the capital letter in 36 points with 14-point leading.

Now it's time to explain how we came up with the value for the drop cap's Subscript Position option. This value varies depending on the font,

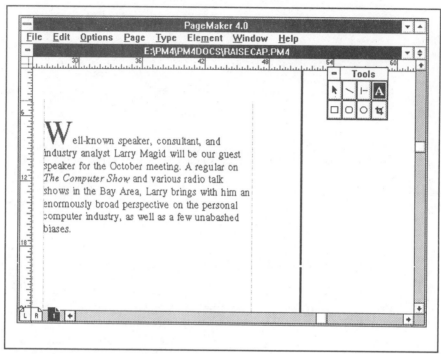

Figure 10.5: A standing cap

size, and leading you are using for the drop cap and the body text. You must adjust the number until the drop cap is embedded in the text properly. After trying several values, we discovered 42% works for this example.

Ideally, the top of the drop cap should line up with the ascenders in the body text, and the bottom should be on the text baseline. The ruler guides in Figure 10.6 illustrate the desired alignment. If the drop cap is too large, you can decrease the Super/Subscript Size value. To get the exact alignment shown in the figure, we set the Super/Subscript Size to 90% and the Subscript Position to 37%.

Although drop caps require a bit of guesswork, once you determine the correct values, you can use the same type specifications for each drop cap in the publication.

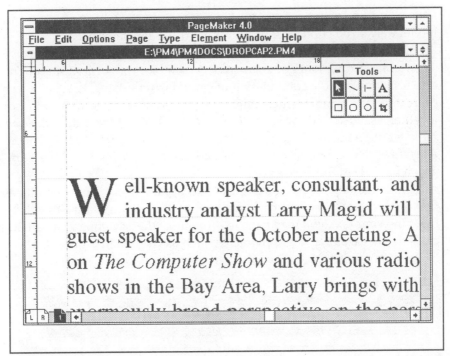

Figure 10.6: Align the drop cap with the body text

ADJUSTING
HORIZONTAL SPACING

PageMaker provides several ways to control the horizontal spacing—the space between words and letters— of your text. Two factors that affect horizontal spacing are alignment and hyphenation. You learned about these controls in Chapter 7. In the following sections, you will learn about kerning, tracking, condensing and expanding character widths, and changing the default word and letter spacing.

Kerning Text

In Figure 10.5, notice the large gap between the enlarged capital *W* and the letter *e*. PageMaker tries hard to correctly control the space between letters, and under normal circumstances, such as straight body copy and moderately sized subheads, its efforts are quite satisfactory.

Not only does PageMaker know how wide each character is, but it also knows that certain pairs of characters need a bit more or less space. The classic example is the combination of capital letters *A* and *V*. When these characters are together, their angles require that they be moved closer together, as illustrated in Figure 10.7. By default, PageMaker does this *pair kerning* automatically. You can see the Pair Kerning setting in the Spacing Attributes dialog box (press Ctrl-M and choose Spacing from the Paragraph Specifications dialog box).

Unfortunately, PageMaker doesn't recognize every single combination of characters, in every conceivable font, that requires adjustment. To fine tune your text, you may have to do some of the adjusting yourself. Increasing the size of a single character, such as the one in Figure 10.5, is a likely situation in which manual letter spacing, or *kerning*, is needed.

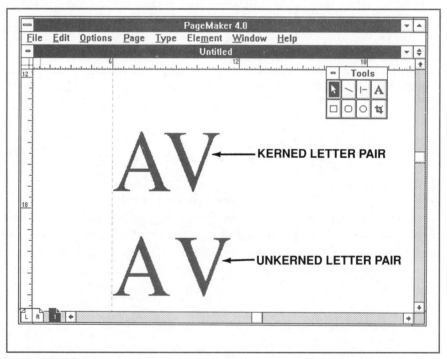

Figure 10.7: The first set of characters is kerned; the second set is not

To kern two characters, place the cursor between the characters and press Ctrl-minus on the number pad to bring the characters closer together. Press Ctrl-minus until you achieve the desired letter spacing. If you bring them too close together, you can press Ctrl-plus to "unkern" the characters.

Now let's try this technique to kern the standing cap *W* you created earlier with the letter that follows it:

1. Place the cursor between the *W* and the *e*.

2. Press Ctrl-minus three times. Figure 10.8 shows the result.

Kerning usually requires accurate screen fonts and some trial and error. You won't really know for sure how accurately you kerned the characters until you print the page. The more accurate your screen display, the fewer rounds of test prints you are likely to need. (Adobe Type Manager's

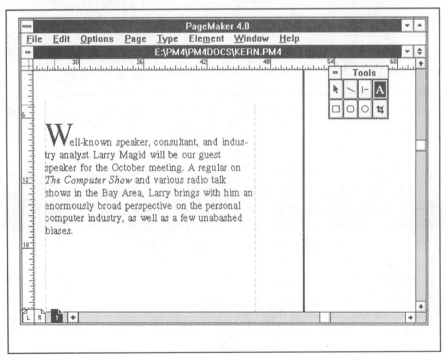

Figure 10.8: The raised capital letter after kerning

screen fonts, which were used for most of the figures in this book, are quite good; see Appendix C for details.)

Tracking Letter Spacing

Another way to adjust letter spacing is with *tracking*. PageMaker's tracking feature lets you adjust the spacing of a selected range of text, such as complete lines or entire paragraphs. If your story is too long to fit in a required amount of space, you can tighten the letter spacing in the story. Large type sizes typically have too much space between the characters; use tracking to tighten up the spacing. Looser spacing is sometimes used for special effects.

Five different levels of tracking are available, as illustrated in Figure 10.9. In the figure, notice that the paragraph's length varies from seven to nine lines, depending on the tracking. By default, PageMaker doesn't use any tracking. Normal tracking is a little tighter than no tracking at all.

You can specify tracking either through the Track option on the Type menu or in the Type Specifications (Ctrl-T) dialog box. First select the quantity of text whose letter spacing you want to change, and then specify the tracking level.

CHANGING
THE CHARACTER WIDTH

The Set Width option, which appears on the Type pull-down menu and in the Type Specifications dialog box, changes the width of the letters as well as the spacing between them. The height of the characters—the type size—remains constant. All character and space widths are changed proportionally so the font is not distorted.

Figure 10.10 shows how different the same type size (36 points) looks with varying character widths. By changing the character width, you give the illusion of choosing a different type size.

You set the width as a percentage of the normal width. To create narrower characters, enter a value less than 100 for Set Width; to create wider characters, enter a value over 100. The standard settings are 70, 80, 90, 110,

No Tracking:

Well-known speaker, consultant and industry analyst Larry Magid will be the speaker for October. A regular on The Computer Show and various radio talk shows in the Bay Area, Larry brings with him an enormously broad perspective on the personal computer industry, as well as a few unabashed biases.

Very Loose Tracking:

Well-known speaker, consultant and industry analyst Larry Magid will be the speaker for October. A regular on The Computer Show and various radio talk shows in the Bay Area, Larry brings with him an enormously broad perspective on the personal computer industry, as well as a few unabashed biases.

Very Tight Tracking:

Well-known speaker, consultant and industry analyst Larry Magid will be the speaker for October. A regular on The Computer Show and various radio talk shows in the Bay Area, Larry brings with him an enormously broad perspective on the personal computer industry, as well as a few unabashed biases.

Normal Tracking:

Well-known speaker, consultant and industry analyst Larry Magid will be the speaker for October. A regular on The Computer Show and various radio talk shows in the Bay Area, Larry brings with him an enormously broad perspective on the personal computer industry, as well as a few unabashed biases.

Loose Tracking:

Well-known speaker, consultant and industry analyst Larry Magid will be the speaker for October. A regular on The Computer Show and various radio talk shows in the Bay Area, Larry brings with him an enormously broad perspective on the personal computer industry, as well as a few unabashed biases.

Tight Tracking:

Well-known speaker, consultant and industry analyst Larry Magid will be the speaker for October. A regular on The Computer Show and various radio talk shows in the Bay Area, Larry brings with him an enormously broad perspective on the personal computer industry, as well as a few unabashed biases.

Figure 10.9: A comparison of tracking levels

70%

80%

90%

Normal

110%

120%

130%

Picture Yourself in Your New House!

Picture Yourself in Your New House!

Picture Yourself in Your New House!

Picture Yourself in Your New House!

Picture Yourself in Your New House!

Picture Yourself in Your New House!

Picture Yourself in Your New House!

Figure 10.10: Proportional character-width changes

120, and 130; however, you can enter any value in $\frac{1}{10}$% increments, up to 250%.

Adjusting Word and Letter Spacing

Another way to control horizontal spacing is through the Spacing Attributes dialog box. (Spacing is a command button in the Paragraph Specifications dialog box.) The Spacing Attributes dialog box, shown in Figure 10.11, lets you define the range of acceptable intra-word and intra-letter spacing. Before you dive into this section, be aware that word and letter spacing are not easy concepts to grasp, and only the most diligent (and brave) typographers will find it necessary to venture into the Spacing Attributes box.

The word spacing values are based on the font's *space band*, which is the amount of space created when you press the spacebar. In word spacing, the default Desired value is 100%. This means that PageMaker tries to keep the space between words equivalent to the size of the font's space band. If you want more or less space between words, you can adjust the Desired value.

When text is justified, PageMaker frequently needs to manipulate the word spacing to something other than the Desired value. It might need to shave off or add a little space between words. The Minimum and Maximum values tell PageMaker exactly how much space it can add or subtract.

A Minimum value of 50% word space indicates that you will allow the intra-word space to be as small as half of the font's space band. A Maximum

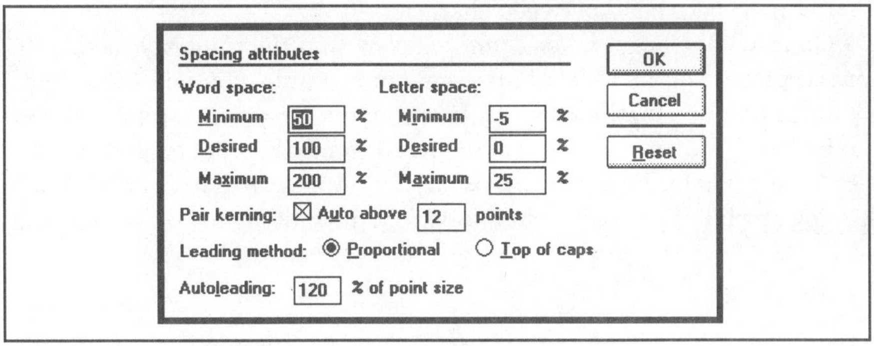

Figure 10.11: The Spacing Attributes dialog box

value of 200% indicates that you will accept a space that is twice the width of the font's space band. By decreasing the Minimum value, you are saying that you are willing to accept a smaller amount of space between words. When you increase the Maximum value, you are likely to see larger gaps between words.

Figure 10.12 compares different word spacing percentages, using extreme values so that you can easily discern the differences. The Desired, Minimum, and Maximum word space settings for each paragraph are shown above it. Notice how the paragraph is longer with 200% word spacing, which places two space bands between each word.

The letter spacing values are entered as percentages of the font's space band. Ideally, each character uses the exact space built into the character; this built-in space is called its *pen advance*. Pen advance is measured from the left edge of one character to the left edge of the next character. The Desired value of 0% indicates that no extra space should be added between letters. Zero percent is the ideal, but PageMaker needs to cheat sometimes to accommodate all the different character widths in a line. It's up to you to tell PageMaker just how much it can cheat.

The Minimum value for letter spacing (entered as a negative number) defines the amount of space you will allow PageMaker to remove from the normal pen advance when necessary. These numbers are not percentages of the pen advance; they are percentages of the space band. Thus, the default value of –5% indicates that character spacing can be narrowed by as much as 5% of the space band. The Maximum value defines the greatest amount of space that can be added to the normal pen advance. The default Maximum value of 25% means that you will allow PageMaker to insert a quarter of a space band between characters.

Occasionally, PageMaker cannot stay within the ranges you specify for acceptable word and letter spacing. For example, you will sometimes see lines that are too loose (with lots of white space in the line) when hyphenation is turned off, or when a word cannot be hyphenated.

To help you locate the lines in which PageMaker had to override your spacing attributes, choose Preferences from the Edit menu and turn on the

Loose/Tight Lines option in the Preferences dialog box. The lines that are looser or tighter than the range in the Spacing Attributes dialog box are then shaded in the publication, as shown in Figure 10.13. You might choose to kern or track these particular lines or to change the hyphenation.

Default Spacing: Desired 100%, Min 50%, Max 200%

Because investors supply the majority of cash, they define most of the terms of the transaction. Blue Chip Realty simply acts as a matchmaker. An investor looks for buyers who have solid cash flow, are credit worthy and debt-free, and are eager to buy a house. Buyers look to match with an investor who fits the buyers' financial needs and desires.

Desired 25%, Min 25%, Max 25%

Because investors supply the majority of cash, they define most of the terms of the transaction. Blue Chip Realty simply acts as a matchmaker. An investor looks for buyers who have solid cash flow, are credit worthy and debt-free, and are eager to buy a house. Buyers look to match with an investor who fits the buyers' financial needs and desires.

Desired 100%, Min 100%, Max 100%

Because investors supply the majority of cash, they define most of the terms of the transaction. Blue Chip Realty simply acts as a matchmaker. An investor looks for buyers who have solid cash flow, are credit worthy and debt-free, and are eager to buy a house. Buyers look to match with an investor who fits the buyers' financial needs and desires.

Desired 200%, Min 200%, Max 200%

Because investors supply the majority of cash, they define most of the terms of the transaction. Blue Chip Realty simply acts as a matchmaker. An investor looks for buyers who have solid cash flow, are credit worthy and debt-free, and are eager to buy a house. Buyers look to match with an investor who fits the buyers' financial needs and desires.

Figure 10.12: Comparison of word spacing percentages

Depending upon your experience with typography, the letter and word spacing could make all the difference in the world or none at all. Rest assured, however, that virtually all documents will have readers who notice and appreciate good kerning.

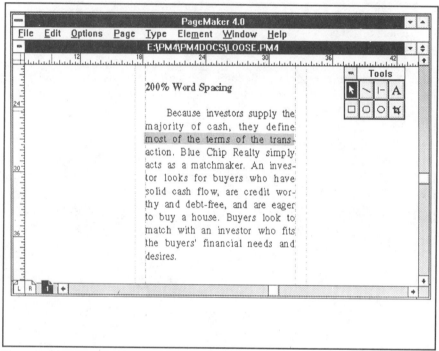

Figure 10.13: Lines that are too loose or too tight are shaded

PART THREE

WORKING
WITH
GRAPHICS

In this part, you will learn how to enhance your publication with graphic elements—ranging from a vertical rule between columns to detailed drawings. In the first two chapters, you will learn how to create graphics with PageMaker's built-in drawing tools and import images created with graphics programs. Chapter 13 explains how to use the Table Editor that comes with PageMaker. It is grouped with the graphics topics because a columnar table becomes a graphic element once you enhance it with lines and shades, and like a graphic image, a Table Editor table must be imported into PageMaker.

C H A P T E R

11

USING
THE
GRAPHICS
TOOLS

This chapter concentrates on the interesting ways graphic elements can liven up your publications. After a brief review of the PageMaker toolbox drawing tools, you'll learn how to set different line widths and styles and how to create graphic effects with fills. We'll also describe how to create two kinds of graphics that will flow with your text: paragraph rules and inline graphics. Finally, you'll learn how to add color to your publications.

In the exercises in this chapter, you will create graphic elements in a short newsletter. The newsletter is shown in Figures 11.1 through 11.4. To save time, you do not need to type, import, and format the text files (unless you would like the practice).

DRAWING GRAPHICS

You've already had some practice creating graphics with PageMaker's tools, and you've seen that they are easy to use. The following sections provide more details on some of the techniques you've used in earlier chapters.

Tool Review

Figure 11.5 identifies each drawing tool in the toolbox. Here's a review of their functions:

- The diagonal-line tool draws a line in any direction.

- The perpendicular-line tool restricts the line angle to increments of 45 degrees. Use it to create horizontal and vertical rules.

- The square-corner and rounded-corner tools draw a box with either square or round corners. To create a square, hold down the Shift key as you draw.

- The circle/oval tool creates circular shapes. By holding down the Shift key as you draw, you can produce a perfect circle.

CLUB NEWS

ReliefWare Auction

While many of us have supported the October 17 earthquake recovery efforts personally, SPAUG was unable to coordinate a proper response last month simply because of the chronology of the events; the quake occurred only one week before the October meeting.

But it is never too late to stretch out a hand, and this month SPAUG calls upon all of its members to participate in ReliefWare '89: An Auction for Action.

Its success depends upon you, the people who will donate computer-related items and buy them. The proceeds will be sent directly to the American Red Cross South Bay Headquarters.

October Meeting

Our meeting started out with a demonstration of three programs. The first, VCD, allows you to visually change directories by moving the cursor around a graphic tree structure. ZDIR displays a directory listing that indicates how much space the files take (unlike DIR which only tells you how much space is remaining). DIRNOTES gives you a way to append comments to filenames, and then view these comments.

Nov - Jan Calendar

Figure 11.1: Page 2 of the newsletter

Several representatives from Technology Concepts demonstrated their unique product called Fax Line Manager. This hardware device enables you to use a fax, a modem, and an answering machine on a single phone line. With this product, you do not have to pay for a dedicated phone line.

The Fax Line Manager automates the answering and detecting process and routes the call accordingly. After the first ring, the device picks up and listens for a tone. If it hears the fax tone, the call will be routed to the fax machine. If it hears a touch tone, it will be routed to the modem. If no tones are detected, the answering machine picks up.

Membership Renewals

For the two months preceding the expiration of your membership you will find a renewal envelope enclosed in your newsletter. Use this envelope to promptly send in your $25 check so that you won't miss an issue of the monthly newsletter.

No December Meeting

Because of the holidays, the club traditionally does not meet in December, nor is the newsletter published. Expect your next PRinT SCreen at the end of January.

This Month

This Meeting Features Us!

In somewhat of a break from tradition, this month's guest will be the inanimate objects that make up the heart and soul of our group: our bulletin board and newsletter.

Now that SPARC has received a facelift, it is time to show it off, and in conjunction with our Disk of the Month, you will be treated to a tour of the bulletin board and all of its nooks and crannies. Those of you who are a bit shy of SPARC, come out and see how easy it can be.

Members will also get to see how the newsletter is put together on the computer.

Disk of the Month

ProComm, the phenomenally popular shareware telecommunications program, will be demonstrated. It is the perfect companion to SPARC. The disk will be available for $1 or you may use your Goodie Coupon.

The Giveaway

Due to our ReliefWare efforts, there will not be a giveaway this month. All products received will be donated directly to the ReliefWare auction.

Figure 11.2: Page 3 of the newsletter

We Love Our Lunchboxes

A New Class of Machine
Makes a Big Impression
On Our Editors

My Lunchbox Does Lotus

by Becky Altman

I bought an AT-compatible portable computer about nine months ago but I've been waiting to write about it to give it time for problems to crop up. I'm still waiting...

My portable is a Sharp PC-7200 and I love it. Because of its size and shape, it's nicknamed a "lunchbox computer." There's nothing especially fancy or powerful about it, but it was cheap ($1500) and it has everything I need. In particular, the machine has a 20-MB hard drive, a high-density 5-1/4" floppy, an 80286 processor, a super-twist backlit LCD display.

Lotus 1-2-3 Release 3 was my impetus for buying a new computer. My desktop computer is an 8088 with a turbo card but Release 3 needs an actual 80286 processor. I decided to buy a portable so that I could lug the computer between my home and office. I also wanted a computer with a 5-1/4" drive so that I could easily exchange data with my desktop computer that has only 5-1/4" drives. The Sharp PC-7200 was the answer.

As it turns out, I don't lug the computer between my home and office all that much. Although my lunchbox stays at home most of the time, its compactness still comes in handy; when I'm not using the computer, I can close the computer up and tuck it away out of sight.

Two computers are useful for many of my writing projects. Sometimes I'll work on one computer while the other computer is printing. Or, I may be writing about one

I bought my

portable last year

but I've been waiting

to write about it to

give it time for

problems to crop up.

I'm still waiting...

Figure 11.3: Page 4 of the newsletter

program while word processing in another. I can use one computer for word processing and the other for the program I am writing about. It sure beats loading and exiting programs every five minutes. I guess this is one alternative to multitasking operating environments such as OS/2 and Desqview!

The computer has a serial port, a parallel port, and an outlet for connecting the portable to an external monitor. It has one free internal slot.

I would highly recommend the Sharp to those on a budget who do not need a super-fast computer with a high-resolution screen. My Sharp has a 10 MHz CPU and a screen that can be switched between monochrome and CGA. Now, if you have more money to burn, you can plunk down $5000 like Rick did...

My Lunchbox Does Everything

by Rick Altman

My lunchbox weighs barely over 20 pounds like Becky's but it is more powerful than most people's first computer. Inside my portable is a 20 Mhz 386 processor, 4 MB of motherboard memory, an additional 3 MB on an expansion card, a 40 MB hard drive, and a VGA Plasma display that can be viewed from any angle. It has EGA and VGA video outputs, two expansion

slots, and so far it has run absolutely every piece of software that I have thrown at it.

Manufactured by Dolch Computers in San Jose, my lunchbox fills a different need than Becky's: mine is for off-site seminars and presentations (like the one I did for the group last month). The more seminars I conducted, the more I tired of bringing a box of floppy disks, installing software, and praying that the presentation would work the way it did on my home computer when I prepared for it. Now I do all of my prep work on the Dolch, close it up, throw it in the car, and I'm ready to demo.

I specifically sought a computer that could hold large quantities of memory so that I could run my applications under Desqview, the multitasking software that allows me to load and store multiple programs in memory. If I digress in the middle of a talk, or if I'm asked an off-the-subject question, I can freeze the current program in memory, start a second one and digress to my heart's content. When it's time to come back on track, two keystrokes brings me right back to the point where I left off. This kind of capability is invaluable in longer presentations, and I am delighted that I found a portable computer that can provide it for me.

Figure 11.4: Page 5 of the newsletter

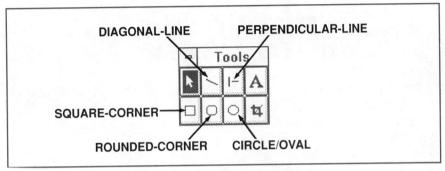

Figure 11.5: The drawing tools

After you choose one of the drawing tools, the pointer becomes a cross-bar shape when you move it onto the page or pasteboard. You draw by clicking and dragging; release the mouse button when the graphic is the desired size.

Tips on Drawing Boxes

After drawing a box, you can use the Rounded Corners option on the Element menu to change the angle of the corners. With this option, you can round the corners of a square-corner box, square the corners of a rounded-corner box, or make the corners less or more round.

With either tool, you can draw a box around text. The boxed column in Figure 11.2 was created with the square-corner tool.

When you draw a box around text, remember to allow space between the lines and the text. If you draw the box on top of the column guides, you need to indent the text on the right and left. One way to indent the text is to adjust the size of the text block with the pointer tool. A more precise way is to select all the text with the text tool and set right and left paragraph indents. In Figure 11.2, 0.5 pica indents were used.

Another way to box text is with the inline graphics feature, described later in the chapter.

SETTING LINE WIDTHS AND STYLES

By default, PageMaker lines—those drawn with the line tool or outlining a shape drawn with another tool—are 1-point solid lines. The Line option on the Element menu allows you to change the width, or *weight,* and style of lines.

Making Line Specifications

You can make your line specifications before or after you draw the graphic. If you specify the line characteristics before you draw the graphic, the graphic will be drawn with that line style. To change the style after you draw a graphic, first select it by clicking on it with the pointer tool. (Actually, if you just drew the object, it's already selected.) A selected line has selection boxes, called *graphic handles,* at the beginning and end of the line. A selected shape is surrounded by eight graphic handles.

Pay close attention to which graphic element, if any, is selected when you choose line specifications. If nothing is selected, you will change the default style—this style will apply to any new lines or shapes you draw. If a line, box, or circle is selected, you will change the line specifications of that particular graphic.

A common mistake that you might make when you want to draw two lines of varying weights is to draw the first line, and then specify the weight of the second line. But because the first line is automatically selected after you draw it, you end up changing the weight of the first line, not the second one. To avoid this mistake, unselect the first line before you specify the weight of the second line. Unselect by clicking elsewhere on the page or pasteboard. This process is called *clicking off.*

Choosing the Point Size

As you can see from the Line menu, shown in Figure 11.6, lines come in a variety of point sizes, ranging from hairline (the thinnest) to 12 points.

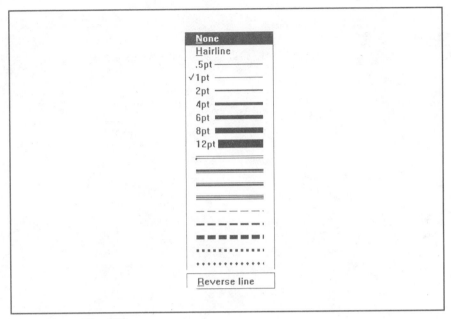

Figure 11.6: The Line menu

The memo form illustrated in Figure 11.7 uses three line weights: the line under the company name is 2 points, the series of thin lines are hairlines, and the heavy line at the bottom is 6 points.

In Figures 11.1, 11.3, and 11.4, the vertical line between the newsletter columns is a 1-point line, which is probably the maximum weight you would use for this type of line. Vertical rules are useful for separating columns, especially when the text is not justified. If you want to repeat between-column vertical rules on every page of a publication, draw them on the master pages, as explained in Chapter 14.

Selecting a Line Style

The bottom choices on the Line menu show the line styles that are available. Some of the line styles create two or three lines of varying weights. For example, one of the styles creates a 2-point line sandwiched between two hairlines.

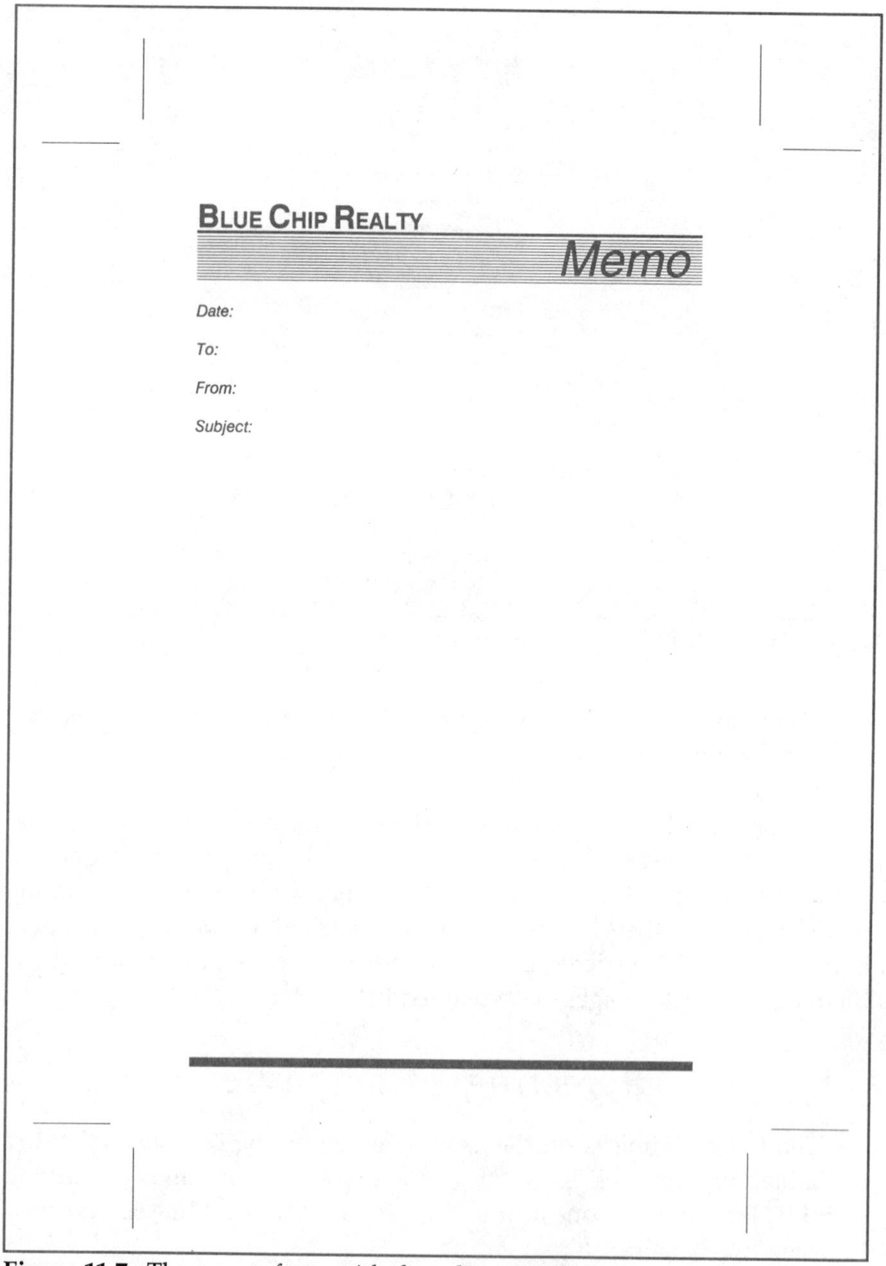

BLUE CHIP REALTY

Memo

Date:

To:

From:

Subject:

Figure 11.7: The memo form with three line weights

The dashed and dotted line styles are frequently used with boxes. Use them to enclose coupons and order forms that you want your readers to cut out.

USING FILLS

Another characteristic of a PageMaker graphic is its *fill*. A fill is a pattern that appears inside a box or circle. By default, your geometric shapes are empty. You can fill them with different shades or patterns by using the Fill menu, shown in Figure 11.8.

As with line specifications, you can make your fill specifications before or after you draw the object. Before you specify the fill, make sure the correct object is selected. Otherwise, you could fill the wrong element or change the default fill (if no object is selected).

Eight different line patterns are listed at the bottom of the Fill menu. You can create vertical, horizontal, diagonal, or criss-cross hairlines in two

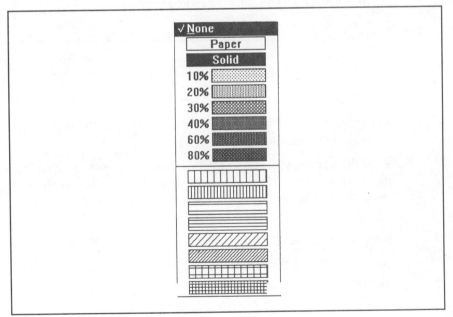

Figure 11.8: The Fill menu

different increments. The number of lines that are created depends on the size of the box you draw. The hairlines in Figure 11.7 are actually a box created with the square-corner tool, using a horizontal-line fill pattern. The following sections describe some other ways to use fills.

Using Screens to Shade Text

The percentages in the Fill menu refer to shades, or *screens*. The higher the percentage, the darker the shade. Unless you are using color, the screens are in shades of gray.

You can create an interesting effect by placing a screen behind text. In the following steps, you will create the shaded heading shown in Figure 11.9:

1. Create a publication with these specifications:

   Page dimensions: 33 by 51 picas (5½ by 8½ inches)
   Number of pages: 5
   Margins: 3 picas all the way around

2. On pages 2 through 5, set up two column guides with a 2-pica gutter.

3. At the top of the first column of page 2, type **CLUB NEWS**.

4. Specify the type as 20-point Helvetica bold.

5. Using the square-corner tool, draw a box around the heading, across both columns.

6. With the pointer tool, select the text block and position it so that its location matches Figure 11.9. Your goals are to center the text vertically inside the box and to allow a little extra space to the left of the text.

7. Select the box and choose a 30% shade from the Fill menu.

8. To remove the outline from the box, choose None from the Line menu.

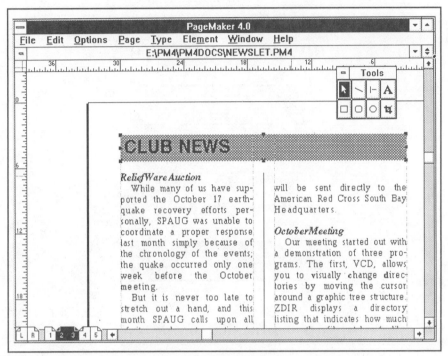

Figure 11.9: A heading that has a 30% gray shade

Because screens are actually made up of many small dots, these dots might be too noticeable on a 300-dpi laser printer. If your page contains a screen and you want the best quality, consider printing it on a high-resolution device, such as a Linotronic 1270-dpi or 2540-dpi typesetting machine. Figure 11.10 compares a 30% shade printed at 300-dpi (on an HP LaserJet II and PostScript printer) with the same shade printed on 1270- and 2540-dpi Linotronic imagesetters. Appendix D describes how to use a typesetting service bureau.

Providing a Background for Reverse Type

As explained in Chapter 5, the reverse type style switches the character color from black to white (or to the current paper color), so this white text needs to be placed against a shaded background. A solid fill, as opposed

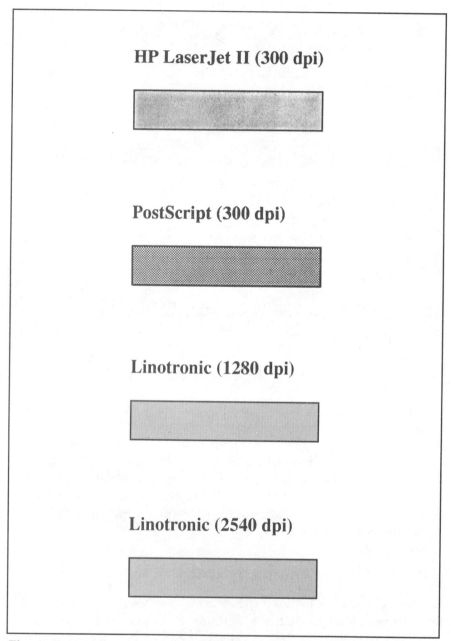

Figure 11.10: A comparison of gray shades

to a percentage shade, provides the greatest contrast and legibility. Unless you are using color, the solid shade is black (adding color is discussed later in the chapter).

The most legible reverse type is large, sans serif, and bold. Do not reverse small body text because it may be unreadable.

Creating reverse type can be difficult because at one stage you either have white text on a white background or black text on a black background. If you reverse the type first, you can't see the text, so you don't know where to draw the box. If you draw the solid-fill box around black type, you can't see the text to reverse it. To see how to solve this problem, we'll create the reversed heading shown in Figure 11.11. Follow these steps:

1. Zoom in on the top of page 3, column 2.

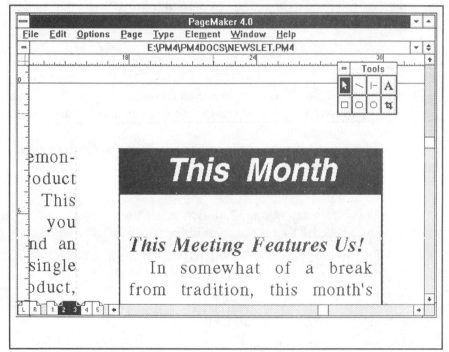

Figure 11.11: A reversed heading

2. Type **This Month** and specify the type as 18-point Helvetica bold italic. Do not reverse the text yet.

3. Center this line.

4. Draw an empty box around the text. Do not add the solid fill yet.

5. If necessary, move the text block so that it is vertically centered within the box you just drew.

6. Select the text with the text tool and then choose Reverse from the Type Style menu.

7. Select the box with the pointer tool and then fill it with the solid shade.

Sometimes when you draw a box with a shaded or solid fill over text, you will not be able to see the text because the box is overlaying it. To solve this problem, you need to place the box behind the text. Select the box and choose the Send to Back option from the Element menu.

Drawing Shadow Boxes

In the quick tour of Chapter 3, you created a shadow box. This effect was created with two boxes: a box in the front that contained text, and a box in the back with a solid fill.

In Chapter 3, you manually drew each of these boxes. Another way to produce the second box is with the Clipboard. Here's how to draw the shadow box shown in Figure 11.1:

1. In the bottom half of page 2, draw a box with a paper fill. *Paper* is an opaque fill that is the color of the paper (usually white).

2. Copy this box to the Clipboard and then paste it. It is now on top of the first box, slightly offset to the right and down.

3. Fill the second box with a solid shade.

4. If necessary, reposition the solid box.

5. Send the solid box behind the first box by using the Send to Back option on the Element menu.

Creating Bleeds

A *bleed* is a graphic element that extends clear to the edge of the page; margins are disregarded. Just glance through a magazine, and you will notice how frequently bleeds are used. You will often see reversed text inside a band of color that bleeds off the top of the page, and photographs and artwork are sometimes bled off the page as well. Occasionally, an entire page is shaded with a color or screen.

To create a bleed, draw an unlined, filled box that extends beyond the edge of the page, as shown in the example in Figure 11.12. This slight oversizing makes sure that the bleed will indeed extend to the very edge of the page after the paper is cut to the page size. In other words, it allows for error in the paper-cutting process.

Creating bleeds on an 8½-by-11-inch page presents a problem because laser printers cannot print to the edge of the page. These printers have

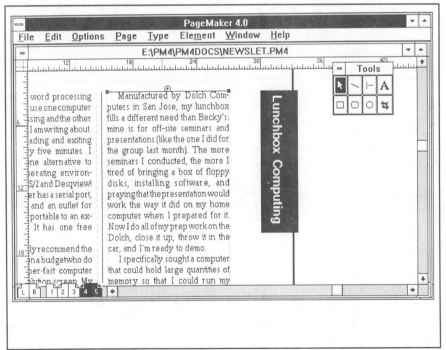

Figure 11.12: A solid shade that bleeds off the page

built-in ¼- to ½-inch margins on all four sides of the page. One solution is to print the publication on a Linotronic typesetting machine that doesn't have this limitation (see Appendix D). Another solution is to set up a slightly smaller page size—for example, 8 by 10 inches. If a final page size of 8½ by 11 inches is necessary, you can tell the print shop to enlarge the page. But keep in mind that enlarging will lower the resolution.

MOVING AND SIZING GRAPHICS

Adjusting the size and placement of a graphic is similar to changing the size and position of a text block. The main difference is that selected text blocks have window shades and selected graphics have *graphic boundaries.*

To select a graphic, use the pointer tool. If the graphic is filled, you can select it by clicking anywhere on the graphic—inside it or on the outline. To select an empty graphic, you must click on the graphic outline. If several graphics or text blocks overlap, and you can't click on a particular graphic, hold down the Ctrl key and click until the graphic you want to change is selected.

Sizing a Graphic

To change the size of a graphic, you simply select it with the pointer tool, and then click and drag one of the handles until the graphic is the desired size.

The selection handles in the middle of the graphic boundary change either the width or the height. The corner handles adjust both the width and the height as you drag. These handles are pointed out in Figure 11.13.

When you change the length of a line, hold down the Shift key as you drag the selection handle. Without the Shift key, the line will be jagged.

Moving a Graphic

To move a graphic, just click and drag it to the desired location using the pointer tool. You don't even have to select it first. However, if the graphic is selected, do not click and drag a handle. If you do, you will end

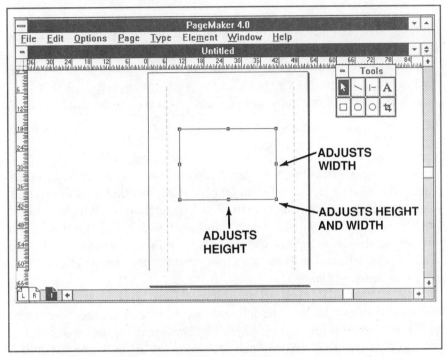

Figure 11.13: Use the handles to change the size of a graphic

up sizing the graphic instead of moving it. Where you click on the graphic depends on whether the graphic is filled or empty. You can click anywhere on a filled graphic (inside or on the outline), but you must click on the outline of an empty graphic.

While you are in the process of moving a graphic, sometimes the actual graphic moves and sometimes a line or box representing the size of the graphic moves, depending on how long you click before you begin dragging. If you click and hold for a second before you start dragging, the actual graphic moves as you drag. If you click and immediately begin dragging, the graphic itself doesn't move; instead a line or box representing the size of the graphic moves. Then when you release the mouse button, the graphic moves to the new location.

If you accidentally move a column guide while moving or sizing a graphic, use the Undo Guide Move option on the Edit menu, or press

Alt-Backspace, to return the guide to its original position. To prevent your-self from inadvertently moving the guides in the future, turn on the Op-tion menu's Lock Guides option. However, you should be aware that this option locks ruler guides as well as column guides, so you can't remove any existing ruler guides you place on the page until you unlock them (al-though you can still add new ruler guides when the guides are locked).

Precise Positioning

While you are drawing a graphic, don't be overly concerned about its exact size and position. Create the graphic in Fit in Window view so that you can position it with respect to the entire page; then zoom in on the area for precise positioning. We recommend that you do all your graphic positioning in Actual Size or even 200% view. Frequently, elements that look properly aligned in Fit in Window view do not appear aligned in a more magnified view.

One way to make sure graphic elements are aligned is to use your column and ruler guides as guidelines (they aren't called guides for noth-ing). The Snap to Guides option on the Options menu ensures that graphic and text elements that are drawn near a guide are actually aligned on the guide. This option creates a magnetic effect between the guides and your graphics (as well as text blocks) so that whenever the element gets near a guide, it is pulled to the guide. With the Snap to Guides feature turned on, you can draw a box around a column guide, and the box will be exactly on top of the column guide. You cannot be assured of this precision when Snap to Guides is turned off.

While it is to your benefit to keep Snap to Guides turned on most of the time, you will need to turn it off to position elements near, but not on, a margin, column, or ruler guide.

Don't forget to use the rulers themselves to help you with graphic alignment. A dotted line in the ruler indicates where the cross-bar is on the page.

Ruler guides—the ones you pull out of the horizontal and vertical rulers—are invaluable tools for lining up graphics with each other or with text blocks. For example, you can use ruler guides to make sure several horizontal lines begin and end at the same point. Ruler guides in Actual Size view provide you with much more accurate positioning than the eyeball method. You can have up to 40 ruler guides per publication, so use them freely.

Depending on the line weight and the page view you are in, you may not see a line you draw on top of a column, margin, or ruler guide. For example, you will not see a hairline drawn on a ruler or column guide in any page view. To make sure that these lines are indeed there, you can turn off all the guides (choose Guides from the Options menu or press Ctrl-J). Or if the line is drawn on a ruler guide, just move the guide out of the way.

Creating a Custom Vertical Ruler

When you are using a leading grid, you want all elements on the page—your graphics as well as the text—to line up on the grid. This alignment becomes almost automatic if you create a custom vertical ruler that matches your body text leading and then turn on the Snap to Rulers option. After you set these two options, the custom ruler is in increments of your magic number, and there is a magnetic effect between your graphic elements and the ruler increments.

To create a custom vertical ruler, follow these steps:

1. On the Edit menu, choose Preferences.

2. For the Vertical Ruler, choose Custom and enter your body text leading (your magic number) next to Points.

3. On the Options menu, turn on Snap to Rulers.

When you are in Fit in Window view, each tick mark on the custom ruler represents one unit of leading; in other words, a single line of text. In the zoomed-in views, the leading tick marks are divided into thirds. Since two-thirds of the leading is above the baseline and one-third is below, your baselines will rest on the second minor tick marks.

As you draw, size, and position your graphics, they will automatically jump to the tick marks on the ruler. The ruler guides you pull out will also automatically line up with these tick marks.

PLACING LINES WITH PARAGRAPHS

The drawing tools aren't the only way to create horizontal lines in PageMaker. The Paragraph Rules dialog box, accessed through the Paragraph Specifications dialog box, has options that place lines above or below paragraphs, without you having to actually draw the lines.

The main advantage to paragraph rules is that they flow with the text. When you draw a line above a subhead with a graphic tool, that line is anchored to the page; if the text reflows, the line doesn't move with the subhead. A paragraph rule, on the other hand, always remains with the text in its paragraph.

Another advantage is that you can precisely control the position and length of paragraph rules. With the drawing tools, you must manually position and size each line.

Creating Pull-Quotes

Pull-quotes are catchy sentences that are pulled out of an article and placed inside rules, a box, or a circle. They have three purposes: to grab the reader's attention, to add a graphic element to a page that looks too gray, and to lengthen an article that is too short for the allotted space. Figure 11.3 shows how a pull-quote can enhance a page.

The text for the pull-quote should be in a separate, unthreaded text block. Decide where you want the pull-quote to go and adjust other text blocks to create space for it. For example, shorten the text block in the column you want the pull-quote to go into.

In the following steps, you'll create the pull-quote shown in Figure 11.14:

1. In the bottom half of column 2 on page 4, type the following text: **I bought my portable last year but I've been waiting to write about it to give it time for problems to crop up. I'm still waiting**…

2. Specify the type as 12-point Times Roman italic, with 24-point leading.

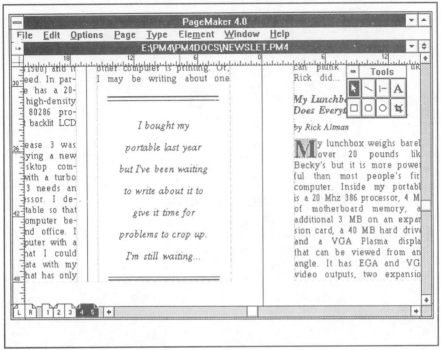

Figure 11.14: A pull-quote

3. Set the paragraph specifications with a 2-pica left indent, 2-pica right indent, and centered alignment.

4. With the text tool, click inside the pull-quote.

5. Press Ctrl-M to display the Paragraph Specifications dialog box.

6. Choose the Rules command button to display the Paragraph Rules dialog box, shown in Figure 11.15.

7. Turn on Rule Above Paragraph.

8. Pull down the Line Style list.

As you can see, paragraph rules can have all the same line weights and styles as lines drawn with the drawing tools.

9. Choose the line style that has a heavy line above a hairline.

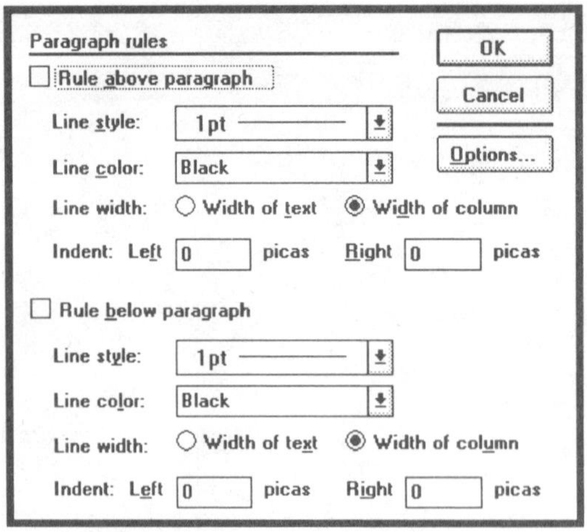

Figure 11.15: The Paragraph Rules dialog box

The length of the rule is controlled by two options: Line Width and Indent. With the default line width, Width of Column, the line spans the entire column width. With the Width of Text option, the rule's length corresponds to the length of the first line in the paragraph (or the last line, for rules below the paragraph). To create rules that are shorter or longer than the line width, use the Indent option. Enter a positive number next to Left or Right to make the rule shorter; enter a negative number to create a longer rule.

10. Set 1-pica left and right indents.

11. Turn on Rule Below Paragraph.

12. Select the line style that has a hairline above a heavy line (the opposite of the rule above the paragraph).

13. Set 1-pica left and right indents.

14. Close the dialog boxes.

Figure 11.16 illustrates another common way of using paragraph rules: below a heading. Notice that this rule spans both columns, a trick that the Paragraph Rules dialog box doesn't handle automatically. To make a line wider than the column width, enter a negative indent value.

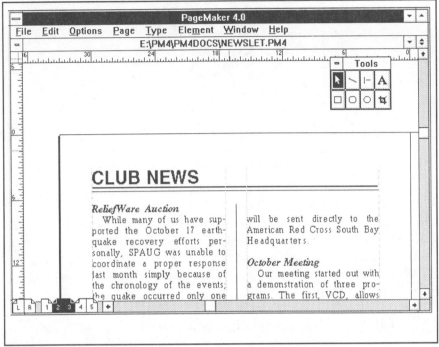

Figure 11.16: A paragraph rule that spans two columns

The rule in Figure 11.16 has a right indent of −14.5 picas (14.5 is the width of the second column plus the gutter).

Adjusting Paragraph Rules

The distance between the rules and the text is a function of the paragraph's leading. If you find that the rules are too close to the text (which they frequently are), you can add extra space by using the selections in the Paragraph Rule Options dialog box, shown in Figure 11.17.

For both the top and bottom rules, the space is measured from the baselines. This measuring system is no problem for the bottom rule because the value you enter is the amount of extra space added below the baseline. But because the rule above is measured from the baseline and not from the top of the capital letters, you need to add the text's cap height to

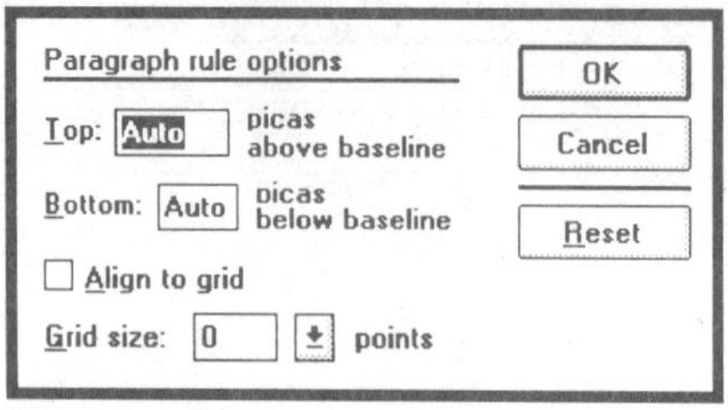

Figure 11.17: The Paragraph Rule Options dialog box

whatever extra space you want between the text and the rule. The *cap height* is the height of the capital letters in a given font and size, usually two-thirds of the point size. For example, if you want 24 points of extra space and your text is 12 points with a cap height of 8 points, specify 32 points of space above the baseline.

Your pull-quote could use some extra space between the text and the rules. Follow these steps to adjust the spacing:

1. Display the Paragraph Rules dialog box.

2. Choose the Options button.

3. Next to Top, type **0p32** (24 picas of extra space plus 8 points of type).

4. Next to Bottom, type **0p24** or **2** picas.

5. Close all the dialog boxes.

There is now an equal amount of space between the rules and the text, both above and below the paragraph.

CREATING INLINE GRAPHICS

Except for paragraph rules, the graphics you have seen thus far are anchored to the page. They don't move unless you move them, so consequently they do not flow with the text. Stationary graphics are the way to go when you want your graphic elements in a fixed location on the page. But sometimes you might want a graphic to be anchored with the text it is associated with and to flow with that text. That's where *inline graphics* come into the picture.

An inline graphic is a graphic that is placed or pasted into a text block so that it becomes part of the text block. You might think of it as a cross between a paragraph of text and a graphic—it shares properties of both. Like any graphic, an inline graphic can be filled with different shades and can be stretched or shrunk with its graphic handles. Like a paragraph, you can define its alignment, indents, leading, and space above and below.

Chapter 12 explains how to import an image and place it in a text block as an inline graphic. Here, we will show you how to shade a paragraph with an inline graphic so that the text remains shaded no matter where it flows.

To create an inline graphic, you paste the graphic into the text while you are using the text tool. The graphic is inserted at the cursor position.

As an example, we'll create a shade behind a paragraph, as shown in Figure 11.18.

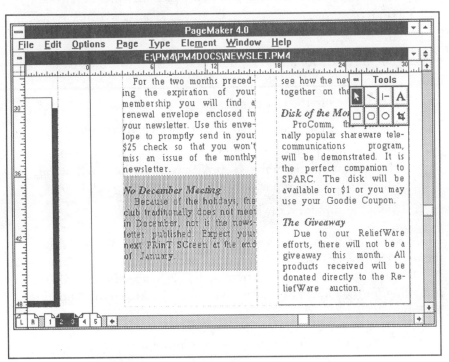

Figure 11.18: The shade behind the text is an inline graphic

1. In column 1, page 3, type the first paragraph:

   For the two months preceding the expiration of your member-ship, you will find a renewal envelope enclosed in your newsletter. Use this envelope to promptly send in your $25 check so that you won't miss an issue of the monthly newsletter.

2. Press Enter, type the head **No December Meeting**, and then press Enter. Specify the type as 12-point Times Roman bold italic, with 12-point leading, and place 1 pica above the heading.

3. On the next line, type the following paragraph:

   Because of the holidays, the club traditionally does not meet in December, nor is the newsletter published. Expect your next PRinT SCreen at the end of January.

4. Specify the body text as 10-point Times Roman with 12-point leading, justified alignment, and a 1-pica first-line indent.

5. With the square-corner tool, draw a box around the heading and the paragraph.

6. Fill the box with a 20% shade and remove the outline by choosing None from the Line menu.

7. Cut the box to the Clipboard.

8. With the text tool, insert a blank line above the subhead.

9. Remove any paragraph attributes (indents, space above) from this line, and turn on the Keep With Next option (so that the shade will not be separated from the text).

10. With the cursor on the blank line, paste the box.

At this point, the box is inserted as an inline graphic and will flow with the text. However, it is not shading the heading and paragraph below it yet. The trick to getting a box to overlay text is to specify a small amount of leading for the inline graphic; we have found that zero or 1-point leading works well.

11. Triple-click on the box to select the entire paragraph.

12. Specify **0** leading and press Ctrl-1 to redraw the screen in Actual Size view. The box overlaps the paragraphs but is not positioned properly.

13. With the pointer tool, drag the box so that it covers the heading and paragraph (refer to Figure 11.18). If necessary, lengthen the box by dragging down one of the bottom handles.

14. Save the publication with the name **NEWSLET**.

For some reason, inline graphics require a lot of screen redrawing. Every time you make a change that affects the inline graphic, you must redraw the screen by issuing one of the page view commands.

To confirm that the shaded box is attached to the text, insert or delete some text above the boxed text. When you redraw the screen, you will see that the box flows with the text.

You can use this same technique to shade a drop cap, as shown in Figure 11.4.

ADDING COLOR
TO YOUR PUBLICATIONS

Along with line and fill style, a third attribute you can assign to graphics is color. You can apply color to text, as well. Spot color adds impact and interest to your publication, but the reason you don't see more of it is simple: it's expensive. Printing in two colors instead of one (for example, black text with spots of red highlighting different areas) can increase the total printing cost significantly.

Assigning Colors

Assigning colors couldn't be easier. Just select the text or graphic you want to add color to and choose the color from the color palette. The color palette, shown in Figure 11.19, works much the same way as the style palette you used in Chapter 8. In fact, the process of defining and editing colors is similar to assigning styles.

Figure 11.19: The color palette

The default color palette contains only a handful of colors. [Paper] refers to the color of the paper (currently white). If you want your screen to simulate the color of paper you will be using in the final publication, you can change this color. The paper color has absolutely no effect on the printing process.

[Black] is the default color of all text. [Registration] refers to the color of the registration marks that are printed in color separations, as explained shortly. The only other colors listed in the palette are blue, green, and red.

Defining Colors

Three ways of defining colors in PageMaker are RGB (Red-Green-Blue), CYMK (Cyan-Yellow-Magenta-Black), and HLS (Hue-Lightness-Saturation). With these methods, you create colors by mixing varying percentages of primary colors; it's up to you to define the percentages.

An easier and more accurate way of defining colors is with the Pantone Matching System (PMS). These colors are predefined printing standards, and there are more than 700 of them. The advantage to using PMS colors is that no matter which commercial printer you use, the colors will have the exact same shade. PMS is the method we are going to describe here.

Suppose that you want to use the color teal in your publication. Since this shade is not in your palette, you need to add it. You would follow these steps to put teal on your palette:

1. From the Element menu, choose Define Colors.

2. Click on the New command button.

3. Click on the PANTONE command button.

A box full of Pantone colors appears, as shown in Figure 11.20. This box has its own scroll bar so that you can peruse the list. If you know the PMS color you want, you can type it in next to the Pantone field.

4. Use the scroll bar to look at the various colors. The color we want is about a third of the way down the list. Its PMS number is 307.

5. Once you find Pantone 307, click on it and choose OK.

6. Edit the name so that it reads **Teal PMS 307**.

It's important to include the PMS number in the name because this number identifies the exact color for the commercial printer to use. Without the number, you are defeating the purpose of using Pantone colors.

7. Close all the dialog boxes.

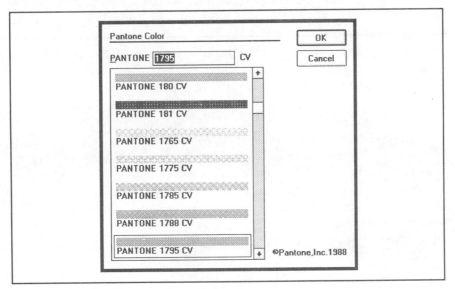

Figure 11.20: The Pantone Color dialog box

8. If you have not done so already, display the color palette by choosing this option from the Window menu.

The new color is now listed in the color palette.

Assigning Colors

Assigning colors is easy: just select the text or graphic that you want to color and click on the appropriate color in the color palette. You must select text with the text tool and graphic elements with the pointer tool.

Printing Spot-Color Overlays

Unless you have access to a color PostScript printer, the standard way of using color is to print the publication in black and white, and then provide the commercial printer with instructions on where to add the color. Actually, you give the printer a set of color overlays for each page in the publication. A *color overlay* consists of all elements on a page that are to be printed in a certain color. You will have an overlay for each color on the page. Color overlays are necessary because the print shop makes a separate printing plate for each color.

This color separation would be incredibly tedious if it weren't for the Spot Color Overlays option in the Print dialog box. This option tells Page-Maker to separate the colors onto different pages. For example, if you printed a page that had several blue objects, all blue elements would print on one page and all black elements would print on another page.

Figure 11.21 shows an example of the overlay for teal elements, and Figure 11.22 shows the one for black elements. Notice that the color name appears at the bottom of the page to let the printer know which PMS color to use for this overlay. Also notice that each page prints with *registration marks* to make sure that the commercial printer overlays the colors in the correct spot. If your page is smaller than standard letter-size paper, turn on the Crop Marks print option (as used for Figures 11.21 and 11.22).

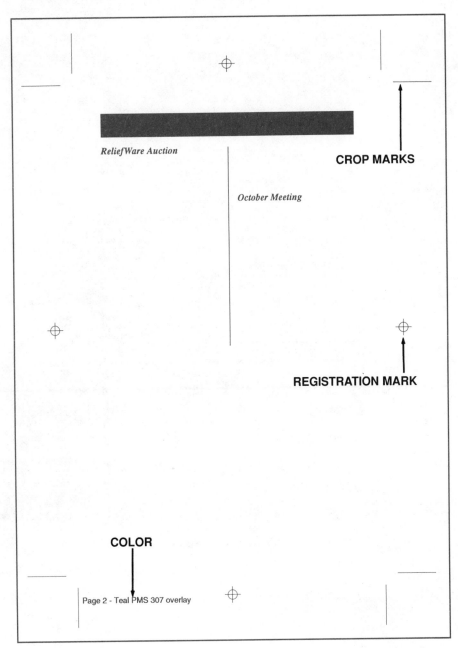

CROP MARKS

ReliefWare Auction

October Meeting

REGISTRATION MARK

COLOR

Page 2 - Teal PMS 307 overlay

Figure 11.21: The teal overlay

CLUB NEWS

While many of us have supported the October 17 earthquake recovery efforts personally, SPAUG was unable to coordinate a proper response last month simply because of the chronology of the events; the quake occurred only one week before the October meeting.

But it is never too late to stretch out a hand, and this month SPAUG calls upon all of its members to participate in ReliefWare '89: An Auction for Action.

Its success depends upon you, the people who will donate computer-related items and buy them. The proceeds will be sent directly to the American Red Cross South Bay Headquarters.

Our meeting started out with a demonstration of three programs. The first, VCD, allows you to visually change directories by moving the cursor around a graphic tree structure. ZDIR displays a directory listing that indicates how much space the files take (unlike DIR which only tells you how much space is remaining). DIRNOTES gives you a way to append comments to filenames, and then view these comments.

Nov - Jan Calendar

Page 2 - Black overlay

Figure 11.22: The black overlay

12

IMPORTING GRAPHICS

While PageMaker's drawing tools can add attractive touches to your publications, they produce only the simplest of graphics. For more sophisticated images and artwork, you need to look to graphic software packages. With a dedicated graphics program, you can either create images yourself or enhance pictures that come with the program. These graphics can then be imported into your PageMaker's publication.

BIT-MAPS VERSUS VECTOR GRAPHICS

Graphic software can be divided into two broad categories:

- Those that create images by a collection of dots, referred to as *paint* programs because you can use your mouse cursor as a brush and mark up the screen however you wish. They create images bit by bit, dot by dot, and so these images are called *bit-mapped graphics*.

- Those that create images by using geometric shapes, such as ovals, rectangles, and lines, known as *drawing* programs. They produce *vector graphic*, or *object-oriented* images.

Drawing programs produce images that are of a decidedly higher resolution than paint programs because they are mathematical shapes, not simply a collection of dots. For instance, when you create a circle with a drawing program, it knows that it is supposed to be a circle, with a certain circumference and radius from the center. If you enlarge or reshape the graphic, it still knows that it is a circle. But a circle from a paint program doesn't know that it is supposed to be a circle; it just happens to look like one at the moment. Resizing usually distorts the image.

Furthermore, paint programs create graphics at a finite resolution, usually between 72 and 300 dpi, depending on the power of the program and the amount of memory your computer has available. The distance between the dots cannot be changed. A low-resolution bit-mapped image will look equally bad on an Epson dot-matrix printer, a LaserJet printer, or an ultra-high-resolution Linotronic imagesetter.

On the other hand, drawing programs produce graphics that are designed to print at the maximum resolution of your printer: 72 dpi on a dot-matrix printer, 300 on a laser printer, and 1200 or even 2500 on high-end typesetting machines. Drawing programs essentially tell the printer: "Make a circle with these dimensions and place the dots as close as you know how."

As a result, drawing programs are excellent for high-precision work, such as CAD drawings and other detailed graphics. The best drawing programs for the IBM PC are, in alphabetical order, Arts & Letters, Corel Draw, and Micrografx Designer. All three programs can produce sharp, complex drawings and store them in a form that is acceptable to PageMaker.

However, you would not use one of these drawing programs to create a scanned image for a PageMaker publication, or to produce a warm and fuzzy scene of a sunset, with ocean waves lapping up against a sandy shoreline. In those cases, you want direct control over each and every dot that makes up the image, and so you would turn to one of the powerful paint programs on the market, such as PC Paintbrush or the Paintbrush program that comes with Windows 3.0.

Compare the two sunbathers in Figure 12.1. These are two clip-art images from Corel Draw. Can you tell which one is bit-mapped and which is object-oriented?

All the screen images in this book are bit-mapped images. Each dot represents a tiny portion of the computer screen; drawing programs cannot produce the same effect.

In many cases, you can take a low-resolution image and convert it into a high-resolution drawing. For example, suppose that you are producing an inventory parts list and you have a dozen low-quality photos of exotic nuts and bolts. Halftoning or photostatting won't work because the coffee stains will show. So you purchase a cheap scanner and turn each photo into a digitized bit-mapped image. Your hand-held scanner produces images that are just as bad as the originals—worse, even—but now you can bring those images into a program like Corel Draw or Micrografx Designer and trace around them with high-quality bezier curve and vector graphic tools.

Presto, you now have high-quality line art that can be precisely sized, scaled, and electronically pasted into your parts list. Your co-workers throw you a party, and your boss gives you a raise.

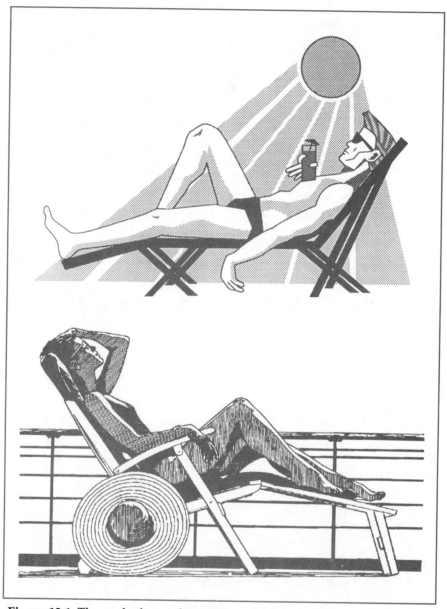

Figure 12.1: The sunbather at the top is an object-oriented image; the one at the bottom is bit-mapped

PREPARING
THE GRAPHIC FOR PAGEMAKER

In order to bring an external graphic into PageMaker, it must be in a format that PageMaker can understand. PageMaker cannot import Corel Draw's .CDR files or Arts & Letters' .GED files. However, all graphics programs offer ways to export their files to standard graphic formats. The most popular formats are Encapsulated PostScript (.EPS), Windows Metafile Format (.WMF), and Computer Graphic Metafile (.CGM). For bit-mapped graphics, picture images (.PCX), and Tag Image File (.TIF) formats are the standards.

Graphic import filters for some of these formats are built into Page-Maker; others need to be installed through the Aldus Setup program. Table 12.1 lists the graphic formats that PageMaker can import, their type, and whether or not filters for them are built-in.

If you have a PostScript printer, the best format to use for your graphic file is Encapsulated PostScript (EPS) because it provides the highest quality art. An image in EPS format is not a good candidate for a non-PostScript printer, although it can be printed under certain circumstances. If you see a shaded box when you import the graphic, you will not be able to print the graphic on a non-PostScript printer because there is no screen rendition of the PostScript code. If you see an image when you import an EPS file, you can print the graphic, but it may be low quality. Except for the most basic of drawings, you shouldn't import EPS graphic files to be printed on a non-PostScript printer (but you have plenty of other formats from which to choose).

Most graphic packages include ready-made drawings and symbols, called *clip art*. Arts & Letters, for example, comes with 5000 clip-art images, including pictures of people, animals, food, maps, home furnishings, buildings, and arrows, to name a few. You can also purchase clip-art packages, such as the ones offered by 3G Graphics, Image Art, Art Right, and New Vision Technologies. Like graphic images in general, clip art can either be bit-mapped or object-oriented.

Some clip art is already in a standard graphic file format, and you can import it directly into PageMaker. However, you may want to import a clip-art image into your drawing program first, so that you can rotate it or add colors, shading, or other enhancements. Do this manipulation and formatting *before* you import the file into PageMaker; once the image arrives in PageMaker, you can only size and crop it.

Table 12.1: PageMaker Graphic Import Filters

FORMAT	EXTENSION	TYPE	BUILT IN
Encapsulated PostScript	EPS	Vector	Yes
Computer Graphic Metafile	CGM	Vector	No
Windows Metafile	WMF	Vector	No
Picture Image	PCX	Bit-mapped	Yes
Tag Image File	TIF	Bit-mapped	Yes
HPGL	PLT	Vector	No
Windows Draw	PIC	Vector	No
Windows PaintBrush	BMP	Bit-mapped	Yes
Lotus 1-2-3 graphic	PIC	Vector	No
Tektronix PLOT-10	PLT	Vector	No
VideoShow (NAPLPS)	PIC	Vector	No
AutoCAD	PLT, ADI	Vector	No
Scrapbook+	ART	Vector or Bit-mapped	No
Excel Chart	XLC	Vector	No
Table Editor	TBL	Vector	No
Micrografx Charisma	GRF	Vector	No
Micrografx Designer	DRW	Vector	No
Micrografx Draw Plus	PIC	Vector	No

To summarize, your objective in the graphic preparation stage is to produce a file that is in one of the standard graphic file formats listed in Table 12.1. Depending on which file format you choose, you might need to run the Aldus Setup program to install additional import filters.

PLACING A GRAPHIC

Placing a graphic is quite similar to placing text, and you even use the same command: Place on the File menu or Ctrl-D. Instead of a text gun, you get a graphic gun, which differs depending on the type of graphic you are placing.

As with text, you have two methods for placing the file: point-and-shoot or drag-place. When you click the graphic gun at the target location (point-and-shoot), the artwork appears in its original size. When you click-and-drag the graphic gun (drag-place), the graphic fits inside whatever size box you draw. The drag-place technique not only changes the size of the graphic, it changes its proportions as well, creating a distorted image. Unless you intend to distort a picture, always place your graphic with the point-and-shoot method. Then you can resize the graphic proportionally, as explained shortly.

Unlike a publication page, which is usually filled with text and other graphic elements, the pasteboard is an uncluttered area that is an ideal target location for an external graphic. You can place the graphic on the pasteboard, resize it, and then move it into position on the page.

Creating a Newsletter Cover Page

To demonstrate the use of external graphics, we will create the cover page for a newsletter shown in Figure 12.2. Every newsletter needs a name, and ours is called PRinT SCreen, after the Prt Sc key on the original IBM PC keyboard. The up arrow refers to the Shift key.

For the cover page, you will need the following graphics (see Figure 12.2):

- An up arrow with the file name ARROW
- Slanted text with the file name SLANT

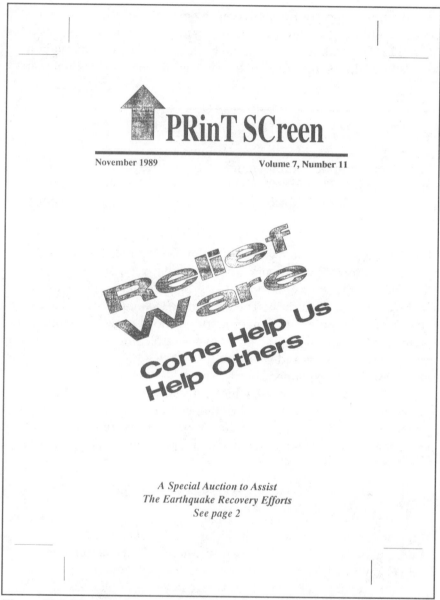

Figure 12.2: The newsletter's cover page has two imported graphics: the large arrow and the slanted text

You can use any graphics or clip-art package to create the files. We used Arts & Letters to create our graphics and exported them to Windows Metafile Format (.WMF).

In the NEWSLET publication you created in Chapter 11, recreate the page shown in Figure 12.3. To make your page match the figure, use the following specifications:

- For the name PRinT SCreen, use 48-point Times Roman bold, 70% width, loose tracking, indented 7p6 from the left.

- Make the horizontal rule a 4-point line weight.

- For the date and volume line, use 12-point Times Roman bold. To align the volume number with the end of the horizontal rule, set a right-aligned tab at the right margin (26p).

- The text at the bottom should be 14-point Times Roman bold, italic, and centered.

The first graphic we will import is the up arrow. This clip art in its original form was pointing to the right, so we rotated it 270 degrees clockwise in Arts & Letters. Follow these steps to import the arrow:

1. Switch to the pointer tool and Fit in Window view.

2. Press Ctrl-D to display the Place File dialog box.

3. If necessary, navigate to the directory containing your arrow.

4. Click on the file name, for example, ARROW.WMF.

Because the file is a graphic, the Place File dialog box shows a new option: As Independent Graphic. The alternative to an independent graphic is an inline graphic, which we described in Chapter 11. An independent graphic has a fixed location on the page; an inline graphic flows with the text. The Inline Graphic option only appears when you have a cursor placed in the text.

5. Choose OK. You then see a graphic gun. The gun has a pencil inside it for vector graphics, a paintbrush for bit-mapped graphics, an *X* for TIFF files, and the letters *PS* for EPS files.

Figure 12.3: The newsletter's cover page before the graphics are imported

6. Click anywhere on the pasteboard to place the graphic there. This allows you to adjust its size before positioning it on the page.

Sizing a Graphic

How you resize a graphic depends on its format (object-oriented versus bit-mapped) and whether you want it to keep its original proportions. In Figure 12.4, the graphic on the left shows the distortion that occurs when an image is not proportionally sized. This happens when you click on a graphic handle and start dragging (the way you have been sizing text and graphic elements so far). The graphic on the right in Figure 12.4 was sized proportionally. To keep a graphic in its original proportions as you adjust its size, hold down the Shift key when you drag a handle. As you drag, the graphic jumps to the next proportional size.

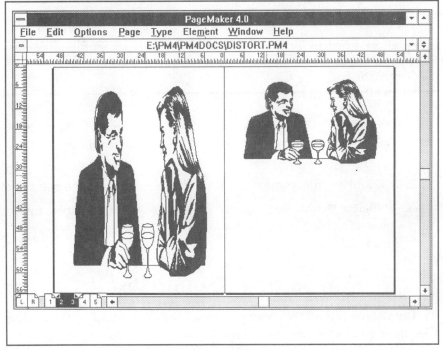

Figure 12.4: The graphic on the left is distorted; the graphic on the right is proportionally sized

Sometimes you might not want proportional scaling. Take the arrow, for example. If you prefer a taller, thinner arrow, you could create this shape by sizing it without the Shift key.

If you forget to hold down Shift as you size a graphic, you don't have to delete the graphic and start over. Just hold down Shift and start dragging a selection handle. The graphic immediately returns to its original size and proportions; you can then finish resizing it, but proportionally this time.

When sizing a bit-mapped graphic, use the *magic-stretch* technique. By holding down Shift and Ctrl as you drag a handle, three things happen at once:

- You change the size of the graphic

- The graphic keeps its original proportions

- The magic part: PageMaker adjusts the resolution of the graphic to match your printer's resolution

The magic-stretch technique provides the best output for graphics produced by paint programs. Figure 12.5 compares a graphic that was stretched with a normal click-and-drag technique with a graphic that was magic-stretched.

Follow these steps to resize your arrow:

1. To proportionally size the arrow, hold down Shift as you drag one of the corner handles. Refer to Figure 12.6 for the arrow's approximate size.

2. Click inside the graphic and drag it into position on the page.

3. Switch to Actual Size view to size and position the graphic more precisely. (You might want to use a ruler guide, as shown in Figure 12.6.)

Importing Graphic Text

The slanted text on the cover page was created in Arts & Letters using a 340-degree clockwise rotation. Similar text can be created in any popular

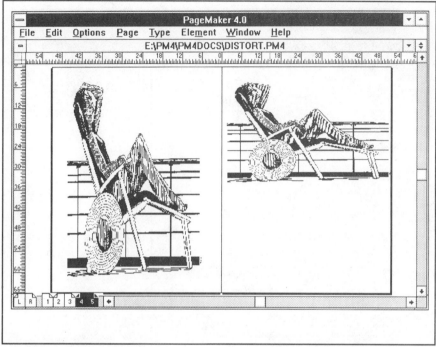

Figure 12.5: The graphic on the right was magic-stretched; the distorted
           graphic on the left was not

drawing program. You cannot create slanted text in PageMaker because it
can rotate text only in 90-degree increments. Thus, it must be imported as
a graphic file.

To import the slanted text, follow these steps:

1. Switch to Fit in Window view.

2. Press Ctrl-D to display the Place File dialog box.

3. If necessary, navigate to the directory containing your slanted text.

4. Double-click on the file name, for example, SLANT.WMF.

5. Click the graphic gun on the page, roughly where you want the
   text to go.

6. Proportionally size the graphic until it fits within the column guides.

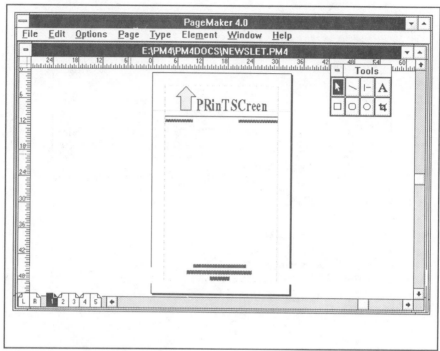

Figure 12.6: The imported arrow

7. Move the graphic so that it is vertically centered on the page, as shown in Figure 12.7.

8. Print the page.

9. Save the publication.

WRAPPING
TEXT AROUND A GRAPHIC

When you are placing a graphic within columns of body text, you need to decide how you want the text to wrap around the graphic. Do you want the text to flow on top of the graphic, above and below the graphic,

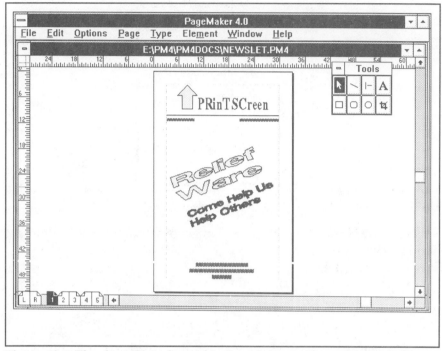

Figure 12.7: The slanted text fits within the column guides and is vertically
centered on the page

above but not below, or on all sides of the graphic? These decisions are
made in the Text Wrap dialog box.

The Text Wrap dialog box, shown in Figure 12.8, contains icons representing the options. First, there are three Wrap options:

- The first icon represents no text wrap; the text flows on top of
  the graphic. This is appropriate for a background image that
  has a very light shade; if it's too dark, you won't be able to read
  the text.

- The second icon turns on the text-wrap feature so that the text
  wraps around the graphic.

- The third wrap icon refers to custom wrap, which you can use
  to adjust the text wrap around graphics with an irregular shape.

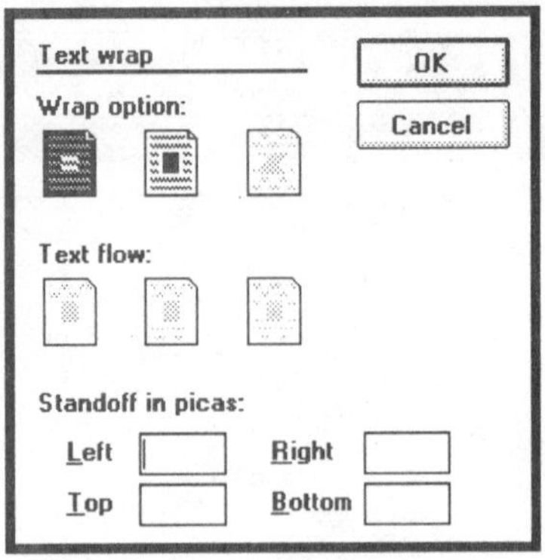

Figure 12.8: The Text Wrap dialog box

Once you turn on text wrap, you can choose from the three different Text Flow options:

- The first icon inserts a column break after the graphic; text does not flow underneath the graphic.

- The second icon flows the text above and below the graphic.

- The third icon flows the text on all four sides of the graphic (assuming there is room for text beside the graphic).

At the bottom of the Text Wrap dialog box there are controls for the amount of white space around the graphic. The *standoff* is the amount of space that separates the text from the graphic. The left, right, top, and bottom sides of the graphic are controlled separately.

Placing a Graphic in a Column

The Blue Chip Realty brochure you've worked on in earlier chapters has room for a graphic on page 2, next to the bulleted list. In the following steps, you'll place the graphic and turn on text wrap. Use a picture of a set of keys from your clip-art collection; we used one from Arts & Letters.

1. Open the BROCHURE publication and switch to page 2 in Fit in Window view.

2. Place the keys graphic on the pasteboard.

3. Proportionally size the graphic until it is approximately the final size. See Figure 12.9.

4. Move the graphic so that it is near the right side of the bulleted list item *We hand you the house keys*. Refer to Figure 12.9 for the exact location. Text flows behind the graphic because text wrap is turned off by default.

Text wrap is an option you apply to a selected graphic, not to the text, so make sure that the graphic is selected before turning on text wrap.

5. From the Element menu, choose Text Wrap.

6. Click on the second text wrap icon to turn on the text wrap feature. The third text flow icon—the one that wraps the text on all sides—is already selected.

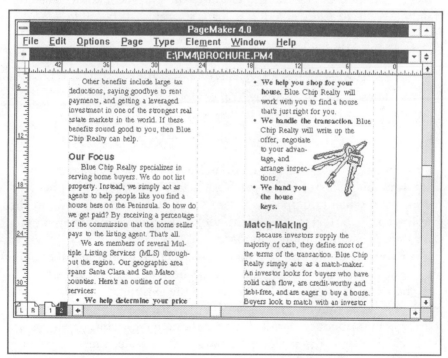

Figure 12.9: The keys graphic placed in the brochure

7. Leave the standoff values at their default setting (1 pica each) and choose OK.

When text wrap is turned on, a graphic has two boundaries. The inner boundary is the *bounding box* you have been using to size the graphic. It is comprised of six square handles. The outer boundary, called the *graphic boundary,* has diamond-shaped handles in each corner. The distance between the two boundaries is the standoff. You adjust the size of a graphic with the square handles. The diamond-shaped handles change the shape of the text that wraps around the text. We'll talk more about custom wrapping in the next section.

8. If necessary, adjust the size of the graphic using the square graphic handles and reposition the graphic.

One way of bringing the text closer to the graphic is to decrease the standoff. We'll set a zero standoff to bring it as close as possible.

9. Display the Text Wrap dialog box.

10. Specify a **0** standoff on all sides of the graphic.

11. Choose OK. The text now comes closer to the graphic.

Customizing Text Wrap

When a graphic is oddly shaped, such as our set of keys, a rectangular text wrap leaves a lot of white space and bad breaks around hyphenated words, even when you specify a zero standoff all the way around the graphic. To get the text to wrap in the nooks and crannies of a graphic, you can create a custom graphic boundary.

For your custom wrap, look for empty space between the text and the graphic, and create new handles in these locations by clicking on the boundary. Then drag the new handles (or any of the existing ones) to bring the graphic boundary closer to the graphic. The more handles you create, the easier it is to get the boundary right up against the actual graphic.

Each time you drag a graphic-boundary handle, the text reflows around the new boundary. This delay can be annoying when you are making a lot of adjustments to the boundary, but you can turn it off by holding down the spacebar as you create and drag handles. When you release the spacebar, the screen is redrawn with the custom text wrap.

Now try your hand at customizing the text wrap around the keys. Figure 12.10 shows the keys with a custom boundary.

1. Click on the boundary to create new handles.

2. Drag the handles so that they lie against the graphic. Remember to hold down the spacebar to prevent screen redrawing.

In the Text Wrap dialog box, the custom text wrap icon is automatically selected when you start adjusting the graphic boundary (you cannot select this icon). If you don't like the results of your custom wrapping, you can return to the original text wrap by choosing the rectangular text-wrap icon and reentering standoff values.

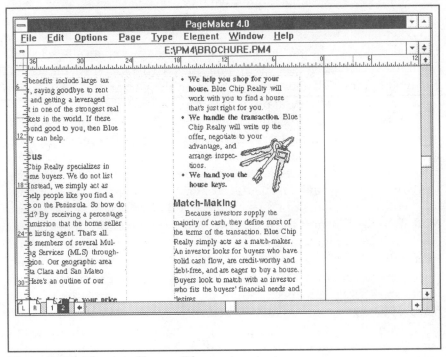

Figure 12.10: The set of keys with a custom text wrap

Customizing a graphic boundary is a skill that requires patience and practice. Try importing a variety of odd-shaped graphics and customizing the wrap. You can also practice wrapping text around a circle or ellipse you have created with PageMaker's drawing tools.

PLACING INLINE GRAPHICS

When you want a graphic to flow with the text, place it as an inline graphic as opposed to an independent graphic. Inline graphics were introduced in Chapter 11, when you pasted a gray shade behind a couple of paragraphs.

To insert a graphic so that it is part of a text block, paste or place the graphic with the text cursor positioned where you want the graphic to go. For example, if you want a graphic to go between two paragraphs, insert a carriage return, and with the cursor on this blank line, place the graphic.

When a text cursor is in a text block, you have a new option in the Place File dialog box: As Inline Graphic. This option is automatically selected. Choose OK. If you don't see the graphic, press Ctrl-1 to refresh the screen. The image is immediately inserted between the paragraphs; you do not see a graphic gun when you place an inline graphic.

Figure 12.11 shows a telephone that was inserted as an inline graphic between two paragraphs. If the telephone were an independent graphic, it would always remain in its current position on the page, even if the text around it flowed to a different position. As an inline graphic, the telephone moves with the text, and it retains its position between the two paragraphs.

Another advantage of inline graphics is that you can use paragraph controls to align them in the text block. To center an independent graphic, you have to move it manually and either eyeball the center or use several ruler guides to help you position it exactly. To center an inline graphic, such as the telephone in Figure 12.11, press Ctrl-Shift-C or enter the alignment in the Paragraph Specifications dialog box. You can also use other paragraph controls such as indents and spaces above and below.

The one limitation to inline graphics is that text wrap options do not apply; a picture cannot be an inline graphic *and* have text flow around it. Also, you must redraw your screen constantly when you are working with

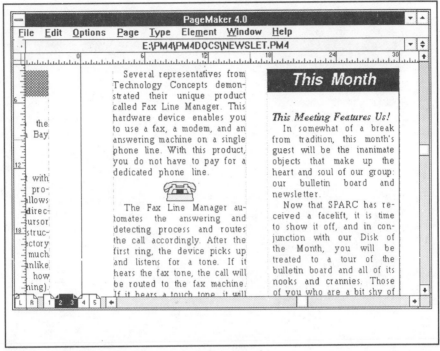

Figure 12.11: The telephone as an inline graphic

inline graphics. The quickest way to refresh your screen is to choose the current page view.

In story view, inline graphics appear as icons, as shown in Figure 12.12. Independent graphics are not indicated in story windows.

FINE TUNING
IMPORTED GRAPHICS

There are a limited number of ways to modify an imported graphic in PageMaker. As you have already seen, you can move and size these graphics. In this section, you will learn a few ways to improve the quality of graphics you have imported from an external graphics program. These features do not work with graphics created with PageMaker's drawing tools.

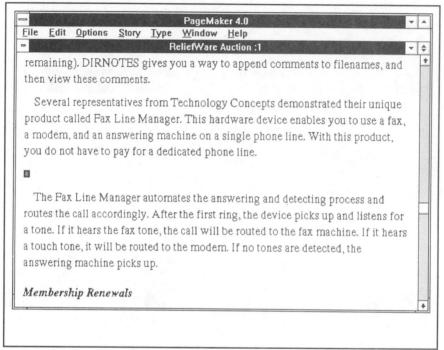

Figure 12.12: An inline graphic in story view

Cropping Images

When you *crop* a picture, you are trimming it to remove an unwanted portion. Here are a few examples of when cropping is appropriate:

- To cut out a distracting person lurking on the side of a photograph
- To focus on a person from the waist up instead of including the full body
- To trim blank space (such as the sky) from the edge of a picture

In other words, cropping lets you zero in on the important or key part of the image. You can crop your artwork in your graphics program or in PageMaker.

When you use PageMaker's cropping tool, the entire graphic is still stored inside the publication; you are simply indicating which part of the graphic you want to see. This fact has its pluses and minuses. On the positive side, you can crop without worrying about deleting part of the image, and if you don't like your cropping job, it's easy enough to uncrop or recrop. On the negative side, a cropped image consumes as much memory and disk space as the original image. If computer memory is at a premium for you, crop the artwork in your graphics program before importing it into PageMaker.

Figure 12.13 shows five different versions of the same image. The graphic at the top of the page is uncropped, and the other images show different ways the picture can be cropped.

Figure 12.13: Different ways of cropping a graphic (the image at the top is uncropped)

Here are the general steps for cropping in PageMaker:

1. Choose the cropping tool in the toolbox (the one to the right of the circle tool).

2. Click on the graphic.

3. Click and drag one of the selection handles. Use the corner handles to crop diagonally, the left and right handles to crop horizontally, or the top and bottom handles to crop vertically.

After you crop a picture to a certain size, you can move the image around inside the bounding box, displaying different parts of the graphic. For example, suppose that you use the cropping tool and click and drag the man in the lower-left corner of Figure 12.13 to the left. The man scrolls out of view, and the woman appears inside the bounding box.

When you click and drag with the cropping tool, you see a grabber hand, which looks like the hand that appears when you hold down Alt and drag the screen. But instead of repositioning what you see on the entire screen, you reposition what you see inside the graphic's bounding box.

Adjusting the Screen Resolution

There is a trade-off between the screen resolution of your imported graphics and the speed at which the screen is redrawn. The Preferences dialog box, shown in Figure 12.14, offers three ways to display images on your screen: Gray Out, Normal (the default), or High Resolution. These options apply to all imported graphics in a publication; you cannot choose a different option for each image. Also, they have no effect on your printed graphics.

Gray Out, shown in Figure 12.15, offers the fastest screen redrawing because it doesn't actually show your images. It displays gray boxes inside the bounding box.

High Resolution provides the best screen resolution for TIFF images. However, screen redrawing is significantly slower.

Figure 12.16 shows a TIFF image in normal resolution. Figure 12.17 shows the same file in high resolution (this image appears in an earlier figure in this chapter). As you can see, the difference in screen resolution is

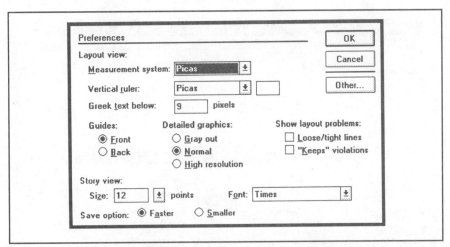

Figure 12.14: Use the Detailed Graphics option to control screen resolution

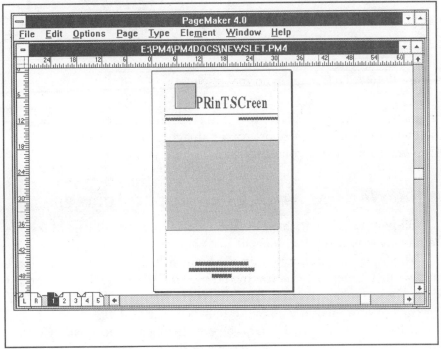

Figure 12.15: The Gray Out screen resolution

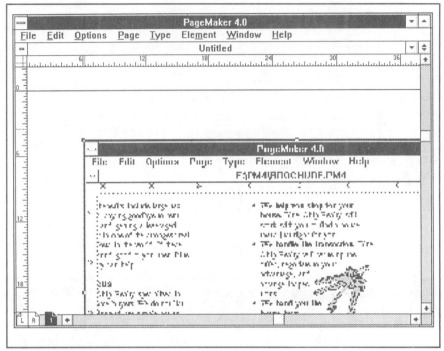

Figure 12.16: A TIFF image in normal resolution

dramatic, as is the time it takes to redraw the screen. Turn on High Resolution when you need to size or crop an image; switch to Normal or Gray Out when you want to concentrate on formatting the text.

Working with Bit-Mapped Images

Bit-mapped graphics have the lowest print quality, but PageMaker offers a way to improve their output.

The Image Control option on the Element menu is specific to black-and-white bit-mapped images (including TIFF files). The Image Control dialog box, shown in Figure 12.18, allows you to control the lightness and contrast of your images (as on your television set).

Select the bit-mapped image before displaying the Image Control dialog box. To lighten the image, enter a positive percentage next to Lightness; enter a negative value to darken it. You can also change the lightness

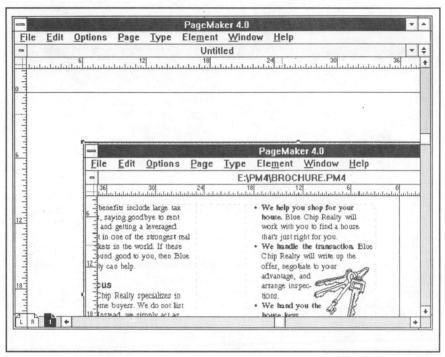

Figure 12.17: A TIFF image in high resolution

Figure 12.18: The Image Control dialog box

percentage with the scroll bar by clicking on the right arrow to lighten, the left arrow to darken.

The imported PCX image on the right side of Figure 12.19 has been lightened by 86%; instead of black and white, the graphic is now in shades of gray. Without the lightening adjustment, the black dots of the figure

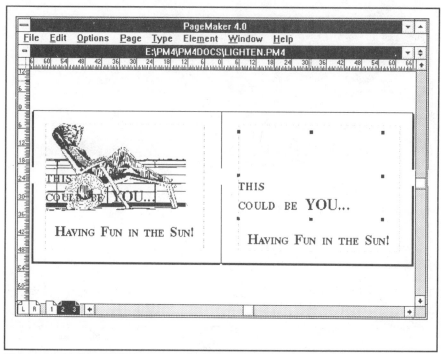

Figure 12.19: The PCX image at the left uses the default lightness setting
(0%); the image on the right has been lightened by 86%

conflict with the black strokes of the type, and you cannot read the text on
top of the image, as shown on the left side of Figure 12.19.

With the Contrast control, you can make the image lighter or darker
in relation to the area behind the image. A 50% setting retains the graphic's
original black-and-white contrast. Higher percentages increase the contrast between the image and its background. A 0% contrast reverses the
black and white.

After adjusting the Lightness or Contrast controls, choose the Apply
command button. This lets you see how the adjustment affects the image
without leaving the Image Control dialog box. If the graphic is hidden
under the dialog box, move the box out of the way (drag the title bar). The
Default button reverts the controls to their original settings (Lightness 0%,
Contrast 50%). When you are satisfied with your results, choose OK.

LINKING FILES

Much of what you learned about text file linking in Chapter 9 applies to the linking of graphic files. File linking helps you maintain a relationship between your publication and the original graphic file you imported. When an imported graphic is linked to its external file, you can avoid having to import and size a graphic each time it is modified in the graphics package.

As with text files, the process of file linking is automatic, but the process of updating the screen image to match the external file is not. You must explicitly issue that command. The Update command button is in the Links dialog box.

When your graphic files match the images in the publication, the status message reads:

This item is up to date.

If you later change one of these external files, the status message reads:

The linked file has been modified since the last time it was placed.

You can then click on the Update button to reimport the file.

Automatic Updating

If you want PageMaker to automatically replace the internal version of the image with the changed external file, turn on the Update Automatically option in the Link Options dialog box shown in Figure 12.20. Link Options is a command button in the Links dialog box, as well as an option on the Element menu. With the Update Automatically option, whenever you open the publication, the image instantly reflects any changes made in the graphic file; you don't need to choose the Update command button

You may also want to turn on the Alert Before Updating option so that as you open a file, PageMaker notifies you when a graphic needs updating. You can then cancel the updating if you want to leave the graphic as it is.

To Store or Not to Store

The Link Options dialog box has another important item: Store Copy in Publication. By default, PageMaker keeps copies of your imported graphic files inside your publication. The graphic is therefore in two places: in the .PM4 file and in its own graphic file. This duplication is a waste of valuable disk space and can sometimes lead to enormous publications.

A less wasteful approach is to tell PageMaker *not* to store a copy of the graphic in the publication. Regardless of whether the files are stored in the publication, you see the graphics because the images are linked to their external files. This approach requires that you keep your graphic files intact—don't delete them! If you delete, rename, or move them, they will not appear in the publication. However, whenever you modify the image in your graphics program, the revised image is automatically used because of the file linking.

By turning off the Store Copy in Publication option, you do two things at once: you minimize the size of your publication and you create an automatic link to the external graphic file. It's up to you to decide which graphics you want to apply the option to. You may want to keep it on for some graphics (such as small clip-art pictures) and turn it off for your larger images.

If you turn off the Store Copy in Publication option, the Update Automatically and Alert Before Updating options are unavailable because, when the graphic is not stored in the publication, PageMaker has no choice but to update. The updating happens automatically, and you are alerted only if it can't find the file.

You cannot turn off the Store Copy in Publication option for EPS files because they are always stored in the publication.

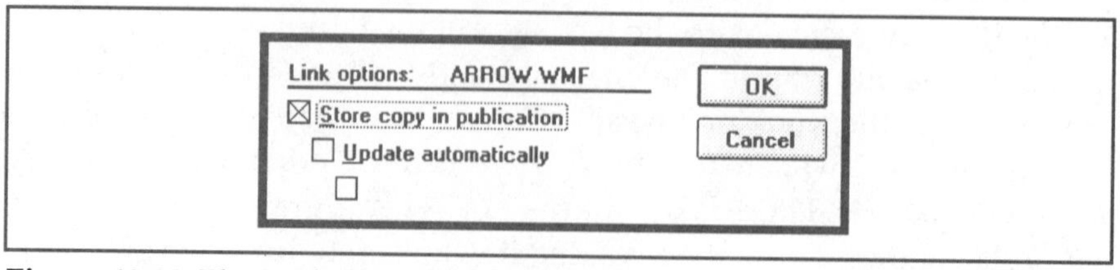

Figure 12.20: The Link Options dialog box

It's important to remember not to delete the graphic files; otherwise, you will see the error dialog box shown in Figure 12.21. If you deleted the file, you have no alternative but to choose the Ignore option, and the image will no longer be in the publication. If you moved or renamed the file, you can use the Files/Directories list to select the new path and name.

Revising and Replacing Linked Files

Suppose that you use your graphics package to modify an image you had previously imported into a publication, and you save the revised image with the same name. How does this revised image get into PageMaker?

- If the Store Copy in Publication option is turned off, or the Update Automatically link option is turned on, the revised image is automatically imported the next time you open the publication.

- If the Update Automatically option is turned off (as it is by default), choose the Update command button in the Links dialog box.

Regardless of which method you use, the graphic's original size, proportions, and cropping are maintained.

Now let's look at a slightly different situation: You want a different graphic (or the same graphic with a different name) in place of an existing

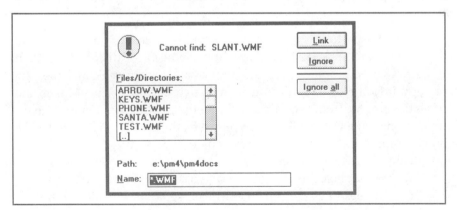

Figure 12.21: This dialog box appears when PageMaker cannot find a linked file

graphic. In order to link this new graphic to the publication, you have several alternatives:

- Delete the existing graphic and then place and size the new graphic. Crop if necessary.
- Select the existing graphic with the pointer tool and choose the new file name in the Link Info dialog box.
- Select the existing graphic, display the Place File dialog box, choose the new file name, and turn on the Replacing Entire Graphic option.

When you use either of the last two techniques, the old graphic is eliminated and the new graphic appears in the same size and location as the original graphic. If the newly imported graphic has the same proportions as the original, the image will be properly proportioned and have the same cropping. However, if the new graphic is proportioned differently (for example, it has a vertical orientation while the original was horizontal), it will be distorted and its cropping will not be retained.

IMPORTING GRAPHICS FROM THE CLIPBOARD

Another way to bring art into your publication is through the Windows Clipboard. This method eliminates the need for disk files. In your Windows-based graphics program, you create your graphic and then cut or copy it to the Clipboard. You then switch back into PageMaker and paste the graphic from the Clipboard into the publication. If a text cursor is positioned in a text block when you paste, the graphic is inserted as an inline graphic. Otherwise, the graphic is independent and can be positioned anywhere on the page.

With the Clipboard technique, you avoid the export–import routine. The graphic doesn't ever need to exist as a separate file, although it's a good idea to save the image in your drawing program in case you need to modify the graphic in the future.

Because you are not importing from a disk file, graphics that you import through the Clipboard are not linked to the publication. You will see the graphic listed in the Links dialog box with the generic name *Graphic*, as shown in Figure 12.22, but you can't use any of the link options. If you later decide to link the graphic to an external file, follow these steps:

1. In the Links dialog box, click on the item labeled Graphic.

2. Choose the Link Info command button.

3. Select the file name in the Link Info dialog box.

If a picture really is worth a thousand words, then PageMaker's ability to include graphic images in a document is an electronic gold mine. Page-Maker recognizes the format of a variety of graphic file formats, enabling it to do business with programs ranging from Arts & Letters to Harvard Graphics.

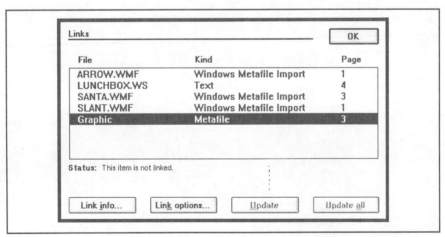

Figure 12.22: A graphic imported from the Clipboard is listed as Graphic in the Links dialog box

13

USING
THE
TABLE
EDITOR

The Table Editor included with PageMaker 4.0 is an alternative way of creating columnar data for your publications. Instead of setting tabs and entering the data with PageMaker's text tool, you can create the table in the external Table Editor program and then import it into your publication.

ADVANTAGES OF THE TABLE EDITOR

Why would you want to use an external program when you can create the table right in PageMaker? Here are a few advantages of the Table Editor:

- You enter the data in a spreadsheet grid of rows and columns.

- You don't have to type commas, dollar signs, and percent signs; numeric punctuation is added with a command.

- You don't have to manually draw horizontal and vertical lines— the borders are there automatically.

- Rather than resetting tab stops, you can change the space between columns by dragging a column boundary.

- The Table Editor can add and subtract numbers.

As you can deduce from the above list, the Table Editor has the look and feel of a spreadsheet program. In fact, if you have used an electronic spreadsheet program, such as Excel, you will find the Table Editor easy to use. It doesn't have the powerful calculating capabilities of a full-blown spreadsheet, but it offers more formatting options. Figure 13.1 shows an example of a table created and formatted in the Table Editor.

LOADING THE TABLE EDITOR

The Table Editor is a stand-alone program that has the file name TE.EXE. It is copied to your PageMaker directory when you run the Aldus Setup program.

Santa Clara County Residential Real Estate Sales

Area	# of Sales	Lowest Price	Highest Price	Median Price	Average Price
Cupertino	9	$215,500	$512,200	$330,000	$320,022
Los Altos	10	420,000	870,000	529,900	582,215
Los Altos Hills	0	0	0	0	0
Los Gatos	11	82,000	755,500	350,000	369,918
Mountain View	12	135,500	447,750	270,000	275,520
Palo Alto	15	165,500	1,200,000	385,500	441,136
Santa Clara	17	86,500	325,500	212,200	219,938
Saratoga	7	278,800	580,000	509,900	469,907
Sunnyvale	16	170,000	440,000	253,300	276,687

This information, recorded in September 1990, is from deeds after the close of escrow. Average housing figure includes single-family homes, condos, townhouses, and mobile homes.

Figure 13.1: A table created and formatted in the Table Editor

You load the Table Editor the same way you load any software program in Windows. From Program Manager, double-click on the Table Editor icon in the Aldus program group. Alternatively, you can choose Run from the File menu and type the path and file name, for example, C:\PM4\TE.EXE.

CREATING A TABLE

The process of creating a table in the Table Editor consists of three basic steps: specifying the table's dimensions, entering the data, and saving the file.

Setting Up a Table

Before you create a new file in the Table Editor, you need to have a good idea of the table's dimensions. The Table Setup dialog box, shown in Figure 13.2, requires you to enter the total number of rows and columns in the table, in addition to its width and length.

For our example, we will create the calendar shown in Figure 13.3. It has three columns and eight rows. Even though the text at the bottom of the calendar appears on two lines, it's considered one row because it is typed in a single paragraph.

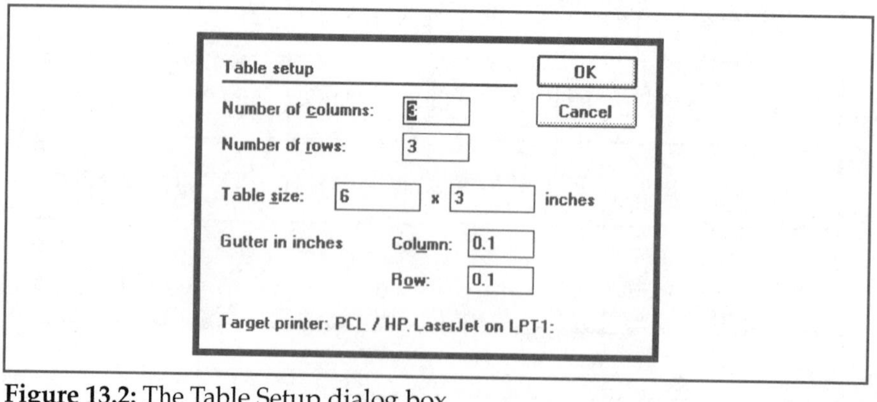

Figure 13.2: The Table Setup dialog box

The dimensions of your table may be more difficult to determine. If you are unsure of a table's final size, make your best guess. Fortunately, you can change the settings later. The dimensions of the sample table are 4½ by 3 inches.

Before creating the table, change the Table Editor's default font to Times Roman.

1. Pull down the Type menu and choose Font.

2. Choose Times Roman.

Now all the tables you create will be in the Times Roman font. Follow these steps to create the table grid for the calendar:

3. Choose New on the File menu. The Table Setup dialog box appears.

4. Specify **3** columns and **8** rows.

5. For the table size, enter **4.5** inches by **3** inches.

Nov - Jan Calendar		
November 27	MS Word SIG	7:30 p.m.
November 29	Group Meeting	8:00 p.m.
January 9	New Users SIG	7:30 p.m.
January 10	Planning Meeting	8:00 p.m.
January 29	MS Word SIG	7:30 p.m.
January 31	Group Meeting	8:00 p.m.
All members are welcome to attend the monthly planning meeting, where we make decisions on the future of the group.		

Figure 13.3: The calendar is 3 columns by 8 rows, and 4.5 by 3 inches

The *gutter* refers to the space between rows and columns. We will keep the default gutter, which is 1/10 inch.

6. Choose OK.

A spreadsheet grid with 3 columns and 8 rows appears, as shown in Figure 13.4. The rows are numbered and the columns are labeled with letters. If you don't see these labels, turn on the Grid Labels option on the Options menu. The intersection of a row and a column is called a *cell*. You refer to a specific cell by its column and row coordinates (for example, A1 or C3). A cell is where you enter your data.

Notice the two tools in the toolbox in the upper-right corner of the screen. Use the text tool to type or edit data and the pointer tool to select cells for formatting.

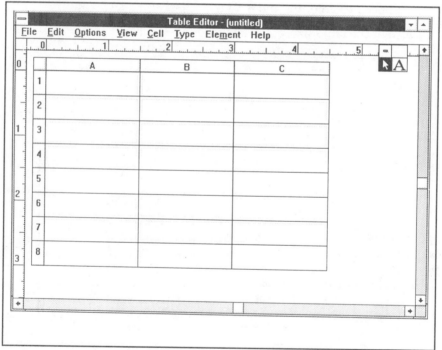

Figure 13.4: An empty table grid

Entering Data

To enter data, you choose the text tool, click the I-beam in a cell, and start typing.

Moving the Text Cursor

You can use any of the following methods to move the text cursor to another cell:

- Press Enter to move down to the next cell
- Press Tab to move to the cell to the right
- Press Shift-Tab to move to the cell to the left
- Click on any cell

If the text cursor is at the bottom of a column when you press Enter, it moves to the top of the next column. If the cursor is at the end of a row when you press Tab, it moves to the beginning of the next row. By using Tab to enter data a row at a time, or the Enter key to type data a column at a time, you can fill in your table quickly and efficiently.

Let's use the row-by-row method first to enter some data in the table.

1. Choose the text tool.
2. Click on cell A2 and type **November 27**.
3. Press Tab and type **MS Word SIG**.
4. Press Tab and type **7:30 p.m.**
5. Press Tab to move to cell A3.
6. Continue using Tab to go row by row, or try pressing Enter after each entry to go column by column, and enter the rest of the data:

November 29	Group Meeting	8:00 p.m.
January 9	New Users SIG	7:30 p.m.
January 10	Planning Meeting	8:00 p.m.

| January 29 | MS Word SIG | 7:30 p.m. |
| January 31 | Group Meeting | 8:00 p.m. |

At this point, your table should look like Figure 13.5.

Grouping Cells

The first and last rows of the calendar have text that spans more than one column. Whenever you want text to appear across multiple cells, use the Group command on the Cell menu. This command creates one long cell from a range of consecutive cells. To group cells together, select the range with the pointer tool and choose the Group command, or press Ctrl-G.

Follow these steps to create a set of grouped cells at the top of the table and another at the bottom:

1. Switch to the pointer tool.

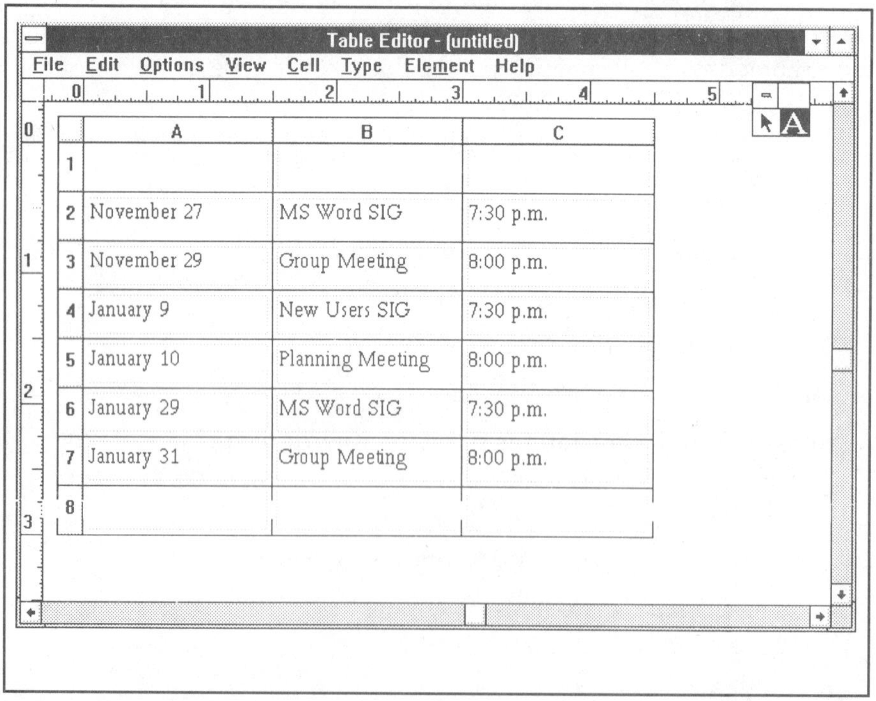

Figure 13.5: The calendar data

2. Click and drag across row 1, from cell A1 to cell C1. The range is blackened except for the first cell, which is outlined in black.

3. Choose Group from the Cell menu, or press Ctrl-G. The three cells are now one long cell.

4. Follow the same procedure to group the cells in row 8.

5. To enter the data, switch to the text tool.

6. Click in row 1 and type **Nov–Jan Calendar**.

The title currently fits within column A, but later on you will be enlarging the text and centering it across all three columns—that's why you grouped the cells.

7. Click in row 8 and type **All members are welcome to attend the monthly planning meeting, where we make decisions on the future of the group.**

The text automatically word wraps within the cell. Automatic word wrap works in all cells, not just grouped ones. Your calendar should look similar to Figure 13.6.

Importing Data

If the data for a table already exists in another file, such as in a spreadsheet or database, you don't need to retype it. The Import option on the File menu will bring in the following types of files:

- Lotus 1-2-3 spreadsheet files (actually, any file in 1-2-3 format that has the extension .WKS, .WK1, or .WK3)

- Symphony spreadsheet files

- Comma- or tab-delimited text files

Although the Table Editor cannot directly import an Excel .XLS file, you can save your Excel spreadsheet in 1-2-3 format and then import the .WK1 file.

Before importing a delimited text file, you must create a new table with dimensions appropriate for the imported data. For example, if the text file contains 30 lines with 6 items of data in each line, you should

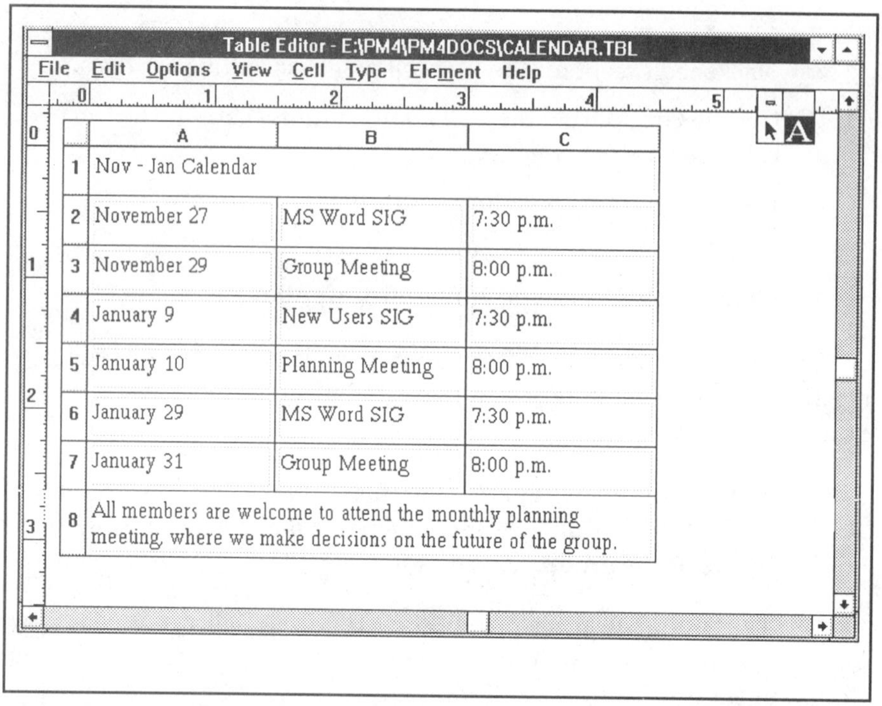

Figure 13.6: The Group command was used on rows 1 and 8 so that data appears across multiple columns

create a table that has 6 columns by 30 rows. This step is unnecessary when you are importing a spreadsheet file because you indicate the range of cells you wish to import. Figure 13.7 shows the Place a 1-2-3 or Symphony Range dialog box. You can either type the range coordinates in the Range field or select the range name from the list of names.

Saving a Table

As in all Windows applications, the Save and Save As options on the File menu save your file to disk. Table files are saved with the extension .TBL.

Now, save your calendar:

1. Choose Save from the File menu.

2. Enter the name **CALENDAR**.

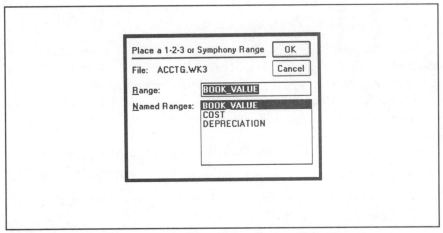

Figure 13.7: The Place a 1-2-3 or Symphony Range dialog box

FORMATTING A TABLE

The Table Editor's Type, Cell, and Element pull-down menus offer numerous ways to format your tables. You can change the font, size, leading, type style, and alignment of text and numbers. You can also specify the style and weight of the lines and add a variety of shades and patterns. The finished calendar in Figure 13.8 has been formatted as follows:

- Most of the text is 14-point Times Roman.

- The title is 22-point Helvetica bold.

- The paragraph at the bottom is 12-point Times Roman italic.

- The title and the paragraph are centered.

- The title has extra space below it.

- The column widths have been adjusted so that the columns are more evenly spaced.

Changing the Type Specifications

The Table Editor does not offer all the typographical controls that Page-Maker does, nor can you format part of a cell. However, you can change the font, size, leading, and type style of a single cell or a range of cells.

To select a single cell to format, click on the cell with either the text or pointer tool. You can select cells several ways:

- With the pointer tool, click and drag to select any rectangular range.

- To select an entire row, click on the row number in the grid-label area.

- To select an entire column, click on the column letter in the grid-label area.

- To select the entire table, click in the upper-left corner of the grid-label area, or press Ctrl-A.

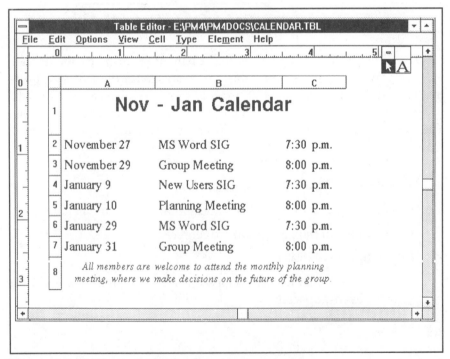

Figure 13.8: The formatted calendar

Unlike PageMaker, you cannot click and drag with the text tool.

Alignment is the only paragraph specification that is available in the Table Editor. Either use the Alignment cascading menu or the keyboard shortcut, such as Ctrl-Shift-C to center. Text is aligned with respect to the cell's right and left boundaries. The boundaries are blue on a color monitor, or light gray on a black-and-white screen.

In addition to left, right, centered, and justified horizontal alignment, the Table Editor offers top, middle, and bottom vertical alignment. For these options, the text is aligned with respect to the cell's upper and lower boundaries. By default, text is aligned with the top of the cell boundary.

Follow these steps to format the table:

1. Click on row 1 with either the text or pointer tool.

2. Press Ctrl-T to display the Table Editor's Type Specifications dialog box, shown in Figure 13.9.

3. Format the title as 22-point Helvetica bold.

4. Choose OK.

5. Press Ctrl-Shift-C to center the title.

6. With the pointer tool, click and drag from cell A2 through cell C7.

7. Press Ctrl-T and format the text in the table as 14-point Times Roman.

8. Click on row 8 with either tool.

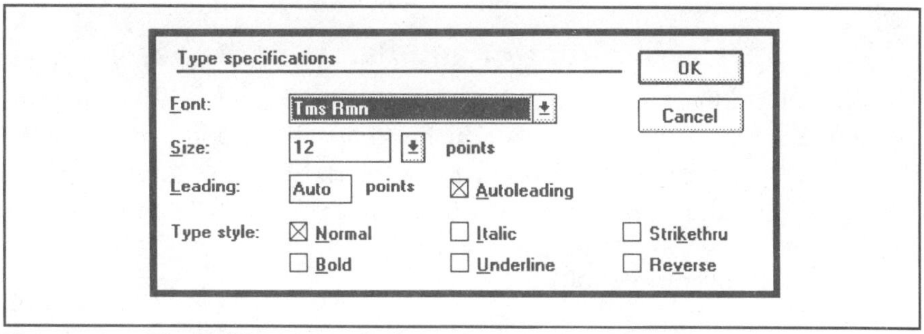

Figure 13.9: The Table Editor Type Specifications dialog box

9. Press Ctrl-T and format the paragraph at the bottom as 12-point Times Roman italic.

10. Press Ctrl-Shift-C to center the paragraph.

Specifying Borders

Borders are horizontal and vertical lines in a table. By default, each cell is outlined with 1-point lines on all four sides. But a complete border is not always appropriate. When the columns are widely spaced, you don't need vertical rules; in a small table with only a few rows, horizontal lines are not really necessary. The Table Editor gives you free reign over where the borders are placed and what line style is used for the borders.

Changing the Line Style

The Line option on the Element menu lets you change the style of existing lines. Most of the line styles offered in PageMaker are available here. The weight of your borders can range from hairline to 12 points, and you can select from several styles of double- and triple-lines.

Just for practice, try a different line style for your calendar:

1. Press Ctrl-A to select the entire table.

2. Choose Line on the Element menu.

3. Select 2pt.

4. Click on any cell to remove the selection highlighting so that you can see the new line weight.

Specifying Interior and Parameter Lines

The cell outlines are now twice as thick and much too heavy for this particular table. A nicer effect might be to specify 2-point lines for the perimeter of the table and 1-point lines for the interior. Now you will specify different line styles for the interior and perimeter of a range.

1. Select the entire table.

2. Choose Borders on the Element menu, or press Ctrl-B.

The Borders dialog box, shown in Figure 13.10, has a set of check boxes for the perimeter (Top, Bottom, Left, and Right) and another set for the interior (Horizontals and Verticals). All boxes are currently checked. Since both the perimeter and interior are already set to 2 points, you only need to change the horizontal and vertical lines in the interior. Therefore, you need to uncheck the perimeter boxes.

3. Click on Top, Bottom, Left, and Right to uncheck these options. Horizontals and Verticals should remain checked.

4. Display the Line drop-down list and choose 1pt.

5. Choose OK.

Your table now has a 2-point border on its perimeter and 1-point lines in the interior. To see the borders more clearly, turn off the Grid Lines option, as in Figure 13.11. (Choose Grid Lines on the Options menu, or press Ctrl-9.)

Removing Borders

Because this calendar does not have many rows or columns, it doesn't really need any borders. To remove border lines, you must first turn on all the border area options (perimeter and interior) and then specify None for the line style.

Follow these steps to remove the calendar's borders:

1. Press Ctrl-A to select the entire table.

2. Press Ctrl-B to display the Borders dialog box.

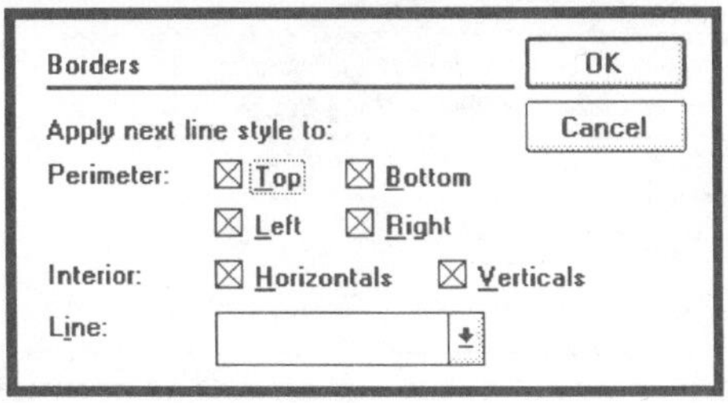

Figure 13.10: The Borders dialog box

3. Turn on *all* check-box options.

4. Display the Line drop-down list and choose None.

5. Choose OK.

The lines are now removed from the table. The thin line that surrounds the table is a nonprinting border.

Adjusting Column Widths

When you create a table and define its dimensions, the Table Editor determines the column widths by dividing the table width by the number of columns. This produces columns with equal widths. For example, the calendar is 4½ inches wide with three columns; thus, each column is

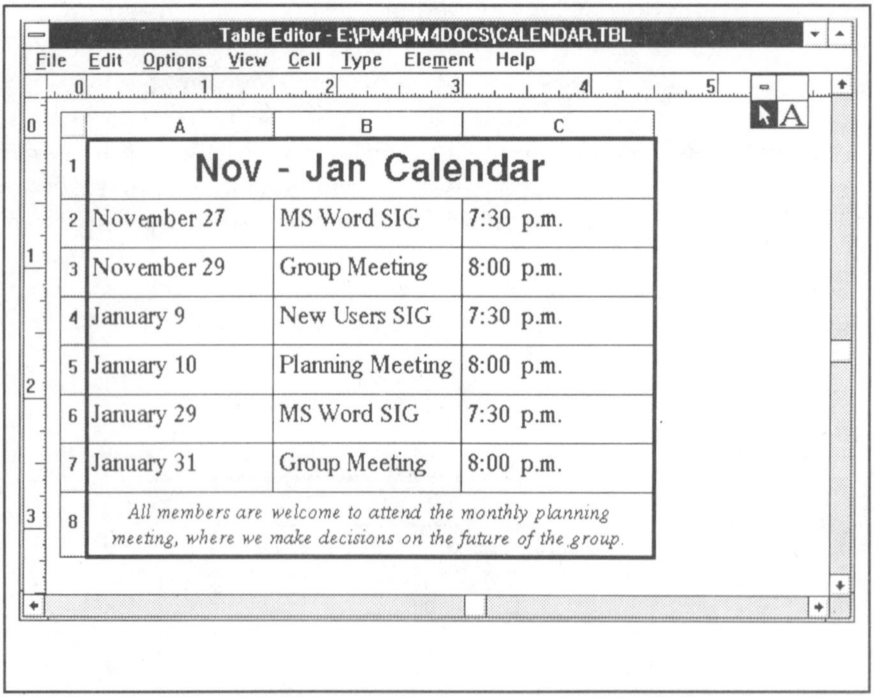

Figure 13.11: The table has a 2-point border on the perimeter and a 1-point border in the interior

1½ inches wide. But equal column widths are rarely appropriate, and most of the time you will want to adjust the widths to fit your data.

When a column is not wide enough to fit the data, it word wraps within the cell, or if only one word is entered, the word is truncated until you widen the column. Because this truncation applies to numbers as well as letters, you might end up with misleading results, so watch for truncated data.

While the current column widths in the calendar are adequate and don't cut off any text, the column spacing is not ideal because columns B and C are too close together. The Table Editor offers two ways to change column widths: by dragging the column boundary with the mouse, or by typing a value in the Column Width dialog box. One advantage to using the mouse is that you can eyeball the column width.

When you use the Column Width dialog box, the width of the entire table is altered. For example, if you widen a column by 1 inch, the width of the table increases by 1 inch.

If you want the table size to remain constant when you adjust column widths, perhaps because it must fit in a fixed area, use the mouse to drag the column border. With this method, the Table Editor adjusts the column to the right so that the width of the table doesn't change. For instance, if you widen column B by ½ inch, column C decrease by ½ inch. However, when you change the width of the last column in a table, you do alter the table width. If you were to drag column C's boundary in the calendar, the table size would increase or decrease by the amount of the change.

Now let's use the mouse to change the width of column B in the calendar. Follow these steps:

1. Place the mouse pointer in the column grid-label area, on the vertical line between the letters B and C. The mouse pointer turns into a double-headed arrow when it is in the proper location.

2. Click-and-drag to the right until the column is the width shown in Figure 13.12, about 2 inches wide. Use the horizontal ruler to measure the column width exactly.

3. Release the mouse button.

Column C is narrowed by the same amount that column B is widened. As shown in the horizontal ruler guide, the net result is that the table remains 4½ inches wide.

Adjusting Row Height

Just as you can adjust the width of columns, you can change the height of the rows. Row height is not a simple issue, and it is determined by a number of factors:

- Largest type size and leading used in the row
- Number of lines of text typed in a cell
- Row gutters specified in the Table Setup dialog box
- Value specified in the Row Height dialog box

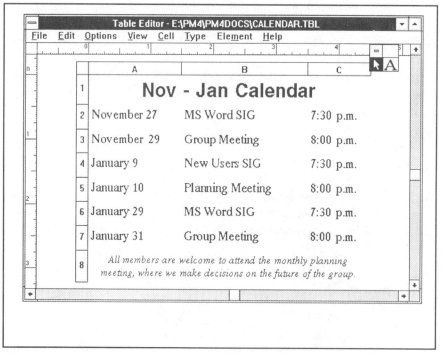

Figure 13.12: The calendar with its new column widths

Increasing the Row Height

Increasing the height of a row is straightforward, so we'll attack this subject first. There are two ways to increase the row height: by dragging the row boundary with the mouse or by typing a value in the Row Height dialog box. Either way, the total length of the table is increased. Unlike with column width, there is no way to automatically keep the table size constant when you change the row height.

Follow these steps to increase the height of row 1 in your calendar:

1. Click anywhere in row 1.

2. From the Cell menu, choose Row Height. The current row height is .47 inches.

3. Type **.7** and choose OK.

The extra space is added below the title since text is vertically aligned at the top of the cell. If you want to vertically center the title, use the Align Middle alignment option. As the vertical ruler shows, the table is now more than 3 inches long. When you increased the row height, the table itself grew taller.

Decreasing Row Height

To keep the table 3 inches high, you need to decrease the height of other rows. One way to do this is to enter the height in the Row Height dialog box. You can also drag the row boundaries with the mouse. Regardless of which technique you use, the leading and the row gutter limit how short you can make the rows. For example, try to reduce the row height from 0.38 to 0.30 inches:

1. Select rows 2 through 7.

2. Choose Row Height on the Cell menu.

3. Enter **.30** and choose OK. A window appears with the message

   Can't reduce one or more row height(s) to specified value given the amount of text in selected row(s). Reduce row height(s) as much as text allows?

This means that, given the current row gutters, a row height of 0.30 is insufficient.

4. Choose OK.

Specifying a Smaller Gutter

To decrease the row height significantly, you must specify a smaller row gutter in the Table Setup dialog box. After changing the row gutter, the row heights do not adjust automatically, but you can decrease the row heights with the mouse or in the Row Height dialog box.

Follow these steps to decrease the row gutters and the row height:

1. From the File menu, choose Table Setup.

2. Change the row gutter to .05, which is half of its current size.

3. Choose OK.

4. Select rows 2 through 7.

The rows are now closer together and consume less space. The table height is very close to 3 inches, as shown in Figure 13.13.

Notice how close the paragraph in row 8 is to the text in row 7. To get a little extra space between the rows without increasing the table length, align the text with the bottom of the cell.

5. Save and close the CALENDAR file.

WORKING WITH NUMBERS

The Table Editor provides some additional formatting options that are specific to numbers. And when your table includes numbers, you can use the Sum option on the Cell menu to total them.

Formatting Numbers

You can enter numeric punctuation (dollar signs, commas, decimal places, and percent signs) yourself, but the Table Editor provides an

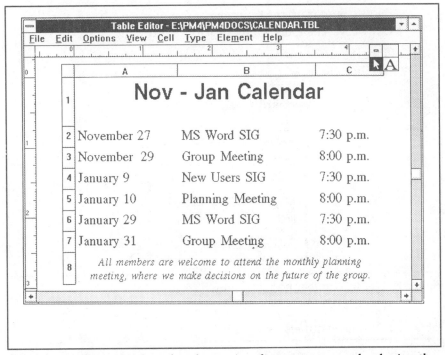

Figure 13.13: The calendar, after decreasing the row gutter and reducing the row heights

easier way: choose the format in the Number Format dialog box, shown in Figure 13.14.

Table 13.1 explains and provides an example of each of the numeric formats. Notice that formatting rounds off the numbers. Because formatting often increases the number of characters in a cell, make sure that the numbers aren't truncated; if they are, adjust the column widths.

Calculating Totals

The Table Editor has one built-in mathematical function: summing a range of cells. If the range contains any negative values, those numbers are subtracted from the total. Here are the general steps for summing numbers:

1. With the pointer tool, select the range of cells to be summed.

2. Choose Sum from the Cell menu. You will see a small icon that says SUM. The total is temporarily stored in this icon.

3. Place the sum icon on the cell where you want to paste the total, and then click.

The total appears, overwriting anything that may be in the cell.

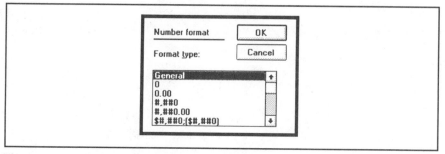

Figure 13.14: The Number Format dialog box

Table 13.1: Number Formats

FORMAT	DESCRIPTION	EXAMPLE
General	No punctuation, variable decimal places	1200.647
0	No punctuation, no decimal places	1201
0.00	No punctuation, two decimal places	1200.65
#,##0	Commas, no decimal places	1,201
#,##0.00	Commas, two decimal places	1,200.65
$#,##0	Dollar sign, commas, no decimal places	$1,201
$#,##0.00	Dollar sign, commas, two decimal places	$1,200.65
0%	Percent sign, no decimal places	34%
0.00%	Percent sign, two decimal places	34.25%

ADDING SHADES

You can shade or fill a cell with a pattern by choosing the Fill option from the Element menu. Figure 13.15 shows the fill patterns that can be applied to selected cells. As in PageMaker, the percentages refer to gray shades, and the solid fill can be used in conjunction with the reverse type style to create reversed text.

At the bottom of the Fill menu are two options specific to the Table Editor: Alternate Rows and Alternate Columns. When these options are turned on, the shade is applied to every other row or column, as shown in Figure 13.16. Alternating shades help differentiate rows and columns in a large table, making it easier to read. To create alternating shades, follow these general steps:

1. Select the entire range in which you want to alternate shades. The shading will begin in the first row or column of the selected range.

2. From the Fill menu, choose Alternate Rows or Alternate Columns.

3. Choose the desired shade from the Fill menu.

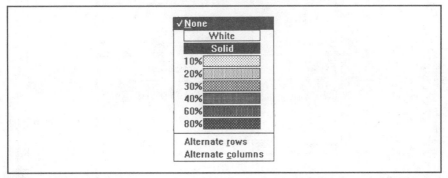

Figure 13.15: The Fill menu

MODIFYING A TABLE

Once a table is created, it is inevitable that you will want to make changes to it. You might need to insert rows or columns, move text to other cells, erase data, or remove rows or columns. This section describes how to make these types of modifications.

Inserting Cells

How you insert rows and columns depends on where you want them to go. To insert additional rows at the bottom of the table, change the number of rows in the Table Setup dialog box. For example, to add another row to the bottom of a six-row table, enter **7** for Number of Rows in the dialog

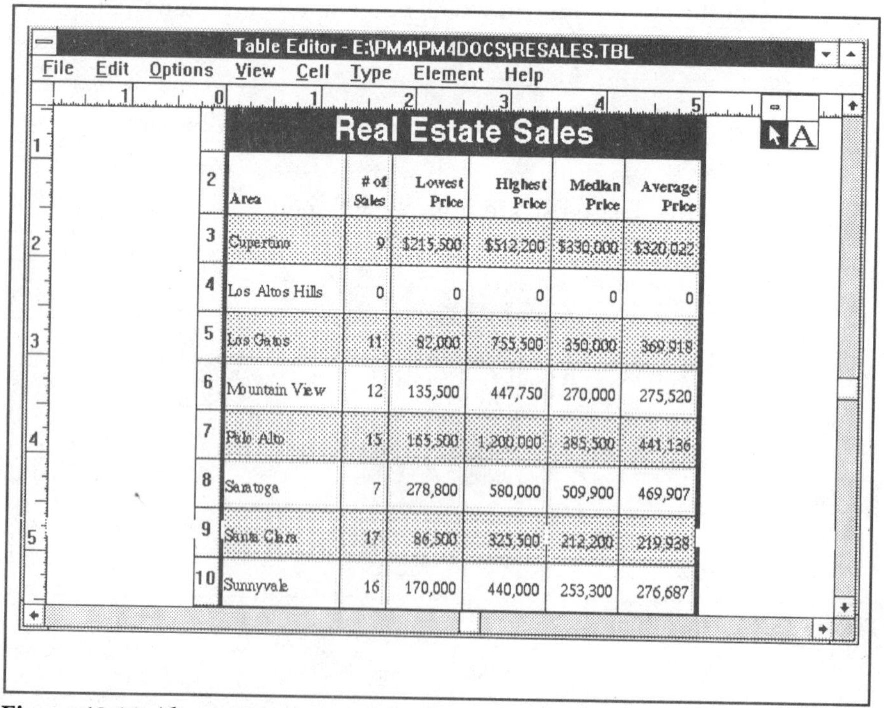

Figure 13.16: Alternating rows of shading

box. Use a similar approach to add columns to the right side of the table. When you choose OK in the Table Setup dialog box, the Table Editor warns you that the table size must be increased to accommodate the new rows or columns. Choose OK to accept the increased table size.

To insert rows and columns anywhere else in the table, use the Insert command on the Cell menu. The Insert dialog box, shown in Figure 13.17, requires two responses: whether you want to insert a row or a column, and how many you want to insert. The Row button is chosen unless you selected an entire column. Rows are inserted above the selected row and columns are inserted to the left of the selected column.

Deleting Cells

Before deleting a row or column, make sure this is really what you want to do. All the data, in addition to the actual cells in the column or row, will be removed. If all you want to do is clear the data so that the cells are blank, don't delete the row or column. Instead, use the Clear command on the Edit menu or press the Del key. You are then presented with the Clear dialog box, where you can select what you want to erase: the text, the lines, the fill, or all of the above. When you want to clear the contents of a range of cells and not the borders, do not accept the default selection (All); choose Text instead. The cells will be emptied, and you can enter new data or leave them blank.

If you want to eliminate the data without leaving empty cells, use the Delete command on the Cell menu. Make sure that the correct button is selected (Row or Column) before you select OK in the dialog box.

The Table Editor does not offer an Undo feature, so be careful with the Delete and Clear commands.

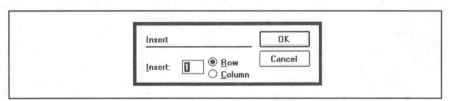

Figure 13.17: The Insert dialog box

Moving Cell Contents

To move the contents of a range of cells to another area in the table, you can use the cut-and-paste method you have already learned. However, moving cell contents in the Table Editor is not quite as easy as moving text in PageMaker.

Because the Table Editor does not automatically insert when it pastes, the range that you paste into should be blank. If it's not, you will overwrite the data that was previously there. Therefore, you will need to insert a row or a column which you will paste into, and then delete the blank row or column which originally contained the data. Thus, the cut-and-paste procedure is actually more of a cut-insert-paste-and-delete routine.

Another tricky part about moving cells is that the selected range you paste into must be the same size as the range that was cut. You can't get away with pasting into the first cell in the range—you must select the entire range.

Follow these general steps to move a row:

1. Select the row to be moved and cut it to the Clipboard.

2. Insert a new row in the new location.

3. Make sure this row is selected, and then paste the data from the Clipboard.

4. Select the blank row and delete it.

IMPORTING
A TABLE INTO PAGEMAKER

The procedure for importing a table is the same as the one for importing a graphic: choose the file in the Place dialog box and indicate where you want to place it. Before you can import a table, you must have previously installed the Table Editor import filter in the Aldus Setup program (see Appendix A for details).

Follow these steps to import the calendar table into the newsletter publication you created in Chapter 11:

1. Exit from the Table Editor.
2. Load or switch into PageMaker.
3. Open the NEWSLET.PM4 publication and go to page 2.
4. Press Ctrl-D to display the Place File dialog box.
5. If necessary, navigate to the directory that contains the calendar table.
6. Double-click on CALENDAR.TBL. You will see an icon with a pencil, which is the object-oriented graphic gun.
7. Place the graphic gun in the upper corner of the shadow box and click.

Exporting and Placing a Table

The calendar comes into PageMaker in its Table Editor size: 4½ by 3 inches. On the page, you can move the calendar as well as drag the handles to size it. Be sure to hold down the Shift key as you drag so that the table is sized proportionally. Your imported calendar should look similar to Figure 13.18. The figure shows a shadow box that was drawn with PageMaker's drawing tools. The steps for creating this box were described in Chapter 11.

When you change the size of an imported table, the type sizes are scaled accordingly. For example, if you make a table smaller than its original size, 12-point type might become 11 points. This scaling can cause problems when you aren't using scalable fonts. If you don't have a certain font size, PageMaker must substitute the closest size you have available. The end result might be text that doesn't fit within the column boundaries.

Printing a Table

If the Table Editor offered a Print command, you wouldn't even need PageMaker to produce a final product. Since there is no way to print in the Table Editor, you must import it into PageMaker.

Once the table is in PageMaker, you can print it in its original size or scale it. There are two ways to scale in PageMaker: proportionally stretch the graphic's bounding box, or enter a percentage next to the Scaling option in the Print dialog box. When using the Scaling print option, place the table in the center of the page so that it has room to grow.

Importing Tables into Other Packages

You can import tables into other software packages by exporting the file to Windows Metafile Format. When you do so, the table looks just as it does in the Table Editor. It has the same borders, shades, fonts, alignment, and so on.

Another export option is Text Only format. A text file does not have any of the formatting you specified in the Table Editor, except for tabs between columns.

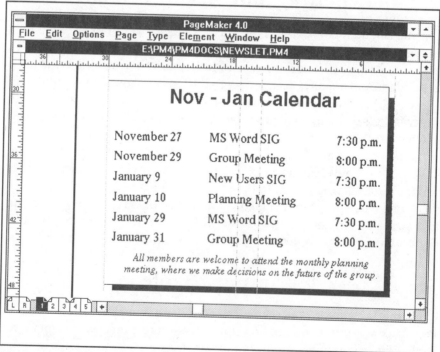

Figure 13.18: The imported calendar

Why would you want to use the Text Only format if it doesn't include any formatting? Text Only offers one major advantage: the table can be edited. If you discover an error in the data, you can fix it on the spot. A table in Windows Metafile format, on the other hand, is a graphic that cannot be edited.

Modifying the Table

The imported table is like an imported graphic, so you cannot directly modify the data. However, as with all imported files, the imported table is linked to its external file, allowing you to easily update the internal copy when you change the original file.

One way to update the table is to load the Table Editor, open the table, make and save the changes, and then use the Update button in the Page-Maker Links dialog box. This is the method you used when you imported external text and graphics files in Chapters 9 and 12. But a less circuitous route is to load the Table Editor and the table itself directly from PageMaker.

In the following exercise, you will go through the steps that are required when you make a change to the calendar:

1. Hold down the Ctrl key and double-click on the calendar. This combination loads the Table Editor (if it's not already in memory) and opens CALENDAR.TBL.

2. Change the meeting time of the New Users SIG to 8:00.

3. Press Ctrl-S to save this change in the table file.

The change is not reflected in the PageMaker publication unless it is saved in the table.

4. Exit from the Table Editor.

5. If necessary, switch back into PageMaker.

6. Display the Links dialog box, highlight CALENDAR.TBL and choose the Update button.

7. Close the Links dialog box.

The internal calendar graphic now matches the external calendar file, without choosing the Update button.

The Table Editor offers an alternative way of producing columnar data for your PageMaker publications. Financial reports, forms, calendars, schedules, and price lists are a few types of tables that the Table Editor can produce with ease.

You will find that data entry into a spreadsheet grid is easier than typing a table with the text tool in PageMaker. More important, the Table Editor specifically addresses the formatting requirements of columnar data. The program's main drawback is that the formatted tables cannot be directly edited in PageMaker.

PART FOUR

▼ ▼ ▼ ▼ ▼ ▼ ▼ ▼ ▼ ▼ ▼

MANAGING
YOUR
PROJECTS

This final section of the book provides you with strategies for managing your publishing projects. Read Chapter 14 to find out how to clone a publication that you will be using over and over again, such as a monthly newsletter. If you are going to be creating a long publication, such as a book, Chapter 15 shows you how to create a table of contents and an index. The last chapter explains how to approach a variety of projects, from menus and invitations to business cards and directories.

14

CLONING YOUR PUBLICATIONS

You finally did it. You generated an issue of your monthly newsletter with PageMaker. You crashed a few times, went through four variations of margins and column widths, and generated enough style names to publish the Bill of Rights. But you did it—all four pages. You're happy and proud, but you can't face the prospect of doing it all over again next month. How do you spell relief? R-E-T-I-R-E-M-E-N-T.

For frustrated PageMaker hackers, there is hope. With a small amount of file management, you can create your newsletter (or any other publication) just once and use it from one issue to the next. When you are through with this chapter, cloning a publication you already created will be as easy as starting PageMaker, opening a file, and making a few modifications. This strategy relies on three PageMaker features: master pages, templates, and file linking.

SETTING UP MASTER PAGES

Consider the text and graphic elements that might appear on every page in a publication. Here are a few that immediately come to mind: page numbers, dates, titles, revision numbers, logos, and horizontal and vertical rules. Rather than manually typing them on every page, you can place these repeating elements on *master pages*.

The master pages are accessed by clicking on the L and R page icons at the bottom of your publication window. Whatever text and graphics you place on these pages appear on all pages in the publication. In a double-sided publication, the items on the left master page are repeated on even-numbered pages; the items on the right master page are repeated on the odd-numbered pages. A single-sided publication has only a right master page.

Master pages can also contain nonprinting elements, such as column and ruler guides. Can you imagine manually specifying column guides for a 50-page publication? Not much fun. But when you set up the column guides on the master pages, you only have to issue the Column Guides command once.

Column guides on existing pages will override the guides you set on the master pages, but any new pages will automatically have the column guides you placed on the master pages.

Adding Headers and Footers

Footers are text or graphic elements repeated at the bottom of each page; headers are repeated at the top. Because headers and footers typically appear within the margins, you should make sure you have ample top or bottom margins before adding these elements.

To include a page number on your master page, press Ctrl-Shift-# wherever you want the page number to print (usually in the top or bottom margin). You will see either LM or RM, depending on whether you pressed Ctrl-Shift-# on the left or right master page. This code is replaced with the actual page number when you leave the master pages.

A footer or header can contain formatted text, such as a newsletter name and date. You might also want to insert a special character, such as the diamond shown in Figure 14.1. This diamond was produced with the

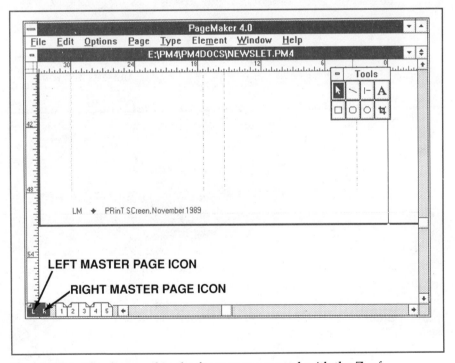

Figure 14.1: The diamond in the footer was created with the Zapf Dingbats font

Zapf Dingbats font. If you don't have this font, you can create a bullet (Ctrl-Shift-8) and format it with the Symbol font.

Turning Off Master Items

While elements on your master pages belong on most pages, they are not appropriate for every page. For example, in a newsletter, the footer does not belong on the cover page. The Display Master Items option on the Page menu lets you turn off the repeating elements for individual pages (in a single-sided publication) or page spreads (in a publication with double-sided facing pages).

Follow these basic steps to turn off the master items on a page:

1. Go to the page or page spread from which you want to remove the master page elements.

2. Pull down the Page menu.

The Display Master Items option is a toggle, and it is automatically turned on (checked) for each page or page spread in the publication.

3. Choose Display Master Items to turn off the option. The master items (except for the guides) will disappear.

Copying Master Guides

When you create, move, or remove ruler guides or set different column guides or gutters for a particular page, that page uses *custom guides* that override the guides on the master pages.

If you decide that you want to replace the custom guides with the column and ruler guides on the master pages, display the page or page spread and choose the Copy Master Guides option on the Page menu. All the custom guides will be removed, and the page or spread will use the master guides.

ADVANTAGES OF USING TEMPLATES

A *template* is a reusable publication that defines the structure and layout of a specific type of document. Templates save you from having to recreate the wheel whenever you need to use the same design for multiple projects. You can create templates for any kind of publication, such as brochures, newsletters, letterheads, memos, and manuals.

Templates can contain any of the following:

- Margins, column guides, ruler guides
- Master pages
- Style sheets
- Logos
- Headings
- Stories
- Graphics (PageMaker-drawn or imported)

Let's look at a simple example. Remember back to Chapter 5 when you created the letterhead for Blue Chip Realty? You saved the letterhead without the body of the letter in a publication called LETHEAD2. The letterhead is essentially a template because it is designed to be used over and over again.

While LETHEAD2.PM4 is a reusable publication, it is not technically a template. To create a template, you turn on the Template option in the Save As dialog box. This option creates a publication file with a .PT4 extension.

How does a .PT4 file differ from a .PM4 file, and what do you actually gain from saving a publication as a template? The difference between the two file types is subtle and mainly one of convenience. When you open a .PT4 file, PageMaker opens an *untitled copy* of the publication, and the original template remains on disk. Because the publication is untitled, you will be prompted for a file name when you save it.

The problem with using a .PM4 file as a template is that you may forget to change the file name when you save your publication, inadvertently altering your template. This is not a concern when you open .PT4 files. Think of .PT4 files as untitled publications that give you a running start.

Because you will be using the template over and over again, it should be as perfect as possible. But mistakes are inevitable, and as you use a template, you might decide to change part of the design. Keep in mind that changes in your .PM4 publication do not affect the .PT4 template file. To make permanent changes to the template, turn on the Original option in the Open File dialog box when you open the template.

CREATING AND USING A LETTERHEAD TEMPLATE

To see how all this works, let's create a letterhead template.

1. Open LETHEAD2.PM4.

2. Display the Save As dialog box.

3. Turn on the Template option.

4. Choose OK.

A file named LETHEAD2.PT4 was created. Now let's take a look at this file.

5. Display the Open dialog box.

6. Click on LETHEAD2.PT4.

Notice that the Copy button is turned on because the selected file is a template.

7. Choose OK.

A copy of the letterhead is displayed, as shown in Figure 14.2. *Untitled* appears in the document window title bar until you save the file with a different name. The file is automatically saved with a .PM4 extension. We are finished with the letterhead now, so close the file.

8. Select Close from the File menu. Do not save the file.

CREATING A BOOK TEMPLATE

In the following steps, you will begin to create a handbook on managing rental properties. Each chapter in the book is contained in its own publication. Because each chapter will have the same layout and style sheet, you will design a template for the book, and then create each chapter by opening the template. The final handbook will have 12 chapters, but you will create only two chapters here. In fact, you are not going to actually type any of the text files; for the example, you will enter only the headings

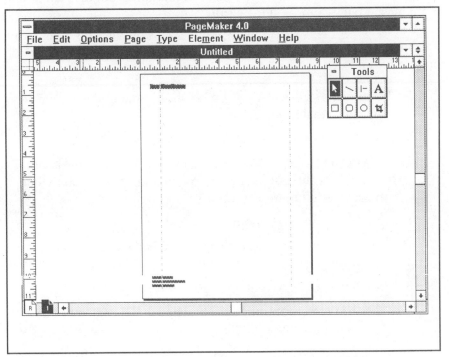

Figure 14.2: The untitled copy of the letterhead template

and subheadings. This minimal amount of text is enough to let you see how to create the template. In the next chapter, you'll add a table of contents and an index to the book.

1. Create a new file and specify the following page setup:

   Size: 24 by 42 picas (4 by 7 inches)

   Number of pages: 5

   Inside margin: 4p6

   Outside margin: 3p

   Top margin: 3p

   Bottom margin: 4p6

2. Click on the master page icons at the bottom of the document window.

Because this publication has double-sided facing pages, the left and right master pages appear side by side.

For our example, we're going to place a page number centered inside the bottom margin of the left and right pages. Figure 14.3 shows the left master page.

3. Position the screen so that you see the bottom of the left master page, in Actual Size view.

4. Pull down a ruler guide at the 40-pica mark.

5. With the text tool, click on the ruler guide. Don't worry about exact placement, but the text cursor should approximately line up with the left margin guide.

6. Specify the type as 10-point Times Roman bold.

7. Press Ctrl-Shift-# to insert a page number code. LM appears on the master page.

8. Press Ctrl-Shift-C to center the page number footer.

9. With the pointer tool, align the baseline of the page number code on the ruler guide.

10. On the right master page, repeat steps 5 through 9 to insert a page number.

11. Remove the ruler guide.

To see the actual page numbers inserted in place of the LM and RM codes, click on one of the page number icons to go to a page spread.

Adding Styles to the Template

As you learned in Chapter 8, paragraph styles allow you to automate the formatting process, and they ensure that your publication is formatted consistently. A style sheet, therefore, is an integral part of a template. With the style sheet in place, you don't have to manually format the imported text. You can assign style names to the paragraphs after you bring in the

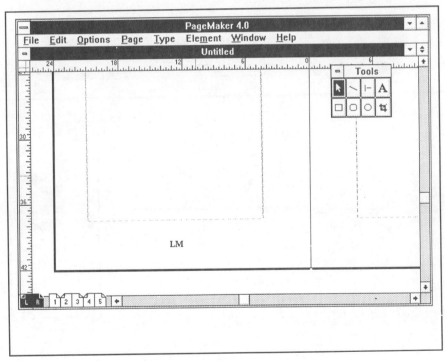

Figure 14.3: Left master page

text. An even easier way is to tag the paragraphs in your word processor, so that the text will be formatted automatically when you import the file.

The book template will have two styles. The Chapter Head style formats a two-line chapter heading, with the chapter number on the first line and the title on the second line, as shown in Figure 14.4. The Subhead style formats the subheadings throughout the chapter, as shown in Figure 14.5. (In reality, a template for a book would have many more styles; for example, to format body text, several levels of subheadings, and bullets.)

Follow these steps to create the Chapter Head style:

1. At the top of page 1, type **Chapter #**.

2. Press Shift-Enter to drop to the next line without creating a new paragraph.

3. Type **Title Goes Here**. This line is the placeholder for the chapter title.

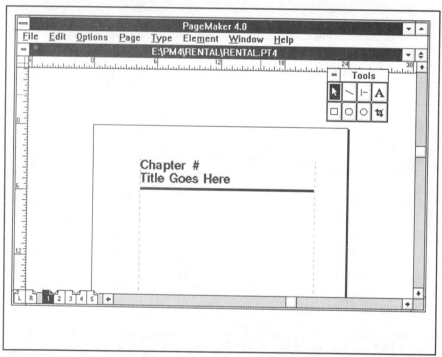

Figure 14.4: The two-line chapter title is formatted with the Chapter Head style

4. Format the text as follows:

   Font: Helvetica

   Size: 14 points

   Leading: 14 points

   Style: Bold

   Rule below paragraph: 4 points, placed 0p9 below the baseline

5. Create a style for this paragraph called **Chapter Head**.

6. Display the style palette and assign this style to the paragraph.

As you can see in the palette, the style sheet contains the five default style names (Body text, Caption, Headline, Subhead 1, and Subhead 2). You should delete them when they are not needed in the publication.

7. Display the Define Styles dialog box and remove the default styles.

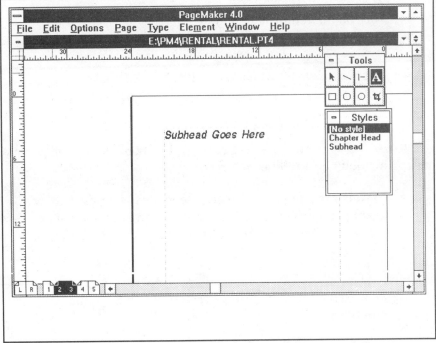

Figure 14.5: The subheading is formatted with the Subhead style

8. To create the Subhead placeholder, at the top of page 2, type **Subhead Goes Here**.

9. Format the text as follows:

   Font: Helvetica

   Size: 12 points

   Leading: 12 points

   Style: Bold, Italic

   Space after paragraph: 1 pica

10. Create a style for this paragraph called **Subhead**.

11. Assign the Subhead style to this paragraph.

The template is complete. Now save the publication as a template.

12. Display the Save As dialog box.

13. Type **RENTAL** for the name.

14. Turn on the Template option.

15. Choose OK.

The template is saved with the name RENTAL.PT4.

Using the Template

To use the template for all the chapters in a book, follow this general procedure (don't do anything just yet):

1. In your word processor, create a separate file for each chapter. Insert paragraph tags, using the same names that are in the template's style sheet. For example, tag each of your subheadings with <Subhead>.

2. In PageMaker, open the template.

3. Replace the Chapter Head placeholder with the actual chapter number and title.

4. Import the text file and graphics (for the sake of simplicity, we are skipping this step in our example).

5. Format the text with the style sheet. This step is not necessary if you tagged the text in your word processor.

6. Save the publication with a unique name.

7. Repeat steps 2 through 6 for each chapter in the book.

Creating the Chapters

Since we are not importing any text into the handbook, all you need to do is type the headings for each chapter. You will place each section heading on a separate page. Follow these steps to create the first chapter:

1. Open the RENTAL.PT4 template.

2. Go to page 1.

3. With the text tool, select the # sign and type **One** to replace the placeholder with the actual chapter number.

4. Select *Title Goes Here* and type **Managing Residents**. Your chapter title should look similar to Figure 14.6.

5. Instead of importing text files, type the following subheadings at the top of pages 2 through 5, and then apply the Subhead style:

   Starting Out Right

   Keeping Good Tenants

   Dealing with Tenant Complaints

   Handling Claims and Disputes

6. Save the publication with the name RENTAL01.

7. To create the second chapter, open the RENTAL.PT4 template and go to page 1.

8. Select the # sign and type **Two** to replace the placeholder with the actual chapter number.

9. Select *Title Goes Here* and type **Marketing**.

10. Type the following subheadings at the top of pages 2 through 5, and then apply the Subhead style:

    Determining a Rental Rate

    Selecting Good Tenants

    Advertising the Product

    Selling the Product

11. Save the publication with the name **RENTAL02**.

We are only creating two sample chapters. Additional chapters could be cloned in the same fashion.

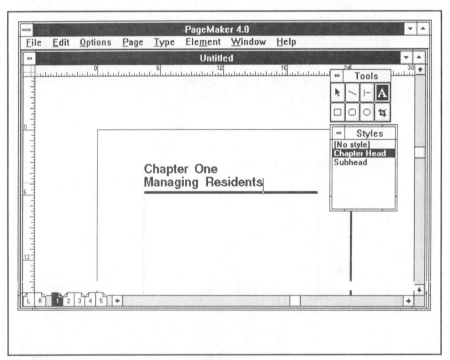

Figure 14.6: The title for Chapter One

CREATING
A NEWSLETTER TEMPLATE

Templates are particularly handy for newsletters. When deciding which elements belong in a template, think of the items that are standard from one issue to the next.

For example, the logo on the cover page of a newsletter is a constant and should be a part of the template. While the date and volume will change each issue, you should keep this line in the template as a placeholder. When you use the template, you replace the placeholder with the new text.

Any standard headings and graphic elements within a newsletter should also remain in the template. Even graphics and stories that will change in each publication are good candidates for a template, because they act as placeholders.

Using a Newsletter Template

To use a newsletter template on a regular basis, follow this basic procedure:

1. Type the new stories and create the new graphics.

2. Open the template.

3. Replace the placeholders with the new stories and graphics.

After you've typed the stories for the next newsletter, open the template and replace each of the stories or graphics with its updated file. One way to do this is to import the file again with the Place command. You don't need to delete the original file. Just click on the story or graphic before displaying the Place File dialog box, choose the file name, and turn on the Replacing Entire Story (or Graphic) option. For text files, turn on the Read Tags option as well.

Alternatively, you can use the file linking feature, as described in the next section.

In a perfect world, the imported stories are the same length as the placeholders. Realistically, you will need to do some *copyfitting*, which is the process of adjusting the length of your stories so they fit in their allotted space. When a story is too long, read through the text and look for sentences or paragraphs that can be cut. (Your writers may scream, but cutting is an inevitable part of the publishing process.) When a story is too short, use pull-quotes, graphics, or *fillers* (short paragraphs to fill space). But don't feel that you must fill every blank spot on the page. A little white space gives your publication a feeling of openness that readers appreciate, even if only subconsciously.

The next step is an easy one to overlook: replace the remaining placeholders with the current text. For example, you may need to type new headlines and pull-quotes for a feature story, as well as change the date in your footer on the master pages and under the logo on the cover page. Select the old text with the text tool and type right over it. The new text will automatically be formatted like the original.

The final step is to import graphics specific to the current newsletter, for example, on the cover page.

Linking Files to Your Template

True automation of your template occurs when your stories and graphics are linked to their external files. As you know, files are automatically linked when you import them with the Place command.

If you imported your newsletter's original stories from text files, the files are automatically linked to the publication. But if you typed the text in the Story Editor, you must export each of the files and reimport them to establish a link. If necessary, follow these steps to create an external file for each story:

1. Place the text cursor in the story.

2. Use the Export command, and turn on the Export Tags option. Choose any of the word processor export filters.

3. Use the Place command, and turn on the Read Tags and Replacing Entire Story options.

4. Display the Links dialog box to see a list of the linked files.

When files are linked to their external files, you do not need to use the Place command to replace the existing files; you just tell PageMaker to update the files in the publication. Actually, the updating can even occur automatically, as explained in the next section.

Ultimate Automation

Here is the ultimate in automation: open a copy of the template, and all the new stories and graphics are automatically in place. There are two keys to making this system work:

- The new files must have the same names as the ones that are linked to the template. For example, if the template is linked to CLUBNEWS.WRI, THISMON.WRI, FEATURE1.WRI, and CALENDAR.TBL, your new files should have these same names. They must also be stored in the same subdirectory as the original files.

- Turn on the Update Automatically link option for each of the files. That way, when you open the template, each of the files is automatically imported.

File management is an important part of cloning a publication. Because each issue's files should have the same names as those in the previous issue, you need to decide what to do with the original files. If you don't want to keep the outdated files, you can simply overwrite the existing files for each issue. On the other hand, if you want to preserve the data, you should develop a system for archiving the files. Either copy the files to another subdirectory or floppy disk, or use an archiving software program, such as LHARC or PKZIP.

Updating the Files Manually

If you want more control over linked files, you can turn on the Alert Before Updating option. When this option is on, PageMaker will ask if you want to import each modified file when you open the template or publication. For even more control, don't use the automatic updating feature at all. Instead, choose the Update command button in the Links dialog box whenever you want to update a linked file.

Linking to a Different File

What if the new files have different names than the ones linked to the publication? One solution is to rename them in DOS or in Windows File Manager. Alternatively, you can tell PageMaker to link to a different file, as follows:

1. Display the Links dialog box and click on the original file name.

2. Choose the Link Info command button.

3. If necessary, navigate the Files/Directories list until you find the new file name.

4. Click on the new name, choose Link, and choose OK to update the file.

USING PAGEMAKER'S TEMPLATES

PageMaker comes with a set of ready-made templates for a variety of publications, including brochures, business cards, calendars, catalogs, phone directories, envelopes, financial statements, employee application forms, invoices, letterheads, mailing labels, manuals, memos, newsletters, price lists, and purchase orders. Like the templates you create, the PageMaker templates contain column grids, style sheets, and placeholders.

All you have to do is open one of these templates and replace the text and graphic placeholders with your files. However, none of the templates are linked to external files, so the Place command is the only way you can import text and graphics. The Links dialog box is not applicable; however, once you place files, a link is created.

Rarely will a ready-made template suit your needs exactly. Most likely, you will need to customize the template for your project. When you modify an existing template, save it with a new name so that the original remains intact, just in case you ever want to refer to it again.

You may want to use these templates to give you ideas on how to design a certain type of publication. For example, if you are going to be creating a price list, open the PRICE.PT4 template to see the page layout, styles, and graphic elements the folks at Aldus used to design their price list.

To use the PageMaker templates, you must run the Aldus Setup program to copy them to your hard disk. There are actually two sets of templates: one for PCL printers (such as the HP LaserJet) and one for PostScript printers. To copy the templates, follow the steps outlined in Appendix A.

The templates are stored in their own subdirectory, in either \PM4\TEMPLATE\PCL or \PM4\TEMPLATE\PSCRIPT. In the PCL and PSCRIPT subdirectories, there are three more subdirectories called AVERY (for the Avery mailing label templates), CALDATES (for the monthly calendar templates), and GRIDS (for the generic grid templates).

In this chapter, you saw several ways that templates can eliminate repetitive work for similar publications. Templates are ideal for newsletters and other publications that you publish on a regular basis. They work equally well for large projects, such as books, that are divided into multiple files. By creating templates, you can be confident that each clone has the same page layout, style sheet, and graphic elements as the original. Well-designed templates automate the publishing process and save you a tremendous amount of time.

15

WORKING WITH MONSTER PROJECTS

The publishing projects we have dealt with so far have been small projects: letterheads, brochures, and newsletters. But what if you have to produce a 70-page document, or a monster-sized 700-page publication? The rules change as the page count increases. Even if PageMaker could handle 700 pages in one publication, you couldn't. Just the amount of time you spend scrolling would be overwhelming. Large documents need to be divided into several smaller publications, for the sake of PageMaker's processing speed, not to mention your own sanity.

THE APPROACH
TO LARGE PROJECTS

When approaching longer jobs, let the content determine the form. If you are producing a book about birds, with discussions of six species, each species could be discussed in its own chapter and stored in its own publication. If you are embarking on a sociological examination of the impact of being left-handed, perhaps each case study would be a separate publication.

PageMaker provides tools for grouping and controlling several publications as a single project. As you might already have guessed, a template is an important part of creating a large project. A template eliminates repetitious work and ensures consistent formatting across all publications. The master template for the project will specify the appropriate page setup, footers, styles, and placeholders. Then to create each publication, open the template, place text and graphic files, and replace the placeholders.

The collection of publications related to a single project is called a *book*. With the book feature, you can create a table of contents and an index that spans all the publications in the book. You can also print the entire book with a single Print command.

Monster projects are made up of many files. Each chapter is in its own publication file, and each publication is made up of at least one text file and any number of graphic files. Consequently, file management is extremely important. We recommend creating a subdirectory for the large project and storing all related files in it.

CREATING A BOOK

In the previous chapter, you cloned a template to create two chapters of a rental property handbook. Now you need to tell PageMaker that these chapters are part of a larger, single document: a *book*. You define a book by creating a list of the related publications in the Book dialog box.

After you have created a book, you can issue commands that will be carried out across all the publications in the book. Presently, there are just two short chapters that we intend to turn into a book, but the process would be the same if there were 40 chapters and 2000 pages.

The book list is created in the first publication in the project. Although this could be in the book's first chapter (for example, RENTAL01.PM4), a better place for it is in a separate introductory publication. This publication might contain a title page, acknowledgments, a preface, and a table of contents. The introductory material, or *front matter*, belongs in a separate publication so that these pages do not affect the pagination of the first chapter.

Let's create a publication for the front matter and book list. We could use the template we created earlier, but you would have to delete the footers, placeholders, and extra pages. Therefore, we'll create a publication from scratch, using the same page setup you specified for the template.

1. Create a new file.

2. Specify the following page setup:

   Size: 24 by 42 picas (4 by 7 inches)

   Number of pages: 2

   Inside margin: 4p6

   Outside margin: 3p

   Top margin: 3p

   Bottom margin: 4p6

3. On page 1, create a title page for the book. Recreate the one shown in Figure 15.1, or be creative and design your own.

4. Save the file with the name RENTBOOK.PM4.

Figure 15.1: The title page

Defining a Book List

Follow these steps to define the publications that are part of the book:

1. Pull down the File menu and choose Book to display the Book
    Publication List dialog box, shown in Figure 15.2.

The book list is on the right, and RENTBOOK.PM4, the current publication, is already at the top of the list. We don't want this file in the book list because it will affect the pagination of the book (more on this later). Let's remove it.

2. Click on the Remove button.

The file names should be listed in the same order they will appear in the book. If they aren't, the table of contents will be out of order, and the

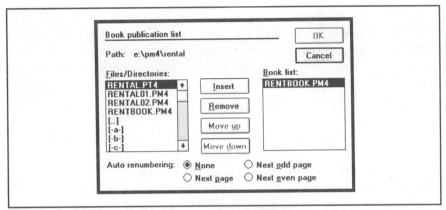

Figure 15.2: The Book Publication List dialog box

page numbering may be off. To add a publication to the list, select the name from the Files/Directories list and click on the Insert command button.

3. In the Files/Directories box, click on RENTAL01.PM4.

4. Click on the Insert button. The file name is added to the book list.

5. Click on RENTAL02.PM4 and choose Insert.

6. Choose OK.

The book list now contains two publications: RENTAL01.PM4 and RENTAL02.PM4, in that order. Because the order of the files on the book list is so important, PageMaker offers two command buttons for rearranging the order of the files: Move Up and Move Down. For instance, to move a file higher up on the list, click on the name and click on the Move Up button until the file is in its correct position.

Numbering Pages Across Publications

Both RENTAL01.PM4 and RENTAL02.PM4 have five pages. If you were to print the publications individually, the pages in each of these documents would be numbered 1 through 5. To number pages consecutively across publications, you could go into each of the documents and change the starting page number in the Page Setup dialog box. This requires that you know the ending page number of the preceding publication. For example, if Chapter One is numbered 1 through 5, you would enter 6 as the starting page number in Chapter Two. You would repeat this process down the line for each publication in the book.

If you have created a book, however, you can have PageMaker number the pages when the book is printed. The Auto Renumbering options in the Book Publication List dialog box (see Figure 15.2) are the key to consecutive page numbering across publications.

By default, PageMaker does not renumber the pages when it prints the book (the None option). Instead, it uses the page numbers in each publication. To turn on autorenumbering, choose one of the three remaining options: Next Page, Next Odd Page, or Next Even Page.

The Next Odd Page option is probably the most common. It makes sure each publication begins on an odd-page number—the right-hand page. If the publication would naturally start on an even page, a blank page is inserted. The Next Even Page option ensures that each publication begins on an even-numbered (left-hand) page. The Next Page option allows the publication to begin naturally, with no regard to whether the page is odd or even.

Remember how we told you to remove the RENTBOOK publication from the book list? Although it would be nice to have the front matter automatically print before the book chapters, you can't have your cake and eat it, too. If you turn on one of the Auto Renumbering options, every page in every publication is renumbered. Thus, the first page in Chapter One would be numbered 3 since RENTBOOK has two pages. To exclude the front matter from the page count, do not include that publication in the book list.

Now let's use autorenumbering to have each chapter begin on a right-hand page:

1. Choose Book from the File menu.

2. Choose the Next Odd Page option.

3. Choose OK.

Printing a Book

Before you tell PageMaker to print all the publications in a book, make sure you have either selected an Auto Renumbering option in the Book

Publication List dialog box, or that you have manually set the starting page number in each publication. If the page numbers aren't correct, you will have to reprint the entire publication.

To automatically print all the publications in a book, you must open the file that contains the book list (RENTBOOK.PM4 in our example), and then issue the Print command. Follow these steps to print the chapters:

1. Display the Print dialog box.

2. Turn on the Crop Marks option (because the pages are smaller than the paper size).

3. Turn on the Print Entire Book option.

4. Choose OK.

Both chapters will be printed. Chapter One is numbered 1 through 5. Because you instructed PageMaker to begin each publication on an odd-numbered page, page 6 is blank, and Chapter Two begins on page 7.

If you open the second chapter, you will see that the page icons reflect the new page numbering. Figure 15.3 shows that RENTAL02.PM4 contains pages numbered 7 through 12. Page 12 is a blank page that forces the next chapter to start on an odd-numbered page.

CREATING A TABLE OF CONTENTS

Creating a table of contents requires three basic steps:

1. Tag each title to be included in the table of contents.

2. Make sure the pages in each publication are accurately numbered.

3. Tell PageMaker to generate the table of contents.

If you turned on autorenumbering, step 2 is taken care of—the pages are correctly numbered. This holds true even if you have inserted and removed pages. If you haven't turned on autorenumbering, you must manually change the starting page number in each publication.

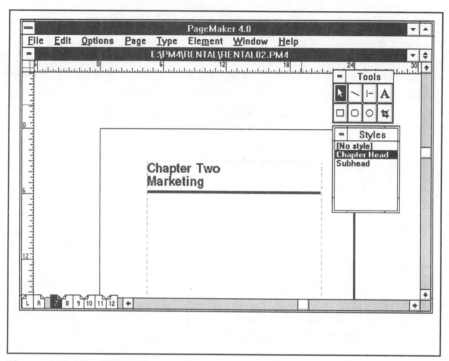

Figure 15.3: The RENTAL02 publication contains pages numbered
7 through 12

Marking a Table of Contents Entry

For your own projects, the template-designing stage is the time to begin planning your table of contents. Including a heading in the table of contents couldn't be easier: you turn on an option called Include in Table of Contents in the Paragraph Specifications dialog box. If this option is part of the style format and the style is part of the template, all the headings in your book will be marked automatically. Because we didn't turn on this option when we created the styles in the template, we need to modify the styles in each publication. Fortunately, we only have two publications (RENTAL01.PM4 and RENTAL02.PM4) and two styles (Chapter Head and Subhead).

Let's modify the styles in the two chapters so that the headings will be included in the table of contents.

1. Save RENTBOOK.

2. Open RENTAL01.PM4.

3. Hold down Ctrl and click on Chapter Head in the style palette. The Edit Style dialog box appears.

4. Click on the Para command button.

5. Turn on Include in Table of Contents.

6. Press Alt and choose OK to close the dialog boxes.

7. Hold down Ctrl and click on Subhead in the style palette.

8. Repeat steps 4 through 6 to modify the Subhead style.

9. Save RENTAL01.PM4.

10. Open RENTAL02.PM4 and repeat steps 3 through 8 to modify the styles in Chapter Two.

11. Save RENTAL02.PM4.

Generating a Table of Contents

When you choose the Create TOC command from the Options menu, PageMaker searches for paragraphs that are tagged for inclusion in the table of contents and makes a note of what page each one is on. You are then presented with a loaded text gun that contains the newly generated table of contents. Click on a page, and you have your table of contents.

The Create Table of Contents dialog box is shown in Figure 15.4. Next to Title is the heading that appears above the table of contents. *Contents* is the default title, but you can change it to *Table of Contents* or any other single line of text. Notice that the Include Book Publications option is turned on. This option looks for table of contents entries in each publication on the book list. To create a table of contents for the current publication only, turn off this option.

With the Format option, you indicate if and where you want the page number placed with relation to its entry in the table of contents. The No Page Number option is useful for creating an outline that displays the structure of a publication or a book.

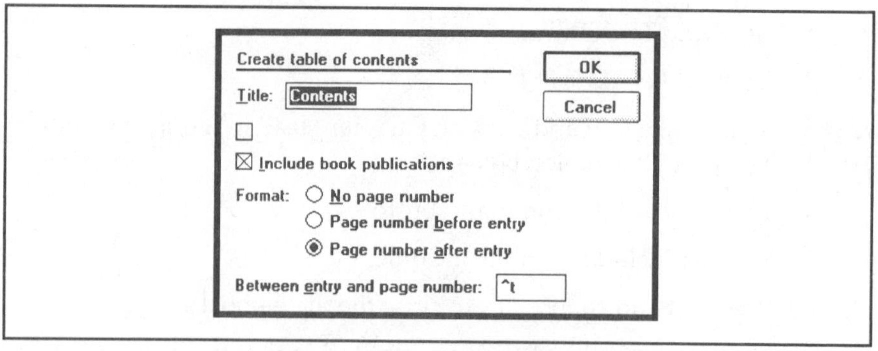

```
┌────────────────────────────────────────────────────────┐
│   Create table of contents _____          ┌──────┐   │
│                                              │  OK  │   │
│   Title: [Contents        ]                  └──────┘   │
│   ☐                                          ┌──────┐   │
│                                              │Cancel│   │
│   ☒ Include book publications                └──────┘   │
│                                                         │
│   Format:  ○ No page number                             │
│            ○ Page number before entry                   │
│            ◉ Page number after entry                    │
│                                                         │
│   Between entry and page number:  [^t  ]                │
└────────────────────────────────────────────────────────┘
```

Figure 15.4: The Create Table of Contents dialog box

The ^t at the bottom of the dialog box indicates that the table of contents entry and the page number will be separated by a tab — by default, a right-aligned tab stop is set at the right margin. The tab also contains *leader dots,* which are a series of periods that appear in the space between the end of the entry and the page number. The leader can be removed or changed, as you will see later.

Although a tab is the most common way to separate the entry and page number, you can replace it with something else, such as a comma and a space. Figure 15.5 shows a table of contents that uses commas as separators.

The table of contents for our handbook should go in the publication that contains the book list. Follow these steps to create it:

1. Open RENTBOOK.PM4.

2. Pull down the Options menu and choose Create TOC.

3. The default settings will work fine for our purposes, so choose OK.

When PageMaker finishes generating the TOC, you will see a loaded text gun.

4. Go to page 2 and click in the upper-left corner of the page.

5. Switch to Actual Size view so that you can see the entries and page numbers.

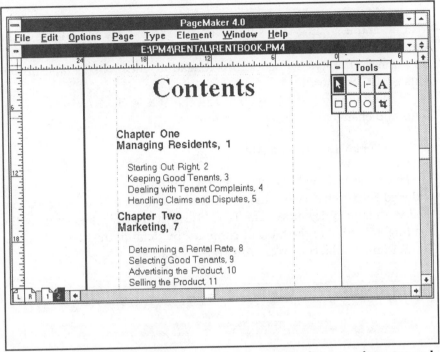

Figure 15.5: Instead of leader dots, a comma appears between the entry and the page number

Your table of contents should look similar to the one shown in Figure 15.6. Notice that both chapter titles are broken into two lines. As you might recall, you placed a line break code in the paragraph, and Page-Maker duplicates this in the table of contents. The second line of the chapter head is indented because, by default, PageMaker creates a hanging indent for multiple-line entries. We will eliminate the indent in the next section.

Formatting the Table of Contents

When PageMaker generates a table of contents, each entry has the same type specifications as the text in the original publication. Thus, the chapter heads are 14-point Times Roman bold, and the subheadings are 12-point Times Roman bold italic. However, these "borrowed" formats are not always appropriate.

PageMaker simplifies the process of formatting a table of contents by creating and assigning styles to the entries. The styles actually have the same names as the original styles, except the name is preceded by *TOC*. For example, the style name for the subheading entries in the table of contents is TOC Subhead.

In the following steps, you will edit the TOC styles to remove the indents and change the type specifications.

1. Display the style palette.

The three TOC style names are shown in Figure 15.7. Notice that we widened the palette so that the longest style name fits. We also removed the five default style names. The TOC title style controls the format of the heading at the top of the table of contents. By default, the title is 30-point Times Roman bold, centered, with 1p6 space after.

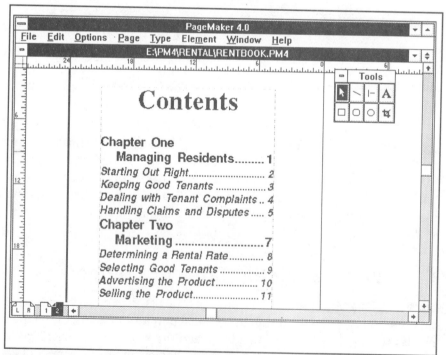

Figure 15.6: The generated table of contents

2. Hold down Ctrl and click on TOC Chapter Head in the style palette. The Edit Style dialog box appears.

3. Choose the Para command button.

4. Change the left and first-line indents to zero.

5. Specify 1 pica before and 0.5 pica after the paragraph.

6. Choose OK.

7. Choose the Type command button.

8. Change the size to 12 points, with 12-point leading.

9. Press Alt, and then choose OK to close all dialog boxes.

Figure 15.8 shows the revised TOC with the new chapter title formatting. Next, we will modify the TOC Subhead style.

10. Hold down Ctrl and click on TOC Subhead in the style palette.

11. Choose the Para command button in the Edit Style dialog box.

12. Change the left indent to 1 pica and the first-line indent to zero.

13. Choose OK.

14. Choose the Type command button.

15. Change the size to 10 points.

16. Choose the Normal type style.

17. Press Alt and choose OK to close all dialog boxes.

Figure 15.7: The style palette, with the TOC style names

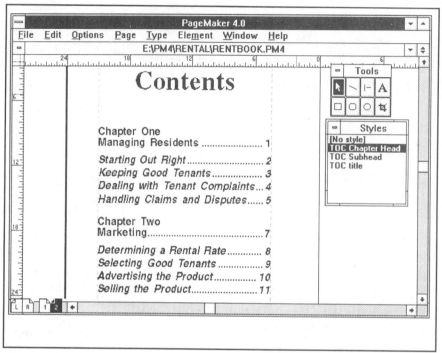

Figure 15.8: The table of contents with reformatted chapter titles

The subheadings are more clearly defined when they are indented from the chapter headings. Also, the chapter titles stand out more when they are the only bold entries. Your table of contents should look similar to the one shown in Figure 15.9.

Changing the Leaders

Leader dots are frequently used in tables of contents to help guide the reader's eye across to the page numbers, but some people feel the page tends to get too busy with so many dots. It's really a matter of personal preference.

To remove the leader dots, you need to edit the TOC styles. Follow these steps to eliminate leader dots for the TOC Subhead style:

1. Hold down Ctrl and click on TOC Subhead in the style palette.

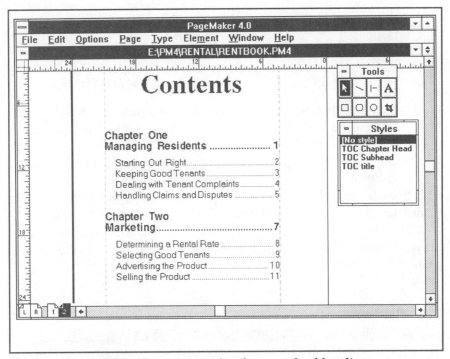

Figure 15.9: The table of contents with reformatted subheadings

2. Choose the Tabs button. You cannot see the tab symbol in the ruler because it is directly on top of the right indent symbol.

3. Click on the right indent symbol, at the 16p6 mark. The field next to Set Leader displays the current leader setting.

4. Click on the Set Leader button.

A drop-down list of types of leaders is displayed. Besides dots, leaders can consist of a series of dashes, underlines, or any character you choose (the Custom option).

5. Choose None to turn off the leaders.

6. Close all dialog boxes.

7. Repeat steps 1 through 6 to remove the leader dots from the TOC Chapter Head style as well.

After completing these steps, your table of contents should resemble Figure 15.10.

Regenerating the Table of Contents

The table of contents is about as undynamic as you can get. After PageMaker generates a table of contents, it is nothing more than an unintelligent story that has no knowledge whatsoever of its roots. If your page numbering were to change, or if you were to change the wording of one of your subheads, your table of contents would not be updated.

The only way to update the table of contents is to regenerate it or manually edit the text. Generally, you shouldn't have to do this more than once or twice because the table of contents (and index) should be one of the very last things that you create, to guarantee that page numbering and content are correct.

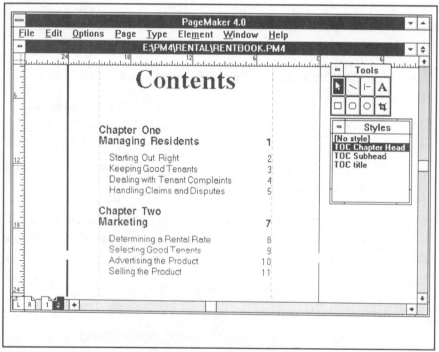

Figure 15.10: The table of contents without leader dots

Regenerating a table of contents is not difficult. First of all, the new table of contents automatically replaces the existing one; the Replace Existing Table of Contents option is turned on automatically when the current publication already contains a table of contents. Also, PageMaker respects the changes you have made to the styles for the table of contents entries, so you will not need to modify the styles again.

Creating a Table of Contents for a Single Publication

You do not need to create a book if all you want to do is create a table of contents for a single publication. Just mark your table of contents entries as described earlier, and then create the table of contents.

Your only problem is where to put the table of contents. If you place it at the beginning of the publication, you change the pagination of the document; but placing it at the end of the document doesn't make any sense.

The best place for the table of contents is in its own publication. Although you have to create an additional file, your pagination is safe. And perhaps most important, you can ignore the table of contents until the end, instead of having to pay attention to it when you would rather be focusing on your document itself.

When you generate a table of contents, the story must be placed in the current publication, but you are free to move it elsewhere. The Clipboard works well here. Follow these general steps to place a table of contents in its own file:

1. Save the publication.

2. At the end of the publication, insert a blank page.

3. Create the table of contents and place it on the blank page. For a long table of contents, insert additional pages and flow the text onto these pages.

4. Select all the text in the story.

5. Cut the text to the Clipboard.

6. Close the publication without saving the changes.

7. Create a new file with the same page setup as the original publication.

8. Paste the table of contents from the Clipboard and position it on the page.

The table of contents, including style names, is imported into the publication. You might want to include other front matter, such as a title page, in this file.

CREATING AN INDEX

Creating an index can be a time-consuming activity, and PageMaker alleviates it only to a small degree. PageMaker will search an entire publication for index markers and generate an index with all entries in place, including the correct page numbers. It does this in the same manner in which it creates a table of contents, except for one very unfortunate exception: you have to tell PageMaker where to embed every single index marker. Marking table of contents entries is easy because you can set it up as part of a style. There is no similar shortcut for marking index entries.

Until PageMaker can read your mind, the task of indexing will remain only slightly more comfortable than root canal work. This section explains how the indexing function works. The hard part is still up to you!

Before we go into the how-to's of indexing, you need to understand PageMaker's indexing terms. Take a look at the index shown in Figure 15.11. An index is divided into *sections* titled with a letter of the alphabet. PageMaker automatically groups your index entries alphabetically and inserts the appropriate letter above the section.

There are two types of index entries:

- A *page reference* lists the page number after the entry.

- A *cross-reference* refers the reader to another topic.

A particular topic can have up to three *levels*. Each level gets increasingly more specific. For instance, the topics *Abandonment* and *Accounting* in Figure 15.11 have only one level each. But the topic *Advertising* has three

Index

A

Abandonment, 137-139
Accounting, 7, 220
Advertising, 115
    apartment rental agencies, 32-35
    types of
        fliers, 34
        newspapers, 33-36
        signs, 34, 36

B

Bookkeeping, 210
Break-even formula, 21-22

C

Certificate of error, 109
Cleaning, 120, *see also* Maintenance
COE, *see* Certificate of error

Figure 15.11: A sample index

levels; *Advertising* is the general topic, and its second-level headings, *apartment rental agencies* and *types of*, are subtopics. The *types of* subtopic has three third-level topics: *fliers, newspapers,* and *signs*. Each level is indented from the previous level.

Marking an Index Entry

You can mark your index entries in either layout or story view, but the Story Editor offers several advantages. First, you can actually see the index markers, as shown in Figure 15.12. These markers are invisible in layout view. Second, you can use the Change command to mark the entries (enter the term to be indexed in the Find What box and type ^; in the Change To Box).

To create an index entry, select the word or phrase you want to mark, and then press Ctrl-; to display the Add Index Entry dialog box, or choose Index Entry from the Options menu. If you want the index entry to have significantly different wording from the text in the publication, don't select the text. Instead, click the text cursor in front of the phrase. You can then manually type the topic in the Add Index Entry dialog box.

Let's mark an index entry in the RENTAL02.PM4 publication:

1. Save the RENTBOOK publication and open RENTAL02.PM4.

2. Go to page 8 (actually the second physical page in the publication) and select *Rental Rate*.

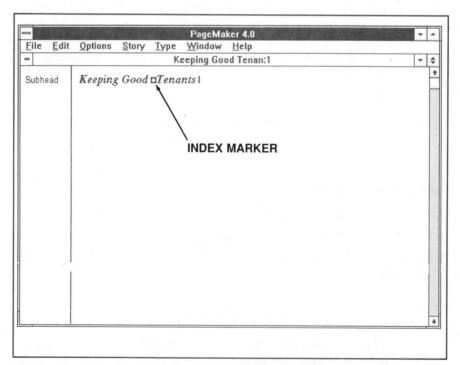

Figure 15.12: The Story Editor shows index markers

3. Press Ctrl-; to display the Add Index Entry dialog box, shown in Figure 15.13.

Rental Rate is already entered into the Topic section, as a first-level topic. The two empty text boxes underneath are for specifying second- and third-level topics. The Page Reference option is selected as the default type.

The various Page Range options let PageMaker know where the topic ends. (The location of your text cursor indicates where the topic begins.) By default, the page reference includes the current page only. To have PageMaker specify a page range (such as 5 through 9), choose one of the other options. For example, if an entire section covers a certain topic, choose the To Next Use of Style option, and select your subhead style from the drop-down list.

4. Turn on the To Next Use of Style option, and select Subhead from the drop-down list.

5. Choose OK.

You don't see the index marker in layout view, but if you were to switch to story view, you would see the index code.

6. Go to page 10 and create an index entry for *Advertising* following the steps described above.

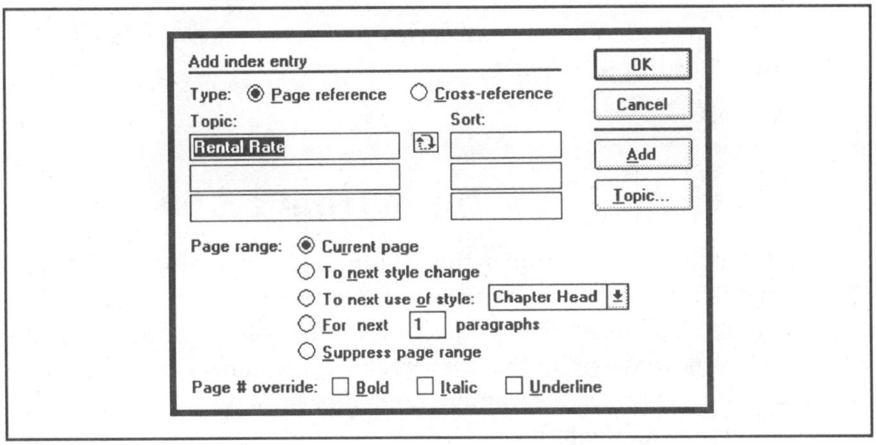

Figure 15.13: The Add Index Entry dialog box

Creating Two-Level Topics

Now we'll create a main topic called *Tenants* and define a second-level entry. Follow these steps:

1. Go to page 9 and select *Tenants*.

2. Press Ctrl-; to display the Add Index Entry dialog box. *Tenants* is automatically filled in as the first-level topic.

3. Press Tab to go to the next line and type **Selecting good**.

4. Turn on the To Next Use of Style option, and then select Subhead from the drop-down list.

5. Choose OK.

6. Save the publication.

Let's move back to Chapter One and mark a two-level index entry in that publication.

7. Open RENTAL01.PM4.

8. Go to page 3 and select *Tenants*.

9. Press Ctrl-;, press Tab to go to the next line, and type **Keeping good**.

10. Turn on the To Next Use of Style option and select Subhead from the drop-down list.

11. Choose OK.

Choosing a Topic from a List

The Topic command button in the Add Index Entry dialog box lets you choose an existing topic from a list instead of typing the topic yourself. The main advantage to this method is that you can be sure the topic is always entered the same way—with the same spelling, capitalization, verb tense, and so on. Otherwise, each variation, no matter how minor, will be listed as a separate topic in the index.

Page 4 also has a reference to the word *tenant*. Since this word already exists as a topic, let's use the Topic button, as follows:

1. Go to page 4 and place the text cursor right before the word *Tenant*. Because we will be choosing the topic from a list, you don't need to select the word.

2. Press Ctrl-; and click on the Topic button.

The Select Topic dialog box, shown in Figure 15.14, displays the existing topics for section T, the only section in this publication thus far. When you have other sections, click on the Next Section button to display them, or type the section letter next to Topic Section.

3. Click on Tenants. The topic fills in next to Level 1, and the subtopic, *Keeping good*, fills in next to Level 2.

4. Delete *Keeping good* from Level 2, and then type **Complaints**.

5. Choose OK.

6. Turn on the To Next Use of Style option and select Subhead from the drop-down list.

7. Choose OK.

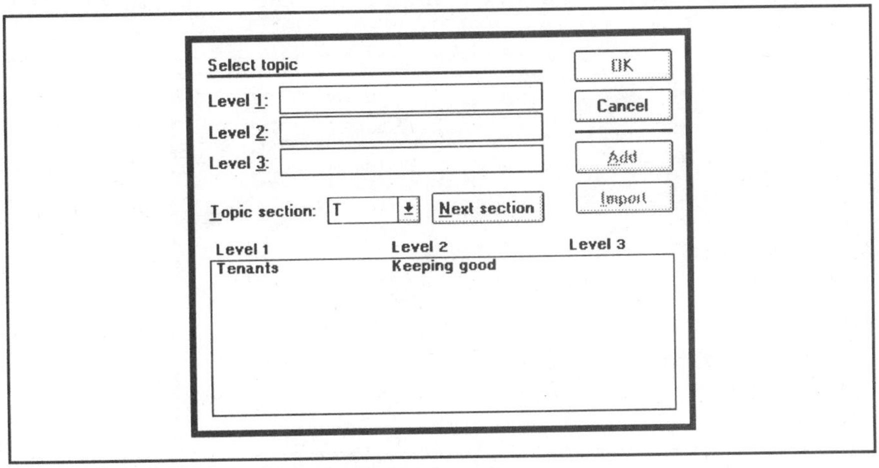

Figure 15.14: The Select Topic dialog box

Creating Cross-References

A cross-reference lists a related topic instead of a specific page number. You see these all the time in indexes; for example, *Actual size, see Page views.* Sometimes an index entry has both a page reference and a cross-reference; for example, *Soft fonts, 125–129, see also Fonts.* Since cross-references do not refer to a specific page in the publication, you do not need to select text or insert a text cursor to include them in the index.

Let's create a cross-reference for the topic *Residents* that refers the reader to the topic *Tenants.* Because you are creating a cross-reference, it doesn't matter where the text cursor is or whether the text tool or pointer tool is selected. Follow these steps:

1. Press Ctrl-; and choose the Cross-Reference option, if necessary. (Cross-Reference is automatically selected when you are using the pointer tool.)

When you select Cross-Reference, the dialog box changes, as shown in Figure 15.15. Since page numbers are not applicable to cross-references, the Page Range options are replaced with a list of cross-reference options.

The See [Also] option, the default, is the most versatile because the cross-reference displays either *See* or *See also,* depending on whether the topic has page references; for example, *Page spread, See Facing pages* or

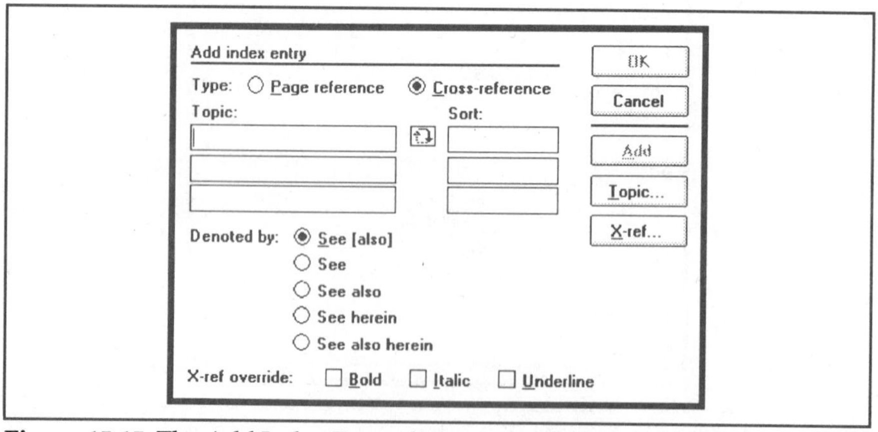

Figure 15.15: The Add Index Entry dialog box for cross-references

Page spread, 26, 119, See also Facing pages. You can force it to choose either *See* or *See also* by turning on the appropriate option. The See Herein and See Also Herein options refer the reader to other levels within the same index entry; for example, *Double-sided pages, See herein Page spread.*

2. For the topic name, type **Residents**.

3. Leave the default Denoted By option (See [also]) and click on the X-Ref command button.

The Select Cross-Reference Topic dialog box appears. This box is identical to the Select Topic dialog box because your goal is the same: to choose a topic.

4. Choose either *Tenants* item.

5. Delete the text next to Level 2.

6. Press Alt, and then choose OK to close all dialog boxes.

Looking at the Index

The Show Index command on the Options menu allows you to peruse the entries before you generate the index. While browsing, you can edit the entries if you discover a mistake or remove unnecessary or duplicate entries. You view the index section by section. In other words, each letter of the alphabet has a separate list.

Show the index for the current publication:

1. Choose Show Index from the Options menu.

The Show Index dialog box displays the first section in this publication, R.

2. Click on the Next Section button to see section T.

The page references are listed next to each topic, as you can see in Figure 15.16. To delete an entry, click on the topic in the list and choose the Remove button. The Edit button takes you to the Edit Index Entry dialog box, where you can modify the name of the topic or change the Page Range option.

3. Click on Next Section. There are no more sections, so the first section reappears.

4. Choose OK.

5. Save the RENTAL01.PM4 publication.

6. Open RENTAL02.PM4.

7. Browse through this publication's index. Use the Edit button to correct any mistakes if necessary.

Creating the Index

Marking the index entries is the grueling part of indexing; generating the index is the part where you can sit back and relax. The process of creating an index is the same as creating a table of contents. When you issue the Create Index command, PageMaker compiles all your index entries and their references into a single story. You are then presented with a loaded text gun that contains the newly generated index. Click on a page, and you have your index.

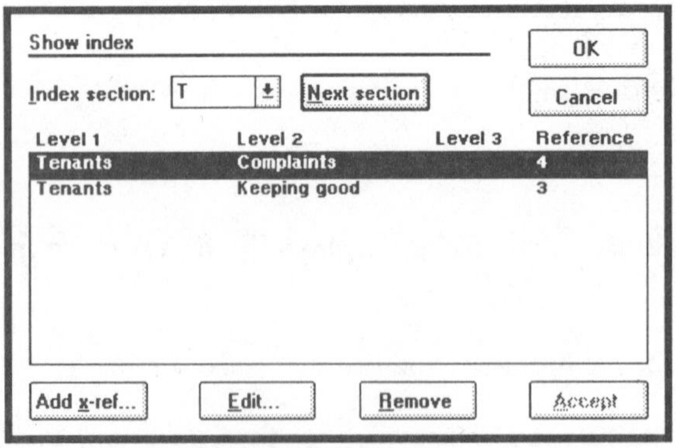

Figure 15.16: The Show Index dialog box for section T

To create an index that spans multiple publications, you must have previously created a book list of these publications, and you must be in the publication that contains this list. In our example, that publication is called RENTBOOK.PM4.

Follow these steps to generate the index:

1. Open RENTBOOK.PM4.

2. Insert a page after page 2 for the index.

3. Pull down the Options menu and choose Create Index.

The Create Index dialog box is shown in Figure 15.17. Next to Title is the heading that appears above the index. Notice that Include Book Publications is turned on. This option compiles index entries for each publication on the book list. The Remove Unreferenced Topics option eliminates entries that do not have page references or cross-references.

4. Choose OK to generate the index.

When PageMaker finishes generating the index, you will see a loaded text gun.

5. Click in the upper-left corner of page 3 and switch to Actual Size view so that you can see the entries and page numbers. Your index should look similar to Figure 15.18.

If you look in the style palette, you can see that several new styles are listed. The Index level 1 and Index level 2 styles control the format of the

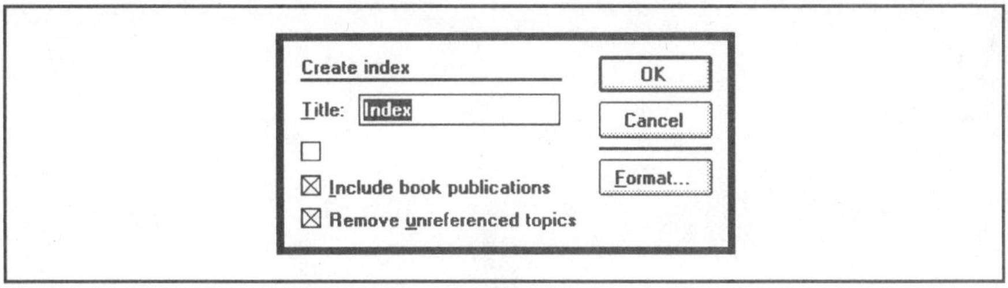

Figure 15.17: The Create Index dialog box

first- and second-level topics. Both levels are 10-point Times Roman, but the second-level topics are indented. The Index section style formats the capital letters preceding each section. By default, the letters are 12-point Times Roman bold with extra space above and below the paragraph. The Index title style formats the heading at the top of the index. It is 30-point Times Roman bold by default. To change the format of the index, edit the appropriate style.

Like a table of contents, an index is not dynamically linked to its entries and must be manually edited or regenerated whenever you add new entries or make any changes that affect pagination. You do not need to delete the outdated index—just go directly to the Create Index dialog box; the Replace Existing Index option is automatically checked.

As always, a bit of experimentation goes a long way toward under-standing the intricacies of this function. PageMaker's indexing tools can make the job of creating an index a bit easier.

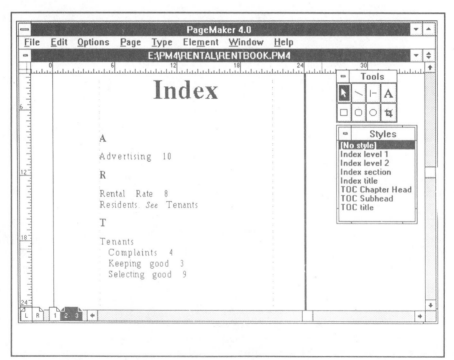

Figure 15.18: The generated index

With the tools discussed in this chapter, you can tame your monster projects. Just design a template, clone it for each chapter, and create a book list. Once you have laid out the pages in each publication, you can use a few PageMaker commands to generate a table of contents and index that reference all the publications in the book.

THE PAGEMAKER COOKBOOK

It's time to put on your chef's hat again. In this chapter, you will find a variety of recipes for producing different types of projects in PageMaker. We'll start with the publications for business applications, and then move on to ones that are fun (menus, invitations, and wedding programs).

INSTANT RESUMES

At the risk of insulting an entire industry of resume-makers, producing resumes does not require state-of-the-art design brilliance. Resumes need to be neat, well-conceived, and readable. Those who receive resumes do not judge them on their aesthetic qualities, but rather on the professionalism and sense of priority that they convey.

If there is any project that calls for recycling, it is the production of a resume. A resume usually follows the same basic structure: it is one page, begins with a name and address, and then describes the applicant's qualifications (objective, education, experience, and so on). Furthermore, there is nothing wrong with making resumes that look the same—they go to different customers and different employers. Aside from the obvious benefit of making production easier, it gives you a visual trademark as a resume-maker. Figure 16.1 shows an example of a resume design.

Making the Perfect Resume

If you're going into the cloning business, your original should be the best you can produce. If you have been producing resumes long enough to recognize a pattern, use it as a guide for your master resume. If you're new to resume-making, don't worry—your "perfect resume" will evolve over time. Pick an existing, typical resume and do the following:

1. For organizational purposes, create a subdirectory that will hold all the files pertaining to resumes. You will store your text files, resume template, and publications in this subdirectory.

2. In your word processor, type the text for the resume. Give this file any name you like (usually the person's last name), making sure to save it in the resume subdirectory.

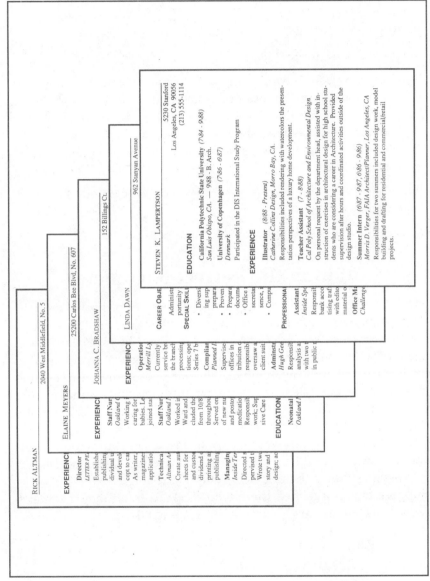

Figure 16.1: A resume assembly line

3. In PageMaker, create a one-page publication and specify the resume's margins, typically 1 inch all around.

4. Place the resume text file.

5. Create styles for the following parts of the resume: the name, address, headings (for example, Objective, Education, and Experience), subheadings (such as university names and job titles), and body text. Resumes should be conservative looking, so don't be extreme with your formatting and use just one or two different fonts.

6. Delete the text file because it doesn't need to be part of the template.

7. Save the file as a template, with the name RESUME.

Cloning the Perfect Resume

Ideally, a resume-maker should spend 90 percent of his or her time writing a resume and 10 percent producing it in PageMaker. For example, let's say a customer hires you to produce a resume. She gives you all the pertinent data, and you create a text file with your word processor. It is here that you earn your keep, applying all your skills to make this resume as professional as possible. Also, you recognize that this resume fits the typical structure, so you should be able to pour it right into your template.

Depending on your preferences, tag the text in your word processor or in PageMaker. The fastest way is to create macros in your word processor and tag the text there. If you decide to wait until you're in PageMaker, you can assign styles with the style palette.

Suppose that you named the file JONES.WP5 (after the customer's name). When the file is ready, here are the steps to take:

1. Start PageMaker and open your resume template, RESUME.PT4.

2. Place the JONES.WP5 text file.

3. Assign style names if necessary.

4. Save the file with the name JONES.PM4.

5. Print. You're done.

With this system, you can actually meet the prescribed 90 –10 propor-
tion of time spent editing the resume to time spent producing it. The
production work is freeze-dried in the template; all you do is add text.

CAMERA-READY BUSINESS CARDS

Business cards may be your simplest PageMaker project. The only
tricky part is ensuring that your final product is truly camera-ready; that
is the focus of this section.

Business cards typically have no borders around them. Therefore, you
must furnish crop marks to ensure that the type is positioned correctly on
the card. By creating a page that is the exact size of your business card and
using the Crop Marks print option, you can let your print shop know
where the type should be placed on the card.

Setting Up a Custom Page Size

Let's say you intend to produce a standard 2-by-3½-inch business
card. Here's how you do it:

1. Create a new file with the following page setup:

    Page dimensions: 12p by 21p (or 2i by 3.5i)

    Orientation: Landscape (unless you want a vertical busi-
    ness card)

    Margins: 1p all the way around

Even though the page size is very small, the page still takes up most
of the publication window. It doesn't look like it, but you are in Fit in Window view. You will even be able to read small point sizes without having
to switch to Actual Size view. In fact, Fit in Window view is larger than the
actual size of the pages.

2. Type and format the text for your business card.

3. Add graphic elements if desired. Extend rules past the edge of the page to create a bleeding effect, as shown in Figure 16.2.

4. Display the Print dialog box, turn on the Crop Marks option, and print the page.

If you want higher quality than your 300-dpi laser printer can produce, print a master business card on a high-resolution typesetting machine (see Appendix D for details).

Creating a Sheet of Cards

Depending on your print shop, you may save time and expense by providing a full page of business cards, all positioned and ready to be cut. That way, your printer does not have to print as many pages, and each pass under the blade cuts up to four cards.

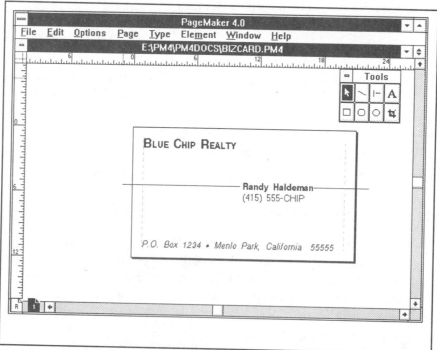

Figure 16.2: Rules extended past the edge of the page create a bleeding effect

In this scenario, you create one business card and copy it seven times to fill out a normal 8½-by-11-inch page. Spacing is critical because each card must be the same exact size. The easiest way to do this is to use the business card template that comes with PageMaker. This file is called BIZCARDS.PT4, and it is located in the PM4\TEMPLATE\PCL or PM4\TEMPLATE\PSCRIPT directory.

The template, shown in Figure 16.3, has placeholders for eight business cards. Each card is delineated with column, margin, and ruler guides, creating eight 2-by-3½-inch boxes. Since these boxes represent the final card size, you need to build margins into the business card text. For example, if you want a 1-pica left margin, set 1-pica left indents. Also, be sure to leave extra space above the first element and below the last element on the card.

If you switch to a magnified view, you can see that this template contains eight different styles of business cards. Choose your favorite style

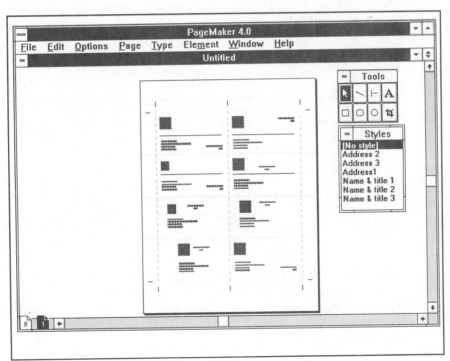

Figure 16.3: The business card template

and replace the placeholders with your name, address, and phone number. If you prefer a different layout, create your own design in a separate file, copy it to the Clipboard, and paste it in the BIZCARDS template.

Once your master card is as perfect as you can make it, you need to make seven copies of it. Follow these steps:

1. Delete all the sample business cards except for your master card.

2. Press Ctrl-A to select all the elements in your card.

3. Copy the selected elements to the Clipboard.

4. Switch to Actual Size view and position the screen so that you can see one of the empty boxes.

5. Press Ins to paste the business card.

6. Move the card into position.

7. Repeat steps 5 and 6 until you have placed a copy of the business card in all eight boxes.

Moving a group of selected objects can be a little tricky. Here are a few pointers:

- If the original object you copied to the Clipboard is on the screen when you paste, the copy is pasted on top of the original, creating confusing text over text. Whenever possible, position the screen so that the original does not show. That way, the copy is pasted on the middle of the screen.

- Make sure you do not click on any of the text or graphic handles; otherwise, you will end up moving or sizing this one object. If this happens, issue the Undo command immediately.

- To make sure you move the entire group of selected objects, click inside one of the text blocks and hold the mouse button for a moment before you begin dragging. That way, you drag the actual card instead of a box representing its size, and it will be immediately apparent whether or not you are moving all the elements on the card.

The Crop Marks print option won't work for the sheet of business cards because you need marks at the corners of each card, not just at the corners of the page. Therefore, the marks must be drawn manually with the perpendicular-line tool. Fortunately, these crop marks are part of the BIZCARDS template. These lines were drawn on the master page. You cannot see all of them because they are drawn on top of the guides. Figure 16.4 shows the master page with the guides turned off so that the crop marks are visible.

EFFECTIVE BROCHURES

Keep in mind that the cover of a brochure is the first thing the reader sees, so you want it to entice your audience to open the brochure and read

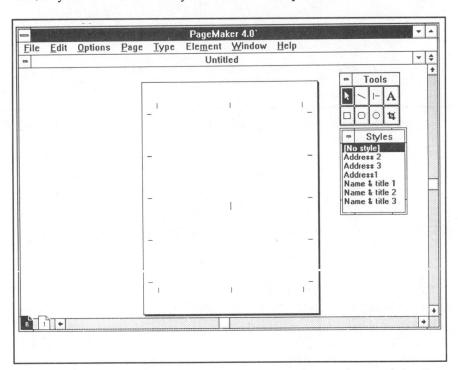

Figure 16.4: The crop marks on the master page indicate where each business card is to be cut

the important information inside. *Do not* call attention to your brochure by using five different fonts in bold and italic—commonly referred to as the ransom-note method of desktop publishing. The most effective front covers contain just a few words and perhaps a photograph. Frequently, as in the brochure you created for Blue Chip Realty, the cover lures the reader with a short, catchy question or statement.

Make the entire brochure light and airy. Don't try to cram too much information on each page. Usually, the purpose of a brochure is to give readers just enough information to spark their interest and encourage them to call for details. If the brochure has too much text, readers might feel overwhelmed or get bored before they finish reading. Allow plenty of white space and use graphic elements to provide visual interest.

A common format is the three-panel landscape brochure on 8½-by-11-inch paper. In the Blue Chip Realty brochure, you laid out the panels as follows:

- The brochure text started on the third column of page 1, and continued to the three columns on page 2.

- The brochure cover appeared in the middle column of page 1.

- The return address was on the first column of page 1.

Figure 16.5 shows another way to lay out the Blue Chip Realty brochure. Here's how this approach works:

- Start the brochure text on the first column of page 2 and place it across all three columns. You can continue it to the first column on page 1, or use a separate story for this panel.

- Create the brochure cover on the third column of page 1.

- Place the return address on the middle column of page 1.

Regardless of which approach you use, remember to follow the rule of thumb for brochure design: the gutters must be double the size of the outer margins. That way, when the inner panels are folded and the inner margins halved, they equal the outer margins. For example, set .35-inch left and right margins and .70-inch gutters between the columns.

Picture Yourself in Your New House!

BLUE CHIP REALTY

P.O. Box 1234
Menlo Park, CA 55555
(415) 555-CHIP

- **We help you shop for your house.** Blue Chip Realty will work with you to find a house that's just right for you.
- **We handle the transaction.** Blue Chip Realty will write up the offer, negotiate to your advantage, and arrange inspections.
- **We hand you the house keys.**

Matchmaking

Because investors supply the majority of cash, they define most of the terms of the transaction. Blue Chip Realty simply acts as a matchmaker. An investor looks for buyers who have solid cash flow, are credit worthy and debt-free, and are eager to buy a house. Buyers look to match with an investor who fits the buyers' financial needs and desires.

Results

If you are interested in owning your own home and would like Blue Chip Realty to help you achieve this goal, call for an appointment now.

BLUE CHIP REALTY

Figure 16.5: An alternate way of laying out the Blue Chip Realty brochure

Do You...?

...want to stop making rent payments?

...want to stop paying so much in taxes?

...want to take advantage of one of the strongest housing markets in the nation?

...feel that you could afford payments if you only owned a house?

If you answered yes to the above questions, keep reading.

Blue Chip Realty is a company whose main goal is to help you buy a house. Our specialty is helping qualified buyers to own their own home. One of these ways is through equity sharing.

Futility

Unlike most areas of the country, buying a home in the Bay Area has become down payment sensitive. There are hundreds of potential homeowners in the Silicon Valley that make great salaries, have good credit, but simply cannot save the lump sum necessary to make a down payment.

Let's assume a couple, who can save $5,000 a year, had $40,000 saved toward a down payment in 1989. They make enough money to cover mortgage payments but need another $10,000 for a 20% down payment on a $250,000 house. So they decide to wait and save.

In the two years it took them to save $10,000, the house appreciated $100,000. Now it's 1991 and they need $70,000 for a down payment on the same house, and they only have $50,000. What can they do? Save another four years? By then the house might be worth $450,000. Chances are they'll never catch up. They need money today. Equity sharing can provide it.

Concepts

Equity sharing is an arrangement where an investor puts up money toward a portion of the down payment. In return, he/she will receive a share of the equity from the home buyer.

For example, suppose a buyer, with the help of an investor, purchases a house in 1991 for $300,000. Here's a hypothetical breakdown of the up-front costs:

	Investor	Buyer
Down Payment	$40,000	$20,000
Closing Costs	5,000	5,000
House Payments	None	All
% of Appreciation	40	60

Numerous benefits accrue to you, the buyer, in return for the portion of the appreciation you relinquish in an equity sharing deal. First, you get to fulfill your own American dream: home ownership.

Other benefits include large tax deductions, saying goodbye to rent payments, and getting a leveraged investment in one of the strongest real estate markets in the world. If these benefits sound good to you, then Blue Chip Realty can help.

Our Focus

Blue Chip Realty specializes in serving home buyers. We do not list property. Instead, we simply act as agents to help people like you find a house here on the Peninsula. So how do we get paid? By receiving a percentage of the commission that the home seller pays to the listing agent. That's all.

We are members of several Multiple Listing Services (MLS) throughout the region. Our geographic area spans Santa Clara and San Mateo counties. Here's an outline of our services:

- **We help determine your price range.** By analyzing your income and savings, Blue Chip Realty uses a computerized worksheet to determine the range of home prices you can reasonably afford.
- **We arrange equity sharing.** If you need cash for a down payment, Blue Chip Realty will match you with an investor.

Figure 16.5: An alternate way of laying out the Blue Chip Realty brochure (continued)

If you have more information than can fit in a three-panel brochure, you can use four panels on legal-size paper (8½ by 14 inches) in landscape orientation.

DIRECTORY ASSISTANCE

Let's say you have a database of names, addresses, and phone numbers, and you want to produce a directory, such as the one shown in Figure 16.6. Can you create this directory in your database or spreadsheet program? Probably not. Database software is designed for sorting, manipulating, and managing information, but report formatting is not its forte; however, this type of formatting is PageMaker's strength.

The data in the directory shown in Figure 16.6 was originally entered in dBASE III Plus, but it was exported to an ASCII file before being placed in PageMaker. Part of the ASCII file appears in Figure 16.7. Notice the two style tags, <Name> and <Address>, embedded in the ASCII file. Because the paragraphs are tagged, the text will automatically be formatted when it is imported. The asterisk between the name and phone number is a placeholder for a tab that you will find and replace in PageMaker's Story Editor. The Smart ASCII Import Filter will eliminate the extra blank lines.

You can also import data from Excel and Lotus 1-2-3. Later in the chapter, we'll describe how to create properly formatted ASCII files in those programs.

Creating the ASCII File in dBASE

The easiest way to design the layout of each directory entry is to use dBASE's Create Label command. The mailing label generator allows up to four lines of text per label. The database in our example has three lines:

- The name and phone number
- The street address
- The city, state, and zip code

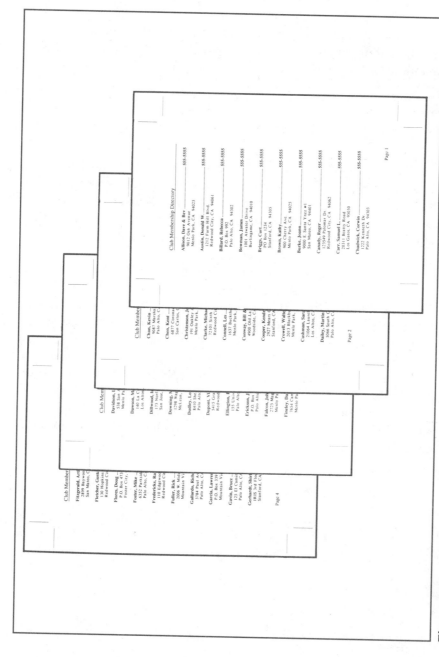

Figure 16.6: A club membership directory

Because you want multiple fields on a line, you need to use *string for-mulas* to place the fields and text together on a single line. A plus sign goes between each item, and text is enclosed in quotation marks. Here are the three string formulas for our phone directory:

"<Name>"+trim(LNAME)+", "+trim(FNAME)+"*"+PHONE

"<Address>"+ADDRESS

Trim(CITY)+", "+STATE+" "+ZIP

```
        <Name>Allison, Dave & Bev*555-5555
        <Address>9012 Oak Avenue
        Menlo Park, CA  94025


        <Name>Austin, Donald W.*555-5555
        <Address>1212 Farm Hill Blvd.
        Redwood City, CA  94061


        <Name>Billard, Rebecca*555-5555
        <Address>P.O. Box 992
        Palo Alto, CA  94302


        <Name>Bowman, James*555-5555
        <Address>1001 Atwater Drive
        Burlingame, CA  94010


        <Name>Briggs, Curt*555-5555
        <Address>PO Box 1234
        Stanford, CA  94305


        <Name>Brown, Kathy*555-5555
        <Address>900 Cherry Ave.
        Menlo Park, CA  94025
```

Figure 16.7: An ASCII file that was exported from dBASE III Plus

The field names are in capital letters; the style names are enclosed in brackets.

To produce the ASCII file, issue the Label Form command, as follows:

LABEL FORM *list* TO *list.txt*

In the above command, *list* is the name of the existing label format, and *list.txt* is the name of the ASCII file that will be created with this command (the file shown in Figure 16.7).

Creating the Directory Publication

The most efficient page size to work with is the standard half-size page of 5½ by 8½ inches. This size doesn't require extra cutting, and you can easily make full-scale proofs and mock-ups on your laser printer. If you prefer a full-size page of 8½ by 11 inches, you can fit two or more columns on a page, depending on the type size you use. Figure 16.8 shows an example of a two-column directory with a vertical rule between columns.

Follow these steps to create a directory publication:

1. Create a new file and specify the page dimensions and margins of your directory. Decide whether the publication is going to be single- or double-sided. Don't worry about the number of pages because extra pages will be inserted automatically when you place the file.

2. Go to the master pages and set up column guides and vertical rules if necessary.

3. Specify headers and footers on your master pages. Be sure to include a page number.

4. Create the styles for the directory. Our directory has the following two styles:

   Name: 12-point Times Roman, bold, tab at 18p7 with leader dots, 1-pica before, keep with next 2 lines

   Address: 10-point Times Roman, 1-pica left indent

Club Membership Directory

Allison, Dave & Bev 555-5555
9012 Oak Avenue
Menlo Park, CA 94025

Austin, Donald W. 555-5555
1212 Farm Hill Blvd.
Redwood City, CA 94061

Billard, Rebecca 555-5555
P.O. Box 992
Palo Alto, CA 94302

Bowman, James 555-5555
1001 Atwater Drive
Burlingame, CA 94010

Briggs, Curt 555-5555
PO Box 1234
Stanford, CA 94305

Brown, Kathy 555-5555
900 Cherry Ave.
Menlo Park, CA 94025

Burke, Joann 555-5555
9000 E. Santa Ynez #1
San Mateo, CA 94401

Canady, Roger 555-5555
123549 Palomar Dr.
Redwood City, CA 94062

Carr, Samuel L. 555-5555
20311 Beatty Road
Los Gatos, CA 95030

Chadwick, Corwin 555-5555
1222 Kenneth Dr.
Palo Alto, CA 94303

Chan, Kevin 555-5555
9087 Marshall Drive
Palo Alto, CA 94303

Chen, Kent 555-5555
6877 Coronado Ave.
San Carlos, CA 94070

Christenson, John 555-5555
191 Oakley Ave.
Menlo Park, CA 94025

Clarke, Michael 555-5555
72101 Sixth Ave.
Redwood City, CA 94063

Connell, Les 555-5555
1637 Buckthorn Way
Menlo Park, CA 94025

Conway, Bill & Jane 555-5555
4900 Old La Honda Road
Woodside, CA 94062

Cooper, Kendric C. 555-5555
2927 Mears Court
Stanford, CA 94305

Crowell, Walter 555-5555
2013 Blackburn Ave.
Menlo Park, CA 94025

Cushman, Sarah 555-5555
21064 Laureles Drive
Los Altos, CA 94022

Dailey, Martin 555-5555
5066 South Court
Palo Alto, CA 94306

Davidson, Larry 555-5555
538 San Antonio Ave.
Menlo Park, CA 94025

Dawson, Martin E. 555-5555
140 La Cresta Drive
Los Altos Hills, CA 94022

Dillwood, Ira S. 555-5555
173 Norfolk Drive
San Jose, CA 95129

Downing, Mark 555-5555
1298 Waggaman Circle
McLean, VA 22101

Dudley, Louise 555-5555
8410 Sheridan
Palo Alto, CA 94306

Dupont, Vladimir 555-5555
5415 Grand St.
Redwood City, CA 94062

Page 1

Figure 16.8: One page of a two-column directory

With these styles, there will be 1 pica of empty space between each listing in the directory, and the address lines will be indented 1 pica from the left. A series of dots will fill the space between the name and phone number because a tab with leader dots is specified as part of the Name style. Turning on the Keep with Next option ensures that a person's name and address will not be split between columns or pages.

Importing the ASCII File

When you place the ASCII file that contains the directory file, turn on the Read Tags option. Then, in the Smart ASCII Import Filter dialog box, turn on the Between Paragraphs option to remove the extra carriage returns in the file.

To flow the text, turn on the Autoflow option. PageMaker will automatically create extra pages for the imported text.

The imported text will already be formatted for three reasons: the file contained style names, you turned on the Read Tags option, and these styles were previously defined in PageMaker.

Cleaning Up the Imported Text

The amount of clean-up work you will have to do in the Story Editor depends on which program you used to create the data file. Lotus 1-2-3 and Excel files require a bit more work because the data is imported in a columnar format, so you must use the Story Editor's Change command to replace the tabs with carriage returns, as explained in the next section.

Because dBASE allows you to set up the data in a format that is similar to the final directory layout, all you need to do in the Story Editor is use the Change command to replace the asterisk placeholder (*) with a tab (^t is the tab code).

In a long directory, you might want to group together names that begin with the same letter and place the appropriate letter above each section. Figure 16.9 illustrates this layout.

Club Membership Directory

A

Allison, Dave & Bev 555-5555
  9012 Oak Avenue
  Menlo Park, CA 94025

Austin, Donald W. 555-5555
  1212 Farm Hill Blvd.
  Redwood City, CA 94061

B

Billard, Rebecca 555-5555
  P.O. Box 992
  Palo Alto, CA 94302

Bowman, James 555-5555
  1001 Atwater Drive
  Burlingame, CA 94010

Briggs, Curt 555-5555
  PO Box 1234
  Stanford, CA 94305

Brown, Kathy 555-5555
  900 Cherry Ave.
  Menlo Park, CA 94025

Burke, Joann 555-5555
  9000 E. Santa Ynez #1
  San Mateo, CA 94401

C

Canady, Roger 555-5555
  123549 Palomar Dr.
  Redwood City, CA 94062

Carr, Samuel L. 555-5555
  20311 Beatty Road
  Los Gatos, CA 95030

Chadwick, Corwin 555-5555
  1222 Kenneth Dr.
  Palo Alto, CA 94303

Chan, Kevin 555-5555
  9087 Marshall Drive
  Palo Alto, CA 94303

Chen, Kent 555-5555
  6877 Coronado Ave.
  San Carlos, CA 94070

Christenson, John 555-5555
  191 Oakley Ave.
  Menlo Park, CA 94025

Clarke, Michael 555-5555
  72101 Sixth Ave.
  Redwood City, CA 94063

Connell, Les 555-5555
  1637 Buckthorn Way
  Menlo Park, CA 94025

Conway, Bill & Jane 555-5555
  4900 Old La Honda Road
  Woodside, CA 94062

Cooper, Kendric C. 555-5555
  2927 Mears Court
  Stanford, CA 94305

Crowell, Walter 555-5555
  2013 Blackburn Ave.
  Menlo Park, CA 94025

Cushman, Sarah 555-5555
  21064 Laureles Drive
  Los Altos, CA 94022

D

Dailey, Martin 555-5555
  5066 South Court
  Palo Alto, CA 94306

Davidson, Larry 555-5555
  538 San Antonio Ave.
  Menlo Park, CA 94025

Dawson, Martin E. 555-5555
  140 La Cresta Drive
  Los Altos Hills, CA 94022

Page 1

Figure 16.9: In this directory, names that begin with the same letter are grouped together

Importing Spreadsheet Data

Directory information can also be imported from a spreadsheet database. The procedure is similar to the one used to bring in dBASE data:

1. Create string formulas that combine the tag names, fields, and text.

2. Produce an ASCII file.

3. Use your word processor or PageMaker's Story Editor to clean up the ASCII file.

4. Create a publication in PageMaker.

5. Place the file.

In an Excel or Lotus 1-2-3 database, each field is in a separate column, and each record is in a separate row. Figures 16.10 and 16.11 show examples of an

	Microsoft Excel - CLUBDB.XLS						
File	**Edit**	**Formula**	**Format**	**Data**	**Options**	**Macro**	**Window**	**Help**

	A	B	C	D	E	F	G
1	LNAME	FNAME	PHONE	ADDRESS	CITY	STATE	ZIP
2	Allison	Dave & Bev	555-5555	9012 Oak Avenue	Menlo Park	CA	94025
3	Austin	Donald W.	555-5555	1212 Farm Hill Blvd.	Redwood City	CA	94061
4	Billard	Rebecca	555-5555	P.O. Box 992	Palo Alto	CA	94302
5	Bowman	James	555-5555	1001 Atwater Drive	Burlingame	CA	94010
6	Briggs	Curt	555-5555	PO Box 1234	Stanford	CA	94305
7	Brown	Kathy	555-5555	900 Cherry Ave.	Menlo Park	CA	94025
8	Burke	Joann	555-5555	9000 E. Santa Ynez #1	San Mateo	CA	94401
9	Canady	Roger	555-5555	123549 Palomar Dr.	Redwood City	CA	94062
10	Carr	Samuel L.	555-5555	20311 Beatty Road	Los Gatos	CA	95030
11	Chadwick	Corwin	555-5555	1222 Kenneth Dr.	Palo Alto	CA	94303
12	Chan	Kevin	555-5555	9087 Marshall Drive	Palo Alto	CA	94303
13	Chen	Kent	555-5555	6877 Coronado Ave.	San Carlos	CA	94070
14	Christenson	John	555-5555	191 Oakley Ave.	Menlo Park	CA	94025
15	Clarke	Michael	555-5555	72101 Sixth Ave.	Redwood City	CA	94063
16	Connell	Les	555-5555	1637 Buckthorn Way	Menlo Park	CA	94025
17	Conway	Bill & Jane	555-5555	4900 Old La Honda Road	Woodside	CA	94062
18	Cooper	Kendric C.	555-5555	2927 Mears Court	Stanford	CA	94305

Ready

Figure 16.10: An Excel database

Excel and a Lotus 1-2-3 database, respectively. You must create string formulas to combine the appropriate fields with tag names and text.

The following string formulas are entered in the cells to the right of the database and copied down the rows for all records:

Excel

="<Name>"&A2&","
&B2&"*"&C2

="<Address>"&D2

=E2&", "&F2&" "&G2

Lotus 1-2-3

+"<Name>"&A2&","
&B2&"*"&C2

+"<Address>"&D2

+E2&", "&F2&" "&G2

The first formula combines the <Name> style tag with the LNAME field in cell A2, the FNAME field in cell B2, an asterisk, and the PHONE field in cell C2. The asterisk will be replaced with a tab in PageMaker. The second

```
A1: [W12] 'LNAME                                                    READY

     A            B           C        D              E          F  G
1   LNAME        FNAME       PHONE    ADDRESS        CITY        STAZIP
2   Allison      Dave & Bev  555-5555 9012 Oak Avenue  Menlo Park  CA 94025
3   Austin       Donald W,   555-5555 1212 Farm Hill Bl Redwood City CA 94061
4   Billard      Rebecca     555-5555 P.O. Box 992     Palo Alto   CA 94302
5   Bowman       James       555-5555 1001 Atwater Driv Burlingame  CA 94010
6   Briggs       Curt        555-5555 PO Box 1234      Stanford    CA 94305
7   Brown        Kathy       555-5555 900 Cherry Ave.  Menlo Park  CA 94025
8   Burke        Joann       555-5555 9000 E. Santa Yne San Mateo  CA 94401
9   Canady       Roger       555-5555 123549 Palomar Dr Redwood City CA 94062
10  Carr         Samuel L.   555-5555 20311 Beatty Road Los Gatos  CA 95030
11  Chadwick     Corwin      555-5555 1222 Kenneth Dr. Palo Alto   CA 94303
12  Chan         Kevin       555-5555 9087 Marshall Dri Palo Alto   CA 94303
13  Chen         Kent        555-5555 6877 Coronado Ave San Carlos CA 94070
14  Christenson  John        555-5555 191 Oakley Ave.  Menlo Park  CA 94025
15  Clarke       Michael     555-5555 72101 Sixth Ave. Redwood City CA 94063
16  Connell      Les         555-5555 1637 Buckthorn Wa Menlo Park  CA 94025
17  Conway       Bill & Jane 555-5555 4900 Old La Honda Woodside    CA 94062
18  Cooper       Kendric C.  555-5555 2927 Mears Court Stanford    CA 94305
19  Crowell      Walter      555-5555 2013 Blackburn Av Menlo Park  CA 94025
20  Cushman      Sarah       555-5555 21064 Laureles Dr Los Altos   CA 94022
```

Figure 16.11: A Lotus 1-2-3 database

formula combines the <Address> style tag with the ADDRESS field in cell D2. The third formula combines the CITY (cell E2), STATE (cell F2), and ZIP (cell G2) fields, inserts a comma between the city and state, and places two blank spaces before the zip code.

Creating an ASCII File in Excel

Figure 16.12 shows the formulas after they have been copied in Excel. Follow these steps to create the ASCII file:

1. Copy the range of formulas to the Clipboard.

2. Paste the range into a new spreadsheet with the Paste Special command, using the Values option to convert the formulas to text.

3. Save the new spreadsheet as a text file (in the Save Worksheet As dialog box, click on the Options command button and choose Text).

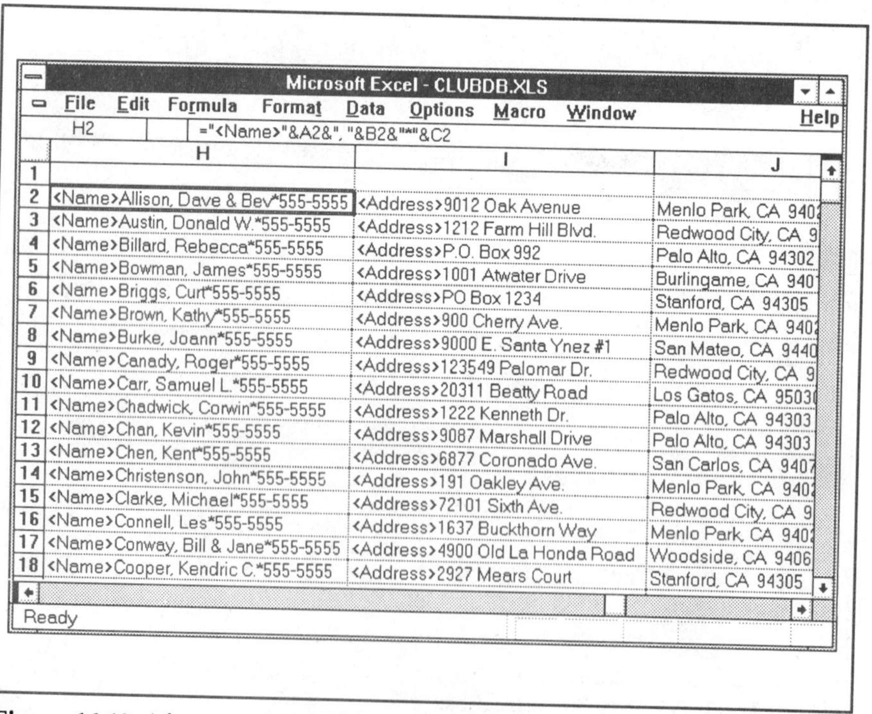

Figure 16.12: After copying the string formulas

This text file, shown in Figure 16.13, has tabs between each column and quotation marks around each field. The tabs need to be replaced with carriage returns, the quotation marks need to be deleted, and the asterisk placeholders should be replaced with tabs. You can make these changes in your word processor or in the Story Editor.

If you didn't use your word processor to clean up the ASCII file, load the Story Editor and import the text file with the Convert Quotes and Read Tags options turned off. Use the Change command to replace the tabs (^{t}) with carriage returns (^{p}), eliminate all the quotation marks by replacing them with nothing, and replace the asterisks with tabs. Then export the text to an ASCII file and exit from the Story Editor. Finally, turn on the Autoflow option and place the text file, making sure to activate the Read Tags option.

Creating an ASCII File in 1-2-3

Figure 16.14 shows the first two string formulas after they have been copied in Lotus 1-2-3. Make sure the columns are at least three characters wider than the longest cell. Follow these steps to create the ASCII file:

1. Issue the /Print File command and enter a file name with a TXT extension.

2. Choose the Range command and highlight the range of formulas.

3. Set the Margins to None and turn on the Unformatted option.

4. Choose Go to create the ASCII file.

```
"<Name>Allison, Dave & Bev*555-5555"        <Address>9012 Oak Avenue "Menlo Park, CA  94025"
"<Name>Austin, Donald W.*555-5555"          <Address>1212 Farm Hill Blvd.    "Redwood City, CA  94061"
"<Name>Billard, Rebecca*555-5555" <Address>P.O. Box 992    "Palo Alto, CA  94302"
"<Name>Bowman, James*555-5555"    <Address>1001 Atwater Drive       "Burlingame, CA  94010"
"<Name>Briggs, Curt*555-5555"     <Address>PO Box 1234       "Stanford, CA  94305"
"<Name>Brown, Kathy*555-5555"     <Address>900 Cherry Ave. "Menlo Park, CA  94025"
"<Name>Burke, Joann*555-5555"     <Address>9000 E. Santa Ynez #1    "San Mateo, CA  94401"
"<Name>Canady, Roger*555-5555"    <Address>123549 Palomar Dr.       "Redwood City, CA  94062"
"<Name>Carr, Samuel L.*555-5555"  <Address>20311 Beatty Road        "Los Gatos, CA  95030"
"<Name>Chadwick, Corwin*555-5555" <Address>1222 Kenneth Dr.         "Palo Alto, CA  94303"
"<Name>Chan, Kevin*555-5555"      <Address>9087 Marshall Drive      "Palo Alto, CA  94303"
"<Name>Chen, Kent*555-5555"       <Address>6877 Coronado Ave.       "San Carlos, CA  94070"
```

Figure 16.13: The ASCII file that was exported from Excel

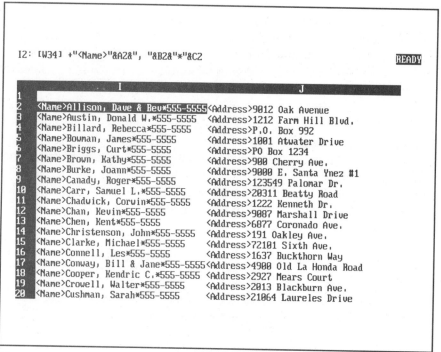

Figure 16.14: After the string formulas have been copied

This text file, shown in Figure 16.15, has spaces between each column. The spaces need to be replaced with carriage returns, so that each field is on a separate line.

Load the Story Editor and import the text file with the Read Tags option turned off. In the Smart ASCII Import Filter dialog box, turn on the Replace 3 or more spaces with Tab option. (This is why you should make sure that there are at least three spaces between the columns in 1-2-3.)

Then use the Story Editor's Change command to replace the tabs (^t) with carriage returns (^p), and replace the asterisks with tabs. Export the text to an ASCII file and exit from the Story Editor. Your last step is to turn on the Autoflow option and place the text file, with the Read Tags option turned on.

```
<Name>Allison, Dave & Bev*555-5555    <Address>9012 Oak Avenue         Menlo Park, CA  94025
<Name>Austin, Donald W.*555-5555      <Address>1212 Farm Hill Blvd.    Redwood City, CA  94061
<Name>Billard, Rebecca*555-5555       <Address>P.O. Box 992            Palo Alto, CA  94302
<Name>Bowman, James*555-5555          <Address>1001 Atwater Drive      Burlingame, CA  94010
<Name>Briggs, Curt*555-5555           <Address>PO Box 1234             Stanford, CA  94305
<Name>Brown, Kathy*555-5555           <Address>900 Cherry Ave.         Menlo Park, CA  94025
<Name>Burke, Joann*555-5555           <Address>9000 E. Santa Ynez #1   San Mateo, CA  94401
<Name>Canady, Roger*555-5555          <Address>123549 Palomar Dr.      Redwood City, CA  94062
<Name>Carr, Samuel L.*555-5555        <Address>20311 Beatty Road       Los Gatos, CA  95030
<Name>Chadwick, Corwin*555-5555       <Address>1222 Kenneth Dr.        Palo Alto, CA  94303
<Name>Chan, Kevin*555-5555            <Address>9087 Marshall Drive     Palo Alto, CA  94303
<Name>Chen, Kent*555-5555             <Address>6877 Coronado Ave.      San Carlos, CA  94070
<Name>Christenson, John*555-5555      <Address>191 Oakley Ave.         Menlo Park, CA  94025
<Name>Clarke, Michael*555-5555        <Address>72101 Sixth Ave.        Redwood City, CA  94063
<Name>Connell, Les*555-5555           <Address>1637 Buckthorn Way      Menlo Park, CA  94025
<Name>Conway, Bill & Jane*555-5555    <Address>4900 Old La Honda Road  Woodside, CA  94062
<Name>Cooper, Kendric C.*555-5555     <Address>2927 Mears Court        Stanford, CA  94305
<Name>Crowell, Walter*555-5555        <Address>2013 Blackburn Ave.     Menlo Park, CA  94025
<Name>Cushman, Sarah*555-5555         <Address>21064 Laureles Drive    Los Altos, CA  94022
<Name>Dailey, Martin*555-5555         <Address>5066 South Court        Palo Alto, CA  94306
<Name>Davidson, Larry*555-5555        <Address>538 San Antonio Ave.    Menlo Park, CA  94025
```

Figure 16.15: The ASCII file exported from 1-2-3

THE MENU, PLEASE

It only seems appropriate to include a menu in our cookbook. The menu in Figure 16.16 was created for a formal dinner party in our new home. Since the meal was being prepared by a friend who is a gourmet chef, we had time to worry about the important details—like designing a menu. Our guests were so delighted with the menu, we thought we would share it with others.

The menu is simple yet elegant. We chose the cursive-like Zapf Chancery font, but if you don't have this font, try Times Roman italic. All the text, which was typed in the Story Editor, is centered. The border is a piece of clip art from Arts & Letters. Most clip-art collections contain a variety of borders. If you can't find a border you like, use PageMaker's drawing tools to create one.

We created the menu on a landscape 8½-by-11-inch page, with½-inch margins all the way around. As Figure 16.17 shows, we made a copy of the perfected menu and placed the two menus side by side. We also drew hairline crop marks with the perpendicular-line tool to indicate the final menu

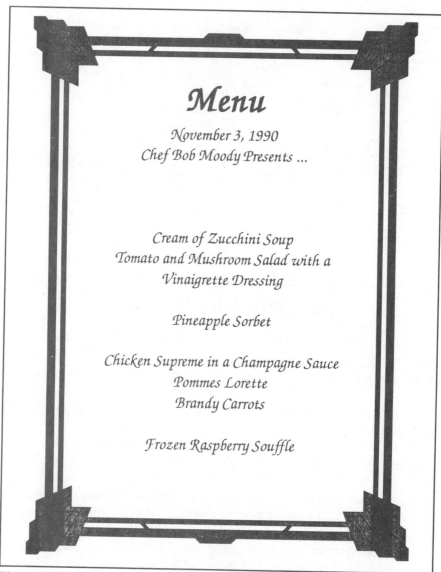

Figure 16.16: A simple menu for a not-so-simple dinner

size. The menus were printed on an ivory-colored card stock and trimmed to 5½ by 7 inches with two swoops of the paper cutter.

If you are creating a restaurant menu, be sure to take the room's lighting and the customers' eyesight into consideration when selecting a typeface, size, and ink color. Eight-point Zapf Chancery in pale rose ink would not be easy to read in candle light. In general, you shouldn't choose a very small typeface.

"I DO" ON THE DESKTOP

Contrary to claims made by those who know us, we did not exchange our wedding vows via fax machine, nor did the proposal take place on the Aldus Forum on CompuServe. On all other counts of electronic romance

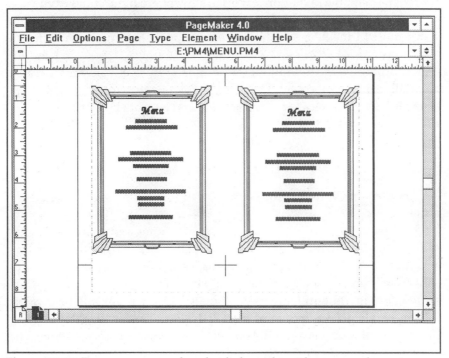

Figure 16.17: Two menus are placed side-by-side with crop marks

during our recent wedding, we plead guilty. Our computers, especially our desktop-publishing software, played a prominent role in the wedding plans. In fact, amid the frustrations and headaches of planning the event, self-publishing our wedding invitations and program proved to be a relaxing experience.

When you are designing your own wedding materials, you can take advantage of the fact that you'll have a sympathetic and forgiving audience. Feel free to create a document that reflects your personalities and have some fun in the process.

Creating an Invitation

Our wedding invitation, shown in Figures 16.18 (the cover) and 16.19 (the inside), has a simple design. The cover was created in Corel Draw and exported to an EPS file. The rose came from the Arts & Letters clip-art collection. The font used for the invitation text is Park Avenue, a light, cursive typeface.

When determining the dimensions of your invitation, keep in mind that it must fit inside a standard-size envelope. Our invitation's dimensions were 6 by 4½ inches.

In addition to the invitation, we designed return envelopes and reply cards, all set in Park Avenue. The master copies were printed on a 1270-dpi Linotronic imagesetter (see Appendix D), and a print shop printed the invitations on a white, textured card stock.

Producing a Program

Another item you can produce for a wedding is a program to hand out at the ceremony.

The cover of our program contained our names and wedding date in addition to the arched type and rose that we used on the wedding invitation. The text on the two inside pages, shown in Figure 16.20, uses only three paragraph styles. The Head style (*The Ceremony* and *The Supporting Cast*) is 20-point University Roman with a 1-point rule below. The Subhead style (*The Processional, Candle Lighting,* and so on) is 13-point University Roman. It is indented on the left and has extra space above. The Body Text style is 9-point Helvetica Light, indented on the left.

Figure 16.18: The front cover of the wedding invitation

Figure 16.19: The inside text of the wedding invitation

Because there wasn't a PostScript Hebrew typeface available at the time, we used a greeting card with the word *Shalom* printed on it to create the background on the inside pages. Using a hand-held scanner, we produced a TIFF file and brought it into Corel Draw. After tracing each letter, we grouped them together as a word and assigned it a 20% shade. This was too dark, so we switched to a 12% shade. When creating background art such as this, it's better to err on the side of too light than to have the artwork overshadow the text.

Again, the masters were printed on a high-resolution typesetting machine. We even matched the ink to the color of the bridesmaid's dresses: teal. We took a swatch of material over to the print shop and matched it to a PMS color. The paper was the color of the bride's ivory wedding dress. How's that for color coordination?

In this book's final chapter, you saw samples of a variety of publications that can be produced in PageMaker. All these projects follow the basic DTP recipe you learned back in Chapter 1:

- Create a file.

- Add your basic ingredients: text and graphics.

- Spice it up with up some formatting.

- Save and print it.

Most of the publication ingredients come from other software packages. For example, the resume text was imported from a word processing file, the data in the membership directory came from dBASE, and the cover of the wedding invitation was created in Corel Draw. PageMaker is simply the kitchen where your publications are prepared.

The Ceremony

Originally, Jewish marriages were separated into two rituals, often a year apart. The first ceremony was the Betrothal, which promised the bride and groom to each other. The second ceremony, the nuptials, was where the couple demonstrated its intention to create a new home and life together. Today, the two ceremonies are merged, both performed under the *huppah* (pronounced "hoopa"), the bridal canopy symbolizing the couple's home.

The Processional

It is customary in Jewish weddings for the bride and the groom to walk down the aisle with their respective parents. Rick, his parents and the wedding party will enter to *Pachelbel's Cannon*, while Becky and her parents make their entrance to *Trumpet Voluntary*.

Candle Lighting

"From every human being, there rises a light that reaches straight to the heavens. And when two souls that are destined for each other find one another, their streams of light glow together and a single brighter light goes forth from their united being."

The Kiddish

Wine is a familiar companion to Jewish holidays and celebrations. The couple will share the wine from their special wedding cup.

Exchange of the Rings

Wedding Vows

Written by each other, for each other.

Lost in Your Eyes

Sung by Rick's sister Jan, accompanied by Bob Doerschuk.

The Blessings

The Cantor will sing the blessings for wine, the universe, humanity, man and woman, children and the love and joy of the bride and groom.

The Breaking of the Glass

There are various interpretations of this extraordinary finale to Jewish weddings. Our favorite is to think of the broken glass as a joyous conclusion that says *Let the Celebration Begin!*

The Supporting Cast

Parents of the Bride
Edwin and Marjorie Bridges

Parents of the Groom
David and Beverly Altman

Maid of Honor
Katherine Fleming was one of Becky's first friends at Stanford. They were sorority sisters, travel companions in Europe and have kept in close touch even though Kathy now lives in Los Angeles.

Best Man
Stephen Lampert is the younger brother that Rick never had. Rick has known Steve for 27 years.

Bridesmaids
Madeline Canepa first met Becky when they were dating men who were roommates. The romances passed, but their friendship has remained. **Jenifer Randall** and Becky met in an aerobics class over four years ago and quickly became best of friends. **Leslie Bell** was Becky's sorority sister at Stanford and her roommate after college. Becky was a bridesmaid in Leslie's wedding.

Groomsmen
Daniel Abrams is Rick's first cousin and closest relative. The two can tell stories about each other that pre-date nursery school. **Harry Johnson** has been a wonderful friend of the wedding couple, hosting both the engagement party and the shower. **Dan Marx** was Rick's best friend through high school and college (even though they went to different schools) and was Rick's first roommate after college. Dan's marriage five years ago has served as continual inspiration to Rick.

"Grand Dad"
James Pollock, Becky's grandfather

Brothers of the Bride (your ushers)
Richard, Brian, and Bruce Bridges

Sisters of the Groom
Jody and Jan Altman

The Cantor
David Unterman, one of the finest voices in Northern California.

Figure 16.20: The inside pages of the wedding program

INSTALLING
PAGEMAKER 4.0

Installing PageMaker on your computer is not difficult; Aldus provides a guided installation that essentially holds your hand through the process of copying the program floppy disks to your hard disk. Installation takes approximately 30 minutes.

HARDWARE
AND SOFTWARE REQUIREMENTS

To run PageMaker on your computer, you need the following hardware and software setup:

- An IBM PC or compatible computer with an 80286, 80386, or 80486 processor

- At least 2 megabytes (Mb) of memory (RAM)

- Windows 3.0

- Depending on how much of the package you install, 4 to 6 Mb of free hard disk space

- One 1.2 Mb 5¼-inch, one 720K 3½-inch, or one 1.44Mb 3½-inch floppy disk drive

- A VGA or Hercules video card

- A Windows 3.0-compatible mouse

- A printer supported by Windows 3.0 (for example, PostScript or Hewlett-Packard LaserJet)

You will also need the disks that came in your PageMaker box. Choose the disk size (5¼ or 3 ½ inch) appropriate for your computer.

RUNNING
THE ALDUS SETUP PROGRAM

The PageMaker disk labeled Disk 1 includes an installation program, called ALDSETUP, which takes you through the complete process of copying PageMaker to your hard disk. Follow these steps to run the Setup program:

1. If necessary, load Windows. The Windows Program Manager should be displayed.

2. Insert Disk 1 into your floppy disk drive.

3. Pull down the File menu and choose Run.

4. Type **A:\ALDSETUP** or **B:\ALDSETUP**, depending on which floppy disk drive you are using.

5. Click on OK.

Choosing Installation Options

When the Setup program is loaded, you see the window shown in Figure A.1. Here, you choose which parts of the program you want to install. At the very minimum, you should select the PageMaker and Filters options. When you choose PageMaker, the entire program and the Table Editor will be installed. Choosing Filters allows you to import and export files to and from other programs (word processors, spreadsheets, graphics packages, and so on).

The Tutorial, PostScript Templates, and PCL Templates choices are optional. You probably won't want to install the tutorial since you are learning PageMaker from this book.

Templates are reusable publications that define the structure and layout of a specific type of document. They are valuable when you need to use the same design for multiple projects. For example, you will use a business card template in Chapter 16. Choose PCL Templates if you have a Hewlett-Packard LaserJet or compatible printer. Owners of PostScript printers should install PostScript Templates.

By default, the PageMaker, Tutorial, and Filters options are selected. To select or deselect an option, hold down Ctrl as you click on the item, as follows:

1. Hold down Ctrl and click on Tutorial to deselect this item.

2. Hold down Ctrl and click on either PostScript Templates or PCL Templates.

The PageMaker, Filters, and one of the Template options should now be selected.

3. Click on Setup.

A Select Directory dialog box appears, with C:\PM4 as the suggested path. This path refers to where PageMaker will be installed.

4. Type a new path if necessary. Be sure to include the drive and subdirectory name.

5. Click on OK.

Personalizing Your Program

The next dialog box you are presented with is called Personalize Your Program. In this box, you need to fill in your name and company name,

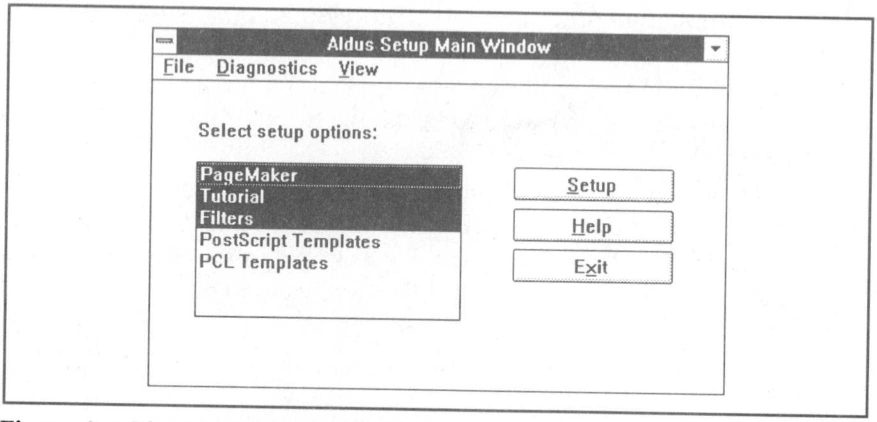

Figure A.1: The Aldus Setup Main window

along with the serial number of your PageMaker program. You can find this number on your registration card and on the box that contained your PageMaker disks.

The information you enter here will appear each time you load Page-Maker. Follow these steps to personalize your program:

1. Type your name in the box underneath Name. You can enter your whole name or just your first or last name. If several people will be using the same copy of PageMaker on the same computer, enter a department name. The name can be from 1 to 63 characters long.

2. Press Tab to move the cursor to the box underneath Company.

3. Type your company name. You can use up to 63 characters.

4. Press Tab.

5. Type your complete serial number, including hyphens.

6. Click on OK.

If you made a mistake in typing your serial number, you will see a message indicating that you entered an invalid serial number. If this happens, click on Continue and repeat steps 5 and 6 above. You cannot install PageMaker until you enter a valid serial number.

Modifying Your System Files

Next, the Setup program displays the Modify Your System Files? dialog box, which asks if you want to modify your AUTOEXEC.BAT and CONFIG.SYS files, as shown in Figure A.2. If you have no idea what these files are, choose Yes so that the changes are made for you. If you understand how to edit your system files, choose No and edit them later.

If you are going to edit your system files, make sure that your CONFIG.SYS file contains the following two lines:

Files=20

Buffers=30

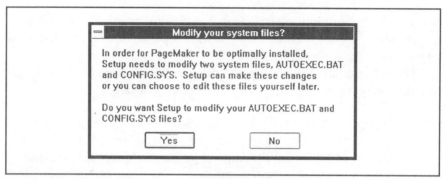

Figure A.2: The Modify Your System Files? dialog box

These are the minimum file and buffer settings; your settings may be higher than those listed above.

The following statement should be added to your AUTOEXEC.BAT file:

SET TEMP=C:\PM4

If you installed PageMaker in a different path, change the above statement accordingly.

Also, the PATH statement in the AUTOEXEC.BAT file should have the Windows and PageMaker directories listed at the beginning, for example:

Path=C:\WINDOWS;C:\PM4;C:\;C:\DOS

Selecting Filters

Filter selection is the most important part of installation. It determines which types of files can be imported into and exported from PageMaker. The available filters are listed on the left side of the Select Filters dialog box, as shown in Figure A.3. Table A.1 lists all the import and export filters.

If you have enough disk space, you can choose the Select All button to install all the filters. However, the complete set of filters consumes about 1.5 Mb of hard disk space, so we suggest that you install only the ones you are likely to use. Also, the more filters you install, the longer it will take to load PageMaker. You should begin by installing a filter for your word processing program (for example, WordPerfect or Word), and for your spreadsheet program (such as Excel or Lotus 1-2-3). Be sure to select the appropriate version number.

In addition, we recommend that you install these filters:

- ASCII Text Import
- PageMaker Pub (.PM4) Import
- PageMaker Template (.PT4) Import
- Table Editor Import
- Windows Metafile Import
- ASCII Text Export
- One of the other export filters, such as Windows Write

When you see the message warning you to install only the filters you need, click on OK to continue. Then follow these steps to select filters:

1. Hold down Ctrl and click on each filter you want to install.

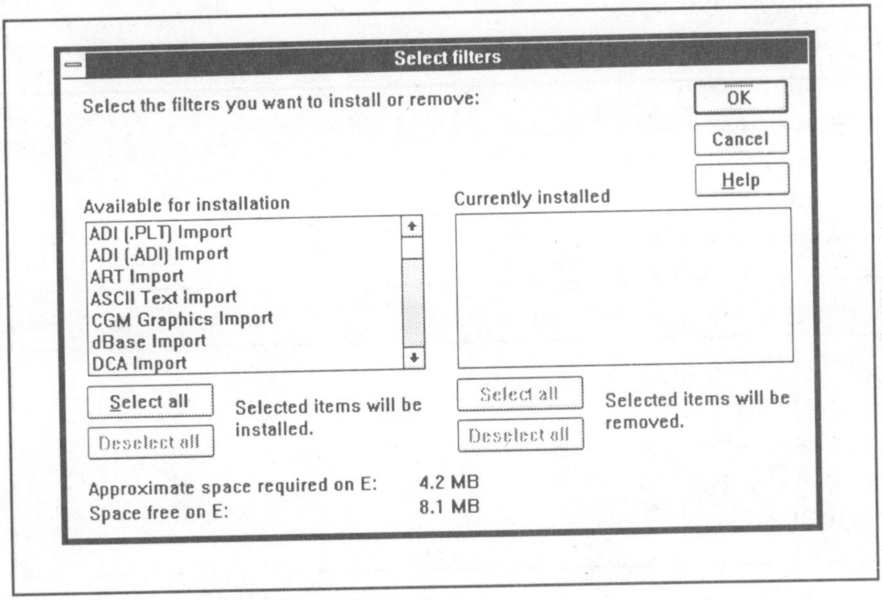

Figure A.3: The Select Filters dialog box

Table A.1: PageMaker Import and Export Filters

TEXT IMPORT FILTERS
Ami
ASCII Text
DCA
DEC-WPS
Microsoft Windows Write
Microsoft Word
MultiMate/Advantage II
Olivetti
PageMaker Pub (.PM4)
PageMaker Template (.PT4)
PC Write
RFT
Rich Text Format (RTF)
Wang (.DOC)
Wang (.IWP)
Windows Word
WordPerfect 4.2
WordPerfect 5.0–5.1
WordStar (.WS)
WordStar (.WST)

GRAPHICS IMPORT FILTERS
ADI (.PLT)
ADI (.ADI)
CGM Graphics
Excel Chart
HPGL

Table A.1: PageMaker Import and Export Filters (continued)

GRAPHICS IMPORT FILTERS (continued)
Lotus 1-2-3 (.PIC)
Micrografx Charisma (.GRF)
Micrografx Designer (.DRW)
Micrografx Draw Plus (.PIC)
Scrapbook + (.ART)
Table Editor
Tektronix PLOT-10
VideoShow (NAPLPS)
Windows Draw
Windows Metafile
SPREADSHEET/ DATABASE IMPORT FILTERS
dBASE
Excel Spreadsheet
Lotus 1-2-3 Rel 1A (.WKS)
Lotus 1-2-3 Rel 2–2.2 (.WK1)
Lotus 1-2-3 Rel 3 (.WK3)
Symphony 1.0–1.01 (.WRK)
Symphony 1.1–2.0 (.WR1)
TEXT EXPORT FILTERS
ASCII Text
DCA/RFT
Microsoft Windows Write
Microsoft Word 3.0–5.X
Rich Text Format (.RTF)
WordPerfect 5.0–5.1

The bottom of the dialog box lets you know how much space is required for the items you have selected, and the amount of space that is free on the drive on which you are installing PageMaker. Keep your eye on these figures to make sure you have adequate disk space.

2. To display additional filters, click on the down arrow in the Filter box.

3. When you are finished selecting filters, click on OK.

Selecting Templates

If you chose to install templates, the Select PCL (or PostScript) Templates dialog box is displayed, as shown in Figure A.4. To install all the templates, click on the Select All button; the complete set of templates consumes about 800K of disk space. To selectively install templates, follow these steps:

1. Hold down Ctrl and click on each template you want to install.

Keep your eye on the disk space figures at the bottom of the dialog box to make sure you have enough room for the templates you select.

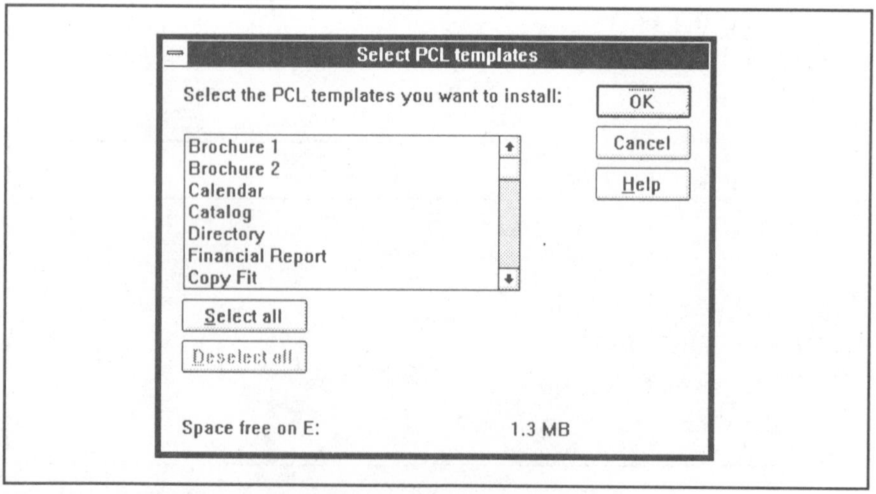

Figure A.4: The Select PCL Templates dialog box

2. To display additional templates, click on the down arrow in the Template box.

3. When you are finished selecting templates, click on OK.

Completing Installation

If your drive has insufficient space to install PageMaker with all the options you specified, you will see the dialog box shown in Figure A.5. As the box suggests, you can delete files to make room for PageMaker. Calculate how much additional space you need by subtracting the space required from the space available, and then choose the Cancel option. Delete files you no longer need with Windows File Manager, or use the DEL command at the DOS prompt, and then repeat the installation procedure. Another alternative is to install fewer options; for example, don't install as many filters or templates.

Assuming you have sufficient disk space, the Setup program will then install the files from the floppy disks to the path you specified. It will prompt you when you need to switch disks. The horizontal bar that you see on your screen indicates how much of the program has been installed. For example, when the bar is halfway across the box, you are halfway through the installation process.

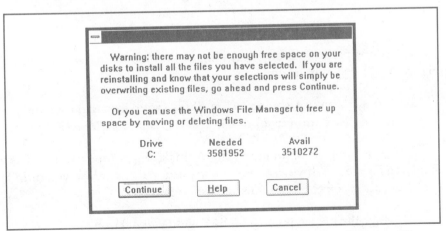

Figure A.5: The warning dialog box that appears when you have insufficient disk space

When installation is complete, you will see the message

Installation complete. Exit Windows and reboot.

Follow these steps to exit from the Setup program:

1. Click on OK.

2. Click on Exit in the Aldus Setup Main Window.

3. If necessary, edit your AUTOEXEC.BAT and CONFIG.SYS files, as explained earlier in the appendix.

4. Reboot your computer by simultaneously pressing the Ctrl, Alt, and Del keys. (Rebooting is necessary whenever the system files are modified.)

STARTING PAGEMAKER

When you install PageMaker, a program group called Aldus is created in your Windows Program Manager. This group, shown in Figure A.6, contains the icons for loading PageMaker, the Setup program, and the Table Editor. Follow these steps to load PageMaker:

1. Load Windows.

The Aldus program group may already be open, as in the example in Figure A.6. If it is, skip to step 3.

2. Move the mouse pointer to the Aldus group icon and click the left mouse button twice quickly. This is called *double-clicking*.

A window appears containing the Aldus group's program icons, as shown in Figure A.6. If you see a menu instead of the window, you didn't click the button correctly. Press Esc and try again.

3. Move the mouse pointer to the PageMaker 4.0 icon.

4. Double-click the left mouse button. The PageMaker program will be loaded, and after 30 seconds or so, you will see the menu bar at the top of the screen.

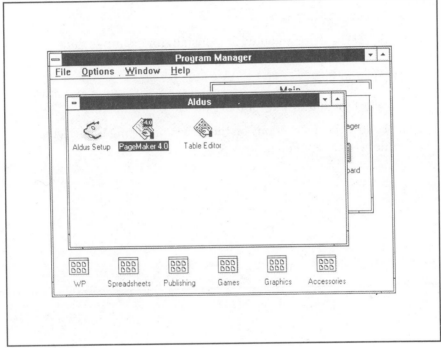

Figure A.6: The Aldus group window

MODIFYING
YOUR PAGEMAKER SETUP

After you begin using PageMaker, you might discover that you need to install additional filters or templates. To install additional items, follow these general steps:

1. Insert PageMaker Disk 1 into your floppy disk drive.

2. From the Windows Program Manager, pull down the File menu and choose Run.

3. Type **A:\ALDSETUP** or **B:\ALDSETUP**, depending on which floppy disk drive you are using.

4. Click on OK.

5. Select the item(s) you wish to install (for example, Filters or Post-Script Templates).

6. Click on Setup.

7. Select the filters and/or templates to be installed.

8. Follow the instructions on the screen, inserting the specified floppy disks when prompted.

WINDOWS 3.0
PRIMER

This appendix condenses the aspects of Windows 3.0 that are important to become a proficient PageMaker user. You will learn how to change the size and position of a window, simultaneously run several applications, and run a DOS application in a window. The Windows Clipboard will also be discussed.

THE ANATOMY OF A WINDOW

Figure B.1 points out the various parts of a PageMaker window. Actually, when you are working on a PageMaker publication, you have a

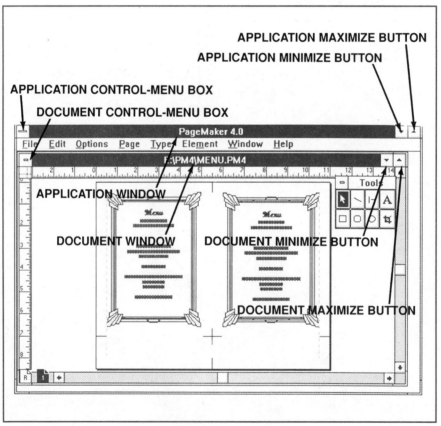

Figure B.1: The anatomy of a PageMaker window

window within a window. The outer window, called the *application window,* is a container for the PageMaker program. This window has the name of the application (in this case, PageMaker 4.0) inside the title bar. The inside window, called the *document window,* holds your publication and is titled with the name of your publication (E:\PM4\MENU.PM4 in the figure). Each window can be sized and moved separately.

Accessing the Control Menu

The Control menu, shown in Figure B.2, is accessed by clicking on the Control-menu box. To access the Control menu with the keyboard, press Alt-spacebar. This menu gives you options for controlling the window. The application and document windows have separate Control-menu boxes because the two windows are controlled independently.

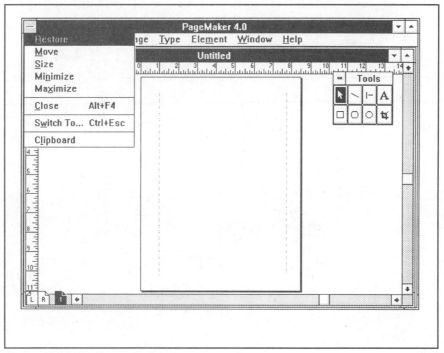

Figure B.2: The Control menu

Using the Maximize and Minimize Buttons

Each window has a set of minimize and maximize buttons, or you can choose these options from the Control menu. If you click on the maximize button in the application window, the PageMaker window fills the entire screen. If you click on the document window's maximize icon, the document expands to fill the entire application window, not the screen. Compare the document windows in Figures B.1 and B.3. The document window in Figure B.3 has been maximized; the one in Figure B.1 has not. Maximizing simply allows you to see more of a page or page spread.

Once you maximize a window, a restore button appears in place of the maximize button. This button, which you can see in Figure B.3, reverts the window to its size before you maximized it.

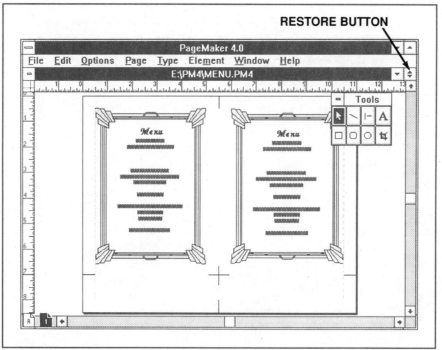

Figure B.3: A maximized document window

The minimize button shrinks the window to a small icon on the desktop. Figure B.4 shows several minimized applications at the bottom of the desktop. When an application is minimized, it is still in memory.

Typically, you will minimize an application when you want to temporarily work with another program. Then, when you are ready to go back into the application you were working with, double-click on the icon, and the window will be restored to its original size. However, you do not have to minimize a window to work on another application, as explained later in the appendix.

MOVING AND SIZING WINDOWS

Windows can be any size, and you can position them anywhere on the screen. Figure B.5 shows a PageMaker window that has been reduced in

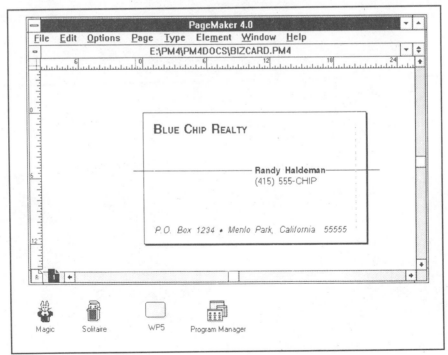

Figure B.4: The desktop with minimized applications

size. Notice how the menu bar wraps onto two lines. Figure B.6 shows two story windows that have been resized and positioned side by side.

The size and screen position of a window are temporary and not saved with the file. If you change PageMaker's window and then exit from the program, the next time you load PageMaker, the window will be displayed at its normal size and in its normal position.

To change the size of a window, drag the window boundary. By dragging a window corner diagonally, you change both the height and width of the window. To adjust the width only, drag the left or right edge of the window boundary. To adjust the height, drag the top or bottom boundary. Follow these general steps to enlarge or reduce the size of your PageMaker application window:

1. Maximize the document window so that both windows are sized simultaneously.

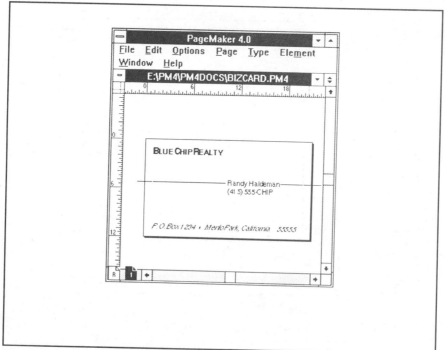

Figure B.5: A resized PageMaker window

2. Place the pointer on one of the window corners or borders. The pointer changes into a doubled-headed arrow when it is positioned in the correct location.

3. Click and drag the boundary until the window is the desired size.

4. Release the mouse button.

To reposition a window on the screen, simply click on the title bar and drag in the direction you want to move the window. Note that you cannot move a window if it has been maximized.

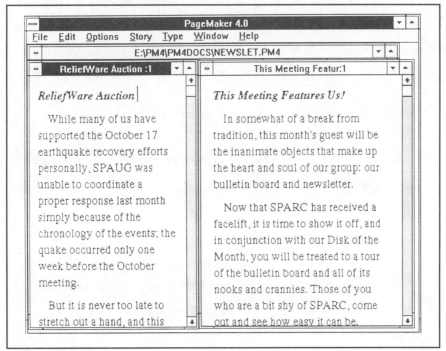

Figure B.6: Two story windows that have been resized and positioned side by side

RUNNING MULTIPLE APPLICATIONS

One of Windows' main assets is its ability to run multiple applications simultaneously, with each program in its own window. Depending on how much memory your computer has, you can have several programs (such as PageMaker, your word processor, and a graphics package) open at once, and then switch between these applications with a couple of keystrokes or mouse clicks.

For example, suppose that you are working in PageMaker and want to switch to your word processor. Here are the basic steps:

1. Press Alt-Tab to return to Program Manager.

2. If necessary, open the program group that contains your word processor icon.

3. Double-click on the program icon to load the application.

Switching Between Open Applications

Windows offers several techniques for switching between open applications:

- When part of the window is displayed, click inside the window.

- When a minimized icon is displayed, double-click on the icon.

- To switch to the last application you were in, press Alt-Tab.

- To cycle through open, nonminimized applications, one at a time, press Alt-Esc.

The Task List, shown in Figure B.7, displays a list of all open applications. *Task* is just another word for application window. There are three ways to display this list: press Ctrl-Esc, double-click on the desktop, or choose Switch To on the Control menu. To switch into one of the items on the Task List, double-click on the application description, or highlight it and choose the Switch To command button.

Closing Windows

To close a PageMaker publication, choose Close on the File menu. To close an application window, you can use one of the following methods:

- Choose Exit from the File menu.
- Press Alt-F4.
- Double-click on the Control-menu box.
- Choose Close from the Control menu.

Keep in mind that when you close the PageMaker application window, you close all open document and story windows. If you haven't saved your latest changes, PageMaker will ask if you want to save them.

DOS APPLICATIONS CAN DO WINDOWS, TOO

Windows applications, such as PageMaker, Excel, and Word for Windows, automatically are contained inside windows. DOS applications, such as Lotus 1-2-3 and WordPerfect, are not. These programs consume the entire screen, just as they do when you are not running under Windows. But if you are using Windows in 386 Enhanced mode, you can

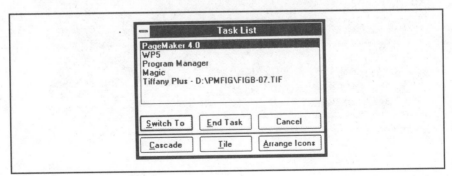

Figure B.7: The Task List

display your DOS applications inside windows. Just press Alt-Enter when you are in your DOS application, and your program appears inside a window.

Figure B.8 shows WordPerfect 5.0 in a window. The WordPerfect window has the same number of lines of text as its normal version, but in about two-thirds the amount of space. The screen characters are smaller, and there is less space between lines.

DOS application windows have many of the same capabilities as Windows applications. You can use the mouse to access the Control menu and to maximize, minimize, move, and size the window. However, there are two limitations. First, you cannot make the window any longer than its default size. Even if you maximize, the window will not fill the screen. Second, depending on how the application icon was set up, you may not be able to close the window with the Control menu or by pressing Alt-F4.

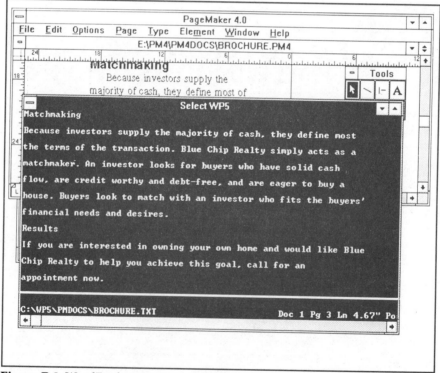

Figure B.8: WordPerfect inside a window

You must use the program's normal exit command (for instance, F7 in WordPerfect or /Quit in Lotus 1-2-3).

To return to your normal DOS application screen, press Alt-Enter again.

CLIPBOARD BASICS

The Clipboard is a temporary data storage area that is used to transfer data within the same document or between different applications. For example, you can use the Clipboard to cut and paste a paragraph in a PageMaker story or to copy a graphic from a drawing program into PageMaker.

Using the Clipboard

The universal gateway to the Clipboard is the Edit menu, which almost all Windows applications have. There are three commands that speak to the Clipboard: Cut, Copy, and Paste. The first two send data; Cut removes it from the current application, while Copy duplicates it. Paste works in the other direction, bringing data into the current application.

You can also use the following keyboard shortcuts:

- Shift-Del cuts the selected data.

- Ctrl-Ins copies the selected data.

- Shift-Ins pastes the contents of the Clipboard (Ins also works in PageMaker).

You can copy text, bit-mapped images, or vector graphics to the Clipboard, but that doesn't necessarily mean that your current application can accept whatever data is in the Clipboard. For example, after we copied a graphic from Micrografx Designer into the Clipboard and pasted it into PageMaker, our system crashed.

You can even cut from and paste to DOS applications, as long as Windows is in 386 Enhanced mode and the program is running in a window. To send data from a DOS application to the Clipboard, select it with the mouse and press Enter. To paste text from the Clipboard into a DOS application, position the cursor and choose Edit from the Control menu. From the Edit cascading menu, select Paste.

Viewing the Clipboard

The Clipboard is actually an application and is located in the Program Manager's Main program group. Double-click on its icon, and you'll see whatever data is currently in the Clipboard. Another way to load the Clipboard is to choose Clipboard on the application window's Control menu. Figure B.9 shows the Clipboard window with a graphic that has been copied to it.

Like any other application window, the Clipboard can be moved, sized, minimized, maximized, closed, or switched to. However, you cannot edit the contents of the Clipboard, except to delete it all with the Delete option on the Edit menu.

Figure B.9: The Clipboard

Saving the Clipboard's Contents

The Clipboard holds only one item at a time. By sending data to the Clipboard, you automatically discard whatever was there previously. However, the Clipboard does have a facility for saving its data to a file for future use. Just choose the Save As command on the Clipboard's File menu. These files have CLP extensions and cannot be used directly by other applications. However, after you open them in the Clipboard, they are available for pasting into other applications.

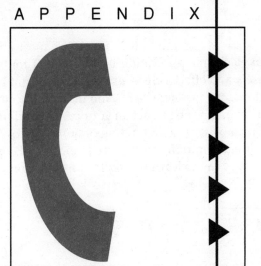

WORKING
WITH FONTS

We don't think it would be an exaggeration to say that the most important element of successful electronic publishing is your use of fonts. Using typefaces and fonts wisely and effectively is almost as important to your success as a communicator as the message itself. And managing fonts in your Windows system will have quite an impact on your peace of mind.

This appendix will give you a better understanding of how Windows and PageMaker handle fonts. Read through this material, and then keep practicing, because that's the only way to learn the skills of font usage.

THE ANATOMY OF TYPE

Before we go any further, we should define a few terms that are frequently confused:

- A *typeface* refers to a name and specific style of characters. For example, Helvetica Italic and Century Bold Italic are two different typefaces.

- A *type family* refers to a group of typefaces with all its various styles. For example, Helvetica Roman, Italic, Bold, and Bold Italic make up the Helvetica type family.

- A *font* refers to a particular type name, a specific style, at a specific size. For example, 13-point Times Bold is a font. So is 10-point Times Italic, as well as 12-point Courier, and 128-point Zapf Dingbats.

The traditional definition for font, as described above, is different from the one used in PageMaker. PageMaker defines a font as a particular type family. To specify a font according to the classical definition, you must choose three options on the Type menu: Font, Size, and Type Style. Alternatively, you can fill in these settings in the Type Specifications dialog box.

Sources of Fonts

Fonts and typeface outlines are generally located in three specific areas:

- Inside the printer
- In cartridges that plug into the printer
- On your hard drive

If you own a PostScript printer, you have 11 type families built in:

Avant Garde	Helvetica Narrow
Bookman	Palatino
New Century Schoolbook	Times
Courier	Symbol
Helvetica	Zapf Chancery
	Zapf Dingbats

Perhaps you have heard it said that PostScript printers have 35 typefaces. This is also true, and because 35 sounds more impressive than 11, most manufacturers advertise that figure. The 35 typefaces are shown in Figure C.1.

It is *not* correct to say that PostScript printers have 35 fonts. In fact, they have 8925 fonts: 35 typefaces in sizes of 1 through 255.

Hewlett-Packard (HP) laser printers use different type families. The LaserJet III offers CG Times, Univers, Symbol, Line Printer, and Courier; the LaserJet II offers just Symbol, Courier, and Line Printer. In addition, Windows 3.0 offers its own set of fonts, consisting of assorted sizes of typefaces named Helv, Tms Rmn, Modern, and Roman. These fonts are good starting points for those new to Windows, because you can begin printing right away, regardless of your printer or choices of typefaces.

The most attractive scenario is to have a printer that has built-in typefaces: PostScript printers, and to a lesser degree, LaserJet III printers. You can use built-in, or *resident,* typefaces without ever having to worry about such nagging issues as pre-downloading or installing fonts.

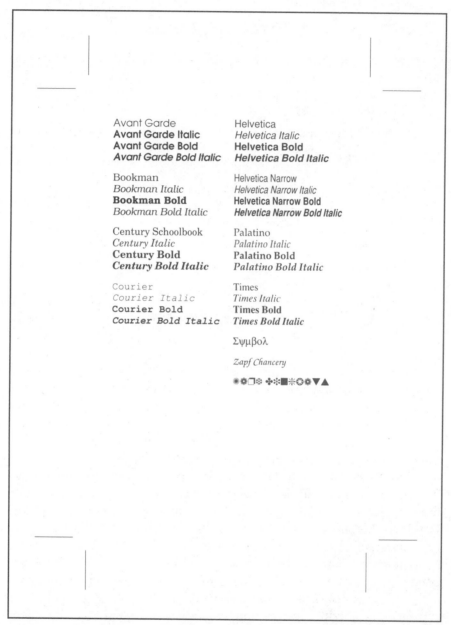

Figure C.1: PostScript printers have 35 built-in typefaces, comprising 11 distinct type families

Cartridges are the next best source of fonts, although most cartridges designed for the LaserJet offer only a selection of fixed-size fonts, not outlines. You have the convenience and speed of resident fonts but not the versatility of scalable outlines.

One of the most versatile cartridges currently on the market is Bitstream's Type City. At the time of this writing, it offers more typefaces and sizes than any other cartridge for the HP LaserJet. Its basic package includes several serif and sans serif typefaces in sizes ranging from 8 to 36 points. One of the unique features of this cartridge is its expandibility. It has four slots into which you can plug add-on cards with additional font selections.

Disk-based fonts, or *soft fonts*, are a necessary evil for serious publishers. A wealth of professional typefaces are offered on disk; it's your job to get them into your printer.

Soft fonts are available both as typeface outlines and bit-mapped fonts. Bitstream is the leading supplier of bit-mapped fonts for LaserJet printers, while Adobe is the king of disk-based PostScript typefaces. (Both manufacturers also cross the fence to support printers outside their primary domain.) There are also several other reliable manufacturers of quality type. If you are interested in purchasing soft fonts, you can refer to desktop publishing magazines, which regularly review various typeface products.

The Two Categories of Type

There are two general categories of type: bit-mapped and outline. In Chapter 12, we discuss two different graphic formats, bit-mapped and vector. Bit-mapped images are of a finite resolution. Vector images can be scaled to any size or shape while still maintaining the highest possible resolution.

The same distinctions apply to the two categories of type. *Bit-mapped type* is typically a collection of fixed-size fonts, such as 6-, 8-, 10-, 12-, 14-, and 18-point Dutch. Each font is contained in a separate file, so installing the fonts just listed adds six files to your system, one per font. After a font is installed, it is available to all your Windows applications, including PageMaker.

Outline type works in a different way. An outline typeface contains the basic characteristics that make up each character. When an application, like PageMaker, requires a font from that typeface, the font is generated automatically from the outline. Therefore, outline typefaces are very flexible. For example, from a Helvetica Bold outline, you could print any point size from 4 to 650, any shade of gray, and any rotation in 90-degree increments.

The outline provides the typeface's basic essence; the rest is up to the software. Outline type is also referred to as *scalable type*. Graphic drawing software, which has more typographic capabilities than PageMaker, can produce stunning effects by manipulating typeface outlines. The components in Figure C.2, created in Corel Draw, are all derived from the same Helvetica Bold outline.

Can you use outline type? It depends on your hardware and software:

- If you use PostScript, scalable typefaces are built in. PostScript typefaces are among the cleanest and most versatile of all.

- If you use an HP LaserJet II, you will need type management software, such as Adobe Type Manager or Bitstream Facelift, in order to use scalable type. Otherwise, you must use programs such as Adobe Font Foundry or Bitstream Fontware to generate bit-mapped fonts in specific sizes.

- If you use an HP LaserJet III, you have two scalable type families built in: CG Times and Univers (similar to Times and Helvetica). Otherwise, you must use bit-mapped type or software that produces outline type.

INSTALLING PRINTER FONTS

Using resident or cartridge type is a piece of cake because Windows 3.0 knows the capability of your printer and supplies PageMaker (and all other Windows applications) with a list of available type choices. After installing a cartridge-equipped HP laser printer, use the Printer Control Panel to choose the cartridges you intend to add.

Figure C.2: This drawing is composed entirely from the outline of a Helvetica Bold lowercase *a*

Installing soft fonts is another matter, requiring patience and a bit of determination, especially if you are adding type from more than one source. The following guidelines cover the basic steps for installing type from Adobe and Bitstream.

Installing Adobe Type

In order to use Adobe typefaces with PageMaker, they must be *Revision 3*. If you have a library full of Revision 1 or 2 typefaces, you must either upgrade them or use Adobe Type Manager, which is described later in the appendix.

All Revision 3 typefaces come with a copy of the Font Foundry Installation Kit. This kit does three things:

- Installs PostScript printer typeface outlines
- Generates screen fonts at the sizes you request
- Creates PCL bit-mapped fonts for LaserJet printers at the sizes you request

Font Foundry creates the outlines, the bit-mapped screen and HP fonts; stores them in subdirectories; and updates WIN.INI.

If you have to install many typefaces, build bit-maps for LaserJet printers, or create lots of screen fonts, be prepared to devote a lot of time and significant disk space to font generation. If your time and disk space are too valuable, consider using one of the outline type managers discussed in the next sections.

Installing Bitstream Type

Installing bit-mapped fonts for LaserJet printers has always been quite a production, and Bitstream has made a career out of cutting through as much of the complications as possible. Its Fontware Installation Kit has probably logged more mileage than all other font packages combined.

The general procedure for using Fontware is the same, regardless of which HP printer you use:

1. Install the Fontware Installation Kit.

2. Configure the Fontware Control Panel for the ANSI character set for both screen and printer fonts. This is very important, and overlooking it is the leading cause of font mishaps.

3. For Ports, select All. This tells Fontware to update all references to HP printers in WIN.INI, including a printer connected to two different ports.

4. Go to Make Fonts and generate the desired typefaces for the screen and printer, in the sizes you choose.

HP LaserJet II users might want to generate a basic set of Swiss and Dutch fonts; LaserJet III users, who already have CG Times and Univers built in, might have other typefaces from which they would want to generate fonts.

5. Exit Fontware and start Windows.

6. Start PageMaker.

7. Choose your HP printer as the target printer.

Screen Fonts: What You See
Is Starting to Look Like What You Get

Six years after the trendy acronym WYSIWYG (what you see is what you get) was invented to describe desktop publishing, we are finally beginning to see developments that actually justify use of the phrase. The font utilities discussed above generate screen fonts as well as printer fonts, but in both cases, the screen fonts are fixed in size and therefore limited in effectiveness.

If you switched to Windows 3.0 because you believed the promise of better-looking screens, your trust was not placed in vain. A new generation of software—outline screen font management — is helping fulfill that promise, particularly the Adobe Type Manager.

USING ADOBE TYPE MANAGER

An inexpensive utility program, Adobe Type Manager (ATM for short) uses one engine to manage all your font requests, including fonts for Post-Script printers, for non-PostScript printers (even dot-matrix), and for the screen.

It uses Adobe Type 1 fonts as the primary engine. Type 1 fonts have long been regarded as the cleanest, sharpest type available. Furthermore, ATM provides outlines, not bit-maps, for all devices, including the screen. If you format a paragraph in 17-point Palatino, ATM instantly does the following:

- At the moment of your request, ATM spins a 17-point Palatino screen font and displays the paragraph with this font.

- For PostScript printers, ATM requests the font from printer memory.

- For non-PostScript printers, ATM creates a 17-point Palatino printer font and downloads it.

You don't have to worry about whether or not you have the specific size; if you have the typeface, ATM makes the size when you need it, "on the fly," as they say.

For a limited time, a special ATM package is included with Page-Maker. It includes the type families called New Times Roman and Gill Sans. When you purchase ATM, you get four families: Times, Helvetica, Symbol, and Courier. You can print all 11 of the type families in PostScript printers, but in order for ATM to show the other seven on screen, you must purchase the Plus Pack. When you get a taste of screens such as the one shown in Figure C.3, you might decide that ATM and its Plus Pack are well worth the expense.

Installing ATM and the Plus Pack

Before you install ATM, you must delete all references to screen fonts produced with Fontware, Font Foundry, or any other screen font manufac-turer. (If you're nervous about this, back up WIN.INI before proceeding.)

The easiest way to delete these fonts is through the Windows Font Control Panel, although you could also edit WIN.INI directly. Make sure *not* to delete the following seven fonts because they are needed for Windows system operation:

Courier   Symbol

Helv   TmsRmn

Modern   Script

Roman

After you have successfully installed ATM, you might also want to delete the FON files from the SYSTEM directory in your hard drive.

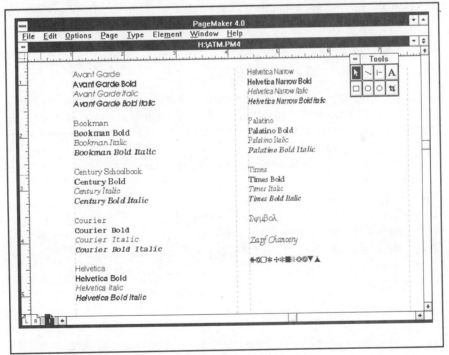

Figure C.3: PageMaker and ATM produce clear results

PostScript Printer Installation

As good as it might be, it is clear that ATM is a rookie to Windows 3.0. When you install the Plus Pack, ATM writes font information into WIN.INI that is superfluous for PostScript printers. Essentially, it tells Windows to treat the seven new families as *not resident* in your printer, even though 95 percent of PostScript owners do have them.

This little bug is more than just wasted effort; it actually prevents the typefaces from being rendered accurately. Furthermore, if there are references to bit-mapped fonts in WIN.INI, ATM might fail. As a result, you must delete the other screen fonts, as explained above, before you first install the Plus Pack.

Now you are ready for the following steps. The only PostScript printer owners exempt from these steps are those with older-model printers that contain only Courier, Helvetica, Symbol, and Times. All others should carry on:

1. Install ATM and then install the Plus Pack, according to the directions that Adobe supplies.

2. Using any text editor (Notepad in Windows works fine, or Sys-Edit), retrieve WIN.INI and search for the collection of lines shown in Figure C.4.

Note that the subdirectory name might not be the same, and you might not have installed all 22 typefaces. When you find these lines in WIN.INI, delete all of them. If you have already installed other disk-based typefaces, leave those and edit the softfont=x number so it reflects the correct number of entries. If this is the first time you have installed type under ATM, these will be the only entries. If you have more than one PostScript device installed, this entire list will be repeated for every PostScript device. Delete the entries at every occurrence.

3. Save WIN.INI and exit Windows.

4. Return immediately to Windows and start PageMaker.

5. Choose your PostScript printer as the target printer.

6. Create some text. You should have very accurate screen fonts, reflecting even subtle changes.

```
softfonts=22
softfont1=d:\psfonts\pfm\agw_____.pfm
softfont2=d:\psfonts\pfm\agd_____.pfm
softfont3=d:\psfonts\pfm\agdo_____.pfm
softfont4=d:\psfonts\pfm\agwo_____.pfm
softfont5=d:\psfonts\pfm\bkl_____.pfm
softfont6=d:\psfonts\pfm\bkli_____.pfm
softfont7=d:\psfonts\pfm\bkd_____.pfm
softfont8=d:\psfonts\pfm\bkdi_____.pfm
softfont9=d:\psfonts\pfm\hvn_____.pfm
softfont10=d:\psfonts\pfm\hvnb_____.pfm
softfont11=d:\psfonts\pfm\hvnbo____.pfm
softfont12=d:\psfonts\pfm\hvno_____.pfm
softfont13=d:\psfonts\pfm\ncr_____.pfm
softfont14=d:\psfonts\pfm\nci_____.pfm
softfont15=d:\psfonts\pfm\ncb_____.pfm
softfont16=d:\psfonts\pfm\ncbi_____.pfm
softfont17=d:\psfonts\pfm\por_____.pfm
softfont18=d:\psfonts\pfm\poi_____.pfm
softfont19=d:\psfonts\pfm\pob_____.pfm
softfont20=d:\psfonts\pfm\pobi_____.pfm
softfont21=d:\psfonts\pfm\zcmi_____.pfm
softfont22=d:\psfonts\pfm\zd_____.pfm
```

Figure C.4: Search for these lines in the WIN.INI file

Figures C.5 and C.6 are before and after pictures. In case you can't tell, Figure C.6 uses ATM.

Non-PostScript Printer Installation

As far as screen rendering is concerned, ATM behaves the same no matter what type of printer you have. At print time, however, it creates bit-mapped fonts from the actual font files and sends those to the printer. Type quality is a shade below true PostScript, but it's very close.

ATM offers a further reward for non-PostScript users: you don't have to worry about incorrect character widths when printing proof copies on a Linotronic. ATM uses the same font metrics (character widths) for all devices. Just make sure to choose your PostScript printer as the target when you create the Encapsulated PostScript (EPS) files (see Appendix D for details).

Installing ATM Soft Fonts

ATM works with any legitimate Type 1 face, regardless of the source. You can easily install these typefaces, provided that two essential files are furnished with them: the .PFM file (Printer Font Metric file), used for calculating character widths, and the .PFB file (Printer Font Binary file), used for printing.

If you have those two files, just double-click on the ATM icon, choose Add, and point ATM in the right direction. It does the rest. After you add fonts, you must close Windows completely, return to Windows, and start PageMaker.

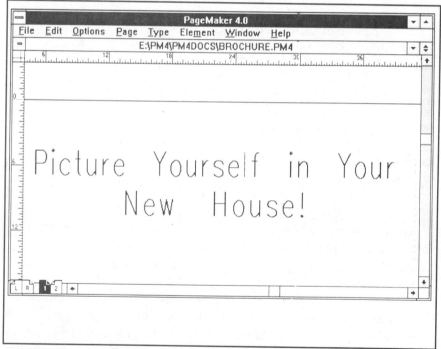

Figure C.5: Before installing ATM

Although you may experience some aggravation with soft fonts, with ATM (or another good type manager), the ecstasy far exceeds the agony. As Figure C.7 shows, decorator and symbol typefaces show exceptional detail in a PageMaker/ATM system.

For more information about using ATM, consult the README.TXT file in your PageMaker directory.

DOWNLOADING SOFT FONTS

The most annoying thing about disk-based type is that it does not live in your printer, so you have to get it there somehow. For non-PostScript

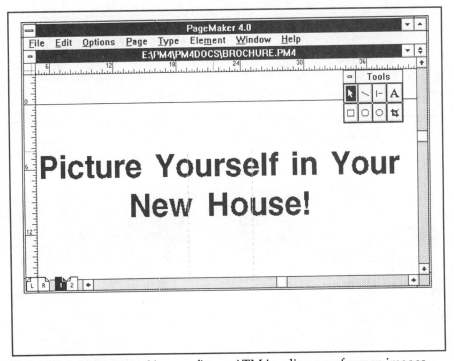

Figure C.6: No contest: You can finger ATM in a line-up of screen images any time

printer owners, this is a fact of life. But PostScript owners are spoiled by the many typefaces that they do have resident. The picture is further complicated for those who regularly produce EPS files for service bureaus, because of the following conflict:

- When you proof on your PostScript printer, you need to download the type.

- When you make the EPS file, you should not download the type because your service bureau already has it (if not, consider switching service bureaus).

To ensure that a typeface is downloaded to your PostScript printer, you can either send it there yourself or instruct Windows to do it for you.

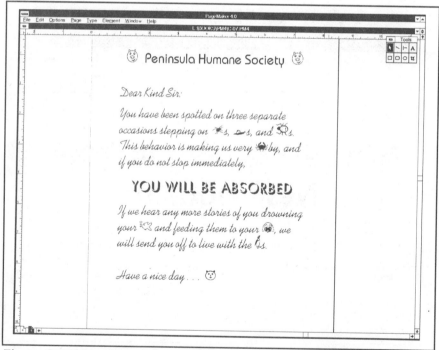

Figure C.7: If it's a Type 1 font, ATM will show it: the script face is Adobe Kaufman, the large outline caps are Umbra, and the animals were exported to Type 1 format from Corel Draw

Instructing Windows to Download Type

Windows stores all type references in WIN.INI, and with a bit of simple editing, you can tell it whether or not you want a typeface to be downloaded to the printer at print time.

Open WIN.INI with a text editor and find the soft font references under each PostScript section. Typically, it will look something like this:

    softfont1=d:\psfonts\pfm\hvl_____.pfm

    softfont2=d:\psfonts\pfm\hvbl____.pfm

    softfont3=d:\psfonts\pfm\hvblo___.pfm

    softfont4=d:\psfonts\pfm\hvlo____.pfm

These lines point to the font metrics that Windows uses for controlling character widths, whether through ATM or not. To get Windows to download fonts to the printer, these expressions should be edited as follows:

    softfont1=d:\psfonts\pfm\hvl_____.pfm,d:\psfonts\hvl_____.pfb

    softfont2=d:\psfonts\pfm\hvbl____.pfm,d:\psfonts\hvbl____.pfb

    softfont3=d:\psfonts\pfm\hvblo___.pfm,d:\psfonts\hvblo___.pfb

    softfont4=d:\psfonts\pfm\hvlo____.pfm,d:\psfonts\hvlo____.pfb

While your subdirectory references might be different, the syntax of the expression must be precise. A comma separates the two parts of the expression, and the second part references the .PFB files, which are the actual printer font files.

If WIN.INI contains the full expression when you print from PageMaker, the fonts are sent to the printer, and your laser printouts will be correct.

The only problem with this approach occurs when you create an EPS file, because you can't just jump into an editing window and change WIN.INI. PageMaker keeps a copy of WIN.INI in memory, and so you must quit PageMaker and restart it.

Do-it-Yourself Downloading

Instead of being a slave to WIN.INI commands, you can take advantage of the wide-open Windows architecture to manage the downloading of your type. If your PostScript printer is connected to a parallel port, you can create a batch file, using Adobe's PCSEND download command, and attach it to icons that represent your typefaces. Here are the steps:

1. In a subdirectory listed in your PATH statement, create a batch file called DL.BAT that looks like this:

   ```
   echo off
   c:
   cd \psfonts
   pcsend -1-v %1
   ```

   The %1 is a *replaceable parameter*, to be filled in when the batch file is run. The −v means to download the font into virtual memory so that it stays there as long as there is power. The −1 stands for LPT1; change that accordingly. Also change the drive and subdirectories to suit your system. Make sure DL.BAT is in a subdirectory in your path.

2. In Windows, use Program Manager to create a new group, called TYPE.

3. Open File Manager and move to the PSFONTS directory (or whichever one you use to store your type).

4. With both File Manager and your new TYPE group visible, select the desired .PFB files and drag them from File Manager into the TYPE group. When you have added all the font files to your new group, close File Manager.

Windows doesn't know what a .PFB file is supposed to be, so it gives each icon the generic DOS emblem.

5. Click on one of them, open File, and choose Properties.

6. For Description, enter the name of the typeface.

7. For Command Line, enter **dl.bat** followed by the name of the file. The dialog box should look something like the one in Figure C.8.

8. Select OK, and then repeat steps 5 through 7 for each typeface in your group.

If you have access to any public domain icons, you can attach them to applications in your group to make your display more attractive, as shown in Figure C.9. To download a typeface, all you would need to do is switch out of PageMaker momentarily, open the TYPE group, and double-click on the icon representing the desired typeface. Your screen will go dark for about 30 seconds or so, as PCSEND downloads the font. Then you are returned to Program Manager, and you can go back to PageMaker and continue. You can print to your laser printer or create an EPS file for remote printing. By pre-downloading your typeface, you have placed the laser printer in the same condition as a remote printer, with all the type resident.

Program Item Properties		
Description:	Helvetica Light	
Command Line:	dl.bat hvl_____.pfb	
OK	Cancel	Browse... Change Icon...

Figure C.8: Teaching Windows what a .PFB file is

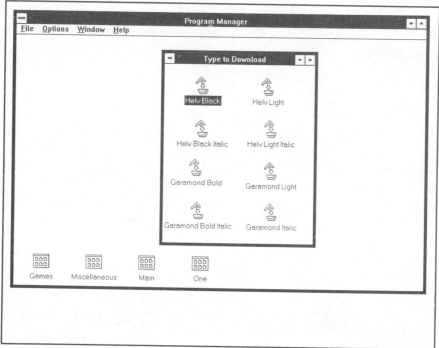

Figure C.9: Under Windows, you can create a personal downloading station

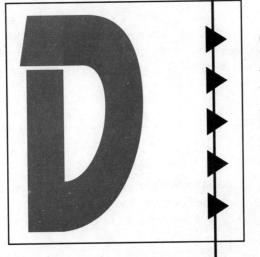

CREATING PRINT FILES FOR REMOTE PRINTING

Few people can afford a 2540-dpi Linotronic imagesetter, and even a $4,000 PostScript printer is beyond the reach of many people. But you don't have to personally own expensive equipment in order to print your documents on high-resolution devices. This appendix will show you how it's done.

FINDING THE OUTPUT DEVICE

First of all, you need to locate a PostScript device. Perhaps someone in your office has one that you can use occasionally. Many copy shops rent time on PCs connected to PostScript printers. Some shops charge by the page, others by the hour.

If you are interested in high-quality typesetting, you need to find a service bureau with 1270- or 2540-dpi imagesetters. Linotronic is the most common. Ask business associates to recommend local service bureaus, or look in your telephone book's Yellow Pages under Desktop Publishing.

When searching for a PostScript printer, you *do not* need to find a computer that has PageMaker installed. PageMaker is unnecessary because you print from the DOS prompt.

CREATING THE FILE

If you know that a publication's ultimate destination is a PostScript device, be sure the target printer is PostScript *before* you build the document. PostScript fonts have different spacing than the ones you are using on your locally connected printer. If you change the target printer *after* you have created the publication, you will discover that some of your line breaks appear in different places, and this could throw off the layout and pagination of the publication.

To create an EPS file, you print to a file. There are two ways to do this. If you own a PostScript printer and have installed it in Windows, you can simply turn on the Encapsulated PostScript option when you print, as described later in the appendix. If you don't have a PostScript printer connected to your computer, you will need to install a printer driver called

PostScript Printer on FILE:. This installation is done in the Windows Control Panel, as follows:

1. From the Windows Program Manager, open the Main program group.

2. Double-click on the Control Panel icon.

3. Double-click on the Printers icon.

4. Click on the Add Printer button.

5. From the list of printers at the bottom of the dialog box, choose any printer that has [PostScript Printer] next to its name. It doesn't matter which you choose, unless you will be printing to a Linotronic *and* your publication requires an oversized page (such as 11 by 17 inches). In this case, choose the Linotronic printer driver.

6. Click on the Install button.

7. When instructed, insert the appropriate Windows program disk and click on OK.

8. Click on the Configure button.

9. In the Ports list, choose FILE; and click on OK.

10. In the Status box, choose the Active option.

11. Click on OK.

12. Close the Control Panel window.

If you go into PageMaker now and display the Target Printer dialog box, you will see a new choice, PostScript Printer on FILE:, as shown in Figure D.1. This is the target printer you should select when composing a document that will be printed on a PostScript device.

After you select this target printer, you have all 11 PostScript type families available to you: Avant Garde, Bookman, Courier, Helvetica, Helvetica Narrow, New Century Schoolbook, Palatino, Times, Symbol, Zapf Chancery, and Zapf Dingbats. However, you may not have the screen fonts associated with each of the printer fonts. In this case, PageMaker substitutes the closest screen font you do have available. For example, if you choose Palatino, PageMaker substitutes a serif font such as Times Roman.

Even though your screen may not display the exact font, it will print correctly on a PostScript device. Furthermore, PageMaker uses the PostScript font's character widths, so your line and page breaks on the screen correspond to the printed output.

If you wait until right before print time to set your target printer to a PostScript driver, you will see the message

Recompose entire publication for PostScript Printer on FILE:?

Choose OK, but be sure to look through the publication to check the different line and page breaks that may have resulted from this recomposition.

Printing a Draft Copy

Even though your target printer is PostScript, you still might want to create a hard copy on your non-PostScript printer so that you can check it. This proof copy won't have the PostScript fonts, but the pagination will be accurate. You will be able to see the overall page layout and review the publication for mistakes. To print a draft copy of your PostScript-composed publication, follow these steps:

1. Press Ctrl-P to display the Print dialog box.

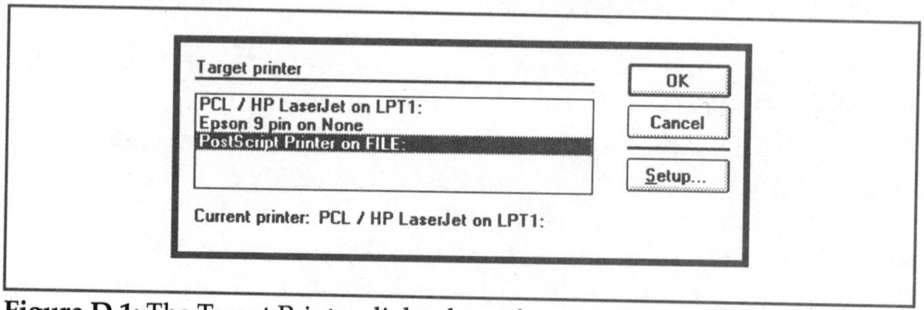

```
 Target printer                          ┌──────────┐
 ─────────────────────────────────────   │    OK    │
 PCL / HP LaserJet on LPT1:               └──────────┘
 Epson 9 pin on None                      ┌──────────┐
 PostScript Printer on FILE:              │  Cancel  │
                                          └──────────┘
                                          ┌──────────┐
                                          │  Setup...│
                                          └──────────┘
 Current printer:  PCL / HP LaserJet on LPT1:
```

Figure D.1: The Target Printer dialog box after installing a PostScript printer driver

2. Check the Printer list at the bottom. Change this to the printer connected to your computer, if necessary.

3. Change any print options.

4. Click on OK. You will then see a message that warns you that the publication was not composed for that printer.

5. Choose OK, and PageMaker will print a draft copy of the publication, using the fonts you have available on your local printer.

Using the PostScript on FILE Driver

When you are ready to create the EPS file, and a PostScript printer is *not* connected to your computer, follow these steps:

1. Press Ctrl-P to display the Print dialog box.

2. The Printer list at the bottom displays the last printer on which you printed—not necessarily your target printer. Change this to PostScript Printer on FILE: if necessary.

3. Change any print options.

4. Click on OK.

5. When prompted for the output file name, enter a name up to eight characters long and include the extension .EPS, such as TEST.EPS.

6. Choose OK.

Unless you are sending the file by modem, you should copy the file to a floppy disk so that you can hand-carry it to another computer—what we fondly refer to as *SneakerNet*.

Turning on the EPS Option

If you have a PostScript printer connected to your computer, the most likely reason you would want to create an EPS file is for imagesetter output. The option to print to an EPS file is buried several dialog boxes deep in the Print dialog box. Follow these steps to create the EPS file:

1. Press Ctrl-P to display the Print dialog box.

2. The Printer list at the bottom displays the last printer on which you printed. Change this to PostScript Printer if necessary.

3. Click on the Setup button.

4. Click on the Options button.

5. For Print To, click on Encapsulated PostScript File.

6. In the File box, enter a name up to eight characters long and include the extension .EPS, as in TEST.EPS. Your Options dialog box should resemble the one shown in Figure D.2. Alternatively, you can leave the File field blank, and you will be prompted for a file name when you print.

7. Select OK in all the dialog boxes.

Unless you are sending the file by modem, copy the file to a floppy disk so that you can take it to the typesetting service.

Note that to print from PageMaker directly to your printer, you must change the Print To option back to Printer. Otherwise, your next print job

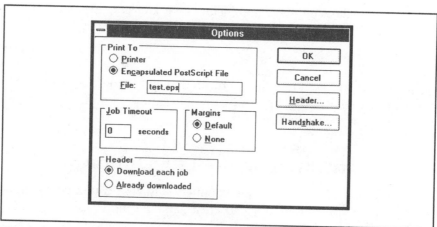

Figure D.2: The Options dialog box, set for EPS output

will be printed to the same EPS file name (unless you left the File field blank; in which case, you will be prompted for a file name). PageMaker will not warn you that you are overwriting an existing file.

PRINTING AN EPS FILE ON A LASER PRINTER

PostScript printers accept data in only one form: PostScript. If you send a PostScript laser printer a generic text file, it will blink a few times and go back to sleep, not showing the slightest interest in such non-PostScript data.

On the other hand, as long as it receives legitimate PostScript code, a PostScript printer doesn't care whether it gets the code from PageMaker, Ventura, Word for Windows, Excel, any other software program, or straight from DOS. A single DOS command is all you need to know. Actually, you might already know it: the familiar COPY command.

Follow these steps to print the EPS file:

1. Insert the floppy disk containing the EPS file.

2. At the DOS prompt, type the command

    COPY a:*filename.eps* LPT1:

Substitute the EPS file's name for *filename.eps*. If the printer is on another parallel port, change this command accordingly (for example to LPT2: or LPT3:). If your printer is connected to a serial port instead of a parallel port, you will need to use telecommunications software to transmit the file.

You should see the printer light blink for a few seconds or minutes, and then DOS will return with the message

1 File(s) copied

Shortly thereafter, your printer should produce the page.

USING A SERVICE BUREAU

EPS files are the standard way to send out your PageMaker documents for high-resolution typesetting. You can either send the service bureau a floppy disk containing your EPS files, or in many cases, dial the bureau with your modem and telecommunicate your data directly to a computer there.

When compared with laser printer output, Linotronic output is startlingly clean and sharp. For your important jobs that need better output than what laser printers can muster, you'll find the extra expense well worth it.

Using Soft Fonts

If you stick with the standard 11 type families built into PostScript, creating EPS files is easy. However, if you plan to use separately purchased typefaces, such as Helvetica Light or Black, Futura, Garamond, or one of about 2000 of the others available, your job might become a bit more involved.

Your PostScript printer already contains the standard 11 type families, but all other typefaces must be downloaded to the printer. Otherwise, you will get Courier where the soft fonts are supposed to go. On the other hand, a well-equipped service bureau possesses more than just the standard 11 families. All of these typefaces are considered to be resident in the typesetting machines—they do not need to be downloaded ahead of time.

When printing to your laser printer, you need to include information about soft fonts, but this information becomes extraneous when using a typesetting machine. Therefore, it is important that you do not include soft font information in your EPS files. You must tell Windows to treat the soft font as resident, or already downloaded.

If you download your soft fonts using an external software program, read no further—you don't have a problem. But if you edited the Windows initialization file, WIN.INI, so that it downloads fonts as you use them, you need to edit the file again. For example, if you installed the typeface Helvetica Black, there would be a line in WIN.INI under the [fonts] section that looks something like this:

softfont1=d:\psfonts\hvbl____.pfm

To instruct PageMaker to include font information during printing, the line would be edited to look like this:

softfont1=d:\psfonts\hvbl____.pfm;d:\psfonts\hvbl____.pfb

This second expression is correct for printing to your laser printer. However, it is not correct for generating an EPS file destined for a service bureau. Remember that the font should *not* be included with EPS files. This is ensured by making the font reference in WIN.INI look like the first (the shorter) expression above. After editing the WIN.INI file, you should reload PageMaker. See Appendix C for more information about using soft fonts.

INDEX

SYBEX ®

FREE CATALOG!

Mail us this form today, and we'll send you a full-color catalog of Sybex books.

Name _____

Street _____

City/State/Zip _____

Phone _____

Please supply the name of the Sybex book purchased.

_____

How would you rate it?

_____ Excellent   _____ Very Good   _____ Average   _____ Poor

Why did you select this particular book?

_____ Recommended to me by a friend

_____ Recommended to me by store personnel

_____ Saw an advertisement in _____

_____ Author's reputation

_____ Saw in Sybex catalog

_____ Required textbook

_____ Sybex reputation

_____ Read book review in _____

_____ In-store display

_____ Other _____

Where did you buy it?

_____ Bookstore

_____ Computer Store or Software Store

_____ Catalog (name: _____)

_____ Direct from Sybex

_____ Other: _____

Did you buy this book with your personal funds?

_____ Yes   _____ No

About how many computer books do you buy each year?

_____ 1-3   _____ 3-5   _____ 5-7   _____ 7-9   _____ 10+

About how many Sybex books do you own?

_____ 1-3   _____ 3-5   _____ 5-7   _____ 7-9   _____ 10+

Please indicate your level of experience with the software covered in this book:

_____ Beginner   _____ Intermediate   _____ Advanced

Which types of software packages do you use regularly?

_____ Accounting	_____ Databases	_____ Networks
_____ Amiga	_____ Desktop Publishing	_____ Operating Systems
_____ Apple/Mac	_____ File Utilities	_____ Spreadsheets
_____ CAD	_____ Money Management	_____ Word Processing
_____ Communications	_____ Languages	_____ Other _____
		(please specify)

Which of the following best describes your job title?

_____ Administrative/Secretarial	_____ President/CEO
_____ Director	_____ Manager/Supervisor
_____ Engineer/Technician	_____ Other _____
	(please specify)

Comments on the weaknesses/strengths of this book: _____

_____

_____

_____

_____

PLEASE FOLD, SEAL, AND MAIL TO SYBEX

SYBEX, INC.
Department M
2021 CHALLENGER DR.
ALAMEDA, CALIFORNIA USA
94501

SYBEX ®

SEAL

SPECIAL CHARACTERS

Bullet	Ctrl-Shift-8
Double quotation mark, opening	Ctrl-Shift-[
Double quotation mark, closing	Ctrl-Shift-]
Single quotation mark, opening	Ctrl-[
Single quotation mark, closing	Ctrl-]
Copyright mark	Ctrl-Shift-O
Em dash	Ctrl-Shift-= (Alt-0151)
En dash	Ctrl-=
Paragraph mark	Ctrl-Shift-7
Registration mark	Ctrl-Shift-G
Section mark	Ctrl-Shift-6

SPACING CONTROLS

Em space	Ctrl-Shift-M
En space	Ctrl-Shift-N
Nonbreaking space	Ctrl-spacebar
Thin space	Ctrl-Shift-T
Kern apart	Ctrl-+ (plus)
Kern closer	Ctrl-– (minus)
Clear manual kerning	Ctrl-Shift-0 (zero)

TOOLBOX

Diagonal-line	Shift-F2
Perpendicular-line	Shift-F3
Text	Shift-F4
Square-corner	Shift-F5
Rounded-corner	Shift-F6
Circle/oval	Shift-F7
Cropping	Shift-F8
Pointer	F9